# Translation of

# ROZANA

## A MEMORIAL
## TO THE RUZHINOY JEWISH COMMUNITY

Originally written in Hebrew and Yiddish

Hebrew: Collected and Edited by
**Meir Sokolowsky**

Yiddish: Supplementary Chapter by
**Joseph Abramovitsch**

Published by JewishGen
An Affiliate of the Museum of Jewish Heritage - A Living Memorial to the Holocaust
New York

Translation of
Rozana - A Memorial Book to the Ruzhinoy Jewish Community

Translated by Jerrold Landau and Lillian Pitkowsky Olshansky

Copyright © 2012 by JewishGen, Inc.
All rights reserved.
First Printing: May 2012, Iyar 5772
Second Printing: August 2019, Av 5779

Editors: Edith Taylor and Brian Zakem
Layout: Janice M. Sellers and Joel Alpert
Image Editor: Jan R. Fine
Cover Design: Jan R. Fine
Publicity: Sandra Hirschhorn
Indexing: Debbie Terman

**This book may not be reproduced, in whole or in part, including illustrations in any form (beyond that copying permitted by Sections 107 and 108 of the U.S. Copyright Law and except by reviewers for public press), without written permission from the publisher.**

Published by JewishGen, Inc.
An Affiliate of the Museum of Jewish Heritage
A Living Memorial to the Holocaust
36 Battery Place, New York, NY 10280

"JewishGen, Inc. is not responsible for inaccuracies or omissions in the original work and makes no representations regarding the accuracy of this translation. Digital images of the original book's contents can be seen online at the New York Public Library Web site."

The mission of the JewishGen organization is to produce a translation of the original work and we cannot verify the accuracy of statements or alter facts cited.

Printed in the United States of America by Lightning Source, Inc.
Original book is available on the New York Public Library site at
http://yizkor.nypl.org/index.php?id=2697

Library of Congress Control Number (LCCN): 2001012345
ISBN: 978-0-9764759-7-2 (hard cover: 468 pages, alk. paper)

Cover photographs: by Michael Pitkowsky, uncle of Edith Taylor, 1913.

## JewishGen and the Yizkor Books in Print Project

This book has been published by the **Yizkor Books in Print Project,** as part of the **Yizkor Book Project** of **JewishGen, Inc.**

**JewishGen, Inc.** is a non-profit organization founded in 1987 as a resource for Jewish genealogy. Its website [www.jewishgen.org] serves as an international clearinghouse and resource center to assist individuals who are researching the history of their Jewish families and the places where they lived. JewishGen provides databases, facilitates discussion groups, and coordinates projects relating to Jewish genealogy and the history of the Jewish people. In 2003, JewishGen became an affiliate of the **Museum of Jewish Heritage - A Living Memorial to the Holocaust** in New York.

The **JewishGen Yizkor Book Project** was organized to make more widely known the existence of Yizkor (Memorial) Books written by survivors and former residents of various Jewish communities throughout the world. Later, volunteers connected to the different destroyed communities began cooperating to have these books translated from the original language—usually Hebrew or Yiddish—into English, thus enabling a wider audience to have access to the valuable information contained within them. As each chapter of these books was translated, it was posted on the JewishGen website and made available to the general public.

The **Yizkor Books in Print Project** began in 2011 as an initiative to print and publish Yizkor Books that had been fully translated, so that hard copies would be available for purchase by the descendants of these communities and also by scholars, universities, synagogues, libraries, and museums.

These Yizkor books have been produced almost entirely through the volunteer effort of researchers from around the world, assisted by donations from private individuals. The books are printed and sold at near cost, so as to make them as affordable as possible. Our goal is to make this important genre of Jewish literature and history available in English in book form, so that people can have the personal histories of their ancestral towns on their bookshelves for themselves and for their children and grandchildren.

*Lance Ackerfeld, Yizkor Book Project Manager*

*Joel Alpert, Yizkor Book in Print Project Coordinator*

Translation of the Title Page of Original Yiddish Book

# ROZANA

## A MEMORIAL TO THE JEWISH COMMUNITY

## Ruzhinoy

Commemoration Book to the Ruzhinoy Community

Written in Hebrew, Collected and Edited by
**Mayer Sokolowsky**

With a supplementary chapter in Yiddish by
**Joseph Abramovitsch**

Published by the
Organization of Ruzhinoy Landsleit in Israel
on the 300th year of the Blood Libel

Printed in Israel in 5717 (1957)
Printing House "Sefer", Tel Aviv

Rozana: A Memorial Book to the Jewish Community

Yiddish Title Page of Original Yiddish Book

# ROZANA

## A MEMORIAL
## TO THE JEWISH COMMUNITY

ראָזשינאָי

א יזכּור בוך נאָך דער אומגעקומענער ראָזשינאָיער קהילה

געשריבן אין העברעאיש, געזאמלט און רעדאַגירט דורך
מאיר סאָקאָלאָווסקי

מיט א צוגאָב קאפיטל אין יידיש פֿון
יוסף אַבראַמאָוויטש

הוצא ע״י
ארגון יוצאי רוז׳ינוי בישראל
בשנה השלוש מאות לעלילת הדם

כל הזכויות שמורות
נדפס בישראל תשי״ז
PRINTED IN ISRAEL 1957
דפוס ״ספר״ בע״מ, תל-אביב

# Preface for the Translation

The copy of the yizkor book of our family's town, <u>Rozana, A Memorial to the Jewish Community (in Hebrew and Yiddish)</u>, was in my parents' possession for a number of years, having first received it from their *landsleit* in Israel in 1957, the year it was published. It came to me after their passing, and being busy with my work, my husband and young children, I did nothing with it. Written in Hebrew, I could not read it. A few years later, after I was widowed and my children were away from home, I began to think more about my parents, the grandparents I never knew, and my own connection to them. I looked at the little book and wondered what it could tell me.

I received an exciting call from my cousin, Lillian Pitkowsky Olshansky, who had her mother's copy of this book. Lillie told me that since she could read Yiddish, she was translating the last chapter (which she discovered was written in Yiddish). I flew up to Walnut Creek, California, edited her work, made copies and a disc. Then I contacted Joyce Field at Jewishgen and got it on line. Unfortunately, Lillie did not live to know that the book has been completely translated and available to all.

What I learned from the chapter written in Yiddish challenged me to get the entire book translated. I then worked with a landsman, Brian Zakem of Chicago, also a Ruzhany descendant, whom I did not know. With his family background of Ruzhany, beginning in the early 16th century, and his knowledge of its history, and with many long telephone conversations and emails, we combined to coordinate our efforts to get the book translated and on the Yizkor Books web page for all to read.

Ruzhany was a market town, which drew vendors and buyers from the entire area. Brian researched the long history of the town. In 1552 the entire area consisted of empty fields. The King of the Polish-Lithuanian Commonwealth gave this future town's lands to the nobles of the Sapeiha family in perpetuity as a reward for great service by Duke Leu Sapeiha to his nation. Under the laws of the Commonwealth, this reknowned and beloved nobleman could develop the land into a private town, where he decided to build a grand, baroque-designed palace suitable for his family's prestige.

He not only invited and welcomed Jews to come and help supply the needed commerce required to support his palace's costs and ongoing expenses, he also did the same for others of German, Scottish, Armenian, etc. background -- residents that would build the town's tax base. All this information helped us prove that this Yizkor book was an important addition to the growing library and the memory of the Jewish communities of Poland and Eastern Europe and the Holocaust.

Brian became my Co-Coordinator of the Ruzhany Yizkor Book Translation Project. Then we had to find a translator. Through Jewishgen we connected with Jerrold Landau of Toronto, whose knowledge of Hebrew, Yiddish, English and probably several other languages, made him the right person for the job. He is a font of knowledge about the way of life in the *shtetlach* and the history of our people living in the Russian-Polish regions. Brian and I agreed on Jerrold, but before he could start, we had to do the fundraising! Jewishgen is dependent upon donations, and each project must be self-supporting. Letters and emails went out to my huge clan and close friends, and thankfully, they came through. The work of translating our book began.

I learned to scan and send the photos in the book. Jerrold translated portions, sent them to us via email, Brian sent me his edits, added to mine, and back to Jerrold.

As I edited, I learned about the history of that small town: its formation over 500 years ago; how the Jewish population grew; the various events through the centuries; the horrible "blood libel"; the first World War and its disastrous affect on the population, both Polish and Jewish; the gradual growth of various social, political, educational and youth organizations, even the formation of the first all-Jewish volunteer fire department -- so many developments in the life of the community that brought about an exciting period between the World Wars. Then the Holocaust! I found this material almost unbearable to read and edit; it affected me very personally. Nevertheless, the project continued. And now it is almost done.

An exciting addition to this story is the trip taken by my cousin Tybie Abrams of Trenton, NJ, who traveled to Minsk, Belarus in December 2010 as a guest of her nephew, Erik Seidel, who was participating in an international poker tournament there. Minsk is a three-hour drive to Ruzhany, and with a driver and translator, they made the trip.

Tybie's story and her emotions as she walked the snowy streets of Ruzhany are recorded in her memoir, now an addendum to this book. It will also be added to *Ruzhany at KehilaLinks* on line at JewishGen.org, together with some photographs of a Passover Hagaddah that was given to her.

I write this preface to the new hardcover translation of a book that has become very precious to me. The entire project has taken twelve years. I added a plaque at the beginning of the on-line book in memory of my parents, Abe and Ida Vegotsky, both of whom were born and raised in Ruzhany, and both lost parents, sisters, their families, and many cousins. I hope my American and South American cousins as well as many *landsleit* will order and own and read the book and learn about the town of their ancestors, their lives and their struggles, and their end. No Jews live in Ruzhany today, yet their descendants can be found throughout the world of 2012.

*Edith (Edie) Vegotsky Taylor*
*March 2012*

**Map of Belarus with current and 1940 borders with Ruzhany indicated**

## History of the Town

The land that the small market town of Ruhzany would inhabit was first the property of the Polish royalty. The first settlement started around 1552. This land and a few parcels surrounding it, was legally "gifted" by the Polish King to the Grand Chancellor Leu Sapieha of what then expanded into the Polish-Lithuanian Commonwealth (1559). Ruhzany then became his private town. Such rewarding of estates was common, usually motivated by significant, meritorious services rendered by established Polish magnates. All of this occurred within a society and culture that was more medieval than that of the emerging "early modern era" of this young, somewhat united, binational alliance. When Duke Sapieha decided to begin to build his grand summer-country palace in Ruhzany (1598), he employed architects from Italy. This beautiful estate retreat charmed his many noble and royal guests! The ruins of that palace are now recognized as a United Nations World Heritage Site. Some of its ruins are being restored to their baroque and later rococo details.

As the long construction and revisions of Ruhzany Palace continued into the 1700s, the Sapieha family-owned market town grew, sometimes prospered as well as sometimes suffering man-made and natural disasters (documented in this book). The Duke invited Jews to the town to become the merchants of his town, so that they could generate collectible taxes. The town enjoyed both the support of the local and national authorities, while also experiencing many various forms of anti-Semitism, as well as the painful and often devastating wars that put it in the "cross-hairs" of enemies from within the region and nation, as well as from outside!

The so-called "golden era" lasted, more or less, till 1648, when this unique, central European commonwealth began to lose its political capacity to protect itself from its surrounding enemies. Ruzhany's fate landed it into the eastern, partitioned parts of the Commonwealth, to the Russian Empire (1775). These lands came to be known as the "Pale of Jewish Settlement." Though owners tried most of the time to protect its subjects, the fate of the Jews deteriorated slowly from 1648 to the Shoah (see historical narratives in this book). False accusations, illegitimate trials resulting in bogus convictions, became more and more frequent, with periodic periods that were slightly better, never without anxiety, when the next act(s) of criminal hate and violence world emerge. Regardless of these patterns of anti-Semitism, it is important to affirm the fact that this weakening Commonwealth, mostly more than all other European lands, provided a great many privileges and relative religious autonomy that made this beloved land to many, between 1659 and 1775, a relatively more secure, economically viable, place to live and practice Judaism, raise a family, and grow a people in numbers, learning, and financial security.

The translation of Ruhzany Yizkor Book (1957), when read as a partial sample of Judaism's broader global history, can be understood as a rich and mostly representative sample of the traditions and dynamics of central European Jewish experience, from the early 1600s to 1942. Readers will find narratives, literary and poems--serious and NOT-- telling the history from multiple points of view. They were written by a number of "Ruhznoyers" who came to "the Land of Israel" before World War II, recalling factually and emotionally, both with great joy along the complex continuum of human emotion, from great tragedy to euphoria, their personal, family, and community remembered experiences, oral histories of some of their ancestors, that we invite you to judge for yourselves, are a pathway into the early modern era of central European history and identity.

*Brian Zakem*

*Co-Coordinator of the translation of the Ruhzany Yizkor Book*

## Dedication for the Translation

On the Jewishgen Ruzhany web site, the first page has two plaques of dedication. The one on the left is in memory of Amy Perlstein Levinson, placed there by her sister, Naomi Kassabian. Amy was the first to place information about Ruzhany on the Jewishgen web site, but unfortunately did not live to see the process and completion of this project.

The plaque on the right is in memory of Edie's parents, Abe and Ida Vegotsky, who lost many of their dear ones; it was placed by Edie Vegotsky Taylor and her brother, Hy Vego.

We dedicate this hard-cover copy of the rich, multii-layered remembrances of our small, yet significant market town, that many of our family described as a "shtetl" -- Ruzhinoy, as we called it -- to the memory of Amy, Abe and Ida, and all the generations of residents and visitors, spanning almost 400 years, who moved to or were born there, studied, prayed, loved. Many died naturally as well as unnaturally, in this once-vibrant, multi-cultural and ethnic town, located about halfway between Warsaw and Minsk.

*Edie Vegotsky Taylor and Brian Zakem, Co-Coordinators*

## Acknowledgements for the Translation

Coming to the completion of this twelve-year project brings me a great deal of satisfaction. It was started as a dedication to my late parents, Abe and Ida Vegotsky, both of whom were born and raised in Ruzhany, and came to the U.S. to make a better life, and to memorialize those of our family—grandparents, aunts, uncles and cousins--who perished in the Holocaust. This loss has remained with me for all my adult life.

Early on I had help from my friend Nurith Brier, a Hebrew teacher at the Pasadena Jewish Temple and Center, to which I have belonged for the past 48 years. Together we translated and recorded the Table of Contents and submitted it to Jewishgen.org. Then my cousin Lillian Pitkowsky Olshansky discovered that the last chapter was in Yiddish, which she could translate. (*Amol is Geven* a *Shtetl* --Once there was a Stetl). So that part also was sent to Jewishgen. I am saddened by the fact that Lillie did not live to see the conclusion of this project.

At the very beginning, in 1999, I had some correspondence with Amy Levinson, who had somehow contacted my cousin Len Solomon, who then referred her to me as the "family historian." Amy had put the first bits of information about Ruzhany on the Jewishgen web site. Unfortunately, she passed away before much more was done, but her sister, Naomi Kassabian, was very generous and encouraged me to continue.

Brian Zakem came on when I attempted to put together the Project Proposal. Brian's knowledge of history and the generations of his family of Za'k (acronym for "*zera kodesh*," Isaiah 6:13) in Ruzhany helped to finally put together a proposal that was accepted by Joyce Field, my first contact at Jewishgen.

I thank our translator, Jerrold Landau, whose work is evident throughout the book. Avraham Groll, the financial officer for Jewishgen, kept track of funds raised and payments made, and sent me a monthly report. Lance Ackerfeld, who lives in Israel, was tremendously helpful as completion neared. Jerrold sent him the edited sections, I sent the scanned photos, and Lance saw to it that all was turned into the translated book on the web site.

Strangely enough, I have never met any of these people in person, the computer age has made it possible for me to be in contact with the wonderful people in all parts of the world who made this happen. One exception is Rose Feldman, whom I did meet on a trip to Israel in 2005. Rose, also a Ruzhany descendant, did the translation of the names of the martyrs in the back of the book, and added the photos I sent in. She is very computer-savvy, not like me, who struggled with every new step in the process.

I also thank my Aunt Dora Pitkowsky (z'l,) who collected many photos of Ruzhany, most taken by her husband Michael on a trip to visit his family before the First World War. These photos may be seen on the Ruzhany at Shetlinks page. Her archives are a treasure and I am grateful to have them on line for all to see.

Now we are working with Joel Alpert, who is guiding us through the last part of our project, as well as his group of volunteers, who are preparing our book to be published in hard cover by an affiliate of Jewishgen. So I also thank Janice M. Sellers for her work on the layout of the text, Jan Fine for creating the cover, and Sandra Hirschhorn for carrying out the publicity on this first hard cover translation.

Special thanks to Warren Blatt, Managing Director of JewishGen and all the staff at JewishGen for their help in making this publication happen.

This is a wonderful climax to these twelve years. My large clan is awaiting its publication. I hope they will learn as much as I have from reading the book and learning about the lives of our ancestors in a small shtetl – Ruzhany.

*Edith (Edie) Vegotsky Taylor*
*Pasadena, California*
*April 2012*

This book is presented by the
Yizkor Books in Print Project
Project Coordinator: Joel Alpert

Part of the
Yizkor Books Project of JewishGen, Inc.
Project Manager: Lance Ackerfeld

These books have been produced solely through volunteer effort of individuals from around the world. The books are printed and sold at near cost, so as to make them as affordable as possible.

Our goal is to make this history and important genre of Jewish literature available in English in book form so that people can have the near-personal histories of their ancestral towns on their bookshelves for themselves and for their children and grandchildren.

Any donations to the Yizkor Books Project are appreciated.

Please send donations to:
Yizkor Book Project
JewishGen
36 Battery Place
New York, NY 10280

JewishGen, Inc. is an affiliate of the
Museum of Jewish Heritage
A Living Memorial to the Holocaust

## Important Notes to the Reader:

Within the text the reader will note "{34}" standing ahead of a paragraph. This indicates that the material translated below was on page 34 of the original book. However, when a paragraph was split between two pages in the original book, the marker is placed in this book after the end of the paragraph for ease of reading.

It should be noted that spellings of names and places may be different than expected because there is much flexibility in transliterating from Yiddish or Hebrew into English. Consequently the reader should not quickly disregard a name that is close to a family name familiar to him just because the spelling is different than his family name. It is most likely the SAME name, only transliterated differently. This is very important to realize.

# Table of Contents

| Subject | Page |
|---|---|
| JewishGen and the Yizkor-Books-In-Print Project | iii |
| Translation of the Title Page of the Original Yiddish Book | iv |
| Yiddish Title Page of the Original Yiddish Book | v |
| Preface for the Translation | vi |
| Map of Belorus with Ruzhany | ix |
| Brief History of the Town of Ruzhany | x |
| Dedication for the Translation | xii |
| Acknowledgements for the Translation | xiii |
| Table of Contents | xvii |
| **The Translation of the Memorial Book of Ruzhany** | 1 |
| Introduction by the Editor | 1 |
| Schematic map of Ruzhany | 4 |
| **History:** | |
| History of the Town of Ruzhany | 6 |
| Ruzhany according to the ledgers of the council of principal communities in the State of Lithuania | 6 |
| Ruzhany according to the General Encyclopedia Orglobarnada from 1884* | 6 |
| Ruzhany according to the Jewish Encyclopedia | 6 |
| **Martyrs:** | |
| The Martyrs of Ruzhany | 11 |
| The Selicha for the Martyrs | 14 |
| Martyrs tomb | 22 |
| Descendents of the Martyrs | 22 |
| The Martyrs of Ruzhany | 23 |
| **Torah:** | |
| Cheders | 29 |
| The Teacher's Union | 31 |
| A Cheder for Girls | 32 |
| Tiferet Bachurim | 32 |
| The Yeshiva in Ruzhany | 33 |
| Various study organizations | 36 |
| Rabbis in Ruzhany | 41 |
| "Shaatnez" | 59 |
| **Labor:** | |
| The economic situation of the town | 68 |
| Lives of the weavers in Ruzhany during the 19th century | 70 |

| | |
|---|---|
| Families of workers in the town | 71 |
| The Labor Movement in Ruzhany in the 19th century | 72 |
| The founding of Pavlova and Konstantinova | 73 |

**G'milut Chassadim (Benevolent Societies):**

| | |
|---|---|
| Popular idealists | 75 |
| Hadaska | 77 |
| Leib Wasz and other members of the Pines family | 81 |
| Yona the shoemaker | 83 |
| Nimele the butcher Bulgatz | 85 |
| Shabtai Shefem of Pavlova | 87 |

**Our Town:**

| | |
|---|---|
| Our town Ruzhinoy | 87 |
| The synagogues of Ruzhany | 89 |
| Public life in Ruzhany | 92 |
| The "Takseh" (meat tax, "Korovka") | 93 |
| From the days of my childhood in Ruzhany | 95 |

**The Fires:**

| | |
|---|---|
| The plague of fires | 98 |
| Leib "Yachid" [the only one] | 103 |
| How the fire brigade in Ruzhany was set up | 104 |
| The voluntary fire brigade in Ruzhany | 105 |
| The drills of the firefighters brigade | 106 |
| Fear of pogroms in the town in 1904 | 108 |

**The beginnings of Zionism:**

| | |
|---|---|
| "Hurry, Brothers, Hurry" written by Yechiel Michal Pines (song still sung in Israel) | 111 |
| Beginnings of Zionism in Ruzhinoy | 112 |
| Yechiel Michael Pines | 113 |
| More on the Activities of Yechiel Michel Pines | 116 |
| Passages from "The Children of My Spirit" by Y. M. Pines | 116 |
| Itta Yellin | 118 |
| Rabbi Ze'ev Wolf Shachor | 119 |
| The founding of Ekron (agricultural settlement south of Tel Aviv) | 120 |
| Yearning for redemption | 123 |

**The years of agitation:**

| | |
|---|---|
| The year 1905--the political parties | 126 |
| The struggle for 12-hour work day | 127 |
| The big strike of 1910 | 128 |

**Public figures and personalities:**

| | |
|---|---|
| Lullaby | 130 |

| | |
|---|---|
| Aharon Libushitzky , Meir Krinsky, Zelig Sher, Melech Epshteyn Dov Shpak Lobzowsky, Avigdor Michal Goldberg, Dr. Meir Pines, Moshe Limon | 132-138 |

**The First World War:**

| | |
|---|---|
| The Days of the First World War | 142 |
| The First Period of the German Occupation | 144 |
| From the Time of the German Occupation | 145 |
| The Forest People | 146 |
| The Big Fire | 147 |
| The Kinderheim (Children's Home) | 149 |
| The Choir | 151 |
| "Hazamir" and "Herzlia" | 151 |
| The Consum Farein (consumers' organization) | 157 |
| Between the Regimes | 157 |
| Pogroms in Ruzhinoy | 158 |

**Way of Life in the Shetl:**

| | |
|---|---|
| The libraries of Ruzhinoy | 161 |
| The library in Pavlova | 162 |
| Memories of Childhood | 163 |
| Longing for Zion | 163 |
| Longing for the Land | 166 |
| Ma'ot Chitim (food fund for needy) | 167 |
| The Eve of Passover in our town | 168 |

**Economic Situation:**

| | |
|---|---|
| The economic situation after the First World War | 173 |
| In Ruzhany | 174 |
| The bank in Ruzhany | 175 |

**Zionist Movements:**

| | |
|---|---|
| Hechalutz Movement in Ruzhany | 177 |
| Activities on behalf of the Jewish National Fund | 182 |
| The General Zionist Organization | 186 |
| The Hashomer Hatzair Movement in Ruzhany | 189 |
| Hashomer Hatzi'r renews its activities | 190 |
| Betar (Jabotinsky's youth movement) | 197 |
| My native town | 197 |

**Educational Institutions:**

| | |
|---|---|
| Educational institutions in the town | 199 |
| The Tarbut School in Ruzhany | 201 |
| The Talmud Torah Institution in Ruzhany | 206 |
| David Miller | 207 |

**Charitable Institutions:**

| | |
|---|---|
| In the 19th century | 208 |
| In the 20th century | 209 |

**Second World War and the Holocaust:** 215

| | |
|---|---|
| Nineteen Days of the German-Polish War, and Russian Jurisdiction in Ruzhany | 215 |
| Echoes in Writing | 217 |
| In Ruzhany During the Time of the Nazis | 219 |
| I Passed Through Ruzhany During the Days of the Nazis | 234 |
| Echoes | 241 |
| Poem: "Everything Precious to Me" | 244 |
| In the German Captivity | 245 |
| What Happened To Me When I Returned Home | 246 |
| Yaakov Meir Maruchnik | 248 |
| In Memory of the Martyrs of Ruzhany | 251 |
| The Beloved and the Pleasant | 253 |

**In Memory of Those Who Made Aliyah:** 256

| | |
|---|---|
| Avraham Yitzchak Chwojnik and his wife | 256 |
| Rabbi Ze'ev Wolf | 257 |
| Leibl Ziskind | 259 |
| Nachum Alperstein | 261 |
| The Organization of Ruzhany Natives | 264 |

**Our Families:**

| | |
|---|---|
| A listing & photos of some of the families | 269 |
| Those Who Fell in the War of Independence: (Israel) | 282 |

| | |
|---|---|
| **Listing of many names and photos** | 282 |
| Poem: The Jewish Body | 288 |
| More names listed | 289 |
| Another poem: Liberty | 297 |

**"Amal is Geven a Stetl" - Ruzhinoy as I Remember:**

| | |
|---|---|
| Once There Was A Shtetl by Yosef Abramowich | 300 |
| In Memory of our Martyrs - Ruzhinoy and Environs | 314 |
| List of Ruzhany Natives Living in Israel | 316 |
| List of Liskova Natives Living in Israel | 323 |
| List of Martyrs from Ruzhinoy | 325 |
| List of Martyrs of Nearby Towns | 373 |
| **Table of Contents of the Original Book** | 394 |

**APPENDIX of Additional Material Not in Original Yizkor Book** 400

My Visit to Minsk and Ruzhany -December 7-12, 2010   401
   By Tybie Abrams

Ruzhany Passover Haggadah   410

Pictures of Ruzhany from the Time of World War I   420

# The Translation of the Memorial Book of Ruzhany

{5}

## Introduction by the Editor

Since the tidings of Job regarding the bitter end of our townsfolk has reached us, we, the natives of Ruzhany in the Land, have set our heart to perpetuate our community that was wiped out, the memories of our parents, brothers and sisters who perished, the efforts of generations of this Jewish community of the Diaspora, tied to tradition and laden with burdens, upon which destruction has come.

For generation upon generation, the Hebrew letter has served as the vehicle of perpetuation, whether it is engraved on a gravestone monument or printed in a book. Since our dear ones have been turned to ashes without a grave and without a monument, it is clear that we must perpetuate the memory of those dear tortured souls by establishing an eternal monument for generations, a monument that is not bound to a specific location and that will stand forever – that is, a monument written as a book.

The members of the Committee of Ruzhany Immigrants were the ones who aspired to realize this perpetuation through this means. However, there was nobody to take on the yoke of this large task. The editor realized that if nobody stands up to take action, even the little bit that could still be gathered would be destroyed; and that with every passing day, additional memories of that dear place where we grew up and where thousands of our dear ones lived are lost. He then started to undertake the work, which he has now being tending to for more than two years.

The members of the advisory committee displayed great astuteness and offered no small amount of assistance. These included: Yosef Abramovich, Elka Rubinowich-Ines, and Zeev Rushkin. They joined forces with him and significantly assisted him in choosing appropriate material from amongst the large selection for our town. An additional thank you is extended to the member Yosef Abramovich, who added a Yiddish chapter to the book.

Similarly, our friend Yosef Shimshoni (Shemshinowich) expended a great deal of effort in collecting the names of our martyrs. Our collective thanks is offered to him for this.

The book does not claim to be complete, for the ledgers of the community of Ruzhany were not before the eyes of the editor during the time of writing. He also did not possess many other sources, which were lost with the onset of the Holocaust. He was therefore forced to seek assistance from the town elders, in order to glean from their memories whatever they still recalled about their town from the early years; and from the younger folk, to record what took place in the town during the latter years, over and above what he knew as a native of the town. He utilized various sources such as newspapers and books from days gone by as well as from the latter years, to the extent that they existed and it was possible to obtain them.

From among the various articles published in the book, we see before us a picture of Jewish Ruzhany with its movements and institutions during its period of flourishing and decline. Not everything that was fitting of such was actually published in the book, and not everything that is published is presented in a complete fashion. This is very clear to the editor, who acted to the best of his ability to fulfill his faithful mission, as he ignited a memorial candle for the community of Ruzhany, which was wiped out as if it never was.

    The Editor

## Schematic Map of Ruzhany

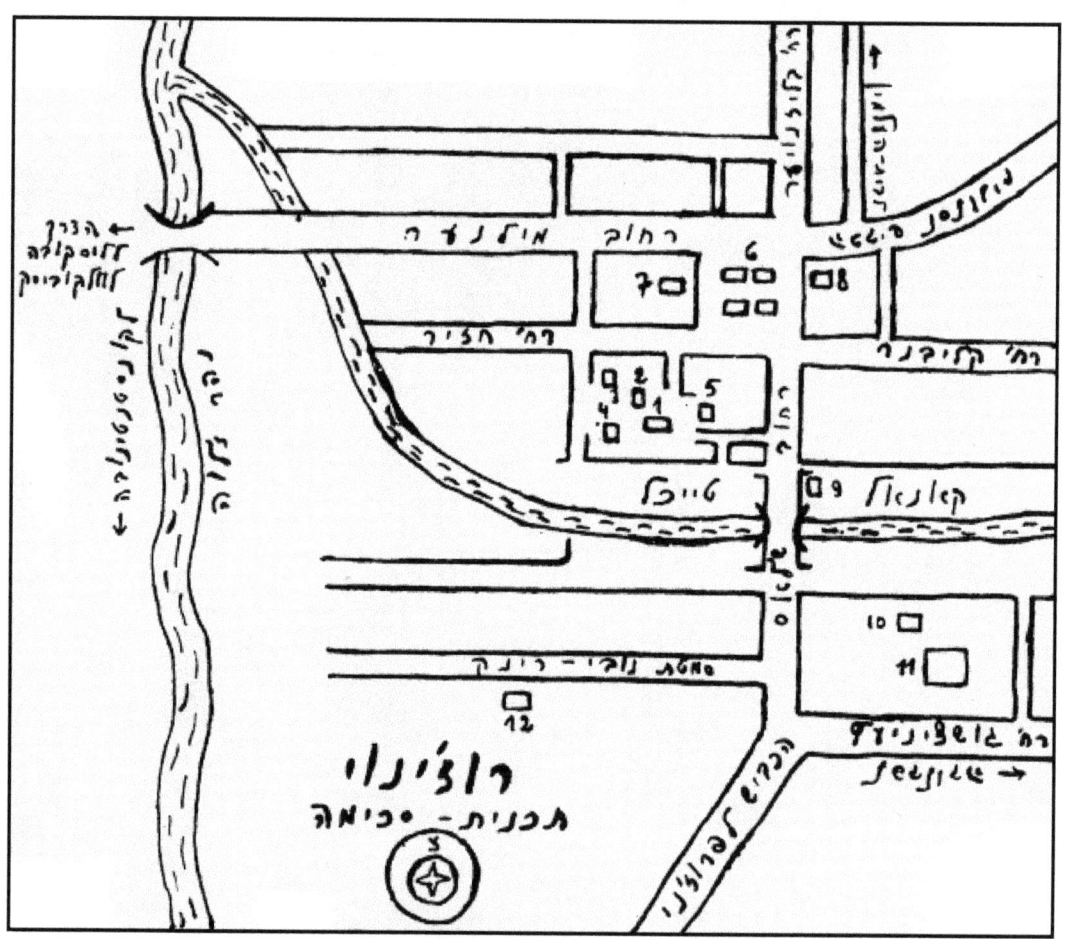

A Schematic map of Ruzhany as I recall it.

The important buildings are noted with the same number on the map and on the list below:

> The Slonim Road also leads to the Slonim Forests that are close to Ruzhany.
>
> The road to Pruzhany also leads to the forests of "Pushcha Belovezhskaya."
>
> The dirt road (the continuation of Goshchiniets) leads to the settlement of Povlava and the nearby city of Kosova.
>
> The dirt road (the continuation of Milner Street) leads to the nearby town of Jaskova and the city of Volkovysk.

There are five synagogues in the areas of the Synagogue Courtyard (Shulhauf)
> 1. The Great Synagogue
> 2. Majar Beis Midrash
> 3. Aguda Beis Midrash
> 4. Tehillim Synagogue
> 5. Talmud Torah
> 6. Shops of the marketplace
> 7. Pravoslavic Church
> 8. Catholic Church
> 9. The headquarters of the Volunteer Firefighters
> 10. The Tarbut Hebrew School
> 11. The palace
> 12. The hospital

There are four other synagogues on other streets of the town:
> The Gershonowich Synagogue on Klibner Street
> The Achim Beis Midrash on Kanal
> The Chikin synagogue on Goshchiniets
> The Ever-Hanahar (*Other Side of the River*) on Milner St.

# History

{7}

## History of the City of Ruzhany

Ruzhany was an ancient Jewish city. It was already known from the time of the kingdom of Poland and the Duchy of Lithuania, and was the property of Duke Sapieha, who built a splendid palace on the hill.

A popular tradition states that the duke had two daughters, Roza and Anna, and that he named his town after both of them: Roza-Anna – Ruzana – which was known as Rozinoy by the Jews.

Ruzhany is located in Eastern Europe, in an area that is settled primarily by "White Russians." It is close to the borders of Poland, Lithuania, and Russia, and on the border of the elevated Grodno District, and the flat, marshy Pulsia District.

We do not know the exact date of the founding of our town, for the town ledgers have been lost and no longer exist. However, we do know that a well-rooted Jewish community already existed in Ruzhany during the 16th century. *Halevanon* from 1875 (8) gives over the following information:

"On the 12 day of Elul, 5635 (1875) a fire broke out from the house of the baker, and spread as a destructive angel. It went on without stopping for five hours, and Ruzhany turned into a valley of the shadow of death. The houses of worship, the Great Synagogue that was built magnificently and that stood in its splendor for 300 years, went up in flames."

If this large synagogue was 300 years old, this implies that there was a significant Jewish community in Ruzhany already in 1575, which had a large, splendid synagogue.

Clear information about the existence of this community at the beginning of the 17th century is given to us by the Ledgers of the Principal Communities in the State of Lithuania in the regulations of the committee from the year 5383 (1623). The Ledgers of the State of Lithuania, in the chapter of "These are the boundaries and environs of the community of Brisk", includes a list of towns that are affiliated with this main community [1]. One of them is Rozanik (Ruzinoy) as it is inscribed there in duplicate form.

In 1657, this town became well-known due to its tragedy – the Ruzhany Blood Libel – which will be described in later chapters.

The Hebrew Encyclopedia (written in Russian) tells us about this blood libel, as well as some facts about the population of this town, as follows:

In the year 1765, there were 154 Jewish souls [2] in Ruzhany according to the official count; according to the census of 1847, there were 1,556 souls; and according to the census of 1897, the population numbered 5,016 souls, of which 3,599 were Jews. There was a Talmud Torah in the town (1910).

{8}

During the time of the Polish Republic, Ruzhany was a city in the district of Slonim, province of Nowogrudek. From the time of the partition of Poland and the establishment of the Czarist Russian government, the city was in the district of Slonim, province of Grodno. When Polish rule returned during the years 1920-1939, the city was declared as a city in the district of Kosowa, province of Pulsia.

Meir Sokolovsky

## Ruzhany According to the Ledgers of the Council of Principal Communities in the State of Lithuania

The regulations of the committee from the year 5383 (1623), <u>Pinkas Medinat Lita</u>

... And these are the boundaries and environs of the community of Brisk and its environs:

Miedzyrzec, Woryn (Wojan), Raszm (Rashi), Lomz (Lomaz), Biala, Beszcz, Wlodowoj, Slawicz (Slowatice), Kodno, Wysaki, Amstybow (Amstibowoj), Kobrin, Horodiec, Pruszna (Pruzhany), Mlatsza (Malcz), Sielec, Czernowicice (Czernowice), Kamenets, Szerseszow, Roznik (Ruzhany), Slonim, Dwarc, Novhorodok (Nowogrudek), Nieswiez, Slutsk, Minczsek, Mohlowony (Mahlowny), Orsza, the settlements of Rus. [3]

## Ruzhany According to the General Encyclopedia Orglobarnada from 1884

(Written in Polish)

Ruzhna, a city in the district of Grodno on the Zlawa River, is the property of the Sapieha family. A splendid palace of the Sapieha dukes existed there until the previous century, which was later designated by the purchaser as partly a textile factory, and partly a grain storehouse.

## Ruzhany According to the Jewish Encyclopedia

(Written in Russian)

During the era of the Polish Republic, Ruzhany was in the district of Slonim, province of Nowogrudek. In accordance with the decision of the Lithuanian committee from the year 1623, Ruzhany belonged to the region of communities of Brisk and its dependencies for internal Jewish matters. From this, we know Ruzhany already had a Jewish settlement in that year.

We know of the Ruzhany blood libel that took place a short time before Passover, 1657. The body of a Christian boy was found in the Jewish quarter. According to the indictment, he was "a victim of the Jewish thirst for blood." The masses prepared to fall upon the Jews and to execute judgment upon them, but the Polish estate owner who also owned the town prevented a pogrom by announcing that the suspect Jews would be brought to trial. Two and a half years passed, and the court case did not take place. It is possible that the Jews were exonerated in court. However, according to the author of the book *Daat Kedoshim*, the Jesuits did not permit the Jews to approach the courtyard of the kingdom and the royal Supreme Court, so they gave over the case to the gentile residents of the town. According to another version, the gentile residents of the city, whose hatred of the Jews was great, took advantage of the absence of the estate owner in September 1657 to transfer the case into their own hands.

Legend states that on the day of Rosh Hashanah, the masses attacked the Jews who were at prayer and threatened to murder them. The local judges accused the community of murder for religious purposes and advised the community to give over two honorable members of the community to be killed. The lot fell upon Reb Yisrael the son of Shalom and Reb Tovia the son of Yosef. (It is possible that both of them offered themselves up as sacrifices for the benefit of the Jewish people.) The martyrs were murdered on the second day of Rosh Hashanah. Reb Shimon the son of the martyr Reb Yisrael described the tragic events with a special *Selicha* (penitential prayer) and memorial prayer (Kel Malei Rachamim). To this day, the natives of Ruzhany make mention of the memories of the martyrs with feelings of holiness. From days of yore, they light memorial candles on the second day of Rosh Hashanah for the elevation of the souls of the tortured martyrs. On Yom Kippur (according to Dubnow, at the time of Neila), they read the special *Selicha* which was written by the son of the aforementioned martyr [4].

{9}

According to tradition, the two martyrs blessed the Jews of Ruzhany before their deaths, and promised to pray before the Dweller On High that there be no more bloody events in the city of Ruzhany.

The grave of the martyrs is located in the cemetery. Its monument was renovated in the year 1875.

Grave of the martyrs in the Ruzhany Cemetery.

**TRANSLATOR'S FOOTNOTES**

1. There is a footnote in the text here, as follows: "At that time, there were three principal communities in Lithuania: Brisk, Horodno (Grodno), and Pinsk. Later Vilna was added as well."

2. There is a footnote in the text here, as follows: "The epidemic which broke out in Ruzhany at the beginning of the 18th century wreaked havoc upon its residents, and therefore their numbers declined."

3. I was not able to verify accurate spellings for all of these settlements.

4. For the text of the Selicha, see the chapter on the Martyrs.

{10}

# The Martyrs

## The Martyrs of Ruzhany

## (According to the book *Daat Kedoshim*)

## Title Page of the Book

*Daat Kedoshim* is the name of the book that is dedicated to the martyrs of Ruzhany, written by one of the descendents of the martyrs, Reb Yisrael Tovia Eisenstadt of blessed memory of Ruzhany. The following is written on the title page of the book, *Daat Kedoshim* includes memoirs of the following family histories: Eisenstadt, Bachrach, Ginzburg, Heilprin, Morawicz, Mintz, Friedland, Katzenelenboigen, Rappaport, and Rokach. They are related through their parents or their wives to the martyrs who gave their lives in the blood libel that took place in Ruzhany in the Horodno Province in the State of Lithuania. It also contains a Selicha for the martyrs who were murdered on the second day of Rosh Hashanah, 5420 / 1659.

It was collected and compiled by Rabbi Moshe Aryeh Leib Friedland from manuscripts and published books that are listed in Kehillat Moshe Friedland Library (Bibliotheca Friedlandiana) and written into a book by Rabbi Yisrael Tovia Eisenstadt of blessed memory of Ruzhany.

The Blood Libel in Ruzhany

By the publisher Shmuel the son of Reb Yirmia Winter of blessed memory, Peterburg, published by Berman and his partners, 5657058 / 1897-98 (*Daat Kedoshim*)

... The city of Ruzhany did not rest and was not calmed from the anger of the oppressor, for the Satan came forth from his hiding place to frighten it one night with a false libel, perpetrated by our enemies. In their zeal they cast a dead Christian boy, with many incisions on his flesh, into the cave of the home of Rabbi Yisrael the son of Rabbi Shalom. (The house with its cave still stands on its foundation in Ruzhany, and was bequeathed to the household of the renowned rabbi and Gaon Rabbi Gershon the son of Rabbi Yaakov of blessed memory Zakheim and his descendents. It was given by his elderly son our teacher Aryeh Leib to the rabbi and Gaon Rabbi Binyamin Wolf the head of the rabbinical court of Yekatrinaslav, because this famous gaon Rabbi Yosef Katzenelenboigen, the head of the rabbinical court of Brisk and its environs, intended to stay over in Ruzhany when he traveled annually to the Zielwa Fair, and he ate the third Sabbath meal (Seuda Shlishit) in this house in memory of the event that took place to his holy forbears, of holy blessed memory.) The next day they attacked the home and went forth screaming, "This is the child whose blood the Jews spilled in order to knead the matzos for their holiday." This claim was made by those fomenters of destruction who fell upon us, spread out, incited wrath, and led the city into an uproar. Many were placed in fetters, bound in chains, and put in prison. Only the wealthy people of the citizens were able to protect themselves with their money so as not to fall into imprisonment. But what? Their property became booty for the enemies, with barely anyone saying to reinstate it. For three years, from the year 5417 to 5420, the city was under a siege. The destruction that came in the wake of the perversion of justice lasted for a significant period of time. Seasons changed without any end, and with no hope for those imprisoned. The city of Ruzhany was perplexed.

{11}

These days were during the reign of Jan Kazimierz II, who at first was a cardinal of the Pope in Rome, and then ruled over Poland and Lithuania in the year 5408, which is 1648 in the secular calendar. The tribulations of Ta'ch [1] took place during his day, and the Cossacks swept through Lithuania during the years 5414 and 5415. The Jesuits spread through the land, and spent half of their zeal against the Jews, inciting the simple folk against them with their libels. Kazimierz, who wished to follow in the ways of the kings who preceded him who were protectors of the Jews, as well as the noblemen, did not exert his rule or expend any energy, for he was an enemy of Karl the king of Sweden, and all of his days were spent in anguish and pain, and he knew no rest. The Jesuits, plotters of evil and short of toil, whose hearts were set on evil toward the Jews, won over the hearts of the nation with a blood libel that they incited. They did not permit the Jews to come to the king. Therefore, throughout the three years that the residents of the city of Ruzhany wished to bring the case to judgment before the king who was their protector and fortress, they were unable to obtain assistance in that manner. The Jesuits arranged matters so that there would be cruel judges from the poor of the people, whom they would be able to flatter in order to promote religious zealotry and Jew hatred, and pervert the case at their will.

At the end of the year 5419, the time came to put an end to the case in the distraught city that was fluttering between life and death.

Then, the farmers of Ruzhany and its environs gathered together to sit on the seat of justice. The masses streamed to the Valley of Jehoshaphat, which is the valley of judgment [2] to deal with the case of the libel, which up to this point had been kept in the Chamber of Secrets. The judges declared, "Let the murderers who murdered the child die, if we know who they are. However, since, after the inquiry and investigation, we do not know who they are, let Judah be guilty! For he was suspected first." Then, the head judge declared that two heads of the Jewish community in Ruzhany should be killed to bear the sin of the community. (There is a family in Ruzhany whose members are snatched by death before they reach the age of thirty. Legend has it that they are descendents of the judges of those days, therefore they do not live out even half of their lifespan. Let those who believe, believe.) Thus did these judges turn off the proper path. In this judgment, the haughty ones placed a trap at the foot of the two good people: Yisrael and Tovia. They were caught in the trap, for they were important men and leaders of the community, as they were in their eyes as well.

These martyrs went out, as if walking with the accompaniment of a flute, to meet their fate, and they accepted the judgment of Heaven with joy. They accepted to give up their lives as a ransom for the nation, to save them from the perplexity of death and destruction. "Oh! How good is our lot! Our inheritance is beautiful for us", they said to each other, "for our souls are being given up to save a large group of people." With hearts full of will and holy desire, they prepared themselves in holiness and purity to be taken out to be murdered, so that they could save their flock, giving their lives for the price of all the residents of the city. They lifted up their hands to Heaven to the G-d who avenges the blood of the oppressed, so that their blood would be accepted as a pure offering to protect the distraught city, so that false accusations and libels will no longer come to its gates, and so that the workers of iniquity will never torture it again.

The sentence against the martyrs was set to be carried out on Friday, the second day of Rosh Hashanah, 5420. On the holy day, when all of the people of the world pass before the Judge of all Flesh as young sheep, these holy martyrs passed by as lost sheep to be taken for slaughter by those that judged them with force, after they poured out their supplication to G-d. How awesome was this terrifying scene! A great and dark pall fell upon the entire people. Their hearts trembled from the voice that emanated from the depths of the heart, as the martyrs of High uttered the sounds of bidding farewell to all the dwellers of earth, and left the world to walk before G-d in the light of life.

{12}

As soon as they had finished their prayer, the ruthless judges approached them to take them to be killed, when a voice was heard from the blasphemers of G-d: "Behold, your good and happiness is in your hands! Give up your religion as a price for your lives, and you will be saved." "G-d forbid! Far be it from us to rebel against the L-rd our G-d and our holy heritage," they answered with holy emotion. "Go away! Go away", they called out, "It is better for us to be a pure sacrifice as an offering of a lamb rather than joining in the heritage of strangers." The martyr Reb Yisrael was taken out first to be slaughtered, as he sanctified the name of G-d. As his soul departed with the word "Echad" [3], his friend Reb Tovia said, "Happy are you, oh Israel! And it is good for you." The holy tongue of Reb Yisrael seemed to be answering Reb Tovia as it was licking the dust, "Your lot will also be for life, my friend! Let us go to the life of the World to Come."

Fathers will tell their sons, the elders of our city will relate to us that after these martyrs were murdered, high government officials arrived to save their lives. However, this was not the will of G-d, for dear to G-d is the death of his holy ones [4], and the decree had already emanated forth from Him, that they should accept upon themselves the judgment. The Rider of the Heavens [5] rejoiced and was glad when the souls of these holy Tzadikim came to cleave with Him, and to grant merit to their children after them and all the residents of the city, whom they would protect with their righteousness.

After these things, the rabbi and Gaon Rabbi Shimon the son of the holy martyr Yisrael, may G-d avenge his blood, formulated the text of a selicha (penitential prayer) to be recited in the synagogues of Ruzhany annually on Yom Kippur, and he formulated a memorial prayer for the souls of the martyrs that should be recited every year on the days that the memorial service (Yizkor) is recited. To this day, the residents of Ruzhany follow this custom in the Beis Midrash Lecha'k Gachsh'a and in the Beis Midrash of Rabbi Gershon. the descendent of the holy martyrs, may their merit stand before us to save the Jewish people from all disasters, until G-d resurrects the dead, rebuilds the Temple, and the redeemer comes to Zion.

## The Selicha for the Martyrs

(According to the book *Daat Kedoshim*. The Selicha was written on a parchment in Hebrew writing and is stored in the Beis Midrash of Ruzhany. It was a donation of the leader Yosef the son of Tzvi of holy blessed memory in the year 5484 (1724) in Ruzhany [6])

There was a false libel on our holy community of Ruzhany, and two righteous, pure men were singled out for death. They went to their deaths for the benefit of the general community. They are Reb Yisrael and Reb Tovia, who gave their lives at the hands of the officers on the eve of the Sabbath, the second day of Rosh Hashanah, 5420. Let their souls be bound in the bonds of eternal life with the souls of Abraham, Isaac and Jacob, and let G-d Almighty put an end to our tribulations, as they promised us when they were still alive that they would pray to G-d that there would be no more libels against our community after their deaths. We recite this Selicha on Musaf of Yom Kippur after the Selicha of "*Elokim al dami ledami*", and before the Selicha of "Emunei Shlomei Yisrael", in memory of their sacrifice, with weeping and broken hearts. May their prayers and ours be accepted with mercy and grace, may their be no more pillage in our borders, and may we quickly merit the coming of our Messiah. May their merit stand before us and our children forever. Amen.

{13}

... Forgive us our Father [7]

For we have erred through our great foolishness

Pardon us our King, for our sins are many.

Our G-d, You are slow to anger, and you have been called the Master of Mercy

You have taught us path to repentance

The greatness of your mercy and goodness

You should remember this day and every day for the children of your close ones.

Turn to us with mercy, for You are the Master of Mercy

We have come before You with supplication and prayer

As you have showed to the humble one (Moses) in times of yore.

Recant your angry wrath

As is written in Your Torah

Let us dwell and be protected in the shade of Your wings

As on the day that G-d came down in a cloud.

Overlook rebellion and wipe out our guilt

As on the day that You stood with him there.

Harken to our prayer and listen to our statements

As on the day that You called out in the name of G-d, as is said there:

And G-d passed before his face and called out: G-d, G-D, a G-d of mercy and compassion, slow to anger and full of mercy and truth. Guarding goodness for thousands of generations, wiping out rebellion, sin and transgression, and forgiving. Please forgive our sins and iniquities, and make us Your inheritance. Forgive us our Father for we have sinned. Pardon us our King, for we have rebelled. For you are a good and forgiving G-d, with much mercy to everyone who calls out to You.

For How long, our G-d, will you forget us forever? For how long will You hide your face from us? Will You, G-d be angry forever, and will the wrath of Your jealousy burn like fire? Arise oh G-d, do not let a man be brazen, that the nations shall judge before you. Arise oh G-d in your wrath, wipe away my enemies. Let the nations witness the vengeance of the spilled blood of Your servants.

As a father is merciful to his children, so may G-d be merciful upon us. To G-d is salvation, Your blessing is upon your people, Selah. G-d of Hosts is with us, the G-d of Jacob is our fortress, Selah. Happy is the person who trust in You, oh G-d of Hosts. G-d saves the king who answers us on the day that we call to him.

Please forgive the sins of this nation, in accordance with Your great kindness, just as you bore this nation from Egypt until now. And there it says: And G-d said, I have forgiven according to your request..

My G-d, turn Your ear and hear, open Your eyes and see our desolation, and the desolation of the city which is called after Your name. For we do not fall before you in supplication due to our own righteousness, bur rather due to Your great mercy. G-d listen, G-d heed, act and do not delay, for your sake my G-d, for Your name is called upon Your city and your nation.

Oh G-d and G-d of our fathers

For How long, our G-d, will You forget us forever? For how long will You hide your face from us? Will you, G-d be angry forever, and will your wrath of your jealousy burn like fire? Arise oh G-d, do not let a man be brazen, that the nations shall judge before you. Arise oh G-d in your wrath, wipe away my enemies. Let the nations witness the vengeance of the spilled blood of Your servants.

As a father is merciful, etc.

{14}

Please, Master of the World [8]

Who acted in days of yore as a warning for the nations.

And now you have hidden your face, and we are dumbfounded and embarrassed.

How great are the troubles that came upon me.

In the year of "My pain is afflicting my heart" (5417)

My enemies around me arose

The laid a trap for me, a false accusation to annihilate my good ones

Is there any pain like my pain?

They took hold of dead bodies

Made incisions on their flesh and spoke evil:

Behold the miserable Jews are drinking the blood of the fallen ones, they juice it out and spill it

And satisfy themselves with the children of the gentiles.

This evil matter dragged out for three years,

We have said that we had a reprieve

For the days dragged on and the anger of our enemies was assuaged.

And then a dark pall fell.

Behold, our enemies judge us, and evil burned in the wicked enemy,

With him was a group of friends, wild beasts and pigs of the forest.

After three years, they came suddenly like a storm

The enemies were going to wreak judgment in the gate

The took council together on the week before Rosh Hashanah

The evil ones made a mockery out of justice.

They judged a crooked and perverted judgment, of which there never was the like

The ears of everyone who hears it will ring.

The evil, wicked wanton one

Judged according to what he saw, without witnesses, without rebellion and without treachery [9]

To cause us to drink the cup of poison,

To spill innocent, righteous blood of those who did no wrong.

The band of wicked ones concluded their perverted judgment.

And said to our enemies who rose up against us:

Choose two Jews who are fitting in their eyes.

They took the people that they chose.

Two good people were caught in the snare,

The martyrs Rabbi Yisrael and Rabbi Tovia were selected from the community.

These men saw the decree of the sharp sword.

Their hands were bound one to the other in their pleasant and beloved lives.

And they swore that their lot in life will be the same

{15}

They were strong, fortified their hearts and offered to be the sacrifices with a joyous heart.

And we were in our eyes like grasshoppers

I will be with you as a sacrifice to G-d, which we will make ourselves.

We will not have mercy upon nor concern ourselves with our bodies.

It is a small thing in our eyes to be the lamb,

And we will dwell under the wings of G-d.

They talked to each other in their house of imprisonment

To strengthen their hearts they girded themselves.

The prepared their souls to die in sanctification of the Divine Name.

Your friends, Oh G-d, how dear are they.

You who are dear in my eye, honored, my brother, my friend, my dear one,

Is your heart the same as mine,

A strong, brave heart like a lion,

See if there is any sadness in me.

They gave themselves over to be killed, and the martyrs took out the two staves of the ark

On Friday they prepared a slaughter, like young sheep.

The anger of G-d went out in wrath and indignation,

And G-d was zealous about the evil in the year of SHLAMIM on the Day of Memorial [10].

The bitterness of death came on the streets of the city.

People gathered together and said, "We have sinned to G-d, and this is its fruits".

They sanctified the name of G-d like Chanania, Mishael and Azaria [11],

No created being had ever seen such a thing.

Everybody said to the captain: Spare us the sword for a bit,

So that we will have about an hour of respite,

And dedicate it to holiness and praise.

G-d dedicated those who call to Him, G-d prepared a sacrifice.

The mouth of the Tzadik shall speak, in place of offering bullocks,

It shall be dearer to G-d than precious sheep.

Let us fall into Your hands, the Creator of the mountains,

And do not give the soul of Your righteous ones into the hands of strangers.

The martyrs accepted their fate before the G-d of the heavens.

We are being killed for Your sake as young kids and goats

Place our tears in your flask.

And protect our children, the descendents of holy ones.

The martyr Yisrael was the first to stretch forth his neck, and he did not face the monster.

He shouted out Shema Yisrael Hashem Elokeinu with his whole soul, with love.

The captain put forth his hand that was holding the blade.

And the golden bowl was shattered [12].

See how the martyr Tovia cried out as he was slaughtered:

Fortunate are you oh Yisrael,

fortunate are you,

For you preceded me in leaving the flock of your friends

{16}

And were the first to enter the light, and I will follow after you.

He also cried out loudly

Shema Yisrael, who protected me like the apple of his eye.

He hastened to sanctify the Divine Name, and was slaughtered like the first one.

These pure peace offerings

The angels shouted out and wailed

Two olive branches were cut off together, alas.

And turned into naught within a moment.

Take note, oh heavens, and call out to the Dweller on High,

About the innocent blood of the Tzadikim who did no wrong,

Which was spilled in a false and deceitful libel

And we do not know the reason.

From the beginning of the libel, our dear ones and our possessions

Were always pillaged by our enemies, as refuse.

Our energy has been exhausted and our money used up,

And their appearance is as bad as it was in the beginning.

About these things we must call out and raise an outcry.

The young people of Israel have been brought low.

G-d is a G-d of vengeance, oh G-d of vengeance appear.

And return them seventyfold into their bosom.

Give them fully what they deserve,

And repay them for what they did on the day of vengeance.

G-d, do not answer us empty-handed.

Take vengeance before our eyes for the blood of your servants that was spilled like a bullock.

And let the land not cover it up.

In the community of the holy and faithful ones, faith flutters about, filled with innumerable corpses.

Our martyred friends Reb Yisrael and Reb Tovia together like two twin gazelles

They are together above among the elevated ones.

The council is great and deeds are mighty

Remember us for good, oh mighty G-d, of mighty deeds

The merit of the martyrs should be a forgiveness and atonement for us.

And hasten our salvation and redemption,

Harken to us oh G-d of Jacob, Selah.

Bring near the vision of Your seers, and let the house of Joseph be a flame,

And let the golden city shine bright

Restore Your city of Zion according to Your will.

Bring us back oh G-d to You, and we will return

{17}

In the book *Daat Kedoshim* it is written:

"The graves of the martyrs were surrounded with a wall from ancient times. When they were about to fall and the inscription on the walls can no longer be made out, holy people headed by the renowned Gaon Moshe Aryeh Leib Friedland of Peterburg, arose themselves to re-erect it upon its ruins. The following words are written upon it:

The inscription on it is as follows:

The Wall of the Daughter of Zion

For the holy and pure soul, our teacher and rabbi, Rabbi

Yisrael the son of the scholar Reb Shalom

And the holy and pure Tovia the son of Rabbi Yosef Shlomo of holy blessed memory

Whose blood was spilled in a libel on Friday

Rosh Hashanah, the year SHLAMIM

May their merit stand for their children and descendents forever


We have renovated and restored this monument in the year

It shall be only good for Israel [13]

Grave of the martyrs in the Ruzhany Cemetery

## Descendents of the Martyrs

In the book *Daat Kedoshim*, the names of the descendents of the martyr Yisrael are listed up to the seventh generation, and of the martyr Tovia up to the eighth generation. These included communal leaders and Torah giants in Ruzhany and other cities. In our book, we will only list the first generation of the aforementioned martyrs.

## Zakheim Family

The generations of the holy Rabbi Yisrael may G-d avenge his blood, the son of Reb Shalom of holy blessed memory. The first generation of the martyr Reb Yisrael consists of three sons:

a) the famous Gaon Rabbi Menachem Nachum Za'k the head of the rabbinical court of Pila and Pluck.

b) The great rabbi, Rabbi Shimon of holy blessed memory. He authored the Selicha and memorial prayer for the martyrs that are transcribed above. His name is included as an acrostic in the heads of the stanzas. He was the leader of the Ruzhany community. He also sat in Torah judgments with the rabbis of Brisk and Ruzhany. He signed together with them in Registry I of the community of Ruzhany in the year 5437 (1677). There is more...

{18}

c) The famous rabbi and Gaon Rabbi Shalom of holy blessed memory, the head of the rabbinical court of Birz and the region in the Zamut province.

## The Bachrach Family

The generations of the holy rabbi Rabbi Tovia may G-d avenge his blood the son of Rabbi Yosef Shlomo of holy blessed memory Bachrach. The first generation of the martyr Tovia consists of two sons and one daughter:

a) The Rabbi and Gaon Rabbi Talma of holy blessed memory Bachrach, the head of the rabbinical court of Tiktyn.

b) Rabbi Natan Nota of holy blessed memory Bachrach of Tiktyn.

c) The wealthy woman Yocheved of blessed memory. In the ledgers of Ruzhany it is written that during her illness prior to hear death in the year 5447 (1687), she commanded that a fund be set up in the community of Ruzhany with the income being used to finance the weddings of the children of her relatives.

## The Martyrs of Ruzhany

(From the book *Neshamot Yisrael*)

The community of Ruzhany takes an honorable place in the annals of blood libels against the Jews. The famous blood libel lasted for several years there after the decrees of Ta'ch ve Ta't [1], or the Chmielnicki tribulations. That blood libel left a very deep mark up on the souls of the Jews of Ruzhany, to the point that even now, several hundred years later, the Jews from there speak about it as if it took place to them yesterday. Descendents of those martyrs who took it upon themselves to be the sacrifices for the community still live in Ruzhany. The townsfolk surround them with honor. In their family, the gloomy legend of the deeds that took place still lives on to such an extent that when you hear it here, in the house that stands silently on the place where the martyrs lived, it seems to you as if all of those events are literally taking place to you and to the descendents who are telling you that terrifying historical legend.

I tell about this as I have heard it here in Ruzhany from the descendents of the martyrs and the elders of the town. I have checked the facts in the old ledgers in which echoes of the blood libel in Ruzhany are collected. Political roots are recognizable in the blood libel of Ruzhany more than in the other blood libels of that unfortunate period.

That time which preceded the tribulations of Ta'ch ve Ta't was one of the bright periods in the life of Polish Jewry, who lived under the shadow of the protection of the kings and powerful leaders of Poland.

The renowned King Kazimierz occupied the throne of Poland at that time. He was favorably inclined to the Jews, and according to legend, he had a Jewish girlfriend, Estherka. Ruzhany was then owned by Duke Sapieha, who, like King Kazimierz also related favorably to the Jews under his rule.

According to the old ledgers, in those days Ruzhany was a city filled with scholars and scribes whose leaders were Reb Tovia and Reb Shmuel Bachrach, who both came from outside, one from Koblenz and the other from Vienna. It is possible that Duke Sapieha brought them there himself, wanting to develop commerce in his domain. In any case, they did not come as uninvited guests, for the duke granted them complete rights of citizenship. They built fine houses for themselves in the heart of the city. Their business expanded in the land; they became wealthy and saw good. Aside from their wealth, they were great in Torah and generous in charitable deeds. They educated their children and raised them in Torah and good character. Before long, the name of these two men spread through the land, and the greats of the generation bound their families to them with marriage.

{19}

These words testify to the general status of the wealthy and middle class among the Jews of Poland of that time. Enlightened Jews such as Reb Tovia and Reb Yisrael Bachrach, who had large-scale business dealings with the highest class of people in the Land of Poland, had a great cultural influence upon the magnates and noblemen. This aroused the wrath of the Jesuits, who did not have great power during the days of King Kazimierz.

The Jesuits did not have the power to openly complain to the king and the powerful magnates. First they put their heart into breaking the power of the court Jews. It was easy to incite the Polish masses, who were prone to be seduced to nonsense, against such people. Thus began the weaving of the threads of the Ruzhany blood libel, through which the Jesuits hoped to build themselves up. A great deal of planning took place in their camp.

The ancient ledger of the community of Ruzhany relates that on one dark night before the holiday of Passover, a dead Christian lad was cast into the cellar of Reb Yisrael. The body of the child was cut in many places. The next day, a large crowd of Poles fell upon the house and shouted that the Jews took the blood of the lad for the matzos that they eat on Passover. Many Jews were bound in fetters and cast into a dark prison. The court case lasted for three years, and the city was in a state of siege throughout that entire time. In the meantime, the Jesuits sowed the poison of hatred amongst the masses, and their power over them increased greatly. It seemed that the magnates as well as the King himself, who certainly did not believe the blood libel, were not able to stand up to this. A great danger hovered over the imprisoned Jews as well as the communal leaders. Their lives hung in the balance, and along with them, the entire Jewish population of Poland was in danger. The Jesuits intentionally dragged out the conclusion of the judgment, in order to increase the anger of the masses. The Jews were plundered of their money. The ledger writes that the blood libel cost the Jews 15,990 zloty. Nevertheless, they were unable to obtain a proper judgment. They finally attained only one thing – that the case not be put off any longer. However, the Jesuits insisted that the judges be only farmers from the area of Ruzhany – that is, people from the group who were already completely dominated by them.

Of course, the guilt of the accused was not proven during the court proceedings; however this did not prevent the judges from issuing a verdict of a death sentence. The words of the judges were as follows: "Since the true guilty people were not identified, but the lad had without doubt been slaughtered by the Jews, we have decided that two people selected by the community should be taken out to be killed for the sin of the entire community."

Reb Yisrael and Reb Tovia willingly accepted upon themselves to be the sacrifices for their community. The ledger writes that the verdict was carried out on Friday, the eve of Rosh Hashanah [14]. The martyrs recited the confession, poured out their prayers to G-d, and then exposed their necks to the executioner. A great, dark pall fell upon all of those assembled. The judges wished to have mercy on them if they would join the Catholic faith, "a religion of love and forgiveness," but the tortured martyrs pushed off this offer with the fortitude of their souls.

{20}

Legend states that the elderly mother of one of the martyrs approached the king and received a royal decree from him to annul the decree of the accused and to set them free. On the way back, she stopped in the synagogue to hear the kedusha. The opportunity was lost during those few moments. She brought the royal decree after the verdict had been executed.

Reb Tovia was the first to be put to death. Legend has it that his severed head did not immediately fall to the ground, but rather circled for some time in the air. When the head of the second martyr went under the axe, Reb Tovia's head called out, "Fortunate are you, Yisrael!"

This did not satisfy the thirst of the Jesuits for Jewish blood. The elders of Ruzhany relate that after some time, they wished to recycle the blood libel before the holiday of Passover. However, that night, the sleep of the duke eluded him. As he was tossing and turning in his bed, he heard the sound of the crowd. He sent his servants to see what was going on outside. The servants returned and told him that several people are carrying something in a sack and tossing it into the cellar of a Jew. The next day, a crowd gathered just like during the first blood libel. However, this time, the duke demanded an exacting trial. During the trial, the servants turned the lies of the false witnesses upon their heads. The witnesses suffered the same verdict that they had intended for the Jews.

There is no doubt that this legend has some basis in fact. The Jews, who knew the feelings in the hearts of the incited farmers, had suspected for many years that a libel might be perpetrated during the timeframe of Passover. Every night of the timeframe leading up to Passover as well as the nights of the holiday itself were literally "nights of watching" for the unfortunate community [15]. The Jews were diligent to preempt the evil and the set up guards, apparently with the knowledge of the duke, who for the most part acted as a protector for the Jews against the hatred of the Jesuits and the farmers. Therefore it is hard to believe that the situation was as it was told in the aforementioned legend.

The residents of the town relate another legend – that not one of the descendents of the judges who sentenced Reb Tovia and Reb Yisrael to death died a natural death. They live near the bounds of the city, and all of the Jews of Ruzhany know them. To this day, the grandchildren of the martyrs relate to grandchildren of the executioners with feelings of anger and hatred. Feelings of unfulfilled revenge fill the hearts of all the Jews of the community of Ruzhany when they see the descendents of the executioners in the marketplace.

Apparently, the feelings of revenge in the tormented souls of the Jews of Ruzhany were forgotten completely only this year [16]. The great-grandchild of the martyr Reb Yisrael told me that this past Yom Kippur during the time of the recitation of the memorial for the souls of the martyrs, someone slinked into the synagogue and said that a gentile who wished to slaughter his pig plunged the knife into his own heart and died. It was quickly established that the gentile who stabbed himself was the last descendent of the judges of the martyrs [17].

Thus are the words of legend and the words of fact intertwined together in the mouths of the Jews of Ruzhany. The mournfulness of the decrees of Ta'ch some 250 years ago is still hanging in the atmosphere as dark clouds and heavy, angry shadows spread over every soul.

A. Leviathan

**TRANSLATOR'S FOOTNOTES**

1. Gezerot Ta'ch ve Ta't (the tribulations of 5408 / 5409) refer to the Chmielnicky uprising, and the massive destruction of Jewish communities that came in its wake.

2. Jehoshaphat was a king of the kingdom of Judah. His name means 'G-d judges', and in the Book of Joel, 3:2, the Valley of Jehoshaphat is mentioned as a place of judgment.

3. The last word of the first line of the Shema, "Hear oh Israel, the L-rd our G-d, the L-rd is one."

4. See Psalms 116:15.

5. A mystical term for G-d.

6. The year is spelled out with a verse from Genesis, "And G-d was with Joseph, and he was a successful man."

7. The entire text of page 13 is the generic text of the Selichot service, that is used for any occasion during the year when Selichot is recited. I believe it is included here for completeness. I have translated it freehand, from my own knowledge, although I did consult the ArtScroll Siddur and the Birnbaum High Holy Day Machzor to compare with their translations. The entire text is generic on this page, except for the paragraph (repeated twice) "For How Long...," which is a medley of Biblical verses. This is also standard in Selichot services, where a different medley of verses, depending on the occasion, is added at this point. The author of this Selichot service evidently chose to add in verses that deal with revenge for martyrdom. Starting on page 14, the Selicha text is unique.

8. There is a footnote in the text here, as follows: Formulated according to alphabet, with the signature at the end of Shimon Chazak. Printed, with some variations, from the parchment manuscript that is found in the manuscript collection of Rabbi Moshe Aryeh Leib Friedland

9. This line is curious – I expect that it means the opposite of what is says (i.e. is meant to be sarcasm).

10. Rosh Hashanah is known in the liturgy and in the Torah as the Day of Memorial.

11. The names of the three friends of the biblical Daniel who were thrown into the fiery furnace.

12. Kohelet 12:6.

13. Tears are often noted on monuments in a cryptic form based on verses and words. SHLAMIM is equivalent to 5420 / 1659. The year of restoration is equivalent to 5635 / 1875.

14. According to all other sources in this chapter, this was on the second day of Rosh Hashanah.

15. The night of Passover is known as "Leil Shimurim", a night of watching, based on Exodus 12:42.

16. There is a footnote in the text here: "This article was written in the year 5672 / 1912".

17. Mr. Abba Leviathan clearly recalls the day that the gentile, the final descendent of the judges of the martyrs, killed himself, as is related here – the editor.

# Torah

{21}

On three things does the world stand: On Torah, on Divine service, and on charitable deeds. (Tractate Pirke Avot, chapter I, Mishna 2.)

## Cheders

The spirit of the martyrs hovered over the atmosphere in our town: the spirit of Torah and Divine service, the spirit of charitable actions and good deeds, and the spirit of dedication for one's fellow. In this chapter we will discuss the spirit of Torah that prevailed there.

## The Cheder

Fifty years ago, Ruzhany did not know any other education institution other than the cheder. A Ruzhany child commenced his studies at a young age. He was brought to the cheder at the age of four or five, where he started to study Hebrew, which meant the reading according of the style of "*kometz aleph oh*" [1]. How did the child come to the school on the first day? His father carried him enwrapped in a tallis, as is described in one of the poems of the poet Ch. N. Bialik. How did the child spend his first day of studies? The Rebbe would show the child the alef beis and say, "See, my son, this is an aleph, and this is a beis." As this was happening, when the child would make efforts with his eyes to look at the strange letters, a coin would suddenly fall on the page of the alef beis. The child would lift his eyes upward in surprise to see from whence it came, and he would then hear the explanation of the Rebbe, "My son, an angel sent you the coin because he knows that you will learn well, and that it is worthwhile to reward you."

## The Talmud Torah

Most of the students of the town studied in the Talmud Torah, which was a government recognized educational institution. This institution had several classes at different levels. The child learned Hebrew in Grade 1. In Grade 2, he learned Chumash and Rashi, and in the higher grades, the student began to swim in the sea of Talmud. In that school, the children also learned to write a little, and they tasted a bit of the subject of arithmetic. The school supported itself by fundraising.

Sh. Shereshevsky, a resident of the city, described the situation of the Talmud Torah in the year 5661 (1901) in his article in *Hatzefira* 1901 (230). He writes as follows:

"It is also worthwhile to praise the local Talmud Torah for its good activities for the benefit of the students, the children of the poor, who number more than 300 souls. They are educated to Torah, the ways of the world, and good character. The superintendent of this educational institution is the philanthropist RA'L (Aryeh Leib) Pines, who concerns himself for the students and all other matters of the institution as a merciful father. Aside from the holy subjects, the students learn the vernacular language and other necessary subjects from the teacher Krupeni. The students were provided with all of their needs: bread, food, as well as clothing and shoes were provided for them. Everything on account of the philanthropists of our city, without receiving any assistance from the outside, as was the way with other educational institutions in other places. The principals did well by also teaching Hebrew grammar in the Talmud Torah. We know that the teachers of the school know grammar and language, so why should they deny the good and beneficial subjects to their students by not teaching them the principals of grammar at the time that they are teaching Bible."

{22}

## Private Cheders

Many students studied in private cheders, including the modern cheder of Avigdor Michel Goldberg (who later was the principal of the Talmud Torah), of Moshe Soltz, of Yaakov Reb Fitil's, Bashin, of Mordechai Aharon Ruchmis, and others. I took my first steps in Torah and secular knowledge in the cheder of Avigdor Michel.

The Teachers' Union was founded in Ruzhany in the year 5662 (1902) to ensure that educational matters would be conducted appropriately. The founding of such a union was very typical of that era. The purpose of that union and its charter will be discussed in the article by Tovia Yosef Shereshevsky in "*Hamelitz*," 1902. We will copy that article later in this book.

**Meir Sokolovsky**

## The Teacher's Union

The purpose of the teachers' union was to organize and establish specific regulations regarding the organization of educational matters in an appropriate manner. These are as follows:

a. No teacher should go to the homes of the parents of the students in order to recruit students for each semester [2], as was the custom until this time.

b. A committee of three honorable, chief teachers should be established, which would choose an appropriate teacher according to the knowledge of the student.

c. The teacher must only conduct one grade in his cheder, and the maximum number of his students is to be established by the committee, unlike the former custom which was to have many grades.

d. To appoint a spiritual committee (supervisory) of three honorable people of our city, who would visit the cheders each month in order to examine the students to see if they are successful in their studies. They would also pay attention to the way the teacher conducts the class.

{23}

e. The teachers would receive their tuition fees each month from the central committee, in accordance with the obligation of the parents of the students to pay tuition every month.

f. If there is a complaint by the teachers against the students, that they are not behaving properly, whether in matters relating to their studies, or whether with respect to the honor of the teacher, then anyone interested in the matter should turn to the central committee, who would be responsible for punishing this errant child in an appropriate fashion.

g. At the end of every month, the spiritual committee must examine those students who excel in their studies and behavior.

Yosef Shereshevsky

("*Hamelitz,*" 1902)

## The Cheder for Girls

(From the book For My Descendents)

There were also cheders for girls in Ruzhany. In her book For My Descendents, Itta Yellin, the daughter of Y. M. Pines, tells about the cheder in which she studied.

"The cheder. I still remember the cheder in which I studied, as well as the attendant who came every morning to take my older sister Sarah Rachel of blessed memory and me to the cheder, which was located at that time in the yard of the Beis Midrash. This cheder was long and narrow. The students sat around the table, listened to everything that the teacher said, and then repeated it. I cannot remember if I ever received a slap on my cheeks from the Rebbe, for I was only a five year old girl then. The Rebbe was always considerate of the well-pedigreed girls of the Pines family, repressed his anger, and put his hands on the table or in his pocket, so as not to give in to his inclination to hit us. The attendant brought us lunch, and at night accompanied us home with a flashlight in his hand, for we had to cross a bridge below which flowed a river, and which connected the city with the synagogue courtyard. There was a danger that one of the naughty girls would want to try to play in the water. However, he guarded us well until we arrived home peacefully.

How pleasant was it to return home and to sit in a warm, clean room after ten consecutive hours of sitting in a narrow, dark cheder. We were approximately ten girls, all of us from the wealthier and noblest families in Ruzhany. My sister and I always reviewed with our father everything that we had learned with the Rebbe... It was not easy for us to review before our father of blessed memory, for he always demanded correct explanations from us, and he was not always satisfied with those that we gave. After some time he decided to bring a tutor to our house who would teach us how to progress in our Hebrew studies."

Itta Yellin

## Tiferet Bachurim

Thus did a portion of the girls study Torah. For the boys, it was not a portion, but rather all of them. Boys who did not succeed in their studies turned to work. The "Tiferet Bachurim" organization assisted them, as Yitzchak Meir Gerber writes in "Hamelitz" 1893 (43):

The Tiferet Bachurim organization has sprouted up. Its purpose is to teach trades to the students of the Talmud Torah who are not successful in their studies, and to fill their lacks so that they would be able to earn their livelihoods through the toil of their hands. It was founded through the hands of the enlightened youths M. Y. Pines and M. A. Pines, fine youths in whose hearts G-d planted a spirit of volunteerism.

Yitzchak Meir Gerber

{24}

## The Yeshiva in Ruzhany

When they concluded their studies in the cheder at age 12, many of the youths who had progressed well in their studies transferred to study in the Yeshiva in town. There were two centers of the Ruzhany Yeshiva. The most important was in the Beis Midrash of the Pines brothers, where Reb Itzele, Reb Avraham Leib Skolnik and Reb Shmuel Epstein taught. The second was the Yeshiva of Reiza Pines on the Nowy-Rynek alleyway, where Reb Natan taught. The Yeshiva of Ruzhany was known in the area, and youths from various towns came to study there.

### The Yeshiva Youths

In those days there were many youths aged 12 and older whose souls desired Torah and knowledge. If the father of such a youth had the financial means and was able to provide him with clothing, transportation costs and board, how nice was his lot. He would go to a place of Torah to study. However, what does a youth do whose parents are caring for young children, and who barely have enough money for a morsel of bread for their children in the house? Such a youth would also go to a place of Torah, but his lot would be poverty, oppression, suffering and bitterness. He would eat on a rotation basis in various houses, and he would have many days of hunger. However, to them study was the wellspring of life. Torah and knowledge revived their soul that thirsted for the words of the Living G-d. Many of them came to Ruzhany where they studied Torah from the Rosh Yeshiva Reb Itzele and others. The wealthy people of the city came to the assistance of the poor youths to the best of their ability, seeing to it that they would not starve and not fail. There were some wealthy people of Ruzhany who provided daily meals for tens of Yeshiva students.

## The Course of Study in the Yeshiva

Mr. Yitzchak Gelber wrote the following interesting words in "*Hamelitz*" (1893) about the studies in Yeshiva.

Approximately 200 students listen to lessons from four teachers. Few of the students are from the city, and many are from other cities. The heads of the Yeshiva are the Ra'n and the Ł'Y [3]. They chose the straight path, preach chapters with wisdom and present before their students things which will penetrate the hearts of any listener. Aside from being proficient in all subjects of the Talmud and its commentators, they also know a great deal about the science of pedagogy...

The students eat on a rotation basis at the tables of the philanthropists of our people. The Yeshiva youths have set up a "Masbiei Reevim" (Satiators of the Hungry) fund for those who are short on their rotation.

A special teacher teaches the Russian language [4], arithmetic, writing and grammar for two hours a day. Only one thing was missing – the teaching of Bible and Hebrew to the youths...

{25}

## When Was the Yeshiva Founded?

We do not know the exact date of the founding of the Yeshiva, but the Yeshiva had already taken root in the life of the town as an established institution and was known in the surrounding area for some time already during the early childhood of Yechiel Michel Pines (who was born in Ruzhany in the year 5604 / 1843). According to the memory of the aforementioned scholar Yechiel Michel Pines, there were five grades in the Yeshiva, in which the youths started with Gemara and Rashi, and concluded with Gemara, Tosafot and the commentators. Young students from near and far towns streamed to it. Students even came from the area of Lomza in Congress Poland.

One of the supporters of the Yeshiva was the wealthy Reb Noach Pines of blessed memory (the father of Y. M. Pines) who died prematurely during his prime in the year 5632 / 1872. ("*Hamelitz*" 1893, written by Yitzchak Meir Gerber).

## The Heads of the Yeshiva

We should especially note Rabbi Binyamin Zakheim from among the Roshei Yeshiva (Yeshiva heads). His broad knowledge in Talmud and its commentaries is demonstrated by the fact that this Rosh

Yeshiva was accepted as the head of the rabbinical court in the large city of Yekatrinoslav in the year 5633 (1873). After his death in the year 5673 (1913), he was designated as a great in Torah and fear of Heaven by the newspaper Hamodia. He was praised and exalted in the community as a great and honorable rabbi.... who had many students when he was the Rosh Yeshiva in the city of Ruzhany.

The residents of the city also gave their honor to their Roshei Yeshiva. We read the following in "*Hamelitz*" number 20 from 1878:

Ruzhany, on the 13th of Tishrei 5639 (1879) the Gaon rabbi Shraga Feivel Berman passed away. He had been the Rosh Yeshiva here and taught Torah with great wisdom. It has already been five years since he was forced to leave his post on account of the illness which afflicted him and prevented him from speaking. He was 48 years old at his death. The residents of our city extended great honor to him. All labor and commerce ceased, and he was accompanied to his rest with bitter weeping. The rabbi and head of the rabbinical court Rabbi Mordechai Gimpel Yaffa and the renowned Rabbi David eulogized him appropriately.

Written with tears by Yaakov the son of the rabbi and Gaon Rabbi Shabtai Wallach.

## Famous Students of the Yeshiva

We should note that two people who later became renowned as expert scholars studied in the Ruzhany Yeshiva during their youths: Rabbi Moshe Sokolovsky, later the Rosh Yeshiva of the Torat Chesed Yeshiva of Brest Litovsk and the author of the *Imre Moshe* book (died in 5691 / 1931); and Rabbi Meir Bessin, the rabbi of Shnipishuk near Vilna and the head of the Ramailis Yeshiva there (died in 5692 / 1932 at the age of 64).

From among the students from outside who studied there, we should mention the father of the poet Shaul Tshernikovsy [5] and Rabbi Moshe Avigdor Amiel, who was known in the Yeshiva as "The lad from Porozovo." From Ruzhany he was accepted as a student into the central Yeshiva of Telz, and after he made aliya to the Land, he was chosen as the chief rabbi of Tel Aviv-Jaffa.

(From various sources)

Meir Sokolovsky

{26}

## Various Study Organizations

Thus was the atmosphere of the town filled with the breath of students of the house of the Rebbe; and the chant of Gemara of the youths who spent their time in the tents of Torah carried itself out to the main streets.

### Chevrat Shas (Talmud Study Group)

It was not only the students of the cheders and the Yeshiva who dedicated their hearts and souls to Torah. Almost all of the town directed their steps in that direction. Many of them studied in the synagogue on the Sabbath after services, and continued with that commandment in the afternoon of the Day of Rest. Many people delved into the Torah even on weekdays, every morning after the Shacharit service. Those whose business affairs forced them to leave the synagogue on the weekdays right after the services returned to the sanctuary for the Mincha service. They did not leave right after that service, but rather sat down to study Gemara as members of the Chevra Shas. There were many studiers especially in the winter, when it would get dark at 3:00 p.m. The class in Gemara was delivered by the rabbi as well as by Torah scholars from amongst the laymen. No small number of the townsfolk possessed rabbinic ordination but did not use the Torah to earn their livelihood. Thus did they fulfill the words of the Mishna: "Love the work but hate the rabbinate." Yudel Berl, Meir Gerber, and others were among these. These people donated their time to teach Torah to their townsfolk, without expectation of renumeration.

### The Mishna and Psalms Organizations, and the Like

There were many people in Ruzhany who did not possess the ability to study Gemara. These people joined the Mishna, Ein Yaakov [6] or Psalms groups. The sounds of Torah broke forth from the windows of the Beis Midrashes of the town between Mincha and Maariv. Whomever entered would see a long table surrounded by heads who are directing their gaze toward the person explaining, listening to every word that emanates from his mouth; or following along in a book to the words that their teacher is speaking.

### The Beis Yaakov Organization

The various organizations were founded by the townsfolk or by emissaries that were sent there. "Hamelitz" from 1898, number 201, tells about the founding of one such learning organization in the town by an emissary.

"Ruzhany (Grodno District), 26 Elul. One additional organization has been added to the organizations that sparkled gloriously in our city, whose holy purpose was Torah and knowledge. This organization was founded by a rabbi who was sent by the author of the Chofetz Chaim [7], Rabbi Asher Herman, may he live, of the community of Dvinsk. This organization was called 'Agudas Beis Yaakov' and 'Tiferet Bachurim'. Each evening crowds of our brethren gathered together. These were people who earned their livelihoods through the toil of their hands, and included the elderly and the youths, old and young together. They came together to study Shulchan Aruch (The Code of Jewish Law) which their rabbi and teacher taught them. How pleasant is it to see at the time of Mincha, at the conclusion of the workday, people streaming to a place of Torah. On their holy days and Sabbaths, they do not stroll in the roads of the town with the crowds, they do not spend their time in laughter, foolishness and idleness, the chief of all sins; but rather these sons of Jacob gather together in one place – to listen to the word of G-d. Oh would it be that this organization, dedicated to such a sublime goal, would instill in the hearts of their members who identify with them the love of Torah and of proper conduct, to grant us the stamp of wholeness. We must extend our blessings and gratitude to the emissary rabbi. May his strength in Torah increase!"

The assistant government rabbi, Eliahu Nota Halevi Berman [8]

{27}

### Shmuel Itche the Wagon Driver [9]

The Gemara and Mishna students, as well as the Psalms readers, came from all strata of the people. Tradesman such as Shlomo the shoemaker and others would come to the Aguda Synagogue every day between Mincha and Maariv to hear Torah from Moshe Reuven Wilensky, an honorable man and a scholar. However, there were also teachers from amongst the simple folk. For example, were you to have followed after the wagon of Shmuel Itche as it was dragged by his thin horse in the afternoons, you would realize that he was not at this time filling up sand or mortar for the oven builders, as in all hours of the day. The thin horse could go faster, but he was not doing so. What happened? His owner did not direct him to the stable, but rather to the Gershonovitz Synagogue. He tied him to a post, and the poor horse knew that he would remain tied in that manner for several hours as he waits for Shmuel Itche to come and untie him, so that he could go to his stable and enjoy his meager meal. What was his owner doing during those hours? He was reading Ein Yaakov or Chayei Adam before 50-60 Jews, who were thirstily soaking up his words.

## Ruzhany is Known as a City of Torah

The extent to which Ruzhany was renowned as a city of Torah is demonstrated by the article of Shlomo Zaltzman about that topic: "Chol Hamoed Pesach" in the Haboker newspaper from April 13, 1944. Among everything, it states.

"It is known that salted fish wafts from the mouth of people of Brisk; from the people of Pruzhany – flakes of fat; from the people of Ruzhany – the aroma of Torah; and from the people of Bialystock – knowledge and wisdom. Jews of Bialystock felt that it was a lowering of their honor to forge a marriage match with a resident of Brisk. Similarly, people of Ruzhany almost considered it to be beneath their honor to forge a marriage match with a native of Pruzhany. It is difficult to delve into the source of and reason for these nicknames, just as it is hard to understand why the Jews of one city felt superior to their brethren in a similar city. This appraisal was a tradition from several generations. Ruzhany among the towns and Bialystock among major cities were known as the most honorable."

{28}

## The Concluding Ceremonies (Siyum) for the Study of a Book

When it came time to conclude a book, one had to arrange a feast. The entire group prepared for the feast, which was like wheat in the place of Torah. In the Synagogue of the Tailors, for example, Tzolis the Tailor would prepare a feast of rice porridge and bean soup for the siyum. He used to say that rice and beans strengthen Torah implies two things: the strengthening of the spirit of the Mishna and Ein Yaakov groups, and the literal strengthening of the body of the group of studiers.

## The Conclusion of the Writing of a Book

There were occasions where one group made a celebration, and occasions where a different one did but there were other occasions where all of the groups of the entire town rejoiced together. When did such a thing occur? On the Jewish holidays and also when a new Torah scroll was dedicated in one of the synagogues. Different people commissioned the Torah scrolls. Once it was Yaakov Chaim the

Shada'l who was childless. The Torah served for him as the "Kaddish" after his death. One another occassion it was a wealthy Jew who wished to perpetuate his name by adding another Torah scroll.

When it was time to conclude the scroll, men and women gathered in the house of the writer. Everyone, including women, purchased a word on the final column, so that they would have a portion in the scroll that was about to be finished. The person concluding the book brought a chupa canopy. Musicians appeared. All of the residents of the town, from young to old, gathered to accompany the scroll to the synagogue. The Torah was carried under the chupa by people who took turns in sharing the honor of carrying the precious holy Torah scroll one after another. The men danced and leaped. Even though the natives of the town were primarily Misnagdim, their dances on such an occasion had the enthusiasm of the Hassidim, or perhaps even more so.

In this manner did the Torah scroll progress toward the synagogue like a groom under his chupa. When the procession approached the synagogue, the most honorable members of the congregation went out with all of the Torah scrolls of the synagogue in order to greet the new Torah Scroll with holy splendor, to the sound of trumpets and shouts of joy of the crowd. Rich and poor, Torah studiers as well as Psalms recitors – the community was united, with their hearts beating together as one person.

Thus did the natives of the town live, choosing the Torah over materialism [10]. They ate sufficient food to strengthen the body, so that it would be possible to occupy themselves with Torah and rejoice in its joy. Lives of Torah and wisdom, of uprightness and righteousness, of honor and dedication to every Jewish holy matter were the desires of the souls and the portion of fate for all of the natives of the town.

(From various sources.)

Meir Sokolovsky

**TRANSLATOR'S FOOTNOTES**

1. A rote, phonetic form of teaching Hebrew letter recognition and reading.

2. There is a text footnote here, as follows: Every half year was known as a semester. The two semesters were from Sukkot until Passover, and from Passover until Sukkot.

3. I assume that R'Y is Reb Itzele and R'N is Reb Natan.

4. There is a footnote in the text here: Since the government mandated the study of Russian, the supporters of the Yeshiva said to teach this language to the point of proficiency in writing (from A. Leviatan).

5. There is a footnote in the text here: Mr. Yosef Abramovich once asked the poet Tshernikovsy if the fact mentioned in one of his stories (he was referring to the story "Shaatnez" which is brought down later) that his father was a native of Ruzhany was indeed true? The poet answered that he meant that his father had studied in the Ruzhany Yeshiva.

6. Ein Yaakov is an anthology of the aggadaic (lore) material of the Talmud, as opposed to the halachic (legalistic) material.

7. The Chofetz Chaim was one of the most illustrious rabbis of the period, Rabbi Yisrael Meir Kagan. He died in 1935 at the age of 95.

8. There is a footnote in the text here as follows: Yaakov Berman, who was one of the leaders of the democratic People's Republic of Poland until prior to 1957, is one of his descendents.

9. There is a footnote in the text here as follows: From the mouth of Abba Leviatan.

10. Literally – wheat.

{29}

# Torah -- Rabbis in Ruzhany

## Rabbi Shlomo the son of Rabbi Elchanan [1]

Rabbi Shlomo the son of Rabbi Elchanan of Zelkow was the rabbi and head of the rabbinical court of Ruzhany from the years 5445-5452 (1685-1692). He was well known in his generation and was called "Reb Shlomo Charif" (Reb Shlomo the Sharp) due to his erudition. As the son of Rabbi Elchanan, who was the rabbi in the two well-known communities of Buczacz and Stryj in eastern Galicia, and the grandson of Rabbi Zev Wolf (the father of Rabbi Elchanan), the head of the rabbinical court of Ulyka in Volhynia (the son-in-law of the Gaon Rabbi Shlomo Luria -- the Rash'al), Rabbi Shlomo had a great pedigree. In the ledger of Ruzhany -- which was prior to author of the *Daat Kedoshim* of Rabbi Yisrael Eisenstadt of Ruzhany -- the signature of Rabbi Shlomo appears as the rabbi of Ruznany in several decisions and enactments of the leaders of that community. From Ruzhany, Rabbi Shlomo was accepted as the head of the rabbinical court of Slutsk, which was the main community of Lithuania at that time, where he ran a famous Yeshiva and died there in the year 5466 (1706).

The approbations of Rabbi Shlomo appear in several books of Torah authors of his time, along side the approbations of other famous rabbis. We find these approbations on "Rosh Yosef" of Rabbi Yosef the son of Yaakov of Saltsi, "Netiv Hayashar" of Rabbi Tzvi Hirsch of Pinsk, the 5460 (1700) edition of the Babylonian Talmud, "Or Yisrael" of Rabbi Yisrael Yaffa the head of the rabbinical court of Shklov from the year 5661 (1701).

We know of the following sons of Rabbi Shlomo Charif, the head of the rabbinical court of Ruzhany and Slutsk: Avraham Abli, the head of the rabbinical court and Yeshiva teacher in the Kloiz of Brest Litovsk, and Reb Aryeh Leib, an honorable resident of Slutsk.

## Rabbi Yechezkel Katzenelboigen

Rabbi Yechezkel the son of Avraham Katzenelboigen was born around the year 5428 (1668). He was raised in Brest Litovsk, where he studied Torah from the rabbi of the city Rabbi Mordechai Ziskind, and already attained fame as a genius during his youth. He became related through marriage to the wealthy Rabbi Shlomo Zalman the son of Rabbi Yoel. Rabbi Yechezkel served as a rabbi in the town of Zetel (Dzyatlava) (near Slonim). From there he moved to Ruzhany, where he served as the rabbi for a few years until the year 5464 (1704). Then he was appointed as the rabbi in the important city of Keidani. From there he was accepted in the year 5473 (1713) as the rabbi and head of the rabbinical court of the three German united communities of Altuna-Hamburg-Wandsbek.

Rabbi Yechezkel Katzenelboigen, who served as the rabbi of Ruzhany for some time, was one of the great rabbis of his generation. Several famous rabbis turned to him with their questions, including the rabbi of Prague, Rabbi David Oppenheim. Many authors also turned to him and requested approbations for their books. His Halacha responsa were published in the book *Knesset Yisrael* (Altuna, 5493 -- 1733). A long time after his death, his book *Mayim Chaim* (Paricek 5546 - 1786) was published. It included commentaries on the Torah in the order of the weekly Torah portions. He died at the age of 80, and the Gaon Rabbi Yehonatan Eibeschutz who occupied the rabbinical seat of those cities for three years, eulogized him twice. His two eulogies were published in his well-known book *Yaarat Dvash*.

{30}

The descendants of Rabbi Yechezkel Katzenelboigen returned to Lithuania and Russia, and became famous as great personalities in Judaism.

## Rabbi Moshe Zeev

After Rabbi Yechezkel Katzenelboigen left Ruzhany, two brothers-in-law appear as rabbis one after the other: Rabbi Moshe Zeev and Rabbi Aharon the son of Rabbi Nathan HaKohen.

Rabbi Moshe Zeev was the son of the famous Rabbi Yehuda Eidel, the head of the rabbinical court of Kowel in Volhynia, and later the head of the rabbinical court of the suburban community of Lwow. This rabbi was related to the family of the Mahar'al of Prague and other people of renown.

Rabbi Moshe Zeev was the head of the rabbinical court of Ruzhany for some time. However, due to the tribulations of the wars in northern Lithuania, he set out for Germany and served as the rabbi and head of the rabbinical court of Fürth, Bavaria. He returned to Lithuania after some time, and served as the rabbi and head of the rabbinical court in the upper district around Minsk, and later in Dolhinów, where he died.

In his book *Yeshua BeYisrael*, the scholarly Rabbi Yehonatan the son of Rabbi Yosef, also from Ruzhany, brings words of Torah from Rabbi Moshe Zeev, the rabbi of Ruzhany.

Rabbi Moshe Zeev's brother was the kabbalistic Rabbi Yosef Jaski, the head of the rabbinical court of Dubno, Volhynia, and the author of the book of moral teachings "Yeshod Yosef". Rabbi Yosef was related to the famous historian Simon Dubnow.

## Rabbi Aharon the son of Rabbi Nathan HaKohen

Rabbi Aharon, who served as the rabbi in Ruzhany following his brother-in-law Moshe Zeev, was the son-in-law of the aforementioned Rabbi Yehuda Eidel, and was related to the renowned Rappaport rabbinical family. His father was Rabbi Nathan HaKohen, who it is believed was the head of the rabbinical court in Lwow and the son of Rabbi Eliahu HaKohen Rappaport of Padua, Italy.

## Rabbi Yehonatan the son of Rabbi Yosef -- a Rabbi and Astronomer

Rabbi Yehonatan the son of Rabbi Yosef served as the rabbi of Ruzhany during a period of great suffering.

The first ten [2] years of the 18th century (1700-1710) were years of civil war in Poland, as well as invasions of two foreign countries on its land. The civil war was between the supporters of King August II and the followers of King Stanislaw Leszczynski. Czar Peter I of Russia was on the side of the former, and King Karl XII of Sweden assisted the latter. As always, the Jews were caught between the hammer and the anvil. Every army brigade and every nobleman who headed an army division placed a heavy yoke upon them and drained the remainder of their strength.

Rabbi Yehonatan the son of Rabbi Yosef tells us about the suffering of the community of Ruzhany in the introduction to his book *Yeshua BeYisrael* in the following words:

{31}

"Many tribulations affected the countries in succession: plague, famine, the sword of nations warring against each other, to the point where we became impoverished, the face of the honorable people of the city and country became diminished, and people lost their possessions. I and my family are among them... And today, G-d is with us, and we have become fruitful in the land, for G-d spoke peace for his nation between the heads of the brigades. Would it be that this situation would last forever."

They not only suffered from wars [3], but also from the aforementioned plagues. Cholera broke out in Ruzhany, and most of the residents of the city died. The survivors left the city and settled in booths on the sand banks on the route to Liskowa throughout the summer. The rabbi and the survivors of his flock lived in tents throughout the entire summer and winter.

"Blessed is G-d who did wonders with me. To my right and left, people were felled from the dark thing; however, I, with my wife and family, survived, and harm did not come to our domain... It was impossible for me to go out from the door of my house and abandon my flock to which I tend and serve as their eyes..." Rabbi Yehonatan made a vow that if G-d were to help him and he was able to return to the rabbinical seat of his town, he would walk by foot to the city of Frankfurt to publish a book that he wrote. G-d was his help, he returned to his position as the teacher of righteousness to his flock, and he fulfilled his vow. Rabbi Yehonatan left Ruzhany, Lithuania and Poland, wandered to Frankfurt, and published his book in the year 5480 (1720). He called the book Yeshua BeYisrael (Salvation in Israel) in recognition of the salvation of the remnants of the community of Ruzhany. This was not an ordinary Torah composition, but rather a scientific book on astronomy, about the concepts of the sanctification of the new moon according to Maimonides [4], with many astronomical drawings.

The following is written about the rabbi from Ruzhany in entry on astronomy in the Hebrew Encyclopedia:

Rabbi Moshe Almoshnino: The Appearance of the Spheres, which is the Hebrew translation of Sphaera Mundi of Havlivud [5]. Later commentaries on that book were produced (in the 16th and 17th centuries) by Rabbi Matityahu Delacroti, Rabbi Manoach Hendel the son of Rabbi Shmaryahu, with glosses by Rabbi Yehonatan the son of Rabbi Yosef of Ruzhany, Lithuania.

(Hebrew Encyclopedia, page 816)

Mr. Yehonatan the son of Rabbi Yosef of Ruzhany, the publisher and commentator on the book Tzurat Haaretz (The Forms of the Earth) by Rabbi Avraham the son of Chaim Nasi (see further on [6] wrote the book Yeshua BeYisrael, an explanation of the laws of the sanctification of the month from Maimonides with illustrations (Frankfurt am Main, 5480, 1720).

(Hebrew Encyclopedia, page 823)

**Rabbi Eliezer**

Rabbi Eliezer was a famous rabbi of fine lineage. His family was the rabbi and parnas Yissachar Berish, who was the son of the renowned Gaon known as "Rabbi Heshel of Krakow". According to the book Daat Kedoshim, Rabbi Eliezer was the rabbi in Ruzhany until the year 5705 (1715). From that year he was the head of the rabbinical court of

Dubno, which was then a primary community of Volhynia. In the year 5479 (1719),

{32}

Rabbi Eliezer left the rabbinate and lived in the city of Brody, where he dwelled within the four ells of Halacha. He died there.

Rabbi Eliezer's daughter Chava was the wife of the wealthy Rabbi Yehuda Yudel Landau of Opatow. They were the parents of the Gaon Rabbi Yechezkel Landau, the head of the rabbinical court of Prague, and the author of the responsa book *Noda BiYehuda* (named after his father, the aforementioned Rabbi Yehuda).

In his introduction to the aforementioned book *Noda BiYehuda*, the Gaon Rabbi Yechezkel Landau describes his maternal grandfather, Rabbi Eliezer of Ruzhany, as "The Rabbi and Gaon, holy, Hassid, who spent all his days in fasting, occupying himself with Torah day and night."

## Rabbi Avigdor

During the 1720s, Rabbi Avigdor, known as "Rabbi Avigdor Charif" due to his great erudition, served as the rabbi and head of the rabbinical court of Ruzhany. Several great rabbis, including Rabbi Shlomo Zalman Murkish, the head of the rabbinical court of Mir, as well as others, found it necessary to beautify their works with the approbation of Rabbi Avigdor.

One of his sons was the famous Rabbi Shmuel of Vilna, and the other was Rabbi Yitzchak Izak, the head of the rabbinical court of several communities of Lithuania.

## Rabbi Yisrael Halpern

Rabbi Yisrael the son of Rabbi Chaim of the well-pedigreed Halpern family was the student of famous Torah giants: Rabbi Menachem Eliezer the author of the book *Yair Kano* and Rabbi Yomtov Lipmann the head of the rabbinical court of Kapolia, the author of the book *Kedushat Yomtov*.

Rabbi Yisrael married the daughter of the Tzadik Rabbi Tovia of Ruzhany, a scion of the holy Rabbi Tovia of our town. Rabbi Yisrael served as the rabbi in Olkinik (Valkininkai), Voranava, and then Ruzhany, where he was the head of the rabbinical court until the year 5579 (1819). Then he was called to the honorable position of serving as the rabbi of Minsk. He died there in the year 5599 (1839), at the young age of 43.

A son was born to Rabbi Yisrael in Ruzhany in the year 5576 (1816), who was the renown Gaon Rabbi Yomtov Lipmann Halpern (named after the rabbi of his father the Gaon Rabbi Yomtov Lipmann, the head of the rabbinical court of Kapolia). This son was the head of the rabbinical court of Bialystok and became famous in the rabbinical world for his well-known Talmudic work *Oneg Yomtov*.

The second son of Rabbi Yisrael Halpern, Rabbi Moshe Tzvi Halpern, was also raised and educated in Ruzhany. He later became one of the great rabbis of Minsk.

## Rabbi Yitzchak Izak the son of Rabbi Yaakov Chaver

Rabbi Yitzchak Izak Chaver served as the rabbi and head of the rabbinical court in Ruzhany for fourteen years, from 5579 to 5593 (1819-1833). He was born in Grodno in the year 5549 (1789) to his father the scholar Rabbi Yaakov Chaver. Rabbi Yitzchak Izak studied Torah in Porozovo, was appointed there as a rabbi, and then moved to serve as the rabbi of Ruzhany.

{33}

In his time, he was one of the famous rabbis of Lithuania, and was given the title "Gaon of the generation". While he was still in Ruzhany, he would respond about matters of Halacha to rabbis of near and far communities. Among those with whom he corresponded was Rabbi Yaakov Moshe of Slonim the grandson of the Gaon Rabbi Eliahu of Vilna, Rabbi Mordechai Epstein a rabbinical teacher in Slonim (one of his descendants, Rabbi Lima Epstein, was an honorable resident of Ruzhany and the son-in-law of Rabbi Shabtai Wallach, the head of the rabbinical court of Ruzhany), and the renowned Gaon and Tzadik Rabbi Yaakov Meir of Jalowka.

While he was the rabbi of Ruzhany, he prepared his well-known Talmudic work *Beit Yitzchak* for publication (published by Sokolow, 5596 / 1836). It included novellae on the laws of forbidden and permitted items, and was published when he was already the rabbi of Volkovisk. Later, he published his responsa book *Binyan Olam*, which was published in Warsaw in the year 5611 (1851), when he was already the rabbi of Suwalki. From that time, the Torah giants of the generation turned to him for every difficult matter.

He was also great in mysticism. His methodology in Kabbala was similar to that of the Gaon of Vilna. He studied mysticism from the Gaon and Kabbalist Rabbi Mendel of Shklov (the student of the Gr'a). In his book *Magen Vetzina* he defended the accepted tradition that ascribes the holy Zohar to the G-dly Talmudic sage, Rabbi Shimon bar Yochai.

Rabbi Yitzchak Izak Chaver was also famous as a Tzadik. The masses revered him as a holy man, a worker of salvations and a man of wonders. While he was still the rabbi of Ruzhany, people came to him from near and far to receive his blessing. His house was open wide to every poor person and every melancholy person. Several legends were created about his wonders that came as a result of his prayers on behalf of all who turned to him at times of trouble.

It should be noted that despite all of his attachment to mystical wisdom and his status as the Tzadik of the generation, he was opposed to the doctrine of Hassidism of the Baal Shem Tov, and did not permit Hassidism to spread in the communities in which he served as rabbi. In this area, he remained faithful to the principles of the Gr'a of Vilna. In his famous testament, he warned his descendants against bringing "unfit books" into their homes, Heaven forbid. He also wrote that they must distance themselves from all new factions that are spreading in our days due to our many sins. The only path is to follow the footsteps of our great fathers and rabbis in the spirit of the Talmud and rabbinical decisors. Indeed, the Hassidic doctrine did not spread in the communities of Ruzhany, Volkovisk and Suwalki, and the Hassidim did not have their own Shtibels for all those years. Only in the latter period did a few of them form their own minyan.

Rabbi Yitzchak Izak Chaver had two children who were rabbis of renown: Rabbi Yosef Chaver [7] and Rabbi Moshe Rabinowicz. Both of them were raised and educated in Ruzhany during the period when their father served as rabbi.

## Rabbi **Efraim Zalman**

Rabbi Efraim Zalman, the rabbi of Ruzhany, was educated in Torah in the Beis Midrash of the wealthy scholar and philanthropist Tzvi Hirsch Simchowicz.

At that time, Rabbi Yomtov Lipmann Halpern, the rabbi of Bialystok and author of *Oneg Yomtov*, was studying in that Yeshiva during his youth. The heads of that Yeshiva at that time were the famous scholars:

{34}

Rabbi Zalman, later the head of the rabbinical courts of Brisk, Pruzhany and Dvinsk [8]. They set the logical methodology of study of their students.

In the year 5615 (1855), Rabbi Efraim Zalman, who already served as the Rabbi of Ruzhany, eulogized in the Beis Midrash of the city the Gaon Rabbi Yaakov Meir Padua, the Rabbi of Brest Litovsk, who was considered to be his relative. Both of them traced their lineage to the family of the prince Rabbi Shaul Wohl and the family of Rabbi Meir of Padua. Rabbi Efraim Zalman died in his prime, around the year 5616 or 5617.

Rabbi Efraim Zalman's son-in-law was Rabbi Ziskind Shachor the son of Rabbi Chaim Leib the leader of Mir. Later, Rabbi Ziskind made aliya to the Land of Israel, and was one of the directors of the Kolel Vilna-Zamot in Jerusalem and one of the honorable members of the old settlement of the capital. He was diligent, and was a disseminator of Torah in his city of Ruzhany, his former place of residence.

## Rabbi Mordechai Gimpel Yaffa

Rabbi Mordechai Gimpel was born in Lithuania in the year 5580 (1820) to his father Rabbi Dov Ber. He studied in the Yeshiva of Volozhin and was one of its best students. He earned his acclaim when serving as the rabbi of Ruzhany for 32 years. His sublime personality is described by his student Rabbi Yerucham Fishel Pines, who served him throughout all of the years that Rabbi Mordechai Gimpel Yaffa was in Ruzhany, in "Misped Mar" at the end of his book *Zichronot Mordechai*. These are his words:

"Rabbi Mordechai Gimpel was a great Gaon in Torah, expert in all aspects of Torah, a man of wide knowledge, more G-d fearing than the masses, an excellent and accomplished orator, knowledgeable in world events, possessing of good and upright character traits, a wonderful researcher and expert in Jewish history of every generation, an intercessor with lucid speech, utilizing concise language and riddles, with the pen of a quick scribe. He had control over his inclination and his heart. He had strong opinions, never missed the mark, conducted his leadership in a lofty manner, never bending to any of the wealthy, strong men in our community. He educated all of the members of his household with Torah, fear of Heaven, wisdom and erudition. He married off all of his daughters to scholars, and did not concern himself with silver or gold."

"Rabbi Mordechai Gimpel was not only a great Talmudist, but a great scholar in general. There is barely one book from the ancient or modern literature that he had not read and studied, and that he had not put under the critic's lens. This is demonstrated by the numerous notes he wrote on the margins of the 4,000 books that he acquired with his own money and livelihood. He collated them, honored them, and valued them with unparalleled dedication and wondrous, deep love. With all of his great, broad wisdom, he feared G-d and worshiped

Him in truth and purity, as one of the simple pure ones who never saw the light of Haskalah. He was exacting in easy commandments the same as difficult commandments in an amazing fashion... He possessed an unparalleled clarity of knowledge. He was stringent upon himself and lenient upon others, hard as a cedar tree in matters of Heaven and soft as a reed in issues of the world. He was exacting about the honor of Heaven and Torah, and always lenient with his own honor. As a private individual, he was always humble and never humiliated anyone. He would tolerate his own disparagement and never respond, or he would respond with words of humor, a parable or riddle, with soft calm language that could break a bone. He constantly mourned over Jerusalem and groaned about it incessantly. Every night he would weep over its destruction with the Tikkun Chatzot service [9], with a weeping voice that would rend the heart and soul... He always agonized over the tribulations of the Jewish people and constantly groaned over its honor. His heart was always alert to any matter that related to the nation in general, and would hasten to send letters to hundreds or thousands of rabbis, wealthy people and noblemen, including the wise men and intelligentsia of the generation who also recognized him and held him in great esteem. He was one of the first people to utilize his sharp, rhetorical pen to fight in the newspapers against those who would revise the religion. He made a name for himself in this..."

{35}

**Rabbi Mordechai Gimpel Yaffa**

"Aside from all this, his home was always wide open to poor people and wayfarers, and he greeted everyone in a friendly manner. With the modesty of Hillel, he drew the hearts of many young people under the wings of the Divine presence, thereby saving many young people from being pushed away..."

"He was also among the first who extended his hand to the Tzadik and Gaon Rabbi Tzvi Hirsch Kalisher [10] of holy blessed memory, and founded an organization for the settlement of the Land of Israel in his city even before the evil days of thunder, afflictions and deportations came..."

Rabbi Mordechai Gimpel Yaffa was one of the first rabbis in Russia to support the Chibat Zion movement. He worked greatly for the settlement of the Land.

## Assisting the Farmers of Pavlova to make Aliya

Rabbi M. G. Yaffa assisted Reb Yechiel Beril, the editor of *Halevanon* who worked as an emissary for Baron Rothschild in selecting Torah observant farmers from the region of Ruzhany to found the Ekron Moshava and to collect money for their travel expenses. In "*Hamelitz*," 1892 (27), Moshe Lewin relates the following:

"He was a true lover of Zion, and the settlement of the Land of Israel was his talk and thought throughout the day. When the rabbi who was the publisher of the *Halevanon* periodical came to get farmers for the Pawlowa Moshava near our city Ruzhany to found the Ekron Moshava, the rabbi removed all obstacles and straightened out all of the difficulties that lay in the path of these farmers, so that they could set out toward the Holy Land. Who else knows as I do how much he toiled and suffered for this. Nevertheless, not only did he not complain about his toil and suffering, but he rather regarded it as a source of pleasure and enjoyment, since he knew that one more Moshava was being founded in the Holy Land with his assistance."

## Making Aliya Himself

He was attracted to the Land with bonds of love. At the end of the year 5648 (1888) he left the rabbinical seat of Ruzhany and made aliya to the Land. It was hard for the residents of Ruzhany to part from their beloved rabbi. In "*Hamelitz*" 1888 (173), Reb Y. Z. Friedman relates the following:

"He was so bound with bonds of love to Chibat Zion and Jerusalem that he actualized his love, and yesterday traveled from there with his entire precious possession -- his packed up library, the price of which exceeds 5,000 rubles (a gigantic sum in those days)..."

"The people of his city, from young to old, made him a great honor on the day he left. Those present included city officials who accompanied him on his way. Great rabbis such as the Gaon and head of the rabbinical court of Volkovisk and other rabbis who lived close to our city came to bless him and to receive his blessing."

{36}

"Our rabbi and teacher, your departure is difficult for us. All of the residents of our city are saddened and your leaving. However our comfort is that you did not reject us or abandon us to dwell in honor in a different city, larger and better than ours; but rather your strong love to the Land of our forefathers and your holy feelings for its soil pulled you with bonds of love to travel to it. Therefore, we offer our farewell blessings to you from the depths of our heart: May G-d guard your goings and your comings -- May G-d bless you from Zion, and may you see the good of Jerusalem all the days of your life."

## The Rabbi in the Land

Rabbi M. G. Yaffa settled in the Mizkeret Moshe neighborhood of Jerusalem. A Talmud Torah was founded in that neighborhood through his efforts. With his influence, Reb Yehuda Horowitz donated a large sum of money to the building of this Talmud Torah, which was called Beit Yehuda. He also succeeded influencing the wealthy Friedland from Peterburg to donate large sums to expand the old age home in Jerusalem.

Rabbi M. G. Yaffa left Jerusalem on account of a dispute that broke out among the rabbis of the city, for he did not want to be caught up within this dispute. He settled in the village of Yehuda. The rabbi moved his many books there, and continued to occupy himself with Torah in peace. He led a small Yeshiva there, which continued on throughout his life.

He felt himself to be in a good situation there:

"Three years before his death, he succeeded in making aliya to our Holy Land, which had always been the desire of his heart. He took with him his many books which were filled to the brim with his notes, and dedicated himself solely to Torah and Divine service in peace and calm, far from the bustle of the city, in the village of Yehud, so as to distance himself from the thicket of the disputes and controversies that were found in the cities of the Holy Land due to our many sins. He would ascend to Jerusalem on the festivals. He loved the Land of Israel, and rejoiced with it in true heartfelt joy in a most sublime manner. Not too many people can understand this type of joy, which literally renewed his youthfulness. He dedicated most of his time to Torah and Divine service. During his free time, he would stroll through the olive groves near Yehud to enjoy the fresh air and the splendid nature of our Holy Land. The Gaon Rabbi Shlomo Mohilever spoke accurately when he said that anyone who wishes to gain a concept of the World To Come should go to Yehud and see the world of Rabbi Mordechai Gimpel there -- a world where there is no jealousy, hatred, or competition, but rather righteous people sitting with their crowns on their heads." (From the volume *Misped Mar* (Bitter Lament) at the end of the book *Zichronot Mordechai*).

A precious man went to his eternal world when he died. Many people, including great rabbis eulogized him: the Rabbi and Gaon of Slonim, the Rabbi and Gaon of Porozova, Rabbi Yerucham Fishel Pines, a naive of Ruzhany and the author of the aforementioned *Misped Mar*, and others. Among other things, Rabbi Moshe Nathan HaLevi, the head of the rabbinical court of Dubno, states the following in his eulogy of M. G. Yaffa of blessed memory:

"A Gaon of Israel, a holy elder, the scion of holy roots, his sharpness and breadth of knowledge were like the early sages, he authored pearls of wisdom. He was an elder, and a man of eminence, who left a blessing after him: many novel ideas in his responsa to his many questioners from all over the Jewish Diaspora (*Klilat Hamenora*, Part I, Berdichev, 5642 / 1882)."

In *Sde Chemed* volume II, Warsaw, 1896, the following is stated about the deceased: "He was a unique man, one of the giants of our generation, a scholar of Jerusalem, a prince of Torah and a light to his nation, who was a holy elder, the wonderful Gaon, a remnant of the Great Assembly [11], our Rabbi Mordechai Gimpel of Ruzhany, whose image was like a lion. From his holy days, rivers flowed from the wine of the Torah to the mouths of the rabbis, life-giving wine.

(From various sources.)

By Meir Sokolowsky

{37}

## Chovev Tzion

The image of Rabbi Mordechai Gimpel Yaffa as a Chovev Tzion [12] is well marked in the tapestry of his character traits. He loved the Land of Israel greatly and deeply. This was not only due to the traditional connection between us and the Land given to us by G-d, but because he felt and believed with true faith that there is no other place in the world aside from the Land of Israel that could serve as a haven and refuge for our nation. One elderly person from Ruzhany told me that on his final Sabbath before leaving the city to make aliya and settle in the Holy Land, he gave a long sermon in his Beis Midrash about the love of Zion and the duty of every Jewish person to acquire some inheritance in our Holy Land. During this sermon about the qualities and holiness of the Land, he told the following story:

There is a story about a poretz (landowner) in Poland who owned many estates, villages and settlements. He leased his estates, liquor distilleries, mills and the inn in every village to Jews. One of these lessees was an intelligent and witty Jew who was not successful in his business and was not able to pay the lease fees to the poretz. One year, and two years passed, and then one winter day, the poretz summoned this Jew and warned him that if he does not pay his debts within a month, he would confiscate all of his property, his efforts and his toil, and would also expel him and his family from the village.

The Jew knew that the poretz was liable to carry out his threat, but he also knew that he had no hope of paying off his debt within a month. Despite all of his wisdom and intelligence, he did not find a way to release himself from his terrible situation. After much thought, he decided to not wait until the end of the month when the poretz would confiscate everything that he had, but rather to salvage anything he could and leave the village within the next day or two. The village Jew gathered up his belongings and his meager property, sat with his family on his winter wagon hitched to one thin horse, left the village and set out along the road that led to the nearby city. They believed that they had already escaped the talons of the poretz, but as is known, Jews have no luck. After traveling only one parsang -- behold the poretz was traveling in his wagon and met them. He called up in surprise:

"Moshke, what is going on today? Why did you suddenly desire to go on a 'vacation' with your family to the city?"

The heart of the Jew shuddered out of great fear, but while the poretz was still surprised, he strengthened himself, thought for a moment, and answered subserviently:

"My master the poretz, this evening and tomorrow is a festival for us Jews. And Your Honor knows that the Jews of the village travel along with their families to the city for the festivals..."

The poretz, who had dealings with Jews on occasion, knew that it was the custom of the Jews of the village to celebrate their festivals in the city. He was also somewhat familiar with the calendar of Jewish holidays, their times and names. He knew that the Jews have three pilgrim festivals with various names, "The season of our freedom", "The season of the giving of our Torah", and "The season of our joy".

He also knew when these festivals fell out during the year. He was surprised to hear that suddenly in the middle of the winter, the Jews have some festival about which he did not know. He asked the Jew:

{38}

"Moshke, what is the name of this festival?"

The Jew immediately answered:

"The name of this festival is 'The season of our escape'"...

The poretz was satisfied with this response, and wrote the name of this festival, which was unknown to him until now, in his notebook. He wished the Jew "A good holiday" and traveled on to the next village, where he also had a Jewish lessee. He entered the village after the stars came out and approached the home of the Jews to warm himself up with a cup of strong liquor. He found "his Jew" in this village standing and chopping wood. He knew that such labor was forbidden to a Jew on a festival, and if he required such work to be done, he would utilize a gentile. He turned to the Jew in anger:

"Zhyd, when did you begin to desecrate your festivals?"

The Jew looked at him with surprise, and thought that the poretz must certainly be drunk. But the poretz continued on:

"Shame on you, zhyd, that you do not keep the festivals of your religion. Moshke from the other village is faithful to his religion. I met him today as he was traveling with his family to the city to celebrate the festival that he called 'The festival of our escape'."

The Jew now understood that the poretz was not asking his question out of drunkenness, and answered him:

"Yes, my master the poretz, this is a Jewish festival from days of yore and from generation to generation, but it does not have a set time. Moshke is celebrating this festival today, and perhaps within a number of days or weeks, I and other Jews will celebrate this festival, the festival of our escape..."

Rabbi Mordechai Gimpel then concluded his sermon:

"My beloved brethren, every Jew in the Diaspora must not forget that there will be times when he will have to, Heaven forbid, 'celebrate' 'The season of our escape'. He must prepare a refuge and a haven for himself in his homeland, for our sages have said (in 'Torat Kohanim' of the portion of Bechukotai) regarding the verse (Leviticus, 26:5), 'And you shall dwell securely in your land' -- in your land you will dwell securely but not outside of it..."

The great and abiding love that Rabbi Mordechai Gimpel Yaffa had for the Land of Israel is especially expressed from the following small episode:

When he made aliya and settled in the land of Israel in the year 5648 (1888), he decided to tour the Jewish settlements that had only started to be built a few years before his arrival. During his tour, he visited Rishon Letzion, a settlement that was involved in a dispute in matters between man and G-d at that time. When the wagon entered the gates of the settlement, Rabbi Mordechai Gimpel stood on his feet, looked to the sides, and said:

"A widow, and somewhat insolent, but in any case, Blessed is He who restores the boundaries of the widow"... [13]

Rabbi Mordechai Gimpel was the first of the second generation of students of the Volozhin Yeshiva to make aliya to the land of Israel, not only to see it in its destruction, but also to assist in its upbuilding. Apparently, Rabbi Mordechai Gimpel Yaffa, with his love of the Land, had a significant influence upon one of his illustrious family members who was a third generation student of the Volozhin Yeshiva, and who made aliya to the Land of Israel, was elevated by it, and assited greatly in both the spiritual and physical development of the Land -- this is none other than the Gaon and Tzadik Rabbi Avraham Yitzchak HaKohen Kook, of holy blessed memory.

By Rabbi Yehuda Leib HaKohen Maimon [14]


{39}

## The Grandchildren of Mordechai Gimpel Yaffa

### Betzalel Yaffa

His second grandson was Aryeh Leib Yaffa, who, like his elder brother, was active in the ranks of Chovevei Tzion in the Diaspora [15], and in his great work for the building and settlement of the Land after he settled there. He was also one of the first builders of the city of Tel Aviv and the expanders of its boundaries. A street in that city is named for him.

### Aryeh Leib Yaffa

His second grandson was Aryeh Leib Yaffa, who, like his elder brother, was active in the ranks of Chovevei Tzion in the Diaspora. In addition, he was well known as a poet and singer. After he made aliya, he dedicated himself, as is known, to work for the Keren Hayesod, and was at the head of its leadership committee.

In this role, he often traveled throughout the world, and was very successful. In one of his visits to Poland, he was received in Lodz by the Ruzhany native Moshe Limon [16] who had moved to that city and headed the Zionist committee of that city. He offered his greetings to the guest in that capacity. He said, among other things, "I recall how the natives of my city Ruzhany parted from your grandfather Rabbi Mordechai Gimpel Yaffa, with weeping and joy. With weeping -- because it was difficult for them to part from their most beloved rabbi, and with joy -- for their rabbi and teacher merited to make aliya to the Land of Israel, the joy of his soul. With great enthusiasm, the people unhitched their horses, hitched themselves up, and carried him to the nearby village. Now I myself have the honor, as a native of Ruzhany, to greet his grandson as he spreads the issues of the settlement to the Diaspora."

## My visit with Aryeh Leib Yaffa

After I made aliya to the Land as a student of the Hebrew University of Jerusalem, I went to visit Aryeh Leib Yaffa in his office at the Keren HaYesod. He greeted me very cordially as a native of the town in which his grandfather had served in the rabbinate for decades.

To this day, I see before me his noble image, as he was bound to his office desk, which he graced and from which his grace exuded. I could not imagine at that time that he would meet his death while on duty at that institution, when a mine that was placed under the national institutions in Jerusalem exploded during the War of Independence

By Meir Sokolowsky

{40}

## The Appointment of Rabbi Shabtai Wallach as Rabbi of Ruzhany

After Rabbi Meir Gimpel left Ruzhany, a meeting was called, and the citizens of the city chose Rabbi Shabtai Wallach as their new rabbi. In *"Hamelitz"* 1888 (188), Reb Y. Z. Friedman tells the following about that meeting:

"The appointment of Rabbi Mordechai Wallach as the rabbi of Ruzhany. Ruzhany (Grodno District), August 19 -- after Rabbi Meir Gimpel left our city (as I reported in issue 173 of *"Hamelitz"*), our townsfolk called a meeting. All of them gathered together in the synagogue to take council: who should be chosen as the rabbi and teacher of righteousness in place of Rabbi Meir Gimpel. All of them, young and old, rich and poor, wished to hear what he had to say. After several hours of deliberations, they agreed unanimously to choose the native of their city, the Gaon Rabbi Shabtai Wallach, to be their rabbi. After their decision, they went to greet their rabbi with great splendor and glory. All the residents of the city, from young to old, left the house of the rabbi, and with shouting, celebration and song, carried their teacher and rabbi on their shoulders under a canopy. From afar, the sounds of the crowd singing the well-known hymn were heard: 'We will depend on you for every legal matter!' They proceeded in this manner to the House of G-d, where they received him in great honor, with lights and musical instruments, and led him to his special place next to the Holy Ark.

**Rabbi Shabtai Wallach**

Who would have believed that the residents of our city, numbering more than 2,000 families (may they continue to increase), including merchants, wealthy people, householders, tradesman and factory workers, divided into factions and organizations, would gather together as one man when the time came to do something good and effective, take council with love and brotherhood, and conclude the matter in a positive fashion, with peace and contentment. In this matter, the residents of our town can serve as a praiseworthy and pleasant example to many others."

## Rabbi Shabtai Wallach

Rabbi Shabtai Wallach [17], the head of the rabbinical court of Ruzhany, was born in the year 5611 (1851) to his father, the Tzadik Rabbi Avraham Yaakov. The family roots were from Germany, and the family gave rise to several individuals renowned in the world of Torah and Judaism. Rabbi Shabtai was known as a genius already during his youth.

{41}

He married the daughter of an honorable citizen of Ruzhany, Rabbi Yomtov Lipmann Epstein of the family of the martyrs of Ruzhany, and he studied Torah there for 22 years. He did not want to accept the yoke of the rabbinate. He earned his livelihood from a store that his wife ran. In the year 5648 (1888), when Rabbi Mordechai Gimpel Yaffa left for the Land of Israel, after the urging of the members of the city and with the recommendation of the aforementioned preceding rabbi, Rabbi Shabtai Wallach agreed to become the rabbi and head of the rabbinical court of Ruzhany.

After his death, his son-in-law Rabbi Zalman Weiss inherited the rabbinical seat. Prior to that, he had served as the rabbinical judge in the community for many years. A dispute arose regarding the seat of the rabbinate after the death of Rabbi Zalman Weiss of blessed memory, which lasted for a long time. Several rabbis wished to be selected as the rabbi of Ruzhany, and opinions in the city were divided.

## Rabbi Ziskind Richtschreiber

Rabbi Ziskind Richtschreiber was great in Torah, like one of the great ones. He was also of good lineage, a descendent of Rabbi Yomtov Lipmann Heller, the author of *Tosafot Yomtov*, of holy blessed memory.

When he was still young, he was accepted as the rabbi and head of the rabbinical court in Ludmir, Volhynia, according to the special recommendation of the Gaon Rabbi Chaim HaLevi Soloveitchik, the head of the rabbinical court of Brest Litovsk.

In the year 5675 (1915), the first year of the first World War, when Ludmir was conquered by Austria, Rabbi Ziskind was forced to move to Liskova due to the tribulations of the war. His father-in-law Rabbi Yomtov Lipmann had previously served as the rabbi of that town.

In the year 5676 (1916), the people of Pavlova (Pawlowo) near Ruzhany invited him to be the rabbi of their community. Even though such a small rabbinate was not in accordance with his value and greatness of his abilities, Rabbi Ziskind agreed to come, and remained with them for a period of 15 years.

Rabbi Ziskind died on the 14th of Tevet, 5691 (1931), and was buried in the Ruzhany cemetery next to the grave of the elder Rabbi Shabtai Wallach. His two brothers-in-law, Rabbi Aryeh Leib Meyerson the rabbi of Liskova and Rabbi Eliezer Harkavi the rabbi of Porozowa, eulogized him, as did Rabbi Abba Swiaticki of Kosowo and Rabbi Zalman Weiss the rabbi of Ruzhany.

<u>Imrei Noam</u> by Rabbi Richtschreiber is known in the world as Torah. This work is mainly a book of sublime exegesis. From among his many writings in Halacha and Aggada that were left behind in manuscript form, we should point out the precious book that explains all difficult passages in the Migdal Oz work on Maimonides.

## Shaatnez [18]

(From the book <u>Thirty Three Stories</u>)

We are living in the era of encyclopedias. There are people who believe that the encyclopedia can define the essence of anything, without question. However I believe that even the finest encyclopedias do not fulfill their obligations. Who is to blame? Of course the publishers. They believe with perfect faith that specifically scholars, experts, German professors or doctors at least are equipped to work in the compilation of an encyclopedia.

{42}

According to me, this is not the case. If the matter is given over to the writers of novels and romances, for example, only then would we have encyclopedias worthy of their name.

I will suffice myself with one example, from which we can learn the rest.

For example, you wish to find out about the city of Ruzhany. You open volume R of the encyclopedia, find the entry on Ruzhany on page so-and-so, and find "Ruzhany -- Region of Grodno, District of Slonim... According to the census of 1847, the Jewish population was 1,556. It had a Talmud Torah (1910)."

Now we will check the article on Pruzhany: "Pruzhany -- Region of Grodno, District of Grodno. According to the census of 1847, the Jewish population was 2,580. It had a Talmud Torah (1910)."

According to the encyclopedia, what is the difference between Ruzhany and Pruzhany?

Nothing.

What is Ruzhany?

Nothing.

Now I will tell you what Ruzhany is -- specifically from a time close to the time of the census -- ten years before or ten years later.

You should know that my father of blessed memory was a native of Ruzhany [19]. What was my father and how did he earn his livelihood? What is the difference! The main thing was that he was a sincerely G-d fearing Jew who observed the commandments. His business affairs were in Riga. That is to say, he earned his money in Riga and spent it in Ruzhany. There in Ruzhany he had a home; there he had a place in the Beis Midrash; there he paid the tuition fees for his children; there he prepared his clothing and those of his family -- with the men's tailor Reb Shmerl. At this time, during my youth, this Shmerl was getting on in age. My grandfather and perhaps my great-grandfather ordered their clothing from him. He had a custom with my father's household. He knew the measurements of every family member by heart -- and this was at a time when measurements were not in vogue. He was able to sew clothing for each person according to his measurements.

It was sufficient for you to bring the merchandise to his home. If someone wanted, a person would not have to trouble himself to go to the shopkeeper to choose the fabric, and certainly not the lining. Everything was awaiting from the outset, and everything was known from the beginning. They would enter the store, choose the merchandise, discuss the sale with the shopkeeper, consult with the tailor, agree on the situation -- and everything was for the benefit of the sale itself. This was for the benefit of the man who was always making sales at the same time as he was coming to purchase.

Reb Shmerl the tailor used to say: "Just as Torah is very deep, the theory of tailoring is very deep."

Indeed, tailoring contains mysteries of wisdom, hidden folds, tall corners. Aside from the "revealed wisdom" -- the outer fabric and the lining, there is the "hidden wisdom" -- known as the ornaments, the purpose of which cannot be grasped by the mind of an ordinary person [20]. Sometimes a thick hair sticks out, specifically near the lapel on the chest, and the ordinary person does not understand from where it comes and what is its purpose.

This "ornament" is not within the domain of the purchaser. After he chooses the fabric and the lining, the shopkeeper calls his assistant, who hastens to bring stacks of fabric patches and joins them together. Nobody asks the purchaser, and nobody shows him anything.

{43}

Father's coat, about which I wish to tell, was also made by Shmerl the tailor. In truth, a person could believe that there is only one type of fabric in the world, one lining, and one cut for all garments, and even only one tailor...

Once my father traveled to Riga at the beginning of autumn and took his good winter coat with him, as usual. First, it was a new garment; second, the cold days were approaching; third, a winter coat would increase the honor of its wearer in the eyes of people, and would be a good portent for credit.

One bitter and unfortunate day, my father was caught in a nail stuck in a pushed-over gate, and the corner of his coat ripped. He entered his inn with a broken heart. The innkeeper, his wife, and several guests who were present at that time gathered around him. All of them were pained and agonized over my father's pain. They talked disparagingly about the owner of the gate and complained about the authorities who do not take care of the things that they should be taking care of. Finally they agreed that the only remedy for the coat would be an expert tailor. After everyone mentioned the name of the best tailor they could think of, the innkeeper sent for one of them that he knew and gave him the coat. Early the next morning, he returned the completed work to its owner, received his fee, and left.

One week later my father had almost forgotten about the incident with the coat. One morning, the innkeeper's wife entered the room and said, "The tailor who fixed the torn coat wishes to talk to you".

"What do I have to do with him", said my father in surprise.

"He does not want to say."

"Tell him to enter."

The tailor entered. Only then did my father take appropriate notice of him. Before him stood an elderly thin man with a fallen chest, prominent eyes, and a pleasant face. His essence was of a pleasant, G-d fearing Jew.

"What is your wish?"

"Do you not recognize me? I am the tailor who fixed the coat."

"Yes", my father said.

The tailor said that he had asked and inquired about my father, from where he came, and who he was. He found out that he was a Torah personality who feared Heaven.

"Why did he go through all this effort? Perhaps he wants to marry into my family?"

"I do not want to marry into your family, and I am also not a matchmaker. But since you are a G-d fearing person, I wish to tell you something that I did not say after I brought the job back to you."

"What is it?"

The tailor answered that it is indeed difficult for a person who is not a tailor to understand the matter. The lining of the coat, the coat that he had fixed, was shaatnez.

My father answered that this is impossible. Heaven forbid that he should purchase shaatnez. The shopkeeper is an upright person, and the tailor who sewed the coat was a proper Jew. Heaven forbid that something like this should happen. Shaatnez! Did his ears hear what he had said? It is forbidden from the Torah... It is unbelievable what he had said!

The tailor answered that he does not suspect proper people, Heaven forbid, but that sometimes it is difficult even for an expert to determine matters such as this. When he realized this, he hesitated and did not know what to do. He thought that perhaps my father was one of the lenient ones -- of the young generation! Certainly that was it... And therefore he said to himself, "it is better that he err than act deliberately." But he did not rest until he investigated and found out who the owner of the coat was. He was told that he was a person meticulous in his religion. Therefore, he is fulfilling his obligation and informing my father of the matter.

{44}

In any event my father could not understand how this could be. Shaatnez! Such is not done among the Jewish people!

The tailor said that he has done what he had to, and if he suspects, Heaven forbid, that he said what he said in order to obtain further work, he is stating from the outset that he would not take on the job of fixing the coat. My father should do what he wants, for he has done his duty.

He said good-bye and closed the door.

The end of the story: my father gave over his coat to check for and eliminate the shaatnez -- specifically to that tailor, for Father saw that he was indeed an upright man and that his intentions were for the sake of Heaven. Heaven forbid that my father should wear clothing that has the suspicion of shaatnez!

On the day that my father returned to Ruzhany, he brought in Shmerl the "long" (to differentiate him from a different Shmerl in Ruzhany who was also a tailor, and who was called the "short").

Shmerl entered our house after a short time and greeted Father. He began the conversation politely, asked about Father's well-being, his business in the city, and the tribulations of the journey. In the recesses of his heart he was certain that Father had another "job" for him. However, my father immediately discussed the matter at hand, and showed him the shaatnez that was in the coat.

Reb Shmerl immediately jumped up from his place as if a snake bit him. He did not grasp the matter.

"Shmerl would put shaatnez in a garment?! He is prepared to swear to his Creator, and by his peyos. This weaver... When did he stop understanding about linings? A man such as he would not do wrong over a piece of cloth worth a penny... So what is it? That lazy tailor in Riga -- how many crazy people are there in the marketplace! He does not wish to hear such things..."

My father held his ground, and Shmerl held his.

At Mincha time, my father entered the Beis Midrash to worship.

A group of acquaintances and friends gathered around him between Mincha and Maariv, for he had just returned from the city! Behold -- the entire group of tailors was also there. Reb Shmerl was at the head of them, with the elder, well-pedigreed tailors behind him, those of the second tier behind them, and the apprentices and youths there as well -- all of them knew the matter, all of them had heard about the shaatnez, and wanted to hear the matter from the mouth of Father himself.

After they heard the matter from Father, they turned to each other, grabbed their shoulders, pulled their beards, and took council with each other: How could this be? It is impossible! Everybody uses this weaver. Our grandparents used him from the time that Ruzhany became a city. Shaatnez! If that is the case, "There is no house where there is no dead person" [21]... That is shaatnez. The entire city wears clothes from the same weaver.

Between Mincha and Maariv in the Beis Midrash -- one person studies a page of Gemara, another looks into a book, another recites Psalms -- each according to his abilities. That night the tables were empty. Everyone turned eastward, surrounding Father and the tailors.

The entire group stood there, even some of the apprentices stood there.

That evening, all eyes were turned to the tailors. Incidentally, they remembered an incident that took place previously with shaatnez. The older people coughed, rubbed red scarves over teary eyes, and told stories about events of past times. The young people, with their hands like a button on a stump [22], and with glittering eyes, also had something to tell.

{45}

"Maariv!", and it was the end of the discussions.

However, the next day, again between Mincha and Maariv, the tailors and householders gathered at the eastern wall. My father spoke, the tailors spoke, and the entire audience spoke and responded.

Not only did this take place between Mincha and Maariv, but also in the market, on the street, in the store and butcher shop, between customers, between dishes, between man and wife, in the kitchen, and the bedroom -- the sole topic of discussion was shaatnez.

The land around Ruzhany was divided: the shopkeepers and tailors on one side, and the householders on the other side.

The householders opened up with "who knows", disparaged the trust in the tailors and accused all of their deeds until they came to the conclusion that there is no more corrupt trade than this, and that the "excess" proves this.

The tailors never had such dismal days as those. The tailors, along with their wives, children, and all that belonged to them became a byword.

Who would have known how noisy the city had become had a good idea not come to the mind of the gabbai: since the city of Lodz stands in its place, and one of his relatives is going to Lodz in a few days and would return after a brief period, and the brother-in-law of the gabbai who lives in that city hobnobs with the merchants or at least would know to whom to turn for this matter -- they should send him one piece of cloth as an example, and he would respond.

They did so, and the city quieted down.

A week passed. It was once again the time between Mincha and Maariv. All of the attendees of the Beis Midrash were in their appropriate places -- one with a book, another with his chapter, a man in a corner, and another man with his study partner -- when the door suddenly opened noisily, and a man burst in and did not shut it behind him despite the fierce cold outside. He entered in haste, while he still had wind, with his mouth open, his eyes popping out, and his hands holding the lapels of his coat. He did not greet anyone or respond to any greetings -- until he came to the center of the room, and shouted out loudly:

"In Lodz they said -- it is shaatnez!!"

Were the sky suddenly to split open in the cold of autumn, lightning flash and thunder crack, this would not have disturbed the congregation more than this frightful call: shaatnez! Those seated turned to stone and those standing froze -- one with his book and another on his podium. Every mouth was open, every hand stretched out with clenched fingers, rubbing and scratching the back and the side.

For the hand of shaatnez was everywhere in Ruzhany: on man, woman, old, young, rich, poor, Hassid, Misnaged, scholar, common person, on the clothes, dresses, jacket, tunic, coat, shirt, lapel, sleeve, edges, trains, pocket, collar -- there was no escape from it, from the shaatnez. The entire world was shaatnez!

After the first commotion passed, and there was deep silence, a great tumult arose, the likes of which there never had been in Ruzhany. Everyone wanted to hear again the terrible word "shaatnez" being said explicitly from the messenger.

{46}

After that, a second commotion arose: here was a "kapote" and here was a zufitza" [23]! Here was shaatnez! What to do?! To strip? Here is the jacket and the coat! It is of course cold outside! It will be cold. But, but... with all due respect to their honor, they must also remove... the pants! Let them bring from home what they can: a shawl, a scarf, as long as it is not shaatnez. But -- how can one go outside without pants? It is impossible to move from the place without pants... Woe woe!

To the great dismay, there was no rabbinical judge in the Beis Midrash, and everyone took off their clothes...

And it was night and it was morning the second day...

The elders of the generation relate: there were no better days than those for the tailors -- for the expert tailor, for the regular tailor, and even the apprentice -- from the time that Ruzhany had become a city, and some people say from the time that G-d had created tailors in the world. Everyone stood at the door of their houses, flattered them, ingratiated themselves to them, and enticed them with words. All the tailors, who just yesterday had stood at a low level, today rose to greatness, and many of the householders "became tailors" [24], for the fear of the tailors fell upon them.

There was no person who did not need a tailor at that time, and there was no article of clothing that did not fall into the hands of a tailor. The tailors were full of work. They arose early in the morning and stayed up late at night, all of them removing every trace of shaatnez.

Whoever did not see Ruzhany in those days has never seen a wonderful city in his days. Until they expunged the shaatnez, repaired the coats and the furs, and rendered the trousers kosher to be worn in the community -- every Jewish person went out dressed in sheets and tablecloths, covered with colors and warm kerchiefs, covered with shawls and dressed in anything they could find -- without a lining, without a collar, without sleeves -- so long as there was no suspicion of shaatnez. Some of the children of the Orthodox people remained at home, and others went out in undershirts and undergarments of their mothers and grandmothers.

This was Ruzhany.

By Shaul Tshernikovsky, Berlin 5693 / 1933.

**TRANSLATOR'S FOOTNOTES**

1. There is a footnote in the text here as follows: To our sorrow, we did not receive any material on the rabbis that preceded him in Ruzhany

2. There is a footnote in the text here as follows: According to E. Yaari, *Haolam*, issue 25 from the year 5698 (1938).

3. There is a footnote in the text here, as follows: According to what Yaakov Ickowicz recalled, from his reading of the introduction of the rabbi's book in the synagogue of Ruzhany.

4. The determination of the New Moon is the basis of the Jewish calendar.

5. I cannot identify the name of this person. *Sphaera Mundi* was written by Johannes de Sacrobosco.

6. There is a footnote in the text here, as follows: On page 818 of the Hebrew Encyclopedia, it states that Rabbi Avraham the son of Rabbi Chiya Hanasi (see entry on him) was one of the great Jewish astronomers who write in Hebrew at the beginning of the Spanish era, and that the influence of his words continued for generations among the Jews.

7. The son of his daughter was Dr. Moshe Yosef Glickson, the editor of *Haaretz* in Tel Aviv.

8. Only one Yeshiva head is mentioned here, even though the sentence is in the plural.

9. Tikkun Chatzot is an optional service, recited privately in the middle of the night. It laments the destruction of the temple and Jerusalem. The custom of reciting Tikkun Chatzot is generally followed only by exceedingly pious individuals.

10. A forerunner of modern religious Zionism. See http://zionism-israel.com/bio/kalischer_biography.htm

11. A reference to early Talmudic sages.

12. Literally, a lover of Zion, but also a reference to the Chovevei Zion movement that was a precursor to the formal Zionist movement.

13. There is a custom to recite this homoletical blessing upon reciting a city in Israel that has been restored and resettled. The 'widow' refers to the desolate city. The rabbi is commenting here that the city itself is acting somewhat insolent (i.e. too modern and has veered away from tradition), but nevertheless warrants the blessing.

14. Rabbi Maimon was one of the signatories of the Declaration of Independence of 1948, a member of the first Knesset, and the one who made the "Shehecheyanu" blessing at the ceremony of the declaration of the State of Israel.

15. This first half of the first sentence is apparently here in error, and refers to the second grandson. The rest of the paragraph appears accurate.

16. There is a footnote in the text here: From Zeev Rushkin.

17. There is a footnote in the text here: Litvinov, the Foreign Minister of Soviet Russia in earlier days, was Rabbi Shabtai Wallach's nephew. Translator's footnote: See Wikipedia article about Maxim Litvinov: http://en.wikipedia.org/wiki/Maxim_Litvinov

18. Shaatnez is a mixture of wool and linen that is forbidden according to the Torah.

19. There is a footnote in the text here: See the footnote at the bottom of page 25.

20. This is a comparison to Torah wisdom. The revealed Torah consists of the Bible, the Talmud, and Halacha, whereas the hidden Torah consists of mysticism and Kabbala.

21. A quote from Exodus describing the situation in Egypt after the plague of the firstborn.

22. I am not sure of the meaning of this euphemistic phrase.

23. Evidently the name of some type of garment.

24. A play on words from the Book of Esther 8:17, where it says that many people "became Jews" for the fear of Mordechai was upon them.

{47}

# Labor

The study of Torah along with a worldly occupation is good (Tractate Avot, Chapter 2, Mishna 2).

## The Economic Situation of the Town

Approximately 70% of the residents of the town were Jews. How did they earn their livelihood? The livelihood of the Jews of the Diaspora was based on commerce and labor, since the other economic endeavors were locked or almost locked before them. These were also the sources of livelihood of the natives of our town.

**The stores of the Ruzhany Market Square**

## The Fairs

The fairs were the most important days for earning a livelihood. The town that was somnolent during the six weekdays was awake with bustling life on that day. The market was full of farmers' wagons with their owners, who brought the goodness of their land to town. In exchange, they purchased all their household needs in the stores of the Jews. The Jewish tradesmen displayed many wares in the marketplace: clothing, shoes, hats, furs, brooms, horses, and other items. Most of these wares were purchased by the farmers from the neighboring villages during the day. The farmers sold a great deal of eggs, chickens, ducks, grain and fruit, as well as sheep, cows, horses, etc.

{48}

Ruzhany was fortunate in that a change in its economic situation took place during the 19th century. It was better off than the other near and far cities of the Diaspora. The livelihood of the Jews was based not only on these two branches of livelihood that were typical in the Diaspora -- commerce and labor -- but also on two additional branches: manufacturing and agriculture.

## Manufacturing

At the beginning of the 19th century, the weaving industry grew in the city. From that time, the livelihood of the local Jews was based on hand-weaving of blankets and material for the fatigues of the army of the Russian Czar. Six weaving workshops and several sewing workshops were established in the town, employing close to 1,000 people, mainly Jews. The wool came from outside, and the blankets and material were exported from the town to far-off places. The pioneer in this line of business was Leib Rishon of the Pines family, who settled in Ruzhany.

Later, the town achieved an important place in the tanning trade. The pioneer in this second area of business was Avraham Yitzchak Chwojnik. Several hundred people worked in his hide workshops.

The livelihood of the Jews of the town was readily available, even though for many it was quite meager. There were barely any Jews lacking in livelihood prior to the First World War.

Several of the Ruzhany residents were also owners of taverns, rope factories, flourmills, and other such enterprises.

Agriculture

A certain number of the Jews of the town occupied themselves in agriculture, as lessees of fruit orchards, growers of vegetables, and other such endeavors. However, the town was not known for those types of farmers, but rather for actual farmers -- workers of the land worthy of the name -- who were residents of the two Jewish villages of Pavlovo and Konstantinovo, which were established around the year 1850. However, this was the lot of only several dozen Jewish families. Nevertheless, this image, unusual in the landscape of Jewish Diaspora life, made a great impression in the region, and brought joy to hearts.

By Meir Sokolowsky

## Lives of the Weavers in Ruzhany During the Nineteenth Century

As has been said, there were several weaving enterprises in Ruzhany. The Jewish workers worked in a primitive fashion at simple looms. They worked on a contract basis, and of course were greatly exploited. There were no set hours of work. People began work early in the morning and ended late at night. The weavers would even come to the Sabbath Mincha service in their work clothes and their outer Sabbath coat, so that they could go out to their work in the factory immediately after the Mincha service. They waited impatiently for the first three stars to come out, indicating the end of the Sabbath. Then they would recite the Maariv service in haste, remove their Sabbath garb, and immediately go to work until well after midnight, for they had rested on the afternoon of the Sabbath and were able to remain at wake until a late hour of the night.

{49}

The wages of work were not sufficient for satiety. Wages were paid semiannually. In the interim, the workers purchased their food supplies in the stores on credit. Therefore, they obviously paid a higher price for every piece of merchandise. The workers received their semiannual pay after the factory owners sold their inventory. How was the merchandise sold? The factories had two agents, whose job was to bring the stock of merchandise to the fairs in Yarmolintz and Nizhin.

The merchandise was loaded upon several rented wagons, each one hitched to a pair of horses, which hauled the heavy load along the Moscow Road in the direction of the two aforementioned cities. However, the merchandise was not always sold to the satisfaction of the factory owners. The agents often stood at the fair with their merchandise, with no purchaser coming to buy. Once it happened that the sun was already setting and nobody had pounced on the merchandise. What could be done? How can one return home empty-handed? How would the weavers sustain themselves for the upcoming half year? Then they saw that there were other agents standing and waiting for purchasers of their merchandise, which was also not sold. The Ruzhany agents asked the other merchants about what they were selling. They responded that they had dried fruits in their sacks. The agents of the two cities decided to swap their merchandise. The merchants of Ruzhany returned home with died fruits -- raisins, apples, and the like -- in their sacks.

They arrived at the inn and lay down to rest. The people in the inn smelled the fruit and could not withstand the temptation. First they tried to taste the fruit, and then they put it in their sacks. The agents finally reached Ruzhany with half-empty sacks. The eyes of the factory owners darkened. What could be done? They took the fruits and divided them up among the weavers instead of paying them money, saying to them: go pay your debts with the value of the money -- that is, with fruit instead of cash.

Heard from the mouth of Abba Leviatan

## Families of Workers in the Town

As is known, the livelihood of most of the residents of the town came from work in the weaving factory of the Pines family. Since the wages of the workers were meager and insufficient to sustain a large family, the wife of the worker would have to assist. How? She opened a small store for groceries and other household necessities. In a store such as this, whose value was only a few rubles, it was possible to find salted fish next to a can of kerosene and rat poison next to a sack of flour. Of course the woman, who was tending to children and the needs of the family, could not devote herself to the home and the family at the same time; so accidents often occurred, sometimes serious. At one time, people were saved from death only through a miracle. The story is as follows:

Pesha Leah, the wife of Reuven the weaver, set aside a corner of her house as a grocery store. We were among her customers. Once when we came to purchase flour for chalah, the shelf with the rat poison moved and some of it spilled into the sack of flour below, unbeknownst to anyone. We baked the challas, ate them, were satiated and went to bed. We woke up a few hours later with pain and tribulations. Our quiet night turned into a night of fear and perplexity. We all felt terrible, and violent vomiting overtook us. Were it not for the fact that we summoned the doctor in time, who knows if we would have survived until the morning. We did not know from where this affliction came. We found out in the morning. Pesha Leah ran to our house and burst in with barely the breath of life. What happened? She had discovered that the rat poison had spilled into the flour. Who can recount the bitterness of her fate and the bitterness of the discussion of the tribulation that she had brought upon us.

{50}

Her husband Reuven, tall and pale, worked in the Pines weaving factory. He worked twelve hours a day. The factory owners regarded this as natural. The statement of one of the factory owners was typical of their way of thinking, "The owners of the factories in Lodz will not maintain their stand, and their factories will close since the workers only work ten hours a day." Reuven was one of the few Hassidim in our town (there was a minyan of them). He was Orthodox, but also was one of the first with a sense of workers' rights. Once when the factory owner said brazenly to his workers, "We need to make you a bit hungry so you will not come to us with exaggerated requests and you will know that your livelihood comes from us," he answered, "We make you wealthy. We strengthen you with our blood and sweat. And you still oppress us." This was the first time that words of this nature were heard in the town.

Thus did Reuven and Pesha Leah live. Both of them worked and never lived in comfort at all.

From the mouth of Bulia Chwojnik

## The Labor Movement in Ruzhany in the 19th Century

In *Historishe Schriftn* (Historical Works) of YIVO 111, on the topic of the "Jewish labor movement in Russia from the beginning of the 1870s until the end of the 1890s" by A. Menes, we find the following article on Ruzhany:

"During the Russo-Turkish war which took place in the years 1877-1878 (the exact date is not in the article), a strike broke out in the Pines Factory of Ruzhany -- as told to us by an article in 'Rezhsoyet'.

During the revival that took place in the wake of the Russo-Turkish War, the workers demanded an increase of wages, and the factory owners shut their ears to this request. The workers declared a strike. This had no impact on the owners despite the fact that it caused a great loss to them -- as has been said, to the sum of 40,000 rubles. The factory owners did not agree to the slightest increase, explaining their stance by stating that they must not allow the workers to 'raise their heads.'"

The strike lasted for eight weeks and completely weakened the workers. The aforementioned article in *Rezhsoyet* 1880 (49) is interesting and important in its various details. The author describes the poverty of the workers and the methods used by the owners. For example: with the agreement of the workers, a factory owner would not hire the employee of another manufacturer, so that the worker would not think that he is able to choose the workplace that he wishes. The writer A. L. Mintz reports harshly about the factory owners, and explicitly intends to publicly attack their behavior toward the workers. That writer writes in an article that appeared several months earlier in *Rezhsoyet* 1880 (28) about the dismal situation of the workers in Ruzhany. The factory owners found it necessary to react to this and to justify themselves in *Rezhsoyet* 1880 (34).

{51}

## The Founding of Pavlova and Konstantinova

During the time of Czar Nikolai I of Russia, a number of Jews were permitted to settle on land in a few places in Russia. Ruzhany was one such place, and two agricultural settlements were founded nearby: Pavlova and Konstantinova. Yosef Starewolsky writes the following about them in "*Hamelitz*" 1887 (242):

"The settlement was founded by thirty families. Fifteen settled there in 1850 and another fifteen in 1851. They came there from Jasionowka, Piaski, Lyskowa, and Volkovisk. At first, we had bad years, for our land did not yield its produce and the expenses were great. Were it not for the Pines factory of woolen garments in Ruzhany, we would have died of hunger. We gained our stand very slowly. The land was improved with fertilizer that we bought in Ruzhany for a great deal of money. Our animals increased, and we earned an honorable livelihood from the produce of our land and the milk of our cows. We now have 25 plots, the same as the number of families. The population consists of 125 males and 124 females. Of the 30 families that settled at the outset, five returned to their cities during the first five years since they were not cut out for agriculture. Their land was confiscated by the government. Each plot is 20 desiatin [1]: 3 of meadow, 1 for their children and a garden, and 16 for cultivating and planting all types of grains. The tradesmen among us include 9 house builders, 7 factory workers, 3 tailors, 4 shoemakers, 3 builders, 1 maker of earthenware vessels, 1 carpenter, 2 smiths, and 3 butchers. During their free time they also serve as wagon drivers in the city.

In the colony of Konstantinova on the other side of Ruzhany, there are 11 families."

## Torah and Divine Service

The Hebrew farmers were diligent, and worked the land for many hours a day. However, they also set times for worship and Torah. Yosef Starewolsky writes about this in "*Hamelitz*" year 2, 1862 (11, 13).

"Twelve years prior to this, 30 familles came to Pavlova. We lived in hunger and want for seven years. Nevertheless, we had already built our own Beis Midrash in the first five years, without requiring help from anyone, not even the late wealthy Aryeh Leib Pines. We did everything with our own power. It has now been five years since we invited a rabbi and teacher to come to us. We give him wheat to sustain his household, a house, wood, and candles, and even one ruble a week. He teaches "Chayey Adam" and Bible every day between

Mincha and Maariv. He teaches the weekly Torah portion on Sabbaths and on Shabbat Mevorchim [2] he teaches morality.

During the spring and the summer, everyone goes to work: men, women, and young girls. The Shacharit service takes place at dawn. Many people are also training for trades. On days when there is a great deal of work, they hire people, including gentile workers. There is great joy at the Harvest Festival [3]. Everybody greets each other, and the Magid preaches.

They study more from the eve of Rosh Chodesh Cheshvan until the spring: Bible, Mishna, and some even learn Gemara. They study normally between Mincha and Maariv, and some remain later to continue learning. The cheder for children is in the women's gallery. It has three levels (classes) and three teachers. Their salary is paid by the parents. The Russian language is also taught there." Starewolski

{52}

## Gemilut Chasadim (Benevolent Societies)

### Popular Idealists

### (From the book *Neshamot BeYisrael*, Souls in Israel)

### People of Ruzhany

Each town of the Jewish people has popular idealists who forgo their own needs and dedicate themselves to the masses with all of their essence. However, none was as excellent as those of Ruzhany. Ruzhany had three people of this type in the previous generation. They all lived at approximately the same time. One is David Melamed, the second is Liba Wasz, and the third is Hadassah.

David Melamed was not only a benefactor who collected from the rich and distributed to the poor, but was also a sort of revolutionary. He remained in a state of open warfare with the wealthy people. At every meeting attended by the city notables that dealt with issues of the poor people, the raging image of David Melamed appeared. He would call them "fat bellies" and "gluttonous gizzards."

### A. David Melamed

At first he was a teacher (melamed). Then he became an agent of wagons. He had a bad wife who made his life difficult, but he patiently suffered her curses and did what he had to. He was a great miser with regard to himself. His food would be a plate of grits, despite the fact that his house was well stocked with goods. He would roam around the streets all day with a sack over his shoulder or a pot under his arm. The householders and even the wealthy people whom he always castigated would meet him and give him bread, potatoes, flour and even cash. He would distribute all these to his people: the elderly, the sick, widows, orphans, poor brides, and students of the Beis Midrash. There was no brokenhearted person whose anguish was not known by David. He did his deeds discretely. Suddenly he moved, tossed his donation to the person, and fled. The donors did not know the recipients, and the recipients themselves did not know the identity of each other. When David the Melamed died, the Jews at the funeral saw -- and the entire town was at the funeral -- to their great surprise that from the alleyways in the midst of the city gentile men and women streamed forth the funeral, pushing their way to the coffin with weeping and wailing: "Our father, our sustainer, the person upon whom we depended!! What shall we do without you!"

It then became clear that David the Melamed sustained their poor families just as he sustained Jewish poor families. His wide heart, full of love for suffering people, did not know the difference between Jew and gentile.

{53}

Above everything, the love of David the Melamed for poor children was known. The Talmud Torah that exists now in Ruzhany was established by him. His greatest pleasure was to hear the sound of the students during their studies, to befriend them, to be with them, and to help them to the extent that was possible. In his will he requested that he be buried among the children, and that garbage from the Talmud Torah and from other cheders be placed at his head.

## B. Hadassah

Hadassah was a daughter of a middle class family. She stemmed from a rabbinical family. Her father Rabbi Eliahu Schik served as the rabbi in Lida, Zagar and Kobryn. Her husband was a wealthy merchant. He lived in Moscow all year, and only returned to his home for Passover. With the money that he sent, she was able to sustain herself amply as a wealthy woman. However, she lived her entire life in a small room, engaged in fasting, and only spent pennies on her needs and those of her family. She distributed all of her money to needy and sick people. When her husband came home once a year, he had to pay her debts.

After her death the people of the city decided that every baby girl that was born that year should be named Hadassah after her.

## C. Liba Wasz

The third popular idealist, Liba Wasz, excelled above those two.

Liba Wasz was from the wealthy class, the son of a factory owner. His nickname Wasz was a short form of the name Warsaw, for he married a woman from Warsaw or traveled there often.

His ways were not as straightforward as David the Melamed or Hadassah. The people of the town used to say that he was not goodhearted by nature, but that he "overcame his temperament." However, it seems that he was truly full of refinement and emotions. If he was not able to resonate entirely among the people and dedicate his life to the people as did David the Melamed and Hadassah, since a good heart was not sufficient for this; he had to separate himself from his group. Such an endeavor requires more than a heart. A lofty soul and iron strength are needed for this.

With his sensitive heart, it was impossible for Liba Wasz not to see the chasm between the two sides of the partition in Ruzhany. Without any socialist study, he was able to figure out for himself who created their own wealth, and who was responsible for the suffering and agony of the thousands of people on the other side of the partition. Since he was not able to change the guard, for he did not create it, he decided that he himself would not benefit from his own wealth, but would rather distribute it to the poor to the best of his ability.

He did not give simple donations. He gave of everything that he had in a discrete fashion so as not to embarrass the recipient. To so-and-so, for example, he would give a present of a box of tobacco, and hidden within the box there would be a gold coin. When he saw a poor person wearing tattered clothes, he would remove his own new clothes and give it to the poor person. So it would not be seen as a gift that would embarrass the poor person, he would "sell" the clothing to him -- that is to say something that cost him tens of rubles would be sold for a few small coins. He would always have new clothes sewn for himself so he could do "business" with the poor people with them. He also wanted to send his son to the army "as a comfort for the poor."

It has now been some decades since these benefactors of the people have passed away, however the Jews of Ruzhany remember their heroes and talk about them warmly and enthusiastically as if they had only passed away recently.

{54}

They name of each of them was perepetuated in the charitable organizations. An honorable place was set up for each of them in the cemetery, and fine stone canopies were erected over their graves. At any time of need, Jewish men and women come to their good benefactors who dwell in the cemetery to pour out their hearts before them and beg of them to be "righteous intercessors for them."

A. Litwin

## Hadaska [4]

The diminutive, thin Hadaska, who was called 'Mother' by all the people of the town, stands before my eyes as if alive. She was the daughter of a famous rabbi, Rabbi Eliahu of Lida, who was known by the people as 'Rabbi Elinka of Lida.'

This Hadaska was a precious person: nothing was for herself, and everything was for other people and strangers.

She would arise early both in the winder and the summer. The morning was dedicated to her soul. She was very much attracted to Barchu and the Kedushas. Her relationship to them knew no bounds. Each morning she would run from one Beis Midrash to the next in order to 'snatch' them. Then she would dedicate all the rest of her essence and time to the poor.

**Hadaska**

She would fast on all weekdays, only tasting a few potatoes and coarse bread after nightfall. Like men, she would only eat on Sabbaths and festivals, when the act of eating is itself a commandment. Her husband would argue with her to stop fasting, but it was to no avail. Once her father, Reb Elinka of Lida, wished to command her to stop fasting, using the pretext of honoring her father. However, she pleaded with him, "Please Father, do not do that. I cannot stand up to such a harsh decree and sin against my soul." Her father, Reb Elinka, retracted and did not make such a command to her. He continued on and said:

"My daughter is a modest woman, and she certainly knows what she is doing..."

All of the people of the town revered her as a holy woman. Rays of light emanated from her image. Many would say, "Reb Elinka did not decree. He said...". People would nod their heads and smack their lips.

{55}

However the fast only applied to her. She did not demand it at all of others. The poor had to eat every day and required clothes. Hadaska was busy all day, including nights, in order to ensure this. It was not for naught that all the people of the town called her 'Mother'.

This name was indeed fitting for her, for she was a merciful mother to all of the poor of the town -- and not just the poor, but also the sick, the mothers who had just given birth, the orphans, and the brides. No obstacle interfered with her actions. She went about her work in rain, snow, summer heat, and winter cold. With a sack over hear head, crossing over to one shoulder, and the other end under her second arm, she would go around to the homes of the wealthy people on behalf of the poor and destitute. If Hadaska had to rock the cradle of a sick orphan, she would sit and rock. If it was necessary to find a wet nurse for an orphan baby, where death snatched away the mother, Hadaska would seek out a wet nurse. Hadaska, the mother of the town, did everything. Whoever did not see her leading a poor orphan girl to the wedding canopy, as a mother or mother-in-law, and dancing and clapping her hands before the bride, has never seen happiness in his life.

When the economic situation worsened and it was difficult to collect money in the town, Hadaska would travel to Warsaw, Lodz or even far-off Moscow, to collect money and clothing for the poor of her town. Her good name always preceded her.

She herself was a G-d fearing woman, but she had great tolerance toward others. She never preached or lectured to anyone that they should fear Heaven. I recall only once when she could not control herself, and told me:

"I am required to admit the truth, that it is very easy to receive a donation from you, and it is always a proper donation, but you are lacking somewhat in the fear of Heaven... Do not imagine that I am, Heaven forbid, asking a great deal from you. No. Only that you pray three times a day, wash your hands before eating, recite the Grace After Meals, and fulfill everything that is written in the Code of Jewish Law (Shulchan Aruch)..." It is clear to me, however, that she did not say these things as exaggerated zealousness, but rather out of goodheartedness. I was close to her, and her heart ached when she saw that I was forsaking my share in the World to Come with my own hands. She could not stand seeing my tribulations, and she had mercy upon me...

When I returned to my city after many years, I discovered that Hadaska had barely changed. It was possible that the wrinkles on her forehead deepened and her eyes became more sunken in their sockets. It is possible that her back also became slightly more hunched. However, the diminutive, thin Hadaska still retained her excitement with respect to Barchu and the Kedushas, she still fasted on all weekdays, and would only eat a few potatoes and coarse bread after nightfall. She spent every day running through the marketplace and the streets to collect money and clothing, and distribute them to the poor, widows, and orphans.

"How are you, Hadaska", I asked her, "How is your health?"

"How am I? Thank G-d, not bad. In truth, I do not have time to be sick. Only my feet have weakened somewhat, may you be spared." She then continued on with her work.

At the end, her diminutive, thin body buckled under the burden of her hard work. It buckled and broke. It was during the period before Passover. During the evening, she was still working on behalf of the poor. She went to sleep, and she woke up in the morning saying that she was not well. Within a half an hour, she had closed her eyes forever. It was as if an angel descended from heaven and kissed her on the lips. As the angel kissed her, he secretly drew her pure soul from her body. She went to her eternal world without pain, without suffering, and without experiencing death throes. She died with the kiss of death, as all righteous people.

{56}

Morning came. The weeping and wailing throughout the entire town were great. The poor felt that they had become even more impoverished with the death of Hadaska. The widows and orphans had become widowed and orphaned once again. All the people of the town felt a searing pain deep in their hearts. All of them came to feel themselves as orphans.

Y. L. Mintz

(*Hayom* from Warsaw, year 1, 1925 / 5685, number 6.)

## Woe to Those Who Have Passed Away but are Not Forgotten

The article about the passing of this wonderful person is found in *Hatzefira* 1901 (61) where it says that the head of the rabbinical court of Ruzhany, Rabbi Shabtai Wallach, eulogized her. Reb Yerucham Fishel Pines also eulogized her, among others.

"The deceased was a holy and pure woman, righteous, and a doer of good deeds in the full sense of the term. She was one of the excellent characters of which Israel takes pride. What the Tzadik Reb Nachum the shamash in Grodno [5] was in the world of men, the deceased of blessed memory was in the world of women. Her death is a loss to the entire generation. I state regarding characters such as this, 'The vintage has ended, and the harvest will not come.'"

Since she was so dear to all of the people of the town, all of the baby girls born that year were named Hadassah in her memory.

**Leib Wasz [6] and other members of the Pines Family**

Reiza Pines

Litwin's book discusses him a great deal. It is further said about him that there was a storehouse near his house, containing firewood for the winter. The storehouse was shaky and had some breaches. The members of the household felt that the amount of wood was dwindling due to theft. One of his sons then repaired all the breaches. The lad entered the home and announced to his father with joy, "From now on, our firewood will not be stolen again. I have sealed all of the breaches in the storehouse."

"You did something bad," his father scolded him. He said, "You do not realize that the thieves are very poor people, shivering in their houses from the winter cold along with their families. Since they cannot purchase the necessary firewood on their own, and they are embarrassed to ask for their needs, they take a few pieces of wood quietly. Go and open up the breaches once again."

Abba Leviathan's father [7] was severely ill. Yom Kippur came. Leib Wasz came and asked the wife of the sick man:

{57}

"With what are you feeding the sick man?"

She replied, "With soup I prepared yesterday." Leib Wasz scolded her, saying that a dangerously ill person must eat fresh food. He got up and chopped wood, lit a fire, and cooked fresh, hot soup.

Indeed, not all members of the Pines family were as charitable as he was. However he, Leib, merited that his wife Reiza was his helpmate in these matters. They also set up a synagogue in their house.

## His Brother-in-law Shmuel

His brother-in-law Shmuel [8], who lived in nearby Kossova, followed in his footsteps. He would go out every year after Simchat Torah with a carpenter, glass maker and builder, make the rounds from the home of one widow to the next, and inspect the windows. If he did not see double windows in preparation for the approaching cold winter, he would order them to be fixed. He would tell the glass maker to put panes into the empty frame. He would tell the builder to fix the oven in the house or rebuild it if he found it weakened to the point that it would no longer function. He would also provide potatoes and other such foodstuffs to the destitute. He would do this every year.

**Yaakov Shmuel Pines and his wife Tzipa-Minia.**

## Noach Pines

The deeds of fathers are a sign for children. Leib Wasz was indeed similar to his father Noach Pines, who was also a great charitable donor. When Noach Pines built a factory in the town of Kossova, they said that he was unable to complete his building due to a shortage of money, for he spent his money for completely different purposes. What were his purposes? If a Jew came before him and complained about his daughter who had come to marriageable age but had no dowry, he would immediately take out a proper sum and give it to him. If another one came and said that winter was approaching, and his house did not have a roof, Noach would open up his wallet and take out the money needed to fix the roof, and the like. They said about him that instead of establishing a factory in Kossova, he built the city itself, for he had a portion in most of the houses.

{58}

## Leib Rishon

Noach Pines inherited this character trait from his father Leib Pines, who was called Leib Rishon, for he was the first (rishon) in this family to arrive in Ruzhany and live there at the beginning of the 19th century. He was numbered among the honorable people of that place due to his good deeds. He established a weaving factory in Ruzhany, which enabled a significant portion of the residents of the city to sustain themselves by working as employees of the factory. The Polish landowner Spicha held him in great esteem and drew him near. When the landowner realized that the battle was lost during the Polish uprising in 1831, he turned to Leib Pines with the request that he purchase his palace and everything around it for a reasonably low price, so that he would be able to support himself in France, where he was going. Then Leib became even wealthier. He used his money not only for the benefit of his family, but also for the benefit of the community. He supported the Yeshiva in Ruzhany. Many of the Torah students of the Yeshiva ate at his table. The sound of Torah was heard in Ruzhany. The Yeshiva students studied Torah from early morning until late at night. They went even further on Thursday nights, when they remained awake all night, so that they would be prepared for the arrival of Leib Rishon, who was a great scholar, and who used to come every Sabbath to examine them and determine their success in Torah throughout the preceding week.

Our mother Tzipa-Minia should also be remembered positively, for she gave charity with a generous hand, and excelled at discrete gifts for those who were in need but were embarrassed to accept gifts in public.

From Sonia and Roza Pines

## Yona the Shoemaker

He lived in a 4 by 4 room on Klibaner Street. The ceiling was so low that it almost hung over the heads. His workspace was in the corner of the room. In that corner stood his shoemaker's table with its poor equipment and with the few extras that he needed. However, this corner was empty all day. This was not because the man was lazy. He worked at night, but he dedicated his days to a different task. All day long he would go from door to door collecting monetary gifts, loaves of bread, and the like. This was not for himself, Heaven forbid, for he was able to sustain himself with the toil of his own hands. He was not a miser. He gathered the money and the food for the youths who spent their days, their evenings and most of their nights at the study of Torah in the Aguda [9] building in Ruzhany.

Yona arrived home after the Maariv service. He never returned home alone, for he was always accompanied by poor people whom he invited to his home on a daily basis. He would share his bread with them and give over his bed to them. He himself would sleep on a straw mattress on the floor. His family of five, the poor people and the guests would all sleep in the bedroom. The room was so crowded that nobody could get by. Yona sat in a corner patching the shoes that had been brought to him for repair. He ate a small portion of bread and drank a meager amount of water. He went about in torn, worn out clothing, but was happy with his lot. Why should a person pay attention to himself and his own needs? He must support those who wished to immerse themselves in Torah despite their state of want. However, it was not only they who benefited from his assistance. He concerned himself with every poor, destitute, ill or depressed person. He would bring whatever was needed to every needy mother who had just given birth.

He would run about even more on the eve of the Sabbath. On that day, he had to find places for the poor people in town to eat. He made sure that the entire Jewish community in the town would greet the holy Sabbath with the additional soul [10], at a set table and with faith that the ultimate redemption would come.

According to Naftali Kantarovich and others

{59}

## Yaakov Limon

Yaakov Limon owned a large store for hides and oilcloths. However, his wife always complained that they had no livelihood. Her husband always took any items from the store and gave it to the needy. He did this all discretely, so that is wife would not notice.

Once Yaakov called me when his wife was present in the store, and advised me to purchase a new oilcloth that would be appropriate for my work. I entered the store, and he took me to the cellar, where the oilcloths were located, according to him. There he filled my pockets: in one pocket he put a bottle of wine, in a second he put sugar, and other items. He took me back up and led me out of the store, thereby smuggling out the provisions that were in my pockets. A few minutes later he also hastily left his store, and went with me to the sick Pinchas "The Yellow" (A wagon driver who would bring people from Ruzhany to the train in Ozernitsa and bring others back in return, who once drank water when he became hot along the way and took ill with tuberculosis) to give him the wine, sugar, and the like.

He helped another sick person, Moshe Dreyfuss the tailor, in the same manner. This was always his custom.

From A. Leviatan

## Nimele the Butcher Bulgatz

He was a simple Jew who owned a butcher shop, as his name testifies. He often enjoyed drinking glasses of liquor, so his nose was always red. He did not excel externally at anything. He was a Jew like all the local Jews. However, an incident once occurred that made him greater in my eyes. I was preparing my lessons with my friend Moshe Berman, whose house was adjacent to the house of Nimele the Butcher. A lantern was burning in the house, and we wrote to its light. Then the light went out, and we were left in the dark. There was no match in the house. We decided to go to our neighbor Nimele the Butcher to request a match from his wife Tsharna.

We entered his house and froze in surprise. Nimele and his wife already went to sleep in the nearby bedroom, and there were poor people in their large room. One was sleeping on the table, the second on the bench. Two others were filling up with borscht in the kitchen and two more were heartily eating a loaf of bread. The room was stifling. The smell of the sweat of people who spent their entire day going from door to door, and the smell of their socks gave off a bad odor that filled the air. The snoring of the sleeping people was earthshaking. We asked ourselves: is it possible that among the gentiles of the world there would be a person who would open his house to poor wayfarers, let them do whatever they wished in the house, while he himself was restricted to some remote corner? Certainly not. Such a thing would only take place with us Jews. How great in my eyes at that time was this simple man and his righteous wife. How happy was I that I too belong to the nation that gives rise to such people.

## Shabtai Shefem of Pavlova

The spirit of the town of Ruzhany attached itself to its suburbs, the neighboring Jewish settlements. Shabtai Shefem lived in the village of Pavlova. Every Friday, he would come to the bathhouse in town with his wagon hitched to his horse. After his customary bath, Shabtai would make the rounds to every Beis Midrash in the city, searching for poor people who were in need of a Sabbath meal. He invited them to ascend to his wagon, and drove them to his home to be his Sabbath guests. He did this every Sabbath.

From Bulia Chwojnik

**TRANSLATOR'S FOOTNOTES**

1. A Russian unit of measure, about 2.7 acres.

2. The Sabbath prior to Rosh Chodesh, the New Moon.

3. This seemingly refers to Sukkot, which is referred to in the Torah as the Harvest Festival, although it may imply a private harvest festival.

4. Hadaska is a diminutive of Hadassah. This person is identical with the aforementioned Hadassah.

5. There is a footnote in the text here, as follows: "See the book <u>Souls of Israel</u>, by A. Litwin.

6. There is a footnote in the text here, as follows: "The brother of Yechiel Michel Pines."

7. There is a footnote in the text here, as follows: "Heard from A. Leviathan."

8. There is a footnote in the text here, as follows: "Heard from A. Leviathan."

9. This house was built by Avraham Yitzchak Chwojniak of blessed memory.

10. Jewish lore states that a person gets an additional soul on the Sabbath.

# Our Town

{60}

## Our Town Ruzhany

Our town Ruzhany remains whole in my memory, without weakness; and to this day remains before my eyes as alive and bustling, as it was when I left it. It does not enter the imagination at all that our town, which raised an entire community of Jews, nurtured many generations, gave rise to hundreds and thousands of sons and daughters, sent many to various lands throughout the seven seas and kept many of them in their own place, was suddenly destroyed completely, wiped off the face of the earth, and remains as a dream in the hearts of those who knew it at that time.

### The Beautiful Landscape

The beauty of Ruzhany's landscape was known throughout the region. When approaching the town, a visitor would already be impressed by the Slonim Valley. A road wound atop this hill between the Christian cemetery with its prominent birch trees on one side, and the green valley of the Klibner Road on the other side. The road enchanted the eye of those beholding it from the higher street. The low houses dotted with numerous gardens laden with fruits and vegetables raised their heads above like white pitched roofs. The burnt castle, some distance away on the hill, rose above everything, adding additional impressiveness to the general view.

Continuing onward on the downward slope of the Slonim hill, the visitor would immediately find himself in the center of the town. He would see a large marketplace with many stores standing in straight rows like soldiers during a practice. The Catholic and Pravoslavic churches stood on the two sides, with their spires and crosses rising up.

Schloss Gasse was considered to be the main street of the town. The importance of this road was that it connected Baranovich with Brisk via Slonim, Ruzhany and Pruzhany. Those walking on the road could also continue their journey on the side streets. This road possessed extra importance due to its fine houses, and especially to the textile factories that were once centered around this road. Even after these factories disappeared from the horizon in the fire of 1915, this road maintained its earlier grace and significance. On Saturday nights, when people went out to chat in the evening, the road bustled with the crowds of people out for a stroll, especially the section that extended from the Slonim Road to the fire hall, and further on to the bridge over the Canal Stream.

The Canal Stream (Kanal Teichl), which wound its way quietly through the heart of the town, added extra grace to this street. This river crossed Schloss Gasse and Milner Gasse, and continued its way peacefully through the green meadows of the alleys of "the other side of the river" until it emptied into the Zlabay River.

The second most important road in the city was the long, broad Milner Gasse.

{61}

**The Napoleon Tower on the Liskova Mountains near Ruzhany**

This street has large houses until the alley of the "other side of the river", and from that point on, it had wooden houses. If you traverse the entire length of the road, you will reach the Zlabay River flowing at its edge. This river was the bathing place of the townsfolk during the hot summer days. As you cross the wooden bridge over the river, you would reach the Liskova Mountains (which were hills that were not too tall, but were called mountains due to the lack of mountains in the region). On one hill there is the remains of a tower that is known as Napoleon's Tower. Popular folklore claims that Napoleon erected this town as a lookout point in 1812 when he crossed through the town on his way to Russia. It is possible that there were battles in the area of Ruzhany at that time.

If you turn left from these Liskova Mountains, you would reach the Jewish settlement of Konstantinova, one of the two Jewish settlements that were established near Ruzhany.

A long and broad road leads northward from the town marketplace to outside the town. Houses surrounded by trees line both sides of that road. As the road continues, there is a broad area covered with wheat fields. Continuing on that road, one would reach the large Bliznaja Forest. From that point, the road is known as Bliznaja Gasse. This forest attracts many convalescents in the summer, who are housed in a building that was set up near the Smolnia (a place where turpentine was extracted from the forest trees).

Going eastward from the intersection of Schloss Gasse and Pruzhany Street, the vista opens to the short, broad Goszcziniec Street. This street leads to a broad road that leads to the other Jewish settlement of Pavlova, two kilometers from the town.

There was a synagogue on almost all of the roads in the town, such as Goszcziniec, Milner Gasse, Klibaner Gasse, and Kanal. However, most of the houses of worship in our town were centered in the synagogue courtyard, called Shul Hauf. From there, the voices of worshippers in the Talmud Torah, the Maier Beis Midrash, the Aguda, and the Tehillim could be heard. Prior to the fire of 1895, the Tailors Synagogue and the Shiva Kruim Synagogue were also located there. The Great Synagogue of the town was at the center of all of the synagogues on the Shul Hauf, rising in all of its splendor.

Heard from Yosef Abramovitch during the memorial to the martyrs of Ruzhany

{62}

## The Synagogues of Ruzhany

As has already been mentioned, our town had a significant number of synagogues. The main one was the Great Synagogue, rising in splendor from the Shul Hauf. It was re-erected after the first fire in 1875, and built in the same place where the Great Synagogue that had been constructed in 1657 in memory of the two martyrs had stood.

During the latter period, Avigdor Michel Goldberg, Moshe Zisking the smith (the jeweler) and, may he live, Abba Leviatan, served as gabaaim (synagogue trustees) during the latter period. Cantor Gershon Kaplan conducted services on special Sabbaths and festivals. Eizenstein served as the wonderful Torah reader on Sabbaths.

The Maier Beis Midrash was located near the Great Synagogue. It was never locked. During the day it served as the place of worship for many members of the community including the rabbi and rabbinical judge, as well as a place of study for the Talmud study group. At night, it served as a hostel for any guest who wished to stay over. Meir Guber and Nota Lisovitzki were the gabbaim. The beadle (shamash) was Leizer der Shamash, one of the four Leizers in the town. The three others were Leizer Liboshitzki, an educated Jew; Leizer Goldin and Leizer Hachanski. All of them lived long. The biggest joker of them was Leizer Liboshitzki. He would say, "A man lives until 70 years, and then he is born again, so a 75 year old is like a 5 year old". Another one of his sayings was, "The table stands on four legs, and the world -- on the four Leizers". When Leizer the Shamash was about to die, Leizer Liboshitzki joked and said, "The table is wobbling -- the world is shaking".

The Tehillim Synagogue was also located on the Shul Hauf. For the most part, tradesmen worshipped there. Leib the Carpenter (der Stoliar) was one of its chief spokesmen for some time.

The nearby Talmud Torah served as a house of worship as well as an educational institution. Aside from the relatively large study rooms, this building had a small room where Aharon Yaakov Pitkowski lived, who served as the shamash in the house of worship and also the first grade teacher in this educational institution. He was dedicated to both jobs.

The two-story Aguda synagogue was also located in the Shul Hauf. The sound of lads reviewing their Gemara lesson would burst forth from the second floor windows. The guest house was located on the first floor of that building. It had been moved from the Maier Beis Midrash by the two righteous women: Lipshe the wife of Shimon the shochet, and Yenta Rushkin. There was also an old age home on that floor.

There was a synagogue on the "Other side of the River" alleyway whose name was the same as that of the street. Many tanners who lived in that area around the Chwojnik tanning factory worshipped there. The gabbaim were Abba Chwojnik and Leizer Segal.

{63}

**The south side of the Maier Beis Midrash**

**In front -- the north side of the Great Synagogue.
On the side -- the east side of the Maier Beis Midrash**

{64}

The Gershonovitch Synagogue was located on Klibaner Street. It was named after the descendent of one of the martyrs of Ruzhany. Aside from the many Misdnagdim, a few "Chaverim" [1] worshipped there. The gabbaim of that synagogue were Hershel Katzin and Yehoshua Soroka.

The Chaikin Synagogue rose above the Goszcziniec. This was far from the center of the city, and the residents of that street worshipped there. The gabbai of that synagogue was Gershon Lipowski. There was a Yeshiva in the Achim synagogue on the Kanal. The gabbaim were the Polak brothers, from whence it derived its name. About ten Hassidim lived in this town, and they gathered for prayer in the house of one of them. Thus, the town was filled with the sounds of prayer from end to end.

By Zeev Rushkin

## Public Life in Ruzhany During the First Half of the Last Half Century Prior to the Holocaust

Until approximately 50 years before the Holocaust, it was not customary for the communal activists to be elected. They would come from the wealthy class, and take the greatness and authority for themselves. For who would run the communal affairs if not they? Indeed, some among them occupied themselves with communal affairs in good faith, but there was no shortage of others who did as they saw fit.

Throughout the latter 50 years, communal life advanced by giant steps. Great changes took place in communal life. The wealthy gabbaim gave way to young activists who from that time stood at the head of the communal institutions and worked diligently to develop them. These young people stemmed from various classes and were elected by the masses of the various parties and organizations that existed in the town.

I wish to point out that our town was already very active in communal affairs 50 years ago. Communal, cultural and even self-defense institutions appropriate to the times were founded. Everything was founded without assistance and without external directions. With all this, the institutions were set up and developed properly, and served as an example to others.

As has been said: for the most part, the communal leaders and activists carried out their duties faithfully. There was never a case in Ruzhany where the communal activists took advantage of their position for personal benefit.

### Rabbis and Rabbinical Judges

When we speak about the community of Ruzhany and its activists 50 years ago, we must mention positively the era when the Gaon Rabbi Shabtai Wallach of blessed memory and the two rabbinical judges Rabbi Hirsch of blessed memory and Rabbi Meir Idel of blessed memory headed the community. We can say that their upright actions were the pride of the community.

## Shochtim and Cantors

The shochtim Reb Shabtai and Reb Shimon, and the cantors Zisel Nishiozinski and Gershon Kaplan, among others, were considered to be among the clergy of the community.

Cantor Zisel Nishiozinski was famous for his pleasant voice. He had a well-organized choir.

{65}

He was he father of the director of the Yiddish theater in New York, and of Mr. Avi-Leah, the professor of music in Israel.

Cantor Gershon Kaplan enchanted the townsfolk with his singing on festivals and the High Holy Days. He was the father of Shlomo Kaplan, who today is the conductor of famous choirs in Israel.

## Other Communal Notables

The following were considered to be among the communal notables:

A) Reb Leizer Liboshitzki, who represented the community before the government and issued passports. He was a learned, scholarly Jew, known for his general knowledge. He was the father of the teacher and writer Aharon Liboshitzki, who was later active in the large city of Lodz.

B) The government appointed rabbi, Eliahu Nota, who also had generous character traits, was educated, and had influence in the city.

By law, the community was only responsible for providing for the religious needs of the population, but in practice, communal life was far richer and variegated due to the fact that numerous important communal institutions were established and fortified.

From where did the community obtain the money needed for this? The principal source was the mean tax, nicknamed the "takseh".

From A. Leviatan

## The "Takseh" (Meat Tax, "Korovka")

As is known, an official Jewish community with the power to impose special taxes on the population in order to maintain the communal institutions established by the community did not exist during the Czarist era. The government only officially recognized the rabbi of the town and the gabbai of the synagogue, who had the authority to collect donations for religious purposes. The rabbi and other members of the clergy received their salary from the "takseh".

This tax did not generally have a good name in the Jewish communities. For many, the word "takseh" implied the strong-handedness of the collectors, of personal privilege and easy profit for the wealthy "owners". This tax was symbolic of a despotic government that took advantage of the poor. However, I can state with full certainty that there was never any incident to justify this opinion in our town, at least during the period that I lived there.

What is the nature of this tax? The authorities of that era permitted the imposition of a tax on Jewish ritual slaughter (shechita), and allowed a certain portion of the income to be given to the community for its religious purposes.

According to the protocols of those days, the government of the city and the district would lease the meat tax to the highest bidder. The official lessee who was sent by the community would then lease this tax to another person who paid an even higher price. In return, the second lessee would have the right, with the agreement of the heads of the community and the gabbai of the synagogue, to impose a tax that would yield some profit for himself as well. Of course, when this tax was set, they would take into consideration the local poor, ensuring that this tax would not be too onerous for them. The difference between the prices of the two lessees would be the income of the community, through which it would maintain the communal institutions, including the Bikur Cholim (society for tending to the sick), the Hospital, the Talmud Torah, and the Beis Midrash. Monthly payments (a form of a bribe) to the Pristov (police chief) and supervising officer, so that they would not cause suffering to the Jews by issuing a command to close the stores on Sundays, issue reports of lack of cleanliness, or order the taverns to be closed due to lack of permits, etc., were also paid from this income.

{66}

In Ruzhany, the collection of the meat tax was organized as follows. On the date set by the authorities, the person designated by the heads of the community to collect the tax was sent from the regional city of Grodno. He would then, without competition, lease the tax for the sum that was agreed upon by the heads of the community at the outset (2,000 rubles).

For many years, the regular purchaser of that tax was the shamash of the Beis Din (court of law) and also the head shamash of the synagogue, Chaim Leib Shifrin. He was a quiet Jew, G-d fearing and intelligent, who was known in the town as someone who suffices himself with little. He was always in good spirits, full of faith, and comforted every person by saying: "If G-d wants, it will be good".

From A. Leviatan

## From The Days of My Childhood in Ruzhany

(From the book For my Descendants)

I was born in Ruzhany in the district of Grodno on the 17th of Kislev 5629 (1869) to my parents Reb Yechiel Michel Pines and Chaya Tzipora, the daughter of the renowned wealthy man Reb Shmarya Luria. Both of these houses were noble in Torah, wisdom, charitable deeds, tending to guests, and other such good traits. To this day, our life in our home in this quiet, small town passes before my eyes.

The Home, The Sukka, and the Festival Days

From my childhood, I remember our large, nice house, with its large yard in which we, the four sisters and our cousins, played. I remember well our Sukka that stood in our yard. I helped decorate it nicely along with the older people. I will never forget when we used to sit in it along with our wise, noble grandmother, my parents, sisters, and many aunts and uncles.

I especially remember the festival of Passover with its large, set table, decorated with flowers and the finest silver and porcelain vessels. There was a splendid chandelier on the ceiling above, which spread light to the entire room. The women were wearing silk and velvet clothing. Their heads, necks and chests were adorned with fine ornaments that suited them well, and added grace and nobility to their appearance. How lovely and how splendid! The men wore kittel (white ritual robes) made out of the finest linen. Their yarmulkes on their heads were made out of the same material. They appeared like angels to me and to all of those around.

### The Nights of Chanukah

How lovely were the nights of Chanuka, as well as all of our national holidays in general. At that time, the nature of these holidays was entirely different from what it is today. The entire family celebrated the holiday inside the home, among friends and acquaintances. The festivities were not brought outside, as is done nowadays, when the splendor and grace of the family are missing, without the holiness of tradition. I remember one specific Chanuka night. My father returned that night from Brisk with several guests. He brought them into the parlor where the family was gathered. They came to the latke party and the card game. Obviously, they also brought gifts to our house.

{67}

## My Uncle's Wedding

I remember the wedding of my uncle Abba. I can still see the large rooms and open doors through which one could go from room to room. The rooms were set up through the length of the house. Crystal chandeliers were hanging throughout the length on the ceiling. Each one had about 20 wax candles. It looked like the whole house was immersed in electric light (at that time, there was still no electricity in our town). The in-laws came from Warsaw, Mohilev, Grodno, and Kovno. All of them stayed over in the rooms that were set up by the local families in their homes. The wedding was celebrated for seven days and seven nights. The entire town was astir.

## Our Family

My grandfather Noach Pines had four brothers. Each of them had sons, daughters, and great wealth. They owned a factory for blankets and woolen textiles for the Russian army. (The Talmud Torah building, the hospital, and other Torah and charitable institutions were run by the Pines family, who ruled over the city and region as a sort of kingdom within a kingdom.) My grandfather Noach of blessed memory had six sons and three daughters. All of them married into the wealthiest and finest pedigreed families of that time. Zev Javitz, Berl Friedlansky and Leibush Davidson were his in-laws. His sons also found wives who were well-pedigreed and wealthy, from the family of Shmarya Luria and others. Three of the sons married into the Pines family itself, for they guarded the honor of the dynasty of this family and did not want to intermix too much with other familles, as was the custom among noble families.

**The entrance to the palace in Ruzhany**

## The Palace

I remember the palace that was called the "Platz". The Russians burnt it down during the last war [2]. Many of the Pines and Mintz family members lived in this palace. We would go there to visit our uncles and aunts every Sabbath. Surrounding it there were buildings built like fortresses and splendid dwellings.

Itta Yellin

{68}

# Fires

## The Plague of Fires

Most of the houses on the main street of the town were made of stone. The minority were wooden houses, with their roofs made of planks or tiles. The city generally appeared new, and there were few old, shaky houses with straw roofs, as in many of the towns of Pulsia. Three fires contributed to the freshness of these houses: the first in 1875, the second in 1895, and the third in 1915. The city was forced to renovate itself after each fire.

## The Fire of 1875

The following is written in *Halevanon*, year 12, 1875 (8) about the fire of 1875:

"On Sunday, 12 Elul 5635, a fire went forth from the house of the baker and spread like an angel of destruction. It spread without stopping for about five hours. Ruzhany turned into a valley of the shadow of death. The smaller synagogues and the magnificently built Great Synagogue that had been standing in splendor for 300 years went up in flames. The hospital, the Talmud Torah, the slaughterhouse and other fine buildings were turned to ashes. The luck of Ruzhany was not good even before the disaster. Its inhabitants did not enjoy treasures of gold, for their source of livelihood was from taverns, small-scale business, work in the woolen clothing workshops and manual labor. Were it not for the benevolent societies that eased the toil of the poor somewhat, it would have perished from poverty by now.

Approximately 200 children found refuge in the Talmud Torah building, from which Torah and wisdom emanated under the supervision of Reb David the Great, a man who excelled in his many deeds. Any bitter, afflicted or tormented person found refuge in the hospital. There, balm and bandages were given to any ill person, and all the needs of the ill person were cared for until he arose from his bed. The upholders of that institution were the two wonderful people who stand out as gems, the wealthy, intelligent brothers, may their names be held in splendor from generation to generation, the Rabbi and Gaon Yechiel Michel and his younger brother who assisted him Rabbi Yerucham Fishel Pines. This building was also destroyed and ruined. Who will now tend to the sick, gather them in, and bandage their wounds?

Our daughter Ruzhany, how great is your injury! Your situation is very serious. Here a call of distress awakens, and there an ear listens to the voice crying out with bitterness. Many hundreds of people are wandering around like sheep without a place to sleep; and for many who do find a place to sleep, the house is too small for them, and they sit in crowded conditions. The Pines brothers do a great deal to help with the burden of the poor, but nevertheless, they are unable to assuage the pain of every tormented soul who sleeps under the open sky.

I hope that even the little that I wrote is enough to arouse the mercy of our Jewish brethren. Act, do not hesitate, come to the assistance of the afflicted, gather donations from everybody and send them to the rabbi and Gaon Rabbi Mordechai Gimpel Yaffa, the head of the local rabbinical court."

Suffering with the agony of his nation: D. B. Starewolski

{69}

We read about another fire, not quite as large, in *Hamelitz* 1886 (27):

From Ruzhany in the region of Grodno, Mr. Yomtov Epstein informs us that on Wednesday night of the Torah portion of Tazria, a fire broke out in the city that consumed approximately 20 houses. All of their residents escaped by the skin of their teeth but did not save any of their belongings.

## The Fire of 1895

The second large fire broke out in 1895. The houses of the city were still small wooden houses with roofs made of straw. The houses were crowded one next to the other. It was the time of the warm, dry summer. Suddenly a flame burst forth from the "Kanal Fabrick" weaving factory. The fire spread to the nearby houses. Within several minutes the entire town was in flames. After about an hour, almost all of the residents of Ruzhany were left without a roof over their heads. It was impossible to save anything from the flames. People lost their entire fortunes and all of their property. They were left naked, and without anything other than the clothes on their backs. They survived, but with only their lives.

There was also one victim of this fire -- a paralyzed woman was burnt alive. The fire took hold of the house from all sides, and people were unable to take her out.

The residents of the town call out for help in "*Hamelitz*" of 1895 (106):

"Ruzhany, Grodno District. The voice of the outcry of the afflicted: men, women and children, the sound of weeping and wailing reaches the heavens over the terrible disaster that took place in our city. On Friday 23 Iyar at 9:00 in the morning fire descended from above, and almost the entire city went up in flames. The flames sprouted from the factory of the Pines brothers-in-law and spread to the entire city. All of the synagogues, Beis Midrashes, benevolent institutions that were always the pride of the Jews and regarding which our community excelled above other smaller or larger cities, were consumed by fire. Even one woman, a merciful mother who was paralyzed and was not able to free herself from the wrath of G-d, was burnt by fire as a sacrifice and a burnt offering. Of the more than 300 houses in our town, including the tanning factory of H. Wolpiansky, the liquor factory, all of the stores and businesses, only about 60 were left intact. The rests are mounds of ruins, a memorial to the destruction. Hundreds of people are wandering in the outskirts of their city without anything, without any shelter from the rain. Therefore, we are greatly anguished as we see honorable people, heads of the community, charitable and benevolent people, extending their hands to request food so that they can satisfy their souls and those of their families.

The nearby cities must be remembered favorably: Pruzhany, Volkovisk, Slonim, Byten, and Byaroza, Shereshevo, and especially Kossava for restoring our souls with bread and food. Thanks must go to the masters, the righteous gentiles, Mr. Dzikonsky, Mr. Ivanov, and especially Mr. Shihen for participating in our agony and for helping us with whatever they could. However, the handfuls did not satiate the lion and the pit was not filled. Therefore, our brethren of the house of Israel, praised as 'merciful ones the children of merciful ones,' wherever they live, please have mercy on your brothers, members of your nation, the residents of our city, who extend their hand to you from afar. Let every person send donations of clothing or money in the name of 'the charitable fund for those afflicted by the fire,' for every coin will add into the total sum, and the blessings of those saved and assisted by you will come to you."

Meir Isser the son of Y. Sh. Pines. Aryeh Leib Pines

{70}

"The aforementioned words are correct and I request that the editors of 'Hamelitz' give them a prominent place in the publication, for one cannot imagine the magnitude of the difficulty. The words written by the aforementioned Mr. Pines are true. The charitable deeds should be in peace, and in this merit, may G-d grant blessing, contentment and calm. As a witness I affix my signature on Monday, 26 Iyar 5655, here in Ruzhany."

"Shabtai Wallach who lives here in this community"

## The Assistance is Delayed in Arriving

Nevertheless, the assistance was delayed in arriving, and the suffering residents of the town write the following in *Hamelitz* 1895 (122):

"Ruzhany, May 31. (After the fire -- great hunger!) Three weeks have passed from the day that the city of Ruzhany was judged with fire and went up with flames heavenward. Food is cut off from thousands of men, women and children. Everyone is moving about, wandering in the outskirts of the city, without anyone asking about their welfare. Then, thank G-d, the nearby towns were the first to send bread and other provisions to restore the souls of those overtaken by hunger. They also sent some clothing, cloaks, kerchiefs and dresses. However, what was the value of all this? The number of weary, hungry people was more than 3,000. How could all the nearby cities such as Pruzhany, Volkovisk, Slonim, Kossova and Malech help? These cities could not provide bread for all of the hungry. Thank G-d, until last week there was no shortage of bread and food, but today, all hope has gone, for a handful does not satisfy the lion. The sources of livelihood and sustenance have dwindled and dried up. Everyone is hungry for bread! Thousands of souls are withering away and bloating from hunger. If our merciful brethren in other places, even far off places, do not have mercy, who knows what will be the end of the victims of the fire of Ruzhany. Our dear brothers, the nation hungers for bread!

Do not be shocked that I am using the word 'hunger' for this is a word that goes forth outward from the language. Know that all the people are dying of hunger -- all the people from the maid to the mistress, rich and poor, child and baby -- they are all begging to restore their souls, and asking for something simple -- bread -- and there is none! They are requesting a cloak to cover their nakedness, they are requesting the spirit of life! Please, oh generous people of the nation! Have mercy upon the city of Ruzhany, for its crisis is great, terrible and very severe. It is weeping and lamenting over the destruction of its Beis Midrashes, Talmud Torah, charitable organizations, and many other institutions. It is wailing, spreading out its hands, and requesting mercy to restore its souls with food and sustenance. It is groaning with a broken heart and a hungering soul, hoping that you will have mercy upon it to revive it, to strengthen it, and to heal it..."

## Help Begins to Arrive

Slowly, the brethren were aroused and began to send help, as is related in *Hamelitz* 1895 (199):

"Ruzhany, 3 Av, 5655. To the editor of "*Hamelitz*." I have received your precious letter with the sum of 236 silver rubles. Many thanks to you for this. May G-d grant to all who donated to this wonderful good deed an abundance of good and eternal success. I request that your honors express thanks on my behalf to the gabbai of the Ana'ch Synagogue in Rostov for donating 100 silver rubles for the victims of the fire here, which was sent by you. I cannot describe to your honors the terrible scene in the city, where only desolation and great destruction is seen. The pressure and difficulties are affecting everyone, and it has literally become a situation of life and death."

"Shabtai Wallach who lives in this community."

{71}

The residents of the city began to restore it. This lasted for months and years. We hear about the continuation of the restoration three years later in "*Hamelitz*" from 1898 (158):

"The community of the city of Ruzhany expresses its gratitude and blessings to the generous, noble philanthropist Rabbi Moshe Aryeh Leib Friedland, may he be well for his generous spirit, for he sent a sum of money after the fire for the benefit of the victims. Now he has sent several hundred copies of his book "Daat Kedoshim" by the author Rabbi Yisrael Tovia Eisenstat of blessed memory, which he published at his own expense. The income from the book is dedicated to finishing the construction of the Beis Midrash of the late Rabbi Gershon Zakheim of blessed memory. This Beis Midrash is very much needed by the residents of the city, for it is still missing five Beis Midrashes, which were not rebuilt after the fire. They are forced to worship in cramped and crowded quarters.

(From various sources)

Meir Sokolovsky

## Leib Yachid

Reb Leib Yachid Pines worked greatly in the area of the development of our town. His nickname Yachid came to him because he was the only son [3] of his parents, for he had only sisters. He was childless. Leib Yachid, the nephew of Leib Wasz, was the head of the Ruzhany community for many years. He worked a great deal for it, and made it his life's passion. After his mother died, he built the Talmud Torah in her memory, where the young children of Ruzhany would study reading and Torah.

**Leib "Yachid"**

He especially rose to the occasion after the great fire of 1895. As we know, most members of the Jewish community were left without clothes, without means, and without a roof over their heads. The few who had insurance on their homes received the insurance money and began their repairs. However, what should be done about the rest? This included 80% of the fire victims, who did not have one penny for their day-to-day needs, let alone the money needed to rebuild their homes. What did Leib Yachid do? He began to help them. He donated large sums himself, but since the handful did not satisfy the lion, Leib Yachid sent letters to all of his acquaintances and friends, including well-known businessmen and manufacturers in Russia, requesting help for the fire victims. Of course all of the many people who knew him understood the need and donated according to their ability, some more and others less. The houses of Ruzhany began to be rebuilt one after the other. Dozens of familles, with their men, women, possessions and children entered their new homes. All of this was thanks to this dear man. He also made efforts to rebuild the Beis Midrashes. He repaired the Great Synagogue that had been mainly destroyed.

{72}

## How the Fire Brigade in Ruzhany was Set Up

Fires in the town often spewed forth their wrath upon the wooden houses with straw roofs, without anyone to help. This situation gave no rest, and demanded a solution.

I recall that in 1901, after I returned from the army, as I bathed in the river enjoying the waters of my town, destruction came. Fire rose up, spreading heavy pillars of smoke that rose up and darkened the sky. I quickly came out of the water, dressed quickly, and hurried to the area of the fire in the shortest way possible. I came and saw the fire spreading from house to house, with the straw being consumed and nobody coming to help. I stood with nothing to do, as did others, for we had no fire fighting tools, and a little bit of water would be of no avail here. You can imagine our mood as we stood helplessly in front of this destructive enemy that took the form of a consuming fire. We then woke up from our helplessness. The fire reached a garden with several rows of trees. If we were to stop it there, there would be hope that the houses on the other side of the garden would not catch fire and burn down. I got to work. People gave me water with any vessel that they had, and I threw it upon the threatening fire. The extinguishing effort went on for several hours in this dismal fashion. At the end, we overcame the flames, but I had no more energy left and I fainted. People carried me out and laid me down on one of the benches outside. They brought me something to drink to restore my soul. The smoke slowly cleared out of my lungs and nose. I opened my eyes and regained my consciousness that had been obscured due to the flames and the smoke inhalation.

The following day, I received a prize of 25 rubles from the city council. I refused to accept it, and stated that I would donate that sum to set up a fire brigade in the town. This proposal met the favor of all the town officials. The city council gathered its honorable members, the factory owners, the merchants, the wealthy people, etc. They organized among themselves the beginnings of a voluntary fire brigade in Ruzhany. Each of them pledged three rubles. A sum of 300 rubles was collected in total. The aforementioned 25 rubles was added to this sum. The brigade came into being and started its first important activities, which yielded great results in the annals of the town.

I was then appointed as the head of the brigade. I remained faithfully in that post until the day when I left the city to make aliya to the Land.

From A. Leviathan

## The Voluntary Fire Brigade in Ruzhany

Today, when we talk about "firefighters" we see red trucks hurrying around with a loud siren blaring through the streets of the city, as it speeds along to offer assistance and put out the fire. Experienced firefighters stand on the truck, who know how to use the fire fighting equipment in their hands in order to stop the destructive menace.

There is no similarity at all between the situation today with what was called the "Voluntary Fire Brigade" in our town. Nevertheless, this brigade had many tasks, not all of which were known to the townsfolk. In theory, the brigade only had to serve the town in the event of a fire, but in practice it gave the Jewish youth of the town the chance to organize as a unit that would protect their independent honor in any contingency.

{73}

The Volunteer Firefighters Brigade of Ruzhany at its inception.

Seated in the bottom row from right to left: Avraham Yitzchak Chwojnik, Kamintsky, Fishel Pines, –, –, –, Mordechai Pines.
Next row up: –, –, –, –, Moshka Kaplinski, Shayka, Yaakov Shemshinowich, Abba Leviatan (the fire chief), Aryeh Leib Pines, Fishel Chwojnik, Leizer Chazatzky, –.}

In theory, this brigade would accept anyone who desired as a member, both Jew and Christian. However, in practice, almost all of the members were Jews. Of course, the organization was officially recognized by the authorities. Therefore, when the district minister visited, it was this brigade that greeted it.

Not only was this brigade able to take credit for the acts of bravery during the extinguishing of fires; it was also able to do so for many independent acts of assistance and self-defense -- the extinguishing of fires of a different sort.

On three occasions when there was a change of government in the country and the town was left as a sheep without a shepherd, the members of this brigade protected the local Jews and prevented disorder and acts of plunder and pillage.

Whenever the young men of the brigade passed by in formation wearing their shiny brass helmets and fine uniforms, the Jewish residents of the town would straighten their backs and, with justified pride, feel an extra measure of safety, according to the verse "Behold, He who does not slumber and does not sleep is the guardian of Israel." [4]

## The Drills of the Firefighters Brigade

When the sound of a trumpet was heard as a sign to summon the firefighters, and I was a young child among the other children, everyone hastened to the headquarters. It was a special delight for me to see the brigade organize itself, and to accompany it in its practices, training and official drills. The instruments of the fire brigade were flashing in their hands and sparking in the sunlight.

{74}

**The Volunteer Firefighters Brigade of Ruzhany after the First World War**

**Third row from the bottom, standing right to left:** –, –, –, Tzvi Epshteyn, –, Heshel Gebzah, Szkliravitz, –, –, –, –, Slutitzky.

**Second row from the bottom, seated right to left:** Alter Epshteyn, –, –, Katzman, –, Aber Liverant, Yisrael Nyumeches.

{75}

Those marching would sing pleasant marching songs.

Our eyes could not see enough of the pleasant sight of our marching youths, and our ears of hearing the lively and encouraging trumpet blasts. The marching songs of the firefighters' band during the parade filled the heart with pride and strength. Visions of the past were awakened in me -- from the time when we were living in our own Land and our soldiers marched outside of Zion and Jerusalem with an upright stature. Hope beat in the heart: we will yet renew our days as old. We wanted for the parade to continue for a long time, and it was a shame when the pleasant moments during which the parade passed by our houses were over.

Meir Sokolowsky

## Fear of Pogroms in the Town in 1904

New winds began to blow in Russia. The workers, whose work to this point had been backbreaking with endless hours and meager payment, began to organize. Strikes broke out. Demands were made. The Russians were concerned about this awakening and decided to direct the wrath of the suffering masses against the Jews. This constant incitement had its effect on the gentile residents of the towns. They prepared to pillage, plunder, and murder their Jewish neighbors. The aroma of revenge against the Jews wafted through the air and also entered the nostrils of our neighbors, the residents of the nearby villages, who were also preparing to rise up against the Jews of the town.

I organized the Jewish members of the firefighters brigade (who were the majority of its members) into a self-defense unit. However, the weapons were few: approximately 12 guns in the entire city and three additional ones in the fire hall, for a grand total of 15 guns. We searched for effective means of defense. If someone says he searched and he found, you should believe him [5]. We decided that in the event of disturbances, we would set a fire in one of the wheat storehouses in one of the neighboring villages, known for its wild people. Since they would have to hasten to put out the fire in their village, they would leave the town.

**Abba Leviatan**

We requested the help of the police force to protect the Jews of the town from the incident hooligans. A new Pristov (police chief) appeared accompanied by several brazen policemen. The police chief related to me in an inimical manner, for they told him that I do not permit him to be given an appropriate bribe each time. One day I was summoned to him. When I arrived, he received me in his room. He was sitting and writing, not paying any attention to me. I was standing the entire time and waiting, for a person does not sit down in front of a high officer before he is requested to do so. He continued his writing. I leaned on his writing table. He raised his head and called out in anger:

"This is not your carpentry table!" (I was a carpenter.)

"My carpentry table is as important to me as your writing table is to you", I answered.

He straightened his head and looked at me, who had been brazen with him, in anger.

{76}

"Who are you?", he asked me.

"A resident of the city of Ruzhany, the head of the volunteer firefighters brigade, and a trustee of the Great Synagogue."

He lowered his voice as he spoke:

"Why did you come?"

"Because you summoned me."

He called his secretary and asked:

"Why did you summon him?"

"Because you wanted to speak to him," answered the secretary.

"Oh yes, I wanted to speak to you, and since you are here, let us discuss: why are you arranging the strikes?"

"This time you did not turn to the correct address," I answered him, "what do I and my organization have to do with strikes?"

"You know that these strikes are causing unrest, and the farmers are getting wild." (The government itself was among the inciters.)

"Perhaps you want us to assist your few policemen?"

"We have no need for assistance. We are able to maintain the order ourselves," was his answer. Our conversation concluded with this.

We organized and were prepared. One bright day, when we saw that matters were not proper, and that the farmers were planning a real activity against us, we sent one of the youths to ignite the wheat storehouse in the village of Vylia. When the fire broke out, and was clearly visible in the town, the farmers cast aside their weapons in their hands and ran to extinguish the fire in their village and in their houses. Of course, they scattered in all directions.

Our plan succeeded. From then, our gentile neighbors in Ruzhany stopped dreaming about pogroms, for they knew that the Jewish youths would pay them back measure for measure.

By A. Leviatan

**TRANSLATOR'S FOOTNOTES**

1. Chaverim means 'friends'. I suspect that there is a typo here, and the intention was Hassidim.

2. There is a footnote in the text here as follows: This refers to the First World War.

3. Yachid in Hebrew means 'only'. Ben Yachid means 'only child'

4. Psalms 121:4.

5. A Talmudic adage.

## Beginnings of Zionism

{77}
Hurry, Brothers, Hurry
by Yechiel Michel Pines
Hurry, brothers hurry
Let us lift up our steps
Rush, brothers, rush
To our native Land

Rest is not for us,
Comfort is not for us
In the land made bare
By the brazen government.
Hurry, brothers, hurry…

My friends mock me
Why are you interested in the Land of your heritage?
There the jackals howl
Find yourself a new land.
Hurry, brothers, hurry…

Fools, do not mock,
Do not do so, children who have forgotten your mother!
Lest bursts forth against you
Our enemies, the strong enemies…
Hurry, brothers, hurry…

{78}

# Beginnings of Zionism in Ruzhany

by A. Leviatan

There was a different spirit around. The Chibat Zion movement appeared on our historical stage. The echo of this movement reached Ruzhany. Several members of the Pines family were among the first who were aroused by this echo. The lions in this area were the two brothers of Leib Wasz: Yechiel Michel Pines and Fishel Pines.

## Fishel Pines

Fishel Pines was one of the 35 delegates to the Chibat Zion convention in Katowice in 5645 (1844). Thus did tiny Ruzhany succeed in entering into a list along with big cities such as Warsaw, Bialystock, Odessa, Riga, and the likes, which sent delegates to this convention.

When Fishel Pines returned home, he would preach about Zion and Jerusalem every Sabbath in the synagogue. On weekdays, he would work to arrange collections for Chibat Zion, and he would donate no small amount himself. We later find Fishel Pines among the delegates to the second convention of the Zionists of Russia that took place in Minsk on 2-8 Elul 5662 (1902).

He continued with his Zionist activity until ties were cut off with the world at the outbreak of the First World War. Fishel Pines died during this war, in 5678 (1918). Ruzhany had then been under German occupation for 3 ½ years. *Hatzefira* number 23 (a weekly published in Warsaw) notes the following about his death:

"In Ruzhany, Reb Fishel Pines passed away. He was the brother of the scholar Rabbi Yechiel Michel Pines of Jerusalem. Reb Fishel Pines was one of the first members of Chovevei Zion, and among the faithful to the idea of national revival. During his brilliant speeches, he would attract many followers to the Zionist idea. He was a scholar from the old Beis Midrash, with deep knowledge of Talmud and Midrashim. He also read a great deal of general literature. He was wealthy and lived comfortably for all his life, but the war took everything from him and also distanced him from his children who were living in Russia. This excellent man lived alone and forlorn in his native city during his last year. May his soul be bound in the bonds of eternal life."

David Noach Pines

The son of Reb Fishel followed the path of his father, and was an enthusiastic Zionist. He would gather the people of the town in the synagogue and preach to them about the settlement of the Land. His mouth would emit flames.

## Yechiel Michel Pines

Fishel's brother decided to actualize Chibat Zion (the love of Zion) in deeds. He made aliya in the year 5638 (1878) and was one of the first builders of the new settlement. The next chapter is about him.

**Yechiel Michel Pines**

Yechiel Michel Pines was born on the 23rd of Tishrei 5604 (1843) in our town Ruzhany, in the Grodno District. In his time, he became famous in the Zionist world as a central figure in the Diaspora and later in the Land. He received a Jewish and general education, and excelled in his talents already during his youth. He was among the influential people already in cheder and Yeshiva. His rabbi, Rabbi Mordechai Gimpel Yaffa, prophesied a future for him. Indeed this was not for naught, for he later became famous as a man of Torah and a maskil blended together, and an enthusiastic lover of Zion, graced with a fine Hebrew style and abilities in publicity. In his articles in *Hakarmel* and *Halevanon* he fought against the demands of the maskilim for revisions to religion, and against the assimilationists and the Reform. His sharp articles, imbued with love of Israel and reverence for the eternal values of Jewish religion and tradition, were collected in a two-volume book called *Yelidei Ruchi* that was published in the year 5632 (1872).

{79}

## His Aliya to the Land

His good name preceded him, and when the "Mizkeret Moshe" fund was established in London in 1874 at the 90th birthday of Moses Montefiore in order to assist the foundations of the Hebrew settlement in the Land of Israel through agricultural work, labor and manufacturing, Y. M. Pines was selected as the spokesman of the group in the Land of Israel. He made aliya and entered his role on the 18th of Elul 5638 (1878). He built the "Mizkeret Moshe", "Ohel Moshe", "Yemin Moshe", and "Zichron Moshe" neighborhoods in Jerusalem. He was one of the founders of the Motza Moshava, where he established a tile factory to employ Jerusalem residents who desired to earn their living from the toil of their hands. The zealots of Jerusalem persecuted him and excommunicated him, but he stood his ground. He founded the "Techiat Yisrael" group in Jerusalem along with Eliezer ben Yehuda and Dr. Zeev Hertzberg, which promoted the revival of the Hebrew Language for the nation. He was one of the founders of the national library. He worked as an official of "Chovevei Zion" during the time of Tyomkin, and he served as a teacher in the "Chevrat Haezra" Teachers' Seminary. He was the author of the poem "Hurry, Brothers, Hurry".

Y. M. Pines helped with the purchase of a section of the land of Petach Tikva. The danger of the annulment of the sale was prevented thanks to the money that he obtained by selling his wife's jewelry. This led to a renewal of this settlement after it was destroyed, and helped the settlers lay the first foundations of Hebrew agriculture. He was the head of the "Chalutzei Yesud Hamaale" committee, and worked for the benefit of its settlers. He was the one who founded, nurtured and improved the Bilu settlement of Gedera. This was the crowning achievement of his actions for the settlement of the Land of Israel. How?

## Helping the Bilu People

The Bilu people were at the threshold of despair. The tribulations of the hard work in Mikve Yisrael under the yoke of Hirsch continued to grow. The hope that their representatives in Kushta [Constantinople] would be able to obtain the desired lot of land to establish their moshav in a proper fashion came to naught. The new light that broke through the darkness with the appearance of Karl Neter, who planned to ameliorate the situation of the pioneers of the nation, was extinguished with his sudden death. Hirsch advised the desperate people only one thing, "Obtain funds for the journey and travel to America." A few of them left the land and the rumor spread, "The Bilu organization is lost, and will not rise again."

{80}

Who knows how far those things would have come had not the star of Pines lit up their way at the appropriate time. He girded his loins and went out prepared to fight for the Bilu people and to establish them on their land. The storm that Pines fomented in the summer of 5644 (1884) bore fruit. Appropriate donations were received. Pines hastened to purchase a large tract of land in the Arab village of Qatra. Pines quickly gathered up the displaced Bilu people. On the second day of Chanukah 5645, a caravan of nine Bilu people set out. After two and a half years of promises and disappointment, hope and despair, they finally succeeded in lighting the candle of redemption of the Macabbees on their own land with soaring emotions. They called their land "Gedera". The happiness of the Bilu people and of Y. M. Pines knew no bounds.

## Woe About Those Who Are Lost [1]

With the death of Yaakov Rabinovitch in the year 5673 (1903), the following words were written in "Hapoel Hatzair" 5673 (24) in "articles":

"... Like Lilienbaum, he too (Y. M. Pines) was also an activist surpassing anyone else. When I once asked him, 'A person such as yourself, with such great knowledge in Torah and science, with such linguistic creativity, with talent, with style and with such writing where every word is a stone -- a person such as you -- why are you involved with the institutes of Jerusalem? How many good books could you have given us?' He then jumped into his place, 'Who told you that one must write books and not forge institutions? Is not the founding of Gedera more important than the best book? We have 20,000 books that were written by people greater and better than us, and if a few more were added by Michel Pines, what difference would it make? But a moshava, an institution -- how many do we have? Are we short on books? If moshavas are founded -- this I understand.'"

Yehoshua Barzilai writes the following in *Hapoel Hatzair* 5673 (25):

"Seventy years ago in a remote town in Lithuania, in a time and place where they did not dream at all about founding a healthy settlement in the Land of the forefathers, could it have been that such a man of strong spirit and a forger of ideas such as Pines had been born, who erected towers of light and beacons in the form of moshavot and cultural institutions in the Land of Israel. How much more so would it be that in the cities, suburbs, moshavot, and farms, in the places where the atmosphere and the sun of the Land of Israel strengthen the landscape and forge the soul -- would be born, or perhaps has already been born, such Pines' who would not only be Pines' but also pillars of light who will light up and forge the paths for the people making aliya to Zion."

Ruzhany merited to have a village in Israel [2] and streets in the Land of Israel named after one of its natives.

By Meir Sokolowsky

## More on the Activities of Yechiel Michel Pines

In the *Davar* newspaper of May 25, 1956, 15 Sivan 5617, on page 6, the following is written:

"Sixty years of war against the mission in the Land.

{81}

Sixty years ago, a group was organized in Jerusalem by Yechiel Michel Pines and Y. D. Frumkin whose purpose was to fight against the mission. The activities of the mission began 100 years ago. A sort of 'Jewish-Christian Community' was organized in Jerusalem already in 1856, consisting of 130 apostates out of 7,500 Jews of Jerusalem.

The missionaries continue to operate in Israel even after the establishment of the state. They rely on clause 2 of the United Nations resolution of November 1947, 'The activities of the religious institutions or charities of any religion are not to be interfered with.'"

## Passages from "The Children of My Spirit"

## People of the Reform

Regarding the people of the Reform, Y. M. Pines says that the "reformers" used to hide the shame of their assimilationist work with a sublime Israelite mission. Pines explained to them that the fulfillment of this mission obligates us with the national experience and the piousness of our Torah... It admits that G-d chose "this nation to bear the flag of rectifying the world and the kingdom of G-d," but "was never sent as a messenger to the gentiles to impose the refined studies upon them with a smooth tongue or the coercion of the sword." It acts upon the nations only indirectly and not directly... As such, this nation is compared to the sun:

The precious sun goes, and shines from its place without realizing that its rays will spread blessing and life. Thus, the providence of the Israelite nation is like the orb of the sun in the heights of the firmament, spreading its light upon all that pass by. Many nations will walk in its light, in their way of life and with its moral teachings, without the source boasting of its activities, and the latter recognizing the source of their good."

Our influence is not intentional, but rather indirect, for the "awakening of the internal force to function itself" can only happen by example. Therefore the Hebrew nation must exist as a "unique group, with the Torah being its ledger, the commandments being its charter, and the basis of its life is proper behavior and just laws. It is forbidden to harm this group, for only in its full essence can it impart its stamp upon the world."

The Demands of the Maskilim Demonstrate a Lack of Understanding

The Maskilim who demand religious reforms demonstrate their lack of understanding, for the commandments flow from "the needs of man's heart for love, recognition of good, doing good, connecting to the sublime, raising up the soul in holiness and purity, and cleaving to G-d."

Against the Assimilationists

Pines states that the Jews are not a religious sect but rather a nation, and therefore "It is impossible for a Jewish person faithful to his Torah and religion to change from nation to nation, for the religion of Israel is like a national charter intertwined with life... If Israel was exiled from its Land and only has the four ells of its Torah, any group rising up against it will not succeed in tearing apart our connection, for the four ells upon which Israel stands is the small area that holds up the large area. It will have a refuge from any wind or storm, until the wrath passes and the sun shines upon him from between the clouds."

Y. M. Pines

{82}

## Itta Yellin

She was born in Ruzhany in the year 1868 to her father Y. M. Pines and her mother Chaya Tzipora of the family of Reb Shmaria Luria. She received a Jewish education in the cheder for girls and general and national education from the home of her parents.

About two years after the aliya of Y. M. Pines, his wife and daughters, including Itta, made aliya along with those who made aliya from the "Bialystock Group" who came to settle in Petach Tikva and to renew its settlement. Reb Yechiel and his wife assisted them with this, as we know.

In the year 5645 (1885) Itta married David Yellin. She was his helpmate who enabled her husband to dedicate himself to his educational, communal, literary and academic activities.

When her mother founded the "Ezrat Nashim" society and took responsibility for the Beit Hamachase institution for the mentally ill in the year 5672 (1902), Itta helped her in her work. From the year 5672 and onward, Itta was the primary person who tended to this institution, raising it up to a high medical standard through the course of 25 years. She ensured its continued existence during the most difficult years, when her fellow directors almost gave up on maintaining it due to lack of funds and buckled under the yoke of debts. She would travel to cities and settlements, increasing the number of members and supporters. She even went to the United States and founded a womens' organization in support of "Ezrat Nashim" of Jerusalem. When the Turkish government attempted to confiscate the building of the Beit Hamachse institution of the mentally ill during the First World War -- among the other communal buildings that they confiscated -- for the purposes of a military hospital, Itta threw the keys of the institution before the director of the department of health, telling him to remove the sick people onto the street himself. With this strong stand, she saved the institution from eviction and destruction.

She also worked to ease the suffering of the residents of Jerusalem. She cared for the ill during the typhus epidemic. She especially worked to provide food and medicine for the starving Yemenite families and the ill people in the "Mishkanot" neighborhood.

Similarly, Itta participated in the founding and leadership of the institution and workshop for Jewish girls in Jerusalem. She was active in the "Gemilat Chesed" organization, in the Brit Bat-Tzion" girls' chapter, and in "Beit Haolim" founded by "Bnai Brith" and "Bnot Brith".

As a token of appreciation for her work, the large Bnai Brith chapter of Israel honored her with the title of Honorary President. The British government, on the recommendation of the Palestine (Land of Israel) government, granted her the title of M.B.E. (Member of the British Empire). She returned the title to the government as a sign of protest at the outbreak of the disturbances of 1936-1939, as did her husband Reb David.

During that period of turmoil, her son Avinoam, who was a government official responsible for the schools in the Land, was murdered. That year, she wrote a memorial book called <u>Letzetzaei</u> (For My Descendants). She finished the second section in the year 5701 (1941). She began to write the third section, but was unable to complete it.

Her grandson Aviezer Yellin was the head of the Teachers Union in the Land for many years.

From David Tidhar

### Rabbi Zeev Wolf Shachor

He was born in Ruzhany in 1869. He made aliya during his cheder years with his parents, who settled in Jerusalem. There, the youth Zeev Wolf continued with his studies in the cheders and Yeshivas. In his adulthood he earned his livelihood from the pharmaceutical trade. He instituted in Jerusalem the scientific medical methodology of relying on accredited physicians and medicine from pharmacies rather than the old methodology of using unaccredited physicians and grandmothers' potions.

{83}

In 5664 (1894) he founded a business in Jaffa called Shachor and Partners with his relative Yitzchak Izersky, which had the rights to distribute chemical fertilizers -- the first business of this type for the assistance of agriculture in the land. He was also the first to export raw materials for the production of fertilizer and aromatic oils.

He continued to conduct his business in Jerusalem. Despite his great occupation in business and communal needs, he set times for the study of Torah in his home or in the Beis Midrash of the Yemin Moshe neighborhood, where he lived for close to 50 years. Even during the times of tribulation when most of the honorable householders left that neighborhood, he remained in that neighborhood that was surrounded by Arab settlements. He gave the following reason for remaining in the neighborhood: Lest his departure cause a mass departure, and therefore the status of the Jewish pioneers would be diminished. He was honored by all of the residents, without distinction between race and creed, due to his generous character traits.

He utilized his good relationships with Arabs for the purpose of redeeming land in the Land of Israel. With his assistance, many areas around Petach Tikva were redeemed. Land in the Talpiot neighborhood was redeemed through him, upon which Kibbutz Ramat Rachel and other areas were built.

He devoted a great deal of time to communal affairs. He was one of the gabbim of the general charitable fund and the "Torat Chaim" Yeshiva, one of the responsible gabbaim of "Talmud Torah" and the "Eitz Chaim" Yeshiva, which was later moved to buildings that were built through his agency in the "Machane Yehuda" area.

During the difficult years of the First World War, he, along with Z. Hofin, David Yellin and Albert Anvati and others bore the burden of responsibility for saving the settlement in Jerusalem. He founded "The House of Bread and Tea" that gave some food to thousands of hungry people. He went there daily to drink tea together with Rabbi Y. M. Tukachinsky so that many of the formerly wealthy people who were now penniless would not be embarrassed to come to eat and drink there.

From David Tidhar

## The Founding of Ekron

From among the founders of the first settlements we know of the founders of Ekron, who originated from the Jewish village of Pavlova near Ruzhany. This is how a few farmers of Pavlova succeeded in being among the first builders of the Land!

The terrible dark days of 5641 and 5642 (1881 and 1882) came. A wave of pogroms passed through the length and breadth of Russia. The Jews in their masses turned to all directions and searched for refuge. Many set out for America. Only the Chibat Zion people attempted to direct the stream of immigration toward the land of Israel.

## Rabbi Mohilever

On one of those days, Rabbi Mohilever was in Paris. He was canvassing the homes of the wealthy people with the constant concern of the idea of the settlement of the Land of Israel. When he met Baron Rothschild, Mohilever told him about the "Chibat Zion" movement and succeeded in swaying him to the idea of the establishment of a settlement in the Land according to the plan of Yechiel Beri'l, the editor of *Halevanon*, who recommended the settling of Jewish farmers from Russia on land that was prepared for them in the Land of Israel. The baron agreed to support these settlers only if it would be proven that they were people who enjoyed and were suited to agricultural work.

Rabbi Mohilever began to search for Jewish farmers in Russia in order to take advantage of the willingness of the baron. He found such in the village of Pavlova next to Ruzhany. Yechiel Beri'l traveled to Ruzhany and, with the assistance of Rabbi Mordechai Gimpel Yaffa, selected ten families, numbering 110 individuals, who would be designated for aliya. However, who would provide them with the sum of money needed for their journey? There is nothing lacking in Israel. Rabbi Mordechai Gimpel Yaffa and the well-known Chovevei Zion activist Mr. Yerucham Fishel Pines of Ruzhany obtained the necessary funds for them.

{84}

## Preparation for Aliya

The days of preparation for aliya were days of double and multiple celebration and joy for them for two reasons: the first was the joy of the imminent aliya and the second as the joy of the many marriages in the settlement. Why did these take place before the aliya. The answer comes in *Hamagid* 1884 935), where Avraham Kasten writes:

"Ruzhany, Rosh Chodesh Elul 5644 (1884). In the previous week, four families, numbering more than 40 souls, set out... The seven remaining families will set out soon. The ten days preceding their journey were days of celebration and joy due to the making of the "tanaim" (pre-marriage) agreements, which they hastened to make before their journey. Many girls who had difficulty finding mates for various reasons including poverty, have now entered into marital relations with young men who know toil and who walk in the good path. One of them is a prayer leader and a shochet. They took the girls without a dowry, so that they could come with them to the Holy Land to work its soil."

At a propitious time, seven families followed the four, for a total of eleven families, leaving the Diaspora and going to the Land. These are their names: 1) Yaakov Orkin, 2) Baruch Orkin, 3) Baruch Tzvi Bernstein, 4) Avraham Yaakov Gelman, 5) Yechezkel Lewin, 6) Yaakov Laskowsky, 7) Moshe Meler, 8) Moshe Chaim Paras, 9) Dov Rudabsky, 10) Yehoshua Rubinstein, 11) Efraim Skolnik.

## The First Period in the Land

Now they had to prove that they could become accustomed to agricultural work in the Land. They worked for about a year in Mikve Yisrael under the supervision of Mr. Hirsch, the director of Mikve Yisrael under the auspices of the "Kol Yisrael Chaveirim" (Alliance Israelite Universelle) [3] organization Since they were strong and accustomed to hard work from their youths, they withstood the tests and proved that aside from being able to work the land, most of them also knew a trade.

"All of them were workers of the land from their youths. Aside from their knowledge of the work of the field, eight of them also have a trade: three of them are house builders, one of them is a wood engraver, two of them are carpenters, and two of them are weavers of wool." (Yechiel Beri'l, "Yesud Haamala").

Mr. Hirsch, whose relationship to the workers who originated from Russia was to this point inimical, was satisfied wit these workers, and gave a good report about them to the baron:

"I am satisfied with them. These people appear calm to me. They continue to work with us, and from the time they arrived, they have not caused me any bitterness. I have authorized several trustworthy people to seek plots of land for them." (From the letter of Sh. Hirsch, the director of Mikve Yisrael, to the Alliance Israelite Universelle -- Sh. Jabnali. <u>Book of Zionism II</u>.)

These farmers were offered an orchard in Wadi el Hanin, but they refused saying: "we requested bread to eat and clothes to wear, not Sabbath fruit (i.e. oranges...)". This was the outlook of these honest farmers. After various recommendations, Mr. Hirsch chose for them 2,700 dunams on the land of the Arabic village of Aqir. The well-known philanthropist kept his promise, purchased the tract of land, settled all of the familles who came from Ruzhany on it, and promised to take care of all of their needs.

{85}

## The Ekronites on their Land

The activists Moyal, through whose assistance the land was purchased, brought them to their inheritance. He led them on their first journey, got them accustomed to the local conditions, and purchased animals and work implements for them, etc.

The settlers called their village Ekron after the Arab village, but the philanthropist called it "Mizkeret Batya" after his mother, who implanted in him the love of Israelite culture.

The land was good for the cultivation of crops, and the farmers were diligent workers of the land who were happy with their lot, as Y. M. Pines said about them in *Hamelitz* 1884 (18):

"They are happy and of good heart, performing their work with diligence, dedication, and patience, as is fitting and appropriate for true workers of the land who were raised from their youth in the bosom of work."

They worked the true work of farmers in this moshava and plowed with oxen. Everyone admitted that this was an agricultural moshava in all its details. The Bilu member Chaim Chisin writes, "Only a man who is a farmer can understand how happy they were at the sight of the bent over stalks of wheat... and full ears" in the fields of the farmers of Ekron.

The small moshava did not succeed in having much written about it in the annals of the settlement of the Land of Israel, for its neighbors Gedera to the south and Rechovot to the north overshadowed it and its modest farmers, despite the fact that their dedication to agricultural village life in its simple meaning (as opposed to an easier farm life) [4] -- with plowing, planting, and harvesting -- was exemplary. They displayed stubborn opposition to the officials who wished to impose the style of planting upon them. Matters came to a rabbinical adjudication, and only the verdict that "with regard to work, farmers must listen to the officials", caused them to submit.

The moshava continued to grow. In 1930, Menashe Meirowitz found there a school for 50 boys and girls, a Mishna study group, a guest house and a loan fund. The support upon which the farmers lived did not move them from their determination, and they continued to display their diligence in their primitive methodologies of planting which their souls desired.

The settlement of Ekron "located on the side" grew and became an area of more than 10,000 dunams. Its population grew to 500 people. During the War of Independence, Ekron served as a transport route on the temporary road between Tel Aviv and the capital of Jerusalem.

Meir Sokolowsky

## Yearning for Redemption

After the aliya of the 11 families of Pavlova, the rest of the families remained on the settlement and continued with their lives. Even though additional families became aroused and wished to make aliya, they did not succeed in their goal. Thus is written in "*Hamelitz*" 1891 (78):

"Pavlova. Approximately 50 Jewish families live in this settlement, working their land with diligence and love, producing seed from the fat of the land [5] which the late Czar Nikolai gave us with his great mercy in his desire to turn us into productive citizens, people of work and action, who bring blessing to them and to the world. Even if the beginning of the settlement was difficult, for there were many who found it difficult to take leave of the life of the spirit and were not easily able to turn their shoulders and bear the burden of physical labor. Some of them left their homes and fields, and went to seek their livelihood with what they might find. However, its later period is very proud, for when disturbances began to take place, our brethren took to the work of the field, the life of a farmer, the life of physical labor and movement. This attracted the hearts of many of us more than the deceptive life of commerce. Whereas earlier they had given up on their fields and given them over to anyone who came to take them without even taking any monetary reward, now the price of each lot is more than 1,000 silver coins or more ere they to want to sell them. All of the farmers of the Pavlova settlement are very diligent in their work. There are people who studied all the ways of civilian farmers in great detail, and make every little matter into a big matter for themselves. When their work in the field finishes, they bring transports from the merchants of nearby Ruzhany that is about two verst [6] away from us, on the railway line, or bring wagons laden with wood to the city to sell. Were it not for the accursed fashion that pervades among the daughters of the farmers, and for the legitimate desires of their hearts, all of our farmers would be happy.

{86}

Our moral situation is also not lacking, for many of the farmers send their children to the large Yeshivas in Ruzhany to study Gemara and Jewish law with the commentaries. There are two Mishna study groups, where the farmers go to study some chapters of Mishna each Sabbath. Thanks are due to the intelligent rabbi Yosef Starewolski, who gathers the naughty children every Sabbath afternoon to teach them Bible with a translation. With his clear language and great knowledge, he won over the hearts of the youths, teaching them to study the holy writings, rather than running around wild forever.

However, you should know that our lots have already grown smaller due to the partitioning of the heirs, and many youths who already built houses for themselves and need to concern themselves for their wives and children find that the fields of their fathers are insufficient to provide for them, their children, and grandchildren. These young people now raise their eyes to the mountains of Zion and Jerusalem, with the hope of restoring to life the destroyed fields of Jerusalem through their diligence and work of their hands. People of this type desire greatly to settle there. However, they are unable to actualize their intentions, for they do not have the required money to purchase a lot there. Therefore some of our youths, including the writer of these lines, have requested that the leaders of Chovevei Zion in our land to stand at our right side and support our honorable group there. However, we were too late.

And now I say: I place the matter in *Hamelitz* before our philanthropists of Chovevei Zion, may they live, so that perhaps one of them will be so generous as to purchase a plot of land for us. We will then return the principle with interest over ten years. It is our fervent hope that within a few years, his donation will flutter high with glory, and we will see his face glow with goodheartedness. You should know that a large moshava in the Holy Land has already been founded by the farmers of Pavlova, which is sprouting among it sister moshavot.

You should know that this is not a meaningless matter for you if you will find people with agricultural experience among the rest of the members, for we know very well that if people who do not understand this work are gathered for this purpose, their hearts will fall and their hands will weaken from the work. Such will not be the case if you find experienced people among them, who will be exemplary in all areas of work. They will also strengthen any weakening hands. Each person will strengthen the other, and the moshava will succeed."

One of the young farmers: Zimmel Lewin

{87}

# Years of Agitation by Yaakov Shimshoni

## The Year 1905 -- the Political Parties

**Yaakov Shimshoni**

Not only did the times of worker unrest at the beginning of the 20th century not skip our town, but rather stirred it up greatly. Even though Ruzhany was a town, it had a few factories in which several thousand workers worked.

At that time I was nine years old, and on occasion I would run to workers' meetings (swadkaot). The meetings took place on Pruzhany and Slonim Streets, especially the latter -- not on the streets themselves but rather on the trenches that conducted the water to the fields. The gatherings took place there, between the nut trees and the other trees. From the party centers in Bialystock and the nearby city of Slonim, delegates came from different parties: Revolutionary Socialists, Social Democrats, "Poale Zion". The guest delegates, the anarchists, were especially numerous. Everyone came to present their case to the workers of Ruzhany, who then went to the householders of the town to ask for money for their party, at times even with physical force. The collectors of these parties would evaluate the means of every person and set the sum that each person should donate to the coffers of their party, even if he was not a member, and even if he was opposed to it. At times there would be attacks of robbery, all for the benefit of their party. Once they attacked the post office in the village of Zalesyany, but they were disappointed when they only found 37 rubles in the till. The postmaster whom they attacked and the wagon driver who brought them to the place of the attack recognized the people who carried out this deed. Therefore, they were forced to hide for a period of time until they moved to America.

## The Year 1905 -- The Struggle for a Twelve-Hour Workday by Yaakov Shimshoni

Motshe (Mordechai) Pines owned a wool spinning workshop in Ruzhany. He signed a contract and was obligated to produce a specific number of blankets. The workers then came and demanded that he reduce the number of work hours per day to 12, or increase their wages. Motshe refused to agree to either of those demands. The unrest of the workers grew. Moshe closed the factory, saying that he was leaving the city. He would somehow arrange things with the people to whom he was supposed to provide the blankets, but now could not. Motshe seated himself in the wagon and traveled. The workers, headed by the sons of the physician Leib Epshteyn and the shoemaker Yitzchak Yaakov, set up guards along the routes and captured him as he was on his way to Byaroza. They returned him to Ruzhany during the night.

{88}

Circassian horsemen were going around the city, guarding the city from marauders. Motshe's capturers drove their wagons opposite the guards. They lay him down in the wagon for fear that he might scream. They sat on him, put a gun to his face, and threatened to kill him if he utters a sound. Motshe was quiet for the entire ride until they brought him to the cellar of Chaim Leib the baker (the daughter of the baker was a "fighter", "Kemperke" in the vernacular). They held him there until evening.

However, Motshe continued to be stubborn. Even in captivity he refused to sign on to a change in the work conditions. The youths did not know what to do with him. They loaded him on the wagon and brought him to Pruzhany. They passed through a forest and entered into the house of the forester. This was near morning, and Motshe rose up to worship. The youths fed themselves. One youth was playing with a gun. A bullet went forth, and struck and killed the forester. The youths were afraid. They took Motshe with them and fled. Along the way Motshe tricked them and advised them to take a side route, for they are likely already being pursued. The frightened youths agreed, and the side route that Motshe showed them brought them close to Ruzhany.

They reached a certain village. Motshe requested to go out to attend to his bodily needs. In the meantime, he entered the house of a gentile who was one of those who worked in his factory (the Jews were the weavers and the gentiles were the spinners) and raised an outcry. The gentile and his neighbors got concerned and held him. Then the youths fled for their lives. Then Motshe informed Ruzhany, from where people came to bring him home. The youths hid for some time until they moved to America.

## The Big Strike of 1910

The working conditions of the hired workers in the weaving factory in Ruzhany were very bad. There was no professional protection, for the workers, who had indeed started to organize, did not conduct this appropriately. The factory owners took advantage of this situation. Not only did they not raise the wages, but they wanted to lower them. This desire caused great bitterness among the weavers, who gathered in the "Majer Beis Midrash" and decided to declare a strike, demanding not only a return to the previous wages, but also a raise. Motshe Pines informed them in a decisive manner that he was about to close the factory and move it to Bialystock, and then the weavers of Ruzhany would die of hunger. He issued an ultimatum to the weavers, saying that if they do not return to work within three days, he would carry out his decision. However, the strikers were not confounded, and continued with their rebellion. What did Motshe do? Rather than move the factory, he brought in strikebreakers from outside. One bright day, several wagonfuls of people from outside arrived to town, and the work in the factory recommenced.

Then something unbelievable took place. The merchants of the town closed their businesses, the tradesmen closed their workshops, and the peddlers left their stalls. All of them streamed to the weaving factory on Schlosse Gasse. It was not the solidarity with the workers that was the factor here, but rather the concern of the merchants and tradesmen for their own livelihood, for their livelihood depended on the workers. Only the intervention of the Pristov (police chief) with all the Ukrainian policemen saved the factory from the wrath of the masses. When the strikebreakers heard about what had taken place in town, they were afraid to leave the factory, and remained there for the night.

The next day, they sent a delegation to the strikers and informed them that they were misled by the factory owner who hired them, who had told them that they were invited due to a shortage of workers in Ruzhany. Therefore, they are releasing themselves from their agreement to work there, and are leaving the factory. When the factory owner saw that his plan did not work, he was forced to enter into negotiations with the strikers. The situation ended with the complete victory of the strikers

{89}

The factory owners did not give up after this incident. Rather, they followed the path of "let us outsmart them" [7]. They instituted contract work. This worked as follows: They chose a few workers as independent workers ("leinketers") as they were called, which led to a reduction in wages. The "leinketers" would hire children between the ages of ten and twelve, and thereby not only caused a setback in the previous gains, but also an actual shortage of work among the veteran workers. The unemployed workers attempted to explain to the "leinketers" that they should raise their prices so that the former workers could return to work instead of the children, but they did not succeed. Then the unemployed workers began to perpetrate acts of destruction against the property of the "leinketers", which forced the factory owners to restore the situation to what it had been previously. These acts of destruction caused the factory owners to slander the most active of the workers. The police began to imprison the workers, especially the activists among them. Many of the workers left the town and escaped to the United States.

From a letter of Yitzchak Shlomo Miller (Mronchik) from United States

{90}

# Public Figures and Personalities

## Lullaby

by Aharon Libushitzky

Lie down, go to sleep my dear child,
Listen, and I will utter a song:
From days of yore, from far away,
There once was a city.

Your predecessors
Used to live there;
They lived a life of happiness
They were indeed a nation.

A land, which beneath their feet
Flowed with milk and honey;
A nation where only very rarely,
Was a poor person found.

But the fathers, from an abundance of good
Abandoned G-d's Torah;
And the sun of their success
Was replaced with thick shadows.

When G-d became angry with them
He expelled them from the city...
Lie down, go to sleep, my dear child,
Listen, and I will utter a song:

In splendid palaces

A strange nation settled;
And your fathers wandered and moved about,
Given over to the hands of an enemy.

They wandered for many hundreds of years
They go here, and also there;
But they hope that the day will come
When they will again become a nation.

For G-d had indeed promised them
On this day of wrath .
That a day will come when they will all return
To once again be a strong nation.
For a day will come -- and will arise from their midst
A man roaring like a lion
His voice will come forth -- and they will all gather
Around him speedily;

Then the roar of a lion will be heard:
Who that is for the nation -- come to me!
Then they will all shout out, all of them:
"The Messiah lives!"

They will fly as quickly as lightning
Through the long path
To that beautiful city,
From which they had been expelled;
And with the will of G-d, they will come
All of them to the city...
Now lie down and go to sleep darling child
Listen, and I will utter a song...

{91}

## Aharon Libushitzky

Aharon Libushitzky was born in Ruzhany in the year 5634 (1874). His father Eliezer (Leizer) was an educated Jew and an honorable man of the town. In his adulthood, Aharon served as the principal of the Tarbut High School in Bialystock. Later he served in that same role in Lodz. He was a poet and a Hebrew writer. In the book <u>Kinor Zion</u> -- a selection of songs of Zion in Hebrew from Biblical times until our day -- that was published by Tushia, Warsaw, 5660 (1900), two songs of Aharon Libushitzky are published among the other chosen songs. The "Lullaby" on the previous page is one of them. Aharon also wrote children's books. He edited a weekly called <u>The Star and the Son of the Star</u> (Warsaw and Lodz, 5684-5, 1924-5).

In addition, he translated into Hebrew and produced an abridged version of Dubnow's history book as a history textbook for the Hebrew schools in Poland and other countries in which Hebrew schools exist.

He apparently perished in the Lodz Ghetto. May his mcmory be a blessing.


## Meir Krinsky

On Hoshana Rabba 5677 (1916) a splendid funeral took place in Warsaw for the teacher and writer Yaakov Meir Krinski, a native of the town of Ruzhany. How did this man come to greatness?

M. Krinsky was born to his father Reb Binyamin Yosef, who was descended from the martyrs of Ruzhany. He studied in cheders and yeshivas in his hometown of Ruzhany and the nearby city of Slonim until age 11. In Slonim, he studied under the supervision of his uncle Rabbi Yitzchak Danzig (later the head of the rabbinical court of Peterburg). He studied in Pinsk under the tutelage of his cousin Rabbi Moshe Zakheim (later the head of the rabbinical court of Kowel) from age 16-19. During that time, he began to become a maskil. When he arrived in Kiev, he became involved in the circle of Hebrew writers, including his relative Yitzchak Yaakov Weinberg. He began to earn his livelihood there by teaching Hebrew. He continued to teach in Bialystock as well, where he went to live later.

He aspired to work to broaden the knowledge of the members of his people and to spread haskala among them. He came to Lodz in 1891 and opened up a school for children. In 1909 he opened up the first Jewish business school in Warsaw, where he went to live. For a long time, this was the only Jewish high school throughout the Russian monarchy. A broad curriculum of the study of the Hebrew language and literature and Jewish history existed in this school. He also opened a girls' school. These schools became famous throughout the Pale of Settlement, and attracted many students from outlying cities, both near and far.

He had a good heart and loved the beauty in everything. He acted as a merciful father to the students of his schools. He never distanced any student from his school because of lack of ability to pay tuition. On the contrary, he made it a point to bring in several students without any tuition obligations at all. He attempted to instill an esthetic style in the school, and he succeeded at that.

His love for the esthetic side in everything was not only expressed in the school, but also in all of his books. He was a teacher and a writer, and his teaching style was the same as his writing style. He attempted to ensure that the content as well as the external appearance of all of the books and newspapers that he published was attractive.

{92}

The man was very fruitful. He was busy in two languages, and he earned the rights of an honorable citizen in both. M. Krinsky wrote various textbooks for Hebrew, starting with basic books for the study of Hebrew reading and ending in an anthology of Hebrew literature and the Talmud. His first work as an author was the publication of the primary textbook _Reshit Daat_ in beautiful, attractive print, and on good paper with pictures. The book had more than 100 editions. He founded the "Haor" publication house, and published many Hebrew books: _Dat Yisrael_ (the Religion of Israel), _Hadibur Haivri_ (The Hebrew Speaking) in three volumes, _Sichot Tevaiot_ (Discussions on Nature), _Torah Latinokot_ (Torah for young children), _Hasignon Haivri_ (the Hebrew Style) -- a large anthology of Hebrew literature in two volumes. He published Hebrew weeklies for youth and children in two parts, called _Hashachar_ and _Ben Hashachar_.

He did not abandon Yiddish. He founded a Yiddish publishing house _Bicher Fur Alle_ (Books for Everyone), and he published the first illustrated weekly in Yiddish, _Roman Zeitung_. He published popular academic books, such as _Der Yiddisher Doctor_. He edited _Di Yiddisher Literature Visenschaft_ (The Science of Jewish Literature) and others. Along with M. Osipov, he published an anthology called _Yiddish Vitzn Un Anekdoten_ (Yiddish Wit and Anecdotes) in 1909. M. Krinski was one of the founders of the _Der Moment_ daily, and helped to establish it.

Even though M. Krinski disseminated learning and knowledge in two languages, he was a supporter of the Hebrew in Hebrew style [8]. He expressed his opinions in his discussions in several pedagogical publications that only that language should be the language of instruction in the schools of the nation.

This man of action did not neglect the social arena. He was an active member in the organization of the Lovers of the Hebrew language, in the Writers and Newspaper Guild, and in various philanthropic organizations.

It is no wonder that the Jews of Warsaw, the capital of Poland and central city of its Jewry, accompanied this very active teacher and writer to his final resting place with large crowds.

(From various sources)

By Meir Sokolowsky

## Zelig Sher (Szereszewski)

In 1909, Zelig Sher was forced to leave his native town of Ruzhany, in which he was born, grew up, and spent his first 20 years. He studied in the yeshivas of Ruzhany, Slonim and Ramailes in Vilna until the age of 15. He also studied weaving in Vilna. When he was working as a weaver, he became involved in the S. S. (Socialist Zionists). He was sent to jail in Slonim and Bialystock a few times.

He immigrated to America in 1909 and began a new life there -- a life of working and writing. He worked in a clothing factory, and published articles and stories in Yiddish in the daily and weekly newspapers in the United States.

During the First World War, he fought as a soldier in the American Army on the French front, and was wounded a few times. He returned to New York, and published various war stories in the "Forwards". He served as a member of the editorial board of the "Di Zeit" Poale Zion daily newspaper. He was also published in "Freiheit" and "Tog". In 1926, he was a permanent assistant at the "Forwards", where he writes to this day. He is active in the Socialist movement in America, and the Territorialist Socialist Movement. For two years he was also the secretary of the cultural division of the "Arbeiter Ring" (Workmen's Circle) in America.

(Lexicon of Zalman Reizin, volume IV, 1929)

{93}

## Melech Epshteyn

One year before the First World War, Melech Epshteyn left his native town of Ruzhany and his native land and immigrated to the United States after a great deal of activity in his native city and country.

He was the son of Shmuel Chaim Epltreger, who was a teacher in the Ruzhany Talmud Torah. Melech Epshteyn received his Torah education in the local Talmud Torah and the Yeshiva. He studied Hebrew and Russian from a private teacher. He had already settled in Bialystock when he was 13 years old. There he completed his education in Hebrew and Russian literature and took interest in the social and political affairs. He was active in the S. S. (Socialist Zionist) movement and in the workers' movement in Warsaw, Lodz, and Bialystock. He tasted the taste of imprisonment in all of those places. He also worked in Kiev for a period of time.

He was one of the founders of the "Di Harpe" workers' musical and dramatic organization in Lodz. For some time, he served as the secretary of "Yiddisher Literatur Gezelschaft" (Jewish Literary Society) under the presidency of Y. L. Peretz in Warsaw, and was imprisoned on account of this. Then he moved to America.

He was appointed as a teacher in a Yiddish school when he arrived in the United States. He went to work for the "Teg" when it was founded. He worked for some time at "Zeit" of Poale Zion and later as one of the editors of the Yiddish "Freiheit" newspaper.

(Lexicon of Zalman Reizin, volume IV, 1929.)

Dov Shpak Lobzowsky

Dov Szpak Lobzowsky, who was born in Ruzhany in 1861, made aliya to the Land in 1911 and was raised up by it. He purchased the Barski farm in Gedera and improved it. He left Gedera and settled in Tel Aviv due to a tragedy in the family.

He brought many of his and his wife's relatives to the Land, and helped establish them economically.

Plots of land were redeemed for urban and agricultural settlement during his tenure as a land dealer. He purchased the lands upon which the Shpak (Bilu Street and its neighborhood) and Montefiore neighborhoods in Tel Aviv were founded; the workers' neighborhood (next to the Keren Kayemet LeYisrael Street) and others; the lands of Gan Meir and Gan Hadassa and others; 2,800 dunams of lands in the Sheik-Munis village, and others. He redeemed agricultural plots in Karkur, Ibn-Yehuda, Herzliya, Kabab village (Ramle region), the land of Joara (Kibbutz Ein Hashofet), land from the village of Tayibe (today Ein Vered and Tel Mond), in Ruchama and near the Egyptian border -- 43,000 dunam. He became involved with purchases in Klansova and Tayibe, but for some reason these did not materialize. Through these transactions he "freed himself" from a large portion of his fortune, but he merited to see the broadening of the settlement in the Land as the fruits of his labor.

From David Tidhar

## Avigdor Michel Goldberg

He was a veteran teacher and scholar. When I arrived in Ruzhany in 1922, I already knew him as the principal of the "Talmud Torah" educational institution, in which many students studied, most of whom were children of parents lacking in means. It was necessary to search for sources of income in order to maintain this religious school. Avigdor Michel maintained a correspondence with his students who had immigrated to America, and would obtain from them a portion of the necessary money for this aforementioned objective. He took interest in this "Talmud Torah" day and night, as a dandled child. The children loved him and held him in esteem.

{94}

He was also loved very much by his family. He was already a widower when I arrived in Ruzhany. However, he was not alone. His daughters and grandchildren, who loved their father and grandfather, always visited him.

He was sickly during his latter years. He underwent an eye operation. He continued to lead the "Talmud Torah" even on his sickbed. The teachers sat by his bed during one of their free hours, listened to and wrote down his impressions on school issues. He led the institution in this manner until his last moment.

Even when all of his dedication to this institution, he found time to work together with Shimon the shochet in "Taz" to canvass people for the Keren Hayesod and other funds.

With his death I lost a friend. I eulogized him in the synagogue. May his memory be blessed.

Avigdor Michel Goldberg

## Dr. Meir Pines

Dr. Meir Pines

The large Pines family never skimped on money for the education of its children. Rrenowned physicians such as the ophthalmologist Dr. Leib Pines, who plied his profession in the large city of Bialystock, and others, stemmed from this family. Dr. Meir Pines also studied and mastered a great deal of knowledge. He excelled in his broad and deep knowledge in the realm of Yiddish literature. His book <u>The Annals of Yiddish Literature</u> is received with appreciation in the literary of circles of our day. He was also known as a communal activist, and was a candidate for the Russian Duma.

While in Germany, he concerned himself with youth aliya after the Nazi ascent to power. He would transfer group after group across the German border, and then return to Germany to continue his deeds of rescue. He was advised to save himself, but he refused with the reason that his task was to continue with the deeds of rescue as long as the possibility of such continued to exist in Nazi Germany. He worked in this area even after the outbreak of the Second World War. The Germans did not harm him since he was a Russian citizen. At the outbreak of the war between Germany and Russia [9], he was transferred to Russia during the exchange of citizens. His tracks were lost there.

From Roza and Sonia Pines

{95}

## Moshe Limon

Moshe Limon was born in 1891. He remained an only son (he had only one older sister, Yenta of blessed memory) to his parents who had lost ten children. Therefore, his mother was nicknamed "The weeper", for she was always weeping for her children who had died in their childhood.

Moshe already excelled in his talents and diligence in his childhood. His father Reb Yaakov Limon did not spare any toil, and gave his son a Hebrew and general education. He was sent to Warsaw to study in high school.

In Warsaw, Moshe befriended the best of the young writers and maskilim, and began to try his hand at writing.

He already published poems in the children's newspaper "Olam Katan" (Small World) at a young age. His children's stories were later published in a special anthology called <u>Meagadaot Zekenati</u> (My Grandmother's Legends).

Due to the death of his father Reb Yaakov of blessed memory and the outbreak of the First World War, Moshe was forced to forego his aspirations and continue with his studies.

He escaped from Ruzhany at the time of the general draft and arrived in Kharkov. There he married Leah the daughter of Cheikel Rotner the inventor.

He underwent many tribulations during the wartime years, especially during the time of the civil war between the "Whites" and the Reds. His life was frequently in danger during the time of the well-known Cheka [10], but he was always saved.

Nevertheless, he always found time to dedicate himself to communal activism. He participated in various assistance committees, for assistance had to be provided for those affected by the war and pogroms.

His home in Kharkov was open to all of the residents of Ruzhany who ended up there. They found support and assistance there.

However, his primary activities were in the realm of Zionism and culture.

He participated in every Zionist and Hebrew meeting. Through his efforts, pedagogical courses were set up in Kharkov under the direction of Dr. Charno of blessed memory. Many teachers and activists graduated from these courses.

He was arrested and sentenced to exile in Siberia for his participation in the "Tarbut" convention, but he succeeded in escaping from there and arriving in Poland in 1924.

He settled in Lodz with the assistance of his many friends. There he found a broad field for his Zionist and cultural activities. He dedicated a great deal of work to the renewal of the sole Hebrew newspaper in the Diaspora, *Hatzefira*. He organized committees for the newspaper in the city. He earned a great deal of gratitude from the wealthy people of Lodz for his great influence and personal charm on behalf of this goal. How great was his sorrow when the paper did not succeed.

With regard to his Zionist outlook, Moshe was one of those who supported Grynbaum, but due to his opposition to narrow factionalism, he did not join any party and remained as a general Zionist in the full sense of the term. The leaders of the Working Land of Israel in the Diaspora and in the Land were among his closest friends. One of his best friends, Avraham Levinson of blessed memory, said the following about him during a memorial evening: "Would it be that we were all general Zionists as he is."

Thanks to his rhetorical talents and his ability to win over the hearts of the masses with his power of speech, he was sent from time to time to speak on behalf of the national funds at various national gatherings.

{96}

**Chaim Nachman Bialik and Moshke Limon**

Moshe Limon was chosen as a member of the Jewish Agency that was founded at the 17th Zionist Congress.

All of the illustrious members of the Jewish nation who visited Lodz, including Nachum Sokolow, Ch. N. Bialik, and others, would visit his home.

Moshe visited the Land in 1934 and attempted to forge his future there. In the meantime, he registered for a dwelling, and left his son there to study in the Land. However, apparently, fate did not have this in mind. Moshe returned to Poland. His business weakened due to the severe depression that pervaded in Poland.

He pushed off his aliya to the Land year by year. He did not wish to take advantage of his Zionist work, which was done without expectation of a reward, in order to set himself up in the Land. This was despite the urging of his friends Grynbaum, Zabursky and others. Finally, it was too late.

The Second World War broke out. His eldest son, who was studying in Switzerland and returned home for the vacation, was killed at the first bombardment. This tragedy and the general Holocaust of Polish Jewry broke him completely.

He moved to Warsaw and remained in the ghetto, where he lived in difficulty and poverty. He spent the rest of his days poor and lacking in everything. He passed away in November 1941. He did not merit to settle in the land to which he dedicated all of his energy and strength. His wife and children later perished in the Holocaust.

Something interesting about the life of Moshe Limon of blessed memory was that despite the fact that he did not receive a traditional education, and despite the fact that during his youth he befriended freethinking youths such as Yaakov Kaplan and others in Ruzhany and other cities, he remained true to his religious convictions and observed the tradition throughout his life. No matter what the situation was, he never missed a day of putting on tefillin, and it goes without saying that, as a pious Jew, he refrained from desecrating the Sabbath. May his soul be bound in the bonds of eternal life.

{97}

# The First World War

## The Days of the First World War

One summer day in 1914, the children were busy covering up pieces of glass with soot so that they could properly watch the solar eclipse that had been predicted in the newspapers. People said that this was a bad omen. A solar eclipse does not affect world events, but it is a fact that the First World War broke out a few days later.

A draft was proclaimed, and sons of Ruzhany also went out to the Russian Army. Difficult days came. Wives and mothers who were waiting for news of their dear ones from the front walked around gloomily. Many of those who went out never returned. Instead, news arrived that led to heartrending screams from bereaved mothers.

Commerce ceased. Help from the relatives who had immigrated to America stopped coming. The Russian Cossack regime tightened its yoke, and the Jews suffered terribly. The Cossacks increased their acts of pillage as they retreated. Stores were broken into and ransacked. Locked doors of houses were broken, and the Cossacks took whatever came to their hand.

The Germans arrived in the town, in the month of Elul, during the time of the blowing of the shofar and the recitation of selichot, the time that the Jewish soul trembles from the fear of the approaching Day of Judgment in general, and from the war and tragedies in particular. When they arrived, quiet was still pervading and the chaos had ceased, but another sevenfold frightful enemy arrived -- hunger. The Germans indeed introduced positive innovations to the life of the town. Residents of Ruzhany saw electric light for the first time, replacing the kerosene lamps. Moving pictures, accompanied by the wonderful sounds of the violin of Tzadok the Ruzhany "band", arrived which brought the wonders of technology to the bored scouts of Ruzhany. A wooden sidewalk sprouted up on Schlosse Gasse. These innovations brought joy, but the hunger afflicted. The farmers of the region, "White Russians", destroyed their crops, and only a portion thereof was hidden in the ground when they fled to Russia. Some of these "underground treasures" were revealed, but the quantity was insufficient to satiate the lion. Since there was no sowing and harvest, there was no bread.

Commerce ceased. Even the stores that were not broken into and not pillaged with the retreat of the Cossacks were emptied of food, and there was no source to replenish them. The merchants walked around with nothing at all to do. The factories also stopped their work and were locked up. Goods that were left after the pillage of the Cossacks were confiscated by the conquerors. The workers lost their places of employment and sources of livelihood. The workshops barely had any activity.

A large fire broke out in the town. Even though there had always been a well-organized group of volunteer firefighters, they were not able to stop the fire, for it was caused by the cannon shells that were exploding and flying around all sides of the arms warehouse which had been set on fire. This caused a large fire.

Despite the fact that the physical situation was in a state of decline and degeneration, the spiritual activity increased at that time. Light shone from darkness -- the light of mutual assistance at a time of distress, as was demonsrated by the activity for the "Kinderheim" school, which gave both Torah and food to the children of the town. A dramatic group called "Hazamir" arose. A good quality choir made the difficult moments more pleasant for the residents of the town. At least for the few hours when the people sat and listened to the sounds of singing and melodies, they forgot the tribulation of hunger. Similarly, the attempt of Pepirmacher to set up the first cooperative agricultural organization in Ruzhany, called "Konsus-Farein" became known.

By Meir Sokolowsky

{98}

## The First Period of the German Occupation

**The period of the First World War. A roll call during the German occupation**

### A. The First Days of Occupation

The Germans entered the town a day or two before Rosh Hashanah. The Germans immediately started to clean the streets. They enlisted almost all of the local Jews for this task. The city was bustling with people. The Russians, who were nearby and could look out at the city from their ambush points, thought that these people were Germans, so they fired at them. There was a theory that the Germans did this deliberately so that the Russians would think that the Jews were German soldiers. The Russian firing caused victims from amongst the cleaners. Moshe Zinskind's son and Shlomo Kozak of the "Ever Hanahar" (Other side of the River) lane were killed at that time.

{99}

### B. The Role Calls and the Deportation of the Youths to the Camp

When the Germans entered, they introduced their own order. Every Russian Jew was considered to be a war captive, and therefore each one of them, over 12,000 people, received a passport of that nature. Twice a day, morning and afternoon, the men of army age had to present themselves. The German Felpewel [11] would enumerate those present and send them to fetch anyone who was missing. This event lasted for some time, then the roll call leader sent everyone back home. One bright morning when the youths assembled themselves, they were not given permission to return. They were transported to the "Landsdorf" Work Camp in Germany. There they worked hard, and ate the leftover food of the German. Many later returned with tuberculosis.

## C. Hunger

There was hunger in the city. The Jews turned to the tanning factory in the city, opened the barrels that contained syrup for tanning hides, and divided it up among the townsfolk to spread on the bread, if such was obtainable.

From Bulia Chwojnak

## From the Time of the German Occupation

### A. Forced Labor

There was no employment, but there was forced labor. The Germans took all Jews from age 14 to approximately 60 for forced labor for two days a week. The work was in the large vegetable gardens that were tended to by the Germans. Within a brief period, forsaken areas began to flourish. The Jews did not look kindly upon this work, which lasted from 7:00 a.m. until 4:00 p.m. They grumbled even more when they were forced to gather up the nettles, the fibers of which the Germans used to make clothing in their factories. The nettles were piled up on the hill of the burnt palace. Since this work was done unwillingly, they acted with cunning and set it up as contract work. Every person had to bring in a specified weight of nettles cut with his own hand throughout the course of the day. Some people hired others to fill the quota.

### B. The Dangerous Business

Commerce ceased. The Jews searched out food and livelihood, and occupied themselves with smuggling across the administrative borders that were set up between the various districts created in their occupied areas. Ruzhany was one district, Volkovysk was another, and Kosova was a third. Each district had its own German army camp and command. The commander of one district was not permitted to encroach upon the borders of his fellow and to transfer goods from one district to another. Since not every district suffered from a shortage of goods, a strange situation was formed where there was plenty in one district and relative famine in another. The Jews smuggled goods from one district to another -- an underground business that was fraught with grave danger.

## C. A Unique Kind of Manufacturing

The factories were silent. Several Jews of Ruzhany had the idea that, since the spirits that the Russians poured out from the various liquor stills in the region had penetrated to the depths of the earth, it was possible to raise it from the belly of the earth by digging wells. The mixed water would be drawn, and distilled into alcohol on the one hand, and pure water on the other hand. They planned this and did this. They requested that the Jewish mayor Zeev (Velvel) Szeresewski obtain the required permit from the German commandant to draw the mixed water. The Jews dug a well, drew the mixed water, and brought it to Mogilenski the pharmacist. The latter distilled it, and there was alcohol.

{100}

A group was immediately set up to take advantage of the permit, and the livelihood of the group was already firmly founded. The Jews of Ruzhany urged on others, who formed additional groups to salvage such blessed waters in the areas of other liquor distilleries in the region. This eased the financial situation of a portion of the residents of the city.

Similarly, the Jews learned to salvage the flax seeds that remained in the burnt factories and extract their oil by using various iron presses.

By Yosef Abramowicz

## The Forest People

There was famine in the town. The Germans divided up the plots of land on the "kanal" in the town and additional plots around the vicinity to work and produce food from the land. Potatoes were divided up and planted.

However, man cannot only live off of potatoes. An additional source of food was found -- the forest. We went out to the forest two or three times a week during the summer. We would stroll among the tall trees with baskets in our hands. The forest was beautiful and full of splendor. As the first man, who dwelled among the trees and blended with them into nature -- so too were we. In the new, green world, we walked proud, lofty and full of thoughts. The trees whispered to us words of love, as if they were greeting us pleasantly and asking us to enjoy the dainties that they had prepared for us. Indeed, we gathered the bounty of sweet fruit in the baskets and boxes that were in our hands. We gathered blackberries and strawberries. The blackberries gestured to us with black eyes from among the many low, green trees, and the strawberries peered at us with smiling eyes in their many freckles. We emptied these bushes from their bounty, and went deeper into the forest to find sources of additional bushes hidden there. The sun peered out at us from between the branches of the tall trees, showing us the return path.

{101}

However, this good sun did not always stand prepared to shine upon us and guide us. Sometimes it hid its face from us. More accurately, the clouds covered it and hid it, and we lost our way in the noisy, frightening forest. The winds strengthened, we suspected that rain would shortly fall, and where would we find refuge from the rainstorm if it comes? It was necessary to quickly find the dirt path that led to town. I, the seven- or eight-year-old child, served as a guide in such cases. I already knew the paths of the forest. I quickly felt my way and found the path upon which we must go to get out of the thicket. I was able to recognize the place of the hidden sun, even through the white appearance of a few clouds that were brighter than others, and I knew the winds of the heavens and the way that would lead us from darkness to light. At that time, there was no small number of forest people like me in the town, who were bound to the trees and foliage of the forest.

We rested from the toil of the day at home. We ate mushroom soup. We swallowed blackberries with or without a piece of bread. The pleasant forest air encouraged us and we were strengthened from the food of the forest. We waited for the end of the lean war years, with the coming of peace, to completely regain our health. In the meantime, we satisfied ourselves with the bit of food that was in the house, which we had brought from the forest with the addition of the food that I received from the "kinderheim".

By Meir Sokolowsky

## The Big Fire

The battle over the town lasted for several days. People lived in their cellars, and the Russian cannonballs exploded one after another in the streets of the town. Several citizens fell victim. The cannon bombardment eventually stopped, and the Russians were beaten and retreated to Slonim. Calm pervaded in the town -- the calm after the storm. People began to leave their hiding places and appear in the streets.

One bright day there was a sudden thundering. The sound of a strong explosion was heard in the vicinity of Pruzhany Street, followed by endless sounds of explosions. At first people thought that the battle over Ruzhany had started again, and they wanted to hide in cellars. Then they saw flames rising up rapidly, with heavy pillars of smoke and flashes of light. The Germans began to flee from the town, carrying with them only light objects. All of the residents fled in their wake. The tumult was great. Fathers lost their children and children lost their fathers. The flight was in the direction of the mountains of Liskowa and in the direction of the cemetery, far from the flames.

The thundering sound increased and strengthened, and within a brief time, most of the Schlosse Gasse street was in flames. The thunder stopped toward evening. The fire slowly quieted down, and the residents began to return. Many discovered that they were left without a roof over their heads.

{102}

The areas of Schlosse Gasse from Pruzhany Road until the bridge over the "Kanal Teichel" especially suffered. Not one house was left standing there.

As was later clear, the fire was caused by the negligence of several German soldiers, who lit a bonfire to brew some coffee in one of the fields next to their arms warehouse. This warehouse then caught on fire and went up in flames.

The Jewish energy and diligence had their effect over several years. The town was rebuilt and the Jewish community continued to weave the threads of its existence.

By Meir Sokolowsky

## The "Kinderheim" (Children's Home)

**The Kinderheim School**
Translator's note, on the photo, the year 5678 / 1918 is noted.

**First row, standing from right to left:** Peshka Wilensky, Sonia Leviatan, Fruma Turn, Peshka Lerman, Ahuva Leviatan, Sonia Bashin, Sonia Rizkin, Dvora Itzkowich, Chasia Ett, Hinda Ditkovsky.

**Second row, seated:** the son of the Brisker melamed (the teacher), Chaim Eliahu Rizkin, Moshe Berman, Tzvi Inker, Yekutiel Moskovsky, Bulia Chwojnik, Yisrael Aharon Bulgatz.

**Third row, seated:** Hadassah Rozen, Rothstyn, Brouda, Itka Selman, Chaya-Rasha Shipitzski, Simcha Rozenstyn, – , Chana Levin, Fruma Ditkovsky.

The Germans arrived, and in their wake, there was also a shortage of work, and hunger. Farmer fled from their villages, taking along the food and sustenance of the town. There was great sadness at home. The pantry was empty. There was no piece of clothing and no shoes. There was darkness in the rooms of the house.

A group of teachers: Y. Moskowski, B. A. Rizkin, Tz. Inker D. Rizkin, B. Chwojnik, P. Szapira, Y. A. Bulgacz, H. Szeresewski, M. Berman, L. Krabczyk, and groups of activists: Misses Epshteyn, Goldin, Mogilenski, Jozelewski, Karelicki, Nechama Szeresewski, Chana Krabczyk, Dova Chwojnik, Rachel Chwojnik, and others organized and opened the "Kinderheim" (Children's Home) school. It was true to its name. This school became a home for the needy and hungry children of Ruzhany. Despite the darkness of the times, the children found light, Torah, happiness and joy in this school in the midst of the heart-piercing sadness, song and dance in place of running about aimlessly, and some food for those who were hungry for bread.

{103}

For the most part, the children came to the school wearing tattered clothing. Several of them received a shirt made out of clean cloth from the school, received as a gift from a German. However, the handful does not satiate the lion, and most of them went about wrapped up in many rags in order to protect the body from the cold of the winter. Even though it was possible to forego a complete set of clothing, it is impossible to go about in the snow and ice barefoot or with worn out shoes with the toes sticking out. Those responsible for the "Kinderheim" asked Sender the shoemaker what to do. After deliberating, it was decided to take care of the issue of shoes.

There were many hides in Chwojnak's factory, but they were confiscated by the conquering authorities and were only under his supervision. Nevertheless, they took out the hides in the darkness of night. Three shoemakers were summoned. The leather cutters cut the skins and the shoemakers made shoes for each of the 200 children in the "Kinderheim". The work was performed in full measure and with great dedication.

Yiddish and German were studied in the school. Sections of the writings of Shalom Aleichem, Y. L. Peretz and others were read in those languages. There was also a choir that sang in the classes and celebrations. From time to time, the students of the institution arranged performances, celebrations and the like. At holidays, they would receive sweets, the like of which had not been seen for some time and which the parents could not find during those times. The Germans were invited to the celebrations, and they often brought gifts of a sack of sugar or groats to the school as a present, which eased the situation of supply for some time.

The hands of the parents were unable to give the children even normal food. The school gave them their primary meal, which consisted of only soup and bread. At times, there was also jam to spread on the bread. This meal was prepared in the school's kitchen, where pleasant warmth was felt in both senses of the word. Young women who volunteered for this holy task, for free, like the teachers of the institution, cooked, prepared, set out and served the meal to the children along with the teachers. The teachers, cooks, leather cutters, shoemakers, and others who assisted carried out their work with goodwill, without thinking at all that they were making some sort of sacrifice. The good spirit of dedication and assistance beat through everyone's hearts.

From Bulia Chwojnik

## The Choir

Despite the great hardship that pervaded under the Germans, song did not stop, and was heard in public. The large choir was organized by Leibel Kessler, who dedicated all of his time to this endeavor. The choir's performances were at a high level. The members included such fine musicians as Shlomo Szipiacki, Moshke Sokolowsky [12], Beilka Egolnik [13], Yentel Fajnman, and others. Just like the organizer, all of the members dedicated much of their time to the choir. For example, Chaim Bass, who was called that name because of his bass, dedicated himself to the choir even though he was a tailor who was burdened with concerns of livelihood in order to sustain his large family.

{104}

From Bulia Chwojnik

## "Hazamir" and "Herzlia"

Bread was lacking during the time of the Germans, but despite this, societal life flourished. At that time, a dramatic group of male and female youths was arranged, called "Hazamir", and conducted many activities. The group performed "Der Vilner Baal Habaisel" (The Little Householder from Vilna) and other plays in Yiddish. In particular, there were many performances of Shalom Aleichem, such as "Shver Tzu Zein a Yid" (It is difficult to be a Jew) and others. The first actors were Yehoshua Szybyc the chief spokesman of the group, Berele-Leibe the doctor's, Leibel Szybyc, the sister and wife of Yaakov Kaplan, Tovia Liwerant, Moshke Szklirowicz, Yentel Pepirmacher, Avraham Limon, Jozelewski, Bilka Egolnik, the wife of Motke Szklirowicz, and others.

The members of "Hazamir" also organized a library that was set up by collecting books in Yiddish, Hebrew, Russian and Germans -- books that were donated by the townsfolk.

After the war, some of the members of "Hazamir" immigrated to America, and the group disbanded. In its place, the youths of the town established "Zelbst Bildungs Farein" in the place of the "Hazamir

Organization for Arts and Culture". Its head was Baruch, the son of the teacher Moshe Solec. The new group continued with the activities of the former "Hazamir" and set up the dramatic group that was conducted by Yaakov Kaplan. The young, excellent actors included Yekutiel Sherman, his wife Peshka Lerman, Hershel Gavoha and others. When Noach Pines, the husband of Roza, returned from Russia, he donated a great deal of his talents toward the success of the group. They performed the plays of Goldfaden, Peretz, Hirshbein, and others. The dramatic group continued its performances even after it changed its name to "The Circle Affiliated with the Yiddish School".

The "Zionist Youth - Herzlia" Group

The hall of "The Organization for Arts and Culture - Hazamir" did not continue long, due to the political ferment that had started. Its organizer, Baruch Selec, had a Communist outlook, and he, together with Moshke Dobrowicki, attempted to turn the movement toward an anti-Zionist leaning. The influence of those two was very noticeable. However, the majority of the youth who belonged to this organization had a Zionist outlook. Therefore, a schism in the organization was unavoidable, and the latter group founded the "Zionist Youth - Herzlia" organization. The organizers of this new organization were the brothers Velvel (he and and his family perished in the Bialystock Ghetto) and Leibel Ziskind (the latter died in the Land), Fishel Chwojnik (died in the Land), and Shmuel Gerber-Burski (died in the Land), and, may they live long: Sonia Leviatan-Moszkowicz, Yosef Abramowicz (both of them in the Land), and Meir Epshteyn (in the United States).

By Yosef Abramowicz

{105}

**Members of Hazamir**

Translator's note: date on photo is February 19, 1918.

First row, right to left, standing: Rachel Kesler, the daughter of Mordechai Shershever, Chana Levinov, Leibel Sheivitz, –, Moshka Wishnivsky, David-Noach Egolnik, Moshka Shipitzski, – .

Second row: Chaya Egolnik, Ethel Kesler, –, –, Rashka Limon, –, Moshka Skliravitz.

Third row: –, Avraham Limon, Yekutiel Chwojnik, Schmidt, Leitcha Guldis, Tzirel Chwojnik, Zeidel, Berl Epshteyn.

Fourth row: Aber Liverant, Beer-Leib Pitkovsky, Moshka Pripstein, Shaya Sheivitz, Yentl Pepirmacher, Leib Kesler, Bulia Chwojnik, Shipitzski, Tovia Liverant.

Fifth row: Chava Kesler, Chana-Sarah Berman, Juzhlovsky, Marishka Stein, Bilka Egolnik, Chana Goldyn, Sarah-Dvora Shipitzski.

{106}

**Arts and Culture Organization – Hazamir**

First row, standing right to left: Liba Leviatan, Bilka Egolnik, Yankel Kaplan, Milia Kaplan, Feigel Shapira, Henia Shereshevsky (Brott).

Second row: Yitzchak Skolnik, David-Noach Egolnik, Moshka Skloiravitz, daughter of Mordechai Shershever, a member from Polonsk, Moshka Wishnivsky, Leibel Rotner, – .

Third row: Leibel Sheivitz, Moshka Kaplan, Tzirel Skloiravitz, Bulia Chwojnik, Bashka Kamintsky, Moshka Shipitzski..

**Herzlia Zionist Youth Group, Tevet 5681 (1921)**

First row, standing right to left: Mulia Gerber (Bursky), Leibel Ziskind, Yosef Abramovich, Zeev Ziskind.

Second row: Fishel Chwojnik, Sonia Leviatan, Efraim Epshteyn.

{107}

**Group at the Yiddish School**

**First row, standing right to left: Joselwicz, daughter of Reuven the owner of the hardware store, Heshel Gebzah, Todzha Epshteyn (son of Leibitshke the feldscher), Zeidel Epshteyn.**

**Second row; David Guldis, Sonia Bashin, the teacher Jeruzolimsky, Milia Kaplan, Yaakov Kaplan.**

**Lying down: Simcha Rozenstyn, Yekutiel Sherman..**

The library also split into two at that time. One part was the foundation of the Y. L. Peretz Library in Ruzhany, and the other part was the foundation of the Hebrew library affiliated with "Tarbut".

The new organization tried to rescue the youth from the claws of Communism, and succeeded at this in no small way. Members of Hashomer Hatzair, Hechalutz, Beitar, and other such organizations later stemmed from it.

## "The Consum Farein" (The Consumers' Organization)

The Consum Farein", the agricultural provision organization, was a unique enterprise. Pepirmacher the dentist gathered around him several youths of the town, such as: David Noach Egolnik, Leibel Chwojnik and others, and set up with them this organization, whose purpose was to till the abandoned plots of land in the abandoned village of Brzenica, so that they can provide all of the agricultural provisions for themselves and the residents of the town. This was an actualization of Pepirmacher's idea, about which he planned and preached. The members of the group, which was established based on the principles of cooperativism, were enthusiastically put into practice. They obtained the required inventory and succeeded in their work. This organization existed for three years, and then disbanded when the food shortage disappeared, and the farmers began to return to their lands.

By Yosef Abramowicz

{108}

## Between the Regimes

Thus did the years of the German regime pass with physical straits and spiritual development, until the breakup of the German occupying army. Even in Germany, this breakup came in the wake of and following the Russian Revolution. When the echoes of the Russian Revolution reached Ruzhany, a great deal of activity began amongst the supporters of Soviet Russia in the town and the surrounding gentile villages. The Communist city dwellers along with their comrades in the villages created the Rawkum (Revolutionary Committee). A large mass gathering took place in the market square, at which Mordechai Karpelowicz and the son of Shmuel Chaim Epltreger the teacher, as well as gentile speakers, spoke. The local Communists declared their participation in Soviet Russia. A similar ferment took place in nearby cities such as Slonim, which the Red Army had already reached.

The new regime did not introduce any change in the life of the town. This was an era of "between the times", where one regime disbanded and the next had not yet succeeded in becoming entrenched and asserting its rule. The local regime functioned for the most part on its own accord, without receiving clear directives from the central government. The local militia was also provisional, and the volunteer firefighters of the town supported them. To their credit, it should be said that their influence on the residents of the town, both Jews and gentiles, was great, and the order was not disturbed.

A sad episode for the Jews of the town at that time was the disturbances by the Polish legionnaires under the command of Zambrowsky. This Polish army division passed through Ruzhany on its way from the Ukraine to Poland to join the Polish Army. One winter night, shots were suddenly heard from the side of the Slonim Road. The small guard of the Red Army that camped in our town and numbered several tens of soldiers attempted to stop the Polish hooligans, but they could not stand up to the power of the greater numbers. The Poles quickly took control of the town, remained there for a few hours, and perpetrated a harsh pogrom against the Jews.

The Soviet regime was felt to a greater degree during the time of the Russo-Polish war. The Red Army that was advancing toward Warsaw filled up the town with its masses, moving through the town in an endless fashion. This was a difficult time for the town, for this army, which was lacking in equipment and supplies, sustained itself from anything that it could find. To this end, it stole the meager portion from the residents, which was small enough even without this.

With the retreat of the Red Army, whose advance had been stopped and reversed by the Polish Army, and with the signing of the peace treaty in Riga in 1921, Ruzhany was included in the State of Poland that had been renewed three years earlier. The years of changing regimes then concluded.

By Yosef Abramowicz

## The Pogroms in Ruzhany

### A. Pogroms in the Town

It was the year 1919. The Russians and Bolsheviks advanced. The Poles organized divisions of fighters under the command of Zambrowsky to fight against the Russians. One of the divisions reached Ruzhany on its route through our town from Dereczyn to Pruzhany and Pinsk. They broke into the town at evening, and in the morning they captured Jews on their way to the synagogue with their tallises under their shoulders. Twelve of them were captured, lined up against her wall, and shot as Jewish Communists. There was a pogrom in the morning! There was murder of innocent people! Six of them fell dead: Asher Pitkowski, Chaim Bass, Kamintzky, Szracyk, the son of Chaim the weaver, and Aharon Yosef Sokolowsky. Six others were wounded, falling below the victims, and acting dead. The hooligans left the city at noon. The bodies were left lying at the place of murder, with nobody to bury them on account of the fear of the enemy.

{109}

Then several youths gathered together and were brazen enough to go outside to see if the hooligans were no longer in the city, and if it was possible to give the final honor to the martyrs. We loaded the bodies onto a wagon and set out in mourning and feeling downtrodden in order to accompany them on their final journey to the cemetery. Suddenly we saw from afar horsemen rushing toward us. Were the murderous Polish gangs returning? Several of us hid. I and my friends remained next to the wagon. The horsemen approached. We realized that they were Russian Cossacks. They asked us the way by which the Poles had left. We showed them the direction, and they quickly disappeared from the horizon in that direction. We brought our martyrs to burial in a common grave. We returned home broken and shaken.

No small number of miracles took place that day. The hooligans asked me to serve as their guide. However, first of all, they asked for straw for the horses, and my wife went with them to show them where the straw was. In the meantime, I got away and left via the back door. When they returned, they searched for me, but in vain. In this manner I was saved, seemingly from certain death.

By Abba Leviatan


## C. Pogroms in Ruzhany

*HaIvri* 1919 (14) writes the following about the pogroms in Ruzhany.

"In Lithuania as well, the Polish legionnaires perpetrated pogroms in many towns, such as: Zelva, Ozernitsa, Dereczyn, Pruzhany, and Ruzhany. The worst pogroms took place in Ruzhany. The Polish legionnaires, 1,500 in number, entered the town toward morning to fight with the Bolsheviks. When they asked the town priest, "Who are the Bolsheviks?", he answered them in brief, "All of the young Jews." Twelve Jews who were on their way to services with their tallis bags under their shoulders were captures and cruelly beaten. Later the legionnaires took them to the Polish house of worship, stood them in four rows with 3 people per row, and shot them. Six of them died, three were severely injured, and three remained intact. One of those murdered had enwrapped himself in his tallis prior to being shot by the legionnaires, and thus did he fall. After the legionnaires had taken out their wrath upon the captured Jews, they began to pillage the homes of the Jews. The pogrom lasted all day. Christian citizens of the town participated along with the legionnaires.

*HaIvri*, 1919 (14)

**TRANSLATOR'S FOOTNOTES**

1. A traditional statement of mourning.

2. There is a village in Israel called Kfar Pines.

3. See http://en.wikipedia.org/wiki/Alliance_Isra%C3%A9lite_Universelle.

4. I believe that this refers to a farm life with more automation and less direct work of the land.

5. Literally, "from the kidneys of the land."

6. There is a footnote in the text here as follows: "approximately a kilometer." A *verst* is an old Russian unit of distance.

7. From Exodus 1:10.

8. A teaching style whereby the language of instruction for the Hebrew language is Hebrew (i.e. Hebrew immersion).

9. This would be in 1941.

10. The All-Russian Extraordinary Commission for Combating Counterrevolution and Sabotage. See http://en.wikipedia.org/wiki/Cheka

11. Likely a corruption of the German rank "Feldwebel" -- Sergeant.

12. There is a footnote in the text here, as follows: My uncle, today in America -- the editor.

13. There is a footnote in the text here, as follows: The daughter of Esther Riva and Moshke Egolnik, today in Canada -- the editor.

{110}

## Way of Life in the Town

### The Libraries of Ruzhany

A. Eliahu Itzkowich the bookbinder ("Eliahu der Einbinder") was the disseminator of literature in our town and the owner of the first library of the town. He had books of all types: from books of Sheme'r [1], which were enjoyed by the girls of the town to the serious book of Smolniskin and others. For five kopecks, one could read for an entire month. If you only wanted a single book, you would pay one kopeck and get it. Great interest was aroused among the youths of the city when Eliahu left the city and returned with a load of new books. They would hurry to grab the books that had not yet been bound, "as a firstborn before the summer" [2]. The books were only bound in some sort of fashion after they had passed through many hands and their pages had become tattered and scattered. Then, they were able to continue to fulfill their honorable task of disseminating knowledge in the city. This first library included many Russian books: approximately 1,500 for adults and 500 for youths. Similarly, there were approximately 200 Hebrew books from the Haskalah period.

From Bulia Chowjnik

B. It had already been stated in the earlier chapters that during the First World War, the members of "Hazamir" set up a library in Ruzhany that included books in Hebrew, Yiddish, Russian, German, etc. The library broke up when the organization broke up. One part formed the foundation of the Y. L. Peretz Public Library and became a Yiddish library, most of whose readers were Bundists or those close to them in spirit. In one corner of that library there were indeed a few Hebrew books published by Shtibel. The second part of the "Hazamir" library formed the foundation of the Hebrew library that was housed in the "Tarbut" Hebrew School and served as a center for nationalistic literature. Most of its readers were active Zionists and their supporters.

C. The Ruzhany youth also did not hide their hands in the plate, and through the efforts of some of them such as Yeshayahu Kaplan, Moshel Eisenstein, Yisrael Yosef Lewiatan and Zeev Ruszkin, a library was set up in the small room of Yeshaya Kaplan, providing books for several tens of youths for a certain period of time.

From Zeev Ruszkin

## The Library in Pavlova

The settlement of Pavlova also followed the path of Ruzhany and founded its own library in the year 1925. There is a story to its founding. A general meeting was called in the women's gallery of the local Beis Midrash, a leadership committee was chosen including progressive members such as the tailor Yom Tov Epshteyn and others. Activity began. A one-time fee was imposed upon all of the members, and membership dues were also set. Raffles were organized, and plays were performed in the barn of Dov Sobolsky. Within a short period the needed funds were collected, which were used to purchase the approximately 130 first books in Yiddish that were ordered from the capital Warsaw.

{111}

There was a private library in our house, which had many books in Yiddish and Hebrew. I gave them over to the public library that had just been founded, raising the number of books in the library to 350. I was chosen as the secretary of the library, and dedicated myself to that task. For two or three hours each evening, I swapped books with those who wanted them. The library maintained itself for a few years, and served as an important cultural institution in the settlement.

Rafael Karelitz

**The Library in Pavlova.**

**Right to left: Leibel Rubenstyn, Mulia Meller, Avrahamel Lissovsky (standing). Yom-Tov Epshteyn, Chaim Berkowich, Zeidel Karlits, Yosef Kaplan (standing).**

## Memories of Childhood

### The Symphony of the Eve of the Sabbath

Captivating sounds rose up from the local Talmud Torah. They were going over the weekly Torah Portion (Sedrah). It was the eve of the Sabbath. The voices of the children were not like on other days. One could sense in them the melody of joy and freedom. The voices of the Rebbes were also quite different. They taught the cantillation of the Haftarah with a melody of sublimeness, joy, pleasant rest, and a feeling of the approaching Sabbath. The voices were those of the teachers: Aharon Yaakov, the Hebrew teacher who was dedicated to the Talmud Torah (who celebrated with the bride and groom at every wedding, and collected donations for the educational institution that was in need, since most of his students were children of poor families); the second teacher was the week and pale Baron, who taught Chumash and Rashi; behind them was the short Chaim Zerach Rotstein, who smoothed his long beard and swayed as a worshipper when he was teaching Bible and Gemara. The broad-shouldered Rebbe Shmuel Chaim Epltreger, who delved into the sea of Talmud with his students, also lifted up his voice. Conducting all of them was Avigdor Michel Goldberg, who had a splendid visage. He was the principal of the institution, and was dedicated to his holy task. He was imbued with sevenfold pleasure on Friday, as if he was rejoicing with the joy of the children and the students together, enjoying the ambiance of the approaching Sabbath that reminds one of the ultimate redemption that will eventually come.

{112}

### Longing for Zion

Indeed, this faith was pulsating in his heart. On Sabbath afternoon she would gather us together in one of the rooms of the Talmud Torah that was empty on that day and sing songs of Zion with us: "On the road there, a rose rolls...", "There in the place of cedars", and others. These first seeds of Zionism fell upon the furrows of my heart, the heart of a young child who grew into a lad and became a man, and did not find rest in the Diaspora until the day of his aliya arrived, when he fulfilled the words of the song that was sung on one of the Sabbath afternoons in the ears of the young children such as him:

I am a small Jew

But filled with strength and might.

My love is great,

To my nation, and also to my land,

That is there, far away.

There, under the azure skies,

Over the sea.

Another year, another two years,

Time passes quickly.

There I will travel and even prepare for myself:

A horse, a plow, a spade.

Then I will work my land,

And I will have a bountiful harvest,

I will also plant a vineyard for myself.

That produces good wine.

{113}

## Friday Afternoon

Now I will return to Fridays. The Rebbe freed us in the afternoon, and I barely touched the stones of the cobblestone road, for I flew, and in an instant I reached my house that was located not far from the Talmud Torah. My mother asks me about the great haste, and serves me aromatic soup, wafting with the aroma of meat and bones, along with a piece of fresh, white challah that had been baked by her hands. These disappeared into my mouth in the blink of an eye.

I was free for a few hours, for my mother was busy with her preparations for the Sabbath. However, how pleasant was this freedom. I "turned worlds" until I was called into the house. Mother was astonished at the filth that clung to me and was happy she had dressed me in old clothes when I had returned from the cheder. Of course, she sentenced me to "boiling water" that cleansed and purified me, combed my wet hear, and dressed me in Sabbath clothes.

The sunset. I went out with father. Quiet! The king and the prince are walking to greet the queen. We directed our steps to the Great Synagogue. We are walking, and we are large in our eyes seeing that we are members of a large nation streaming together with us from the Schloss Gasse, and the Kanal to the holy place. We are not a small stream of people. Additional masses are coming from Bliznajer and Klibner Streets through the marketplace to the house of worship. Many householders from Chazir Gasse, Milner Gasse and other streets between the house of Shimon the shochet and the Aguda synagogue. The rabbi, tall and with a splendid aged appearance is seen leaving his home next to the Tehillim Synagogue and approaching the Great Synagogue that is near to our home, with the throngs clearing a way from him and greeting him with "Peace be upon you, our Rabbi."

## The Synagogue

I enter the lofty synagogue. When I was small, I imagined it as a splendid, high palace resting on four gigantic supporting pillars, with a high platform between them upon which they place the Torah scroll when it is read. When I got older I imagined it as a giant fortress in which the Jews gathered during times of tribulation, therefore its windows are so tall and it has an additional door as an emergency exit. Indeed, the frightful stories of what took place to us in the Diaspora that I learned in school caused this change of image.

We approached our place in the synagogue. My father had his place in the second row behind the eastern wall, next to the cantor's lectern. It was an excellent spot. From there we could see the cantor Gershon Kaplan and his young and old choir singers. I was one of them for some time.

The service of the welcoming of the Sabbath commences. The voice of the cantor and his singers rings in our ears, comforting our hearts. We participate with them as we sing the Lecha Dodi prayer ("Come my beloved to greet the bride, let us greet the Sabbath") and welcome the Sabbath Queen that fills our synagogue with its honor.

## In the Home

We feel its presence also when we return home after services. The street is lit up with rays of sparkling light breaking forth from the windows of the house.

We enter our house that is full of light shining forth from the chandelier hanging from the ceiling, lit in honor of the holy evening; from the eyes of Mother greeting us with love; from the bottle of red wine on the table waiting for father to recite Kiddush; from the white cloth covering the challas, resting on a tablecloth as white as snow. The words of the Kiddush then rise up, bringing us under the wings of the Divine presence that is filling the room and turning it into a miniature sanctuary.

{114}

The tasty food, the hymns that broaden the mind and bring joy to the heart with their sublime melodies, the words of Torah spoken at the Table about the weekly Torah portion and what the children had learned during the week — merge together to form the table of the Dweller on High.

## The Sabbath Symphony Continues

The meal concludes. Father and Mother start singing Yiddish songs about a Jew, the son of a king who is content with his lot — on his Sabbath, with a mother waiting for a letter from her son who wandered to far-off places, about the exodus from Egypt, etc. Songs of the Sabbath, songs of longing from the wandering child, songs of redemption fill our hearts with alternating feelings of sadness and joy.

Your tunes, oh Father, and your songs oh Mother, flow through my veins and sing themselves to this day.

Slowly the songs of my parents cease. They go to their room and go to bed. We also go to sleep with a feeling of a night of restfulness. The hours of sleep have no bounds. Outside, however, on nearby Schloss Gasse, the older youths stroll, talking vibrantly, conversing loudly, and singing.

Sleep falls upon us, while the Sabbath symphony continues outside

Meir Sokolowsky

## Longing for the Land

I spent some time in the Land as a tourist and returned home. My decision was to liquidate my affairs in the Diaspora and make aliya to the Land. I rented a carriage in Slonim (there were no cars yet) and traveled slowly to Ruzhany, for the horses did not pay attention to the fact that I was hurrying to return to my family. I had already gone most of the way, and had exited the Slonim Forest that was about four kilometers from Ruzhany. It was midnight. I suddenly sensed someone walking in the darkness of the night. Who could it be? Was it not a robber? Then this man raised his hand and requested that we stop the carriage. We responded to his request, looked at him, and recognized him. It was Nota Lisowicki. I asked him what he was doing at such a time so far from the city. His answer was that he wanted to be the first

Jew to greet his friend who was returning from the Land of Israel. I said to him, "Have not many Jews already shook hands with me in Slonim". He answered that he wanted to be the first from among the Jews of Ruzhany.

I brought with me about ten packages of Israeli cigarettes. I gave two packages to my relative Leib Lerman the carpenter. He lit a cigarette and closed the window. I asked him to explain his actions, and he did not hesitate with his answer, saying that he did not want the smoke of the Israeli cigarette to be scattered in the winds. I distributed the rest of the cigarettes among my acquaintances, giving each person one cigarette. They thanked me profusely.

Go forth and see how great was the longing of the Jews of Ruzhany for the Land of Israel.

From Tzvi Lerman

{115}

## Maot Chittim (Charity for Passover) [3]

The holiday of Purim passed, and Passover was approaching. One must prepare everything needed for this holiday, and the needs of the Jewish people for this holiday are great. However, there are those who do not have the means to celebrate this holiday appropriately — for they cannot afford it! Therefore the concept of "Maot Chittim" was instituted, an enterprise to rectify what fate had denied. From where do the "Maot Chittim" funds come? Every resident of Ruzhany donated generously to Mr. Leib Tzadik (Mrucnk) who sat in a small side room of the Great Synagogue, issuing a receipt for every sum of money that was received from each person.

However, exceptional things also took place. I was an eyewitness to two such events, about which I will now relate. I was sitting next to Leib Tzadik after I had brought my contribution to "Maot Chittim" when Levi the weaver entered. After exchanging greetings, he asked:

"How much should I give to the Maot Chittim fund?"

"Like last year."

"And how much did I give then?"

"Thirty kopecks."

"For you it is easy to register amounts. I cannot give that much, I will give only 25 kopecks."

I knew that his situation was not bad. The sum that was set for him was low for his status, but his heart did not move him to give what was asked of him, so he disputed the amount to lessen it. I was embarrassed and thought, "It is not from such people that the poor of my nation will be saved."

However, I had already said that the majority gave generous donations to Maot Chittim, and some even gave more than asked. Here is the second incident:

Yerucham Marminski entered. His means had declined in the latter period. He was an independent weaver, not the owner of a factory. However, as he did possess a few looms, he was entered into the list of the wealthy of the town. He would bring a very proper donation each year with a full heart. However, the wheel of fortune turns about. That year had been difficult for him. The cloth for uniforms that had been manufactured had not been sold. The previous orders had been canceled, and new ones had not arrived. His machines were idle. The bundles of material that had already been prepared remained as stones without anyone to turn them over, and coins disappeared from his pocket. When I saw him entering, I wished to exit, so as not to see him in his straits and embarrass him. I was sure that he would not be able to bring his donation this year, and, on the contrary, perhaps he would receive assistance this time. However, he removed a silver ruble and gave it over for Maot Chittim, as in previous years. I was certain that he himself did not have the means to purchase the needs for Passover. But our sages were wise when they said, "G-d wants hearts" — it is not the pocket that donates, but rather the heart!

From A. Lewiatan

## The Eve of Passover in our Town

The pleasant aroma of the Passover holiday was already wafting through the air. One must prepare fine flour, from the best of the best, for the purposes of baking matzos. Our hearts swelled and rejoiced at the sight of the holiday preparations. We impatiently awaited the great day that was approaching — the day of the baking of matzos. Who can describe an enjoyment greater than this? All the people of the town had the same feelings that we did. There was excitement.

{116}

There were a few matzo bakeries in town. The bakeries were cleaned and made kosher for this purpose. The families of the city took turns baking their matzos there. Who could imagine when our turn would come?

Father removed the flour from the wagon and brought it to the bakery. The horses pushed the wagon from our house, through the Kanal, until the bridge next to the bathhouse. The precious cargo crossed the bridge over the Kanal Stream, and we arrived at the bakery. Mother and we children accompanied the wagon.

The Baking of the Matzos

We entered the bakery, which was filled with men, women and youths. One woman kneaded the dough in a shiny copper bowl. Two boys stood next to her and brought her the correct measure of flour and water so that the kneading would not stop and the dough would not become leavened. Another woman apportioned the dough to the women who were dividing up the dough into the portions for the matzos. From then, the matzos passed to a table covered with a clean metal sheet, upon which several youths are making holes in the dough with hollow rolling pins.

During the work, the girls conducted conversations spiced with local gossip. Laughter filled the rooms. Laughter and diligence of the hands. The perforated matzos were transferred to the hands of the baker, who used a baker's shovel to put them into the oven. He would remove the baked matzos in about a minute. Most of them were white, but a few were brown as they were slightly singed. We received some of both. They were hot, and the heat spread to all parts of the body. We spent most of the day in the bakery, and when the day was finished, we were sorry that such a happy day had passed.

Preparing the "Mead"

We had other such days before the festival arrived. One of them was the day of the preparation of the mead.

The day of the preparation of the mead was a holiday for us. Mother cooked the honey, tasting it from time to time, but the drink was already good and fitting to be served on the table of kings. We children did not put our hands into the plate. Rather, we surrounded Mother, cupping our hands and asking her if we could taste the steaming liquid. We drank it and praised the drink, for it was good. This was not Mother's opinion, for she continued to cook and taste, and we continued to request and receive additional portions of this sweet, sweet drink.

## Whitewashing the House

The days of cleaning the house were additional days of joy. The order of the world changed when they arrived. Everything that filled the rooms of the house until this time was taken outside. Only the walls and ceiling could be seen. Where was the floor? It was covered with straw so that it would not get too dirty during the whitewashing.

The white angels — that is the whitewashers — appeared, wearing clothing that was white from the whitewash that stuck to them. The work began. Our empty rooms, which grew and broadened in our eyes due to the removal of the furniture, continued to grow with their new whitewash and shining white. We entered the rooms and stretched out our necks to see the whitewashing. However, we were chased out by the adults who asked that we do not run between their legs and not dirty ourselves from the drops of whitewash that were dropping all over the place. We fled outside, wandered around the furniture, and played hide-and-seek. We were served food at irregular times. We ate at times eating on a bookshelf and at times standing next to a table, all outside. After the hasty meal, we were free. What was demanded of us further? How good was it for us? How good was our lot.

{117}

## Splendor, Beauty, the Glory of the World [4]

The vacation was complete. The month of Nisan was the month between school semesters. G-d did a kindness for the school children, and the yoke of studies was lifted from them. We no longer sat in the closed cheder from morning until evening. We were able to enjoy the glory of the world. How many interesting, attractive things were there!

The day shone down from hour to hour. Look up. The winter clouds have disappeared. The sun, which had hidden its face for weeks and months, appeared. It was bright and brilliant, warm and caressing. Look down. The white covering had melted and the earth was exposed. Puddles gathered on the ground, sparkling with the colors of the sun. Many images were scattered over the face of the earth. Pleasant aromas arose from it and spiced the air.

How high was the sky! The firmament of the sky! It is blue! An azure sea atop your head. And a sea also beneath your feet. This was the small river that passed close to our house, the "Kanal Teichl" changed its form and became a mighty river. It had a meager flow all year, and now it overflowed all of its banks. Its quiet flow turned into a mighty, noisy stream.

## Guests for the Festival

Now you raise your head again, and a family of storks had arrived, passing sleepily from their peaceful kingdom. They arrived, and with them came the month of Nisan, the month of spring. A pair of storks were nesting in the tall chimney rising up from between the buildings of the liquor still on Schloss Gasse, heralding the advent of spring.

However they are not the only ones that arrived. Many birds of all types fill the sky with joyful chirping, a new song. There are so many of them! Who told them about the renewal of our world? Who told them about its return to life? From where did they appear? Indeed, they came from the lands of the south for the festival of spring and renewal, the time when our town is filled with song and melodies (of the matzo bakers, the house whitewashers, the children on vacation, with splendor in their eyes, songs in their ears, and desire for redemption in their hearts). They, the birds, tell me about our Land and our birthplace where we came from. The heart is filled with pangs of longing. If the joy of Passover is so great here, how great would our joy be if we celebrated it there, in our native Land.

Oh, would it be soon!

## In the Synagogue

The eve of Passover arrives. After bathing, we don our new clothes and new shoes. The sun is about to set. We walk with Father with deliberate steps to the synagogue, like the sons of kings with their king. People are streaming to the house of worship from all sides. The Great Synagogue is filled with joy and light. Thousands of candles light up this holy place. Thousands of bright eyes are lit up with the joy and happiness of the Festival of Freedom. The synagogue is filled with song and joy. Cantor Kaplan and his choir perform splendidly. The echoes of freedom emanate from their throats with wide hearts and clear intellect.

{118}

The service ends, and the masses of Jews stream to their houses to conduct the Seder and tell about the Exodus from Egypt. There is a pleasant tumult in the streets. Light is planted along the entire route, bursting forth from the windows of the houses lit up with extra lights.

## In the Home

We arrive to our home, which is not far from the synagogue. The house is filled with light and joy. The Seder plate is set up, the goblets are arranged, with the cup of Elijah rising above them. The wine for the four cups is on the table. Father puts on his white kittel [ceremonial garment] and his appearance is that of an angel. He reclines on a pillow like a king. Mother is dressed up as a queen. The faces of my mother and father are beaming. They look upon us children with satisfaction, joy and bright eyes. It is good for us, and our hearts are warm. The youngest child asks the questions in a festive voice, and father reads the answer with a sense of great importance, as we read after him. A unified voice, lofty and festive, a voice filled with faith in the freedom that will yet come continues until a late hour of the night; a voice saturated with love, from which the Song of Songs [5] naturally emanates.

   Meir Sokolowsky

{119}

# Economic Situation

## The Economic Situation After the First World War

The First World War ended. Poland returned to life. The weaving factories of Ruzhany were burnt down during the war, and those that were not burnt lay idle, since the Russian marketplace for textiles was no longer available. The hide factories continued with their work, but the majority of the Jews did not earn their livelihood before the war from these, but rather from the weaving factories that lay idle.

Commerce and labor were virtually the only branches of livelihood in our town, but the Polish authorities assaulted the economic status of the Jews in the country. The status of the Jews was weakened through heavy taxes and through the enabling of the gentiles to take control of the commerce and labor. Even without this, they would have been weakened. The marketing possibilities for the merchandise of the Jews shrank, and their market area became constricted. Only a few of the merchants were able to earn a sufficient livelihood from their work. The rest lived from hand to mouth despite their great efforts, business talents, and diligence.

Their sons and daughters ambled idly through the streets of the town, without work and empty of Torah, since only a few of them were accepted to the high schools, and even those with great difficulty. Commerce had already betrayed their parents, and they had no hope to build themselves up in that area. There were also very few chances of being accepted into labor-based jobs. The heavy taxes that were impoverishing their parents demanded that they find their own independent means of existence, but there was none. This was a circle of cruel spells from which there was no exit, so they searched for means of immigration. Since only a few of the locked doors of the world were open to them, the youth wandered about the streets of the town idle and with nothing to do.

The farmers of the settlements of Pavlova and Konstantinova also came down from their greatness, as we learn from the letter of David Pinski, the emissary of Hechalutz and member of Givat, who visited Ruzhany and its settlements in 1930.

Meir Sokolowsky

## In Ruzhany

Hello friends!

— — — During those days, things have been most difficult for me here. I am already tired of the traveling and the wandering. Now, when I am en route, I am looking at the fields: the farmers are plowing, planting, and hauling fertilizer. I feel a pain in my heart. I am now wandering around here as an "emissary". A great deal of agricultural work is taking place. It is hard for me to look at the poverty and difficulty that I find in every city and town, and even more difficult for me to look at the youths walking around idly, wandering about outside with nothing to do. In every place I hear the same refrain: it is a depression, there is no work, there is no end to the sea of tribulations.

{120}

I arrived in Ruzhany on Friday. The members of "Hechalutz" were waiting for their confirmation in Hachsharah, and in the meantime, they were wandering idly about the city. The town had declined and was dead. A deathly silence pervades the market in the middle of the day. The youth are leaving the city and searching for a place to which to immigrate.

I heard that there are two Jewish agricultural settlements near Ruzhany. I was happy to hear about this, and I asked my friends to take me there. I wanted to see the fields of the Jews, and Jewish agricultural work. I went there, and along the way I saw farmers hauling fertilizer, plowing and planting potatoes, but I did not meet one Jewish worker along the way. I entered the village. The settlement was founded approximately 100 years ago, during the time of Nikolai I. It had dilapidated houses that were liable to fall down. There was a dilapidated house of worship in the middle of the settlement. I met one Jew who was standing next to an empty potato pit, covering it. An official of the I.C.A. [Jewish Colonization Association] passed by in a wagon. I asked the Jew if the I.C.A. was helping them to any extent. "Absolutely no help," was the response. The farmer began to complain, "The earth is poor and of inferior quality, the harvests are scanty, the prices are low, and it is impossible to maintain oneself." I looked in the yards. Gentile workers were hauling fertilizer and picking potatoes — clearly doing all the work. The Jew was not working. He was looking for auxiliary sources of income. Before, they used to work a bit in commerce. Now, due to the tribulations of the times in the midst of the depression, they await money from America. The cultivation was very primitive. There was no concern for ensuring a variety of crops. They did not plant flax, for one needs to invest a great deal of manual labor in that crop, and since the family members do not work in the field and one must hire workers, it would not be economically feasible to do this. "Agriculture is not for Jews," agreed one farmer, "It is for gentiles. They are born as farmers, and can earn their livelihood from this." — "But you were also born a farmer," I asked him. "Indeed, but our needs are greater, agriculture is not for us."

I remembered our old settlements in the Galilee. How great are the similarities. Here too, the youth leave the settlement. Here too, it is strange labor, and there is despair and lack of faith. I did not gain any satisfaction from my visit to the settlements. I returned to town dejected and disappointed...

Hershel Pinski

(Givat, Sources and Events — published by Hakevutza. One of the letters of H. Pinski, Slonim, May 2, 1930.)

## The Bank in Ruzhany

At first it was a charitable fund. Anyone in need could receive an interest free loan for a security pledge, and sometimes without one.

Later, the bank was set up. One of the first founders was Pepirmacher. A special emissary from the central banks in Warsaw passed through various towns and set up bank branches. He also visited Ruzhany and authorized the new branch. Pepirmacher's brother Reuvke was the accountant of the bank. Shmelke "Stires" was his assistant. The bank was opened in the Shulhauf Lane in the house of Finkel the baker ("Der Piaker"). When Reuvke left Ruzhany, Yaakov Kaplan was appointed as treasurer. He also served as a member of the directorship. From that time, Simcha Rozenschein served as accountant. His assistant was Yaakov Asher Rabinowich, and the bank emissary was Yitzchak the son of Eliahu Rodcki the tinsmith.

{121}

From among the founders of the bank we must mention Mordechai Karpels, Berl Chwojnik, Moshka Michels, Aharke Gamerman, Yaakov Michel Leb the shoemaker, and Hershel Lerman. Later Katzman, Szereszewski's son-in-law, also joined.

The bank provided great value for impoverished Ruzhany, even though it was only able to give small loans during the early years. The bank continued to develop after the First World War until it became quite large. With the economic depression that aflictd Ruzhany after the birth of the State of Poland, the bank assisted several of the merchants in no small manner and kept them from bankruptcy.

Tzvi Lerman

**The Ruzhany Bank Committee**

**First row, standing right to left: Yaakov-Asher Rabinowich, Shmuel Hirsch Stein, Yaakov Kaplan, – , Yaakov Michel Leib the shoemaker, Zelig Rudetsky, Yom-Tov Leviatan, – , – , Yitzchak Epshteyn, Simcha Rozenschein.**

**Second row: Yitzchak Wilensky, Yoel Epshteyn, Moshka Kaplan, Meir Guber, Nachum Fineman, Avraham Katzman, Tzvi Lerman, Moshka Guldin..**

### TRANSLATOR'S FOOTNOTES

1. This is likely "Shemot Rabba" — a Midrashic exegetical work on the book of Exodus.

2. I am not sure of the etymology of this phrase. Obviously, it expresses haste.

3. Literally "Money for wheat", referring to the wheat needed for the baking of the Passover matzos.

4. A quote form one of the Sabbath hymns.

5. It is customary to read the Song of Songs following the Seder.

{122}

## Zionists Movements

**Hechalutz Movement in Ruzhany**

At the end of World War I, the echoes of the call of Hechalutz to the young people of our nation to arise, make aliya and build up the Land of our Fathers began to reach the town. There was already a Hechalutz group in Ruzhany in 1920, which had its headquarters with Yehuda the Printer ("Der Drucker") on Liznajer Street. Courses in Hebrew and the study of Zionism took place in that room. However, matters did not reach the point of aliya, and the activity quieted down.

The actual Hechalutz chapter in Ruzhany went through different phases of development. It was first established in 1924. The youths of Hashomer Hatzair in the town had graduated from the movement and felt that the time for actualization had arrived. In those days, a Keren Kayemet (Jewish National Fund) convention took place in Warsaw, in which Yosef Abramovich served as the delegate of Hashomer Hatzair from Ruzhany. At this convention, the call of Mrs. Ben-Dror was issued to set up local Hechalutz chapters in places where none existed. Yosef returned from the convention and founded the Hechalutz chapter in Ruzhany along with Leibel Ziskind, Yaakov Kletzki, Yehudit Sokolovsky, and Fruma Ditkovsky.

Hachshara farms in our area still did not exist, but two of the aforementioned Hechalutz organizations and Rivka

{123}

Shapira organized a pioneering group of female seamstresses, who advertised regarding various sewing jobs in the town — something that left a great impression in Ruzhany.

Yaakov Kletzki, a member of the committee and a candidate for aliya, traveled to the regional convention of Hechalutz in Pulsia, which took place after some time in Brest Litovsk. However, when three certificates were later received, he and the other two youths were not able to travel, since their age made them eligible for the draft and therefore they were unable to obtain passports for the journey. Yehudit Sokolovsky, Fruma Ditkovsky, and Gisha Rudetski (today in Afula, and her sister is in Kfar Yechezkel) went in their place.

After their aliya, the Tel Chai Hachshara Kibbutz was set up in the village of Michlin. The members of the kibbutz tried their hands at all types of difficult labor in order to prepare themselves for hard work in the Land.

**A group of seamstresses of Hechalutz in Ruzhany**

**Standing right to left: Rivka Shapira, Fruma Ditkovsky, Pitkovsky, Sonia Rizkin, Hodel Rabinowich, Yehudit Sokolovsky.**

**Sitting: Gisha Rudetsky, Bilka Brazovsky.**

A short time later, an additional group of young women went on aliya to the Land: Dvora Itzkowich (Givat group), Rivka Kletzki, Raya Kaplinski (in Moshav Mishmar Hashiva), and Rivka Shapira.

The influence of these olim left their imprint on the youth and instigated a growing influx to Hachshara. However, the crisis in the Fourth Aliya [1] somewhat dampened the enthusiasm of those who aspired to actualization. The activities in the chapter once again weakened.

However, the enthusiasm of the students of the Tarbut Hebrew School and the members of the Zionist youth movement, in whom the spirit of aliya and upbuilding had already been absorbed in their blood, did not cease. The elders of Hashomer Hatzair renewed the activity of Hechalutz in the winter of 1929. The members of the new committee were:

{124}

Yona Epshteyn, Yudel Sokolovsky, Elka Rubinowich, Chinka Grabolsky, Miriam Epshteyn, and Motel Katz. The teacher Nybursky assisted them greatly. Nachum Alperstein, Gedalia Epshteyn of blessed memory, and may they live long — Zeev Rushkin and Rivka Bashin were active later.

Tel Chai Hachshara Kibbutz in Michlin

**First row, standing right to left: Aharon Egolnik, — , Chaim Isser Abramovich, Heshel Gezbah, Sonia Kaplinsky, Efraim Gustovcki, — , — , — .**

**Second row: Yosef Rushkin, — , Rivka Kluchky, Itzel Chwojnik, — , — , — , — , Yosef Abramovich, Yosef Kaplan.**

**Third row: — , — , Bilka Brazovsky, — Fruma Gustovcki.**

Life in Hechalutz was vibrant. The lively debates and the Hebrew songs from the Land of Israel strengthened the longing of the members for the homeland and their aspirations toward actualization. Guest speakers were invited, and we drank up their words with thirst. Herschel Pinsky and others visited us. We arranged lectures, celebrations and memorial days. For example, there was the Trumpeldor celebration, which took place on 11 Adar 1931, where Yehoshua Vishnitzer and Ben Porat from the Hachshara farm in Iwacewicze spoke. These were hours of internal awakening and an ascent of the soul. Many of the members of Hechalutz then went out to Hachshara in Iwacewicze, Janów, and Shacharia [2], and actualized their aspirations not in words, but rather in deeds by following their Hachshara with aliya. At that time the following people made aliya: Zeev Rushkin, Rivka Bashin, Beilka Shipitzki, David Pitkovsky, David Noach Gvurin, and — may they rest in peace — Nachum Alperstein of blessed memory who died two years ago, and Shmuel Rubinowich of blessed memory who fell in Ramat Hakovesh during the War of Independence in 1948.

Committee of the Hechalutz chapter in Ruzhany, 1929

**Standing right to left: Motel Katz, Miriam Epshteyn, Elka Rubinowich, Chinka Grabolsky, Yudel Sokolovsky.**
**Sitting: the teacher Yitzchak Nybursky.**

Later olim included Yosef Egolnik, Fruma Gustovsky, Elka Rubinowich, Yosef Abramovich, and Meir Sokolovsky. Most of them made aliya as tourists, with the intention of remaining in the Land and not leaving it. Meir Sokolovsky made aliya as a student of the Hebrew University, which provided special certificates for its students that were not included in the meager general quotas that were known as "Shadiul" in the lingo of the Mandate.

From Y. Abramovich, A. Rubinowich, and Z. Rushkin.

{125}

Hechalutz organization in Pulsia

First row, standing right to left: Esther Shemes, Yudel Sokolovsky, Shimon Sydlenitsky, Nachum Alperstein, Sheindel Ett, Roza Egolnik, Hinda Klebensky, Chasia Ett.

Second row: Yaakov Pitkovsky, Liba Zemach, Gedalia Epshteyn, Sonia Levinov, Motel Bayr, Berl Ett, Chaim Sapir, Noach Gvurin, Hershel Kolodany, Meir Yidel Itzkowich, Gashelwich.

Third row: Teibel Alperstein, David Pitkovsky, Feigel Pripstein, Zeev Rushkin, the teacher Yitzchak Nybursky, Mulia Rubinowich, Moshe Lissibitsky, David Zakheim, Yone Epshteyn.

Fourth row: Kreina Zakheim, Breina Burovsky, Shlomo Pitkovsky, Tzadok Skolnik, Miriam Epshteyn. Fruma Gustovcki, Sheindel Joselwicz, Dvora Pitkovsky.}

{126}

## Activities on Behalf of the Jewish National Fund

**Jewish National Fund (Keren Kayemet) Committee in Ruzhany**

First row, standing right to left: Shmerkowich, —, —, —, Nuchem Alperstein, Yudel Sokolovsky, Gedalia Epshteyn.

Sitting: Yosef Kaplan, Roza Kaplinsky, the teacher Yitzchak Nybursky, Shmuel Mogilnesky, Guldis, Zeev Rushkin, Yona Epshteyn.

The activity for the Jewish National Fund broadened from 1924 and on, even though it existed in a restricted fashion prior to then. At that time, the blue box was brought into most of the homes of the town. The boxes were emptied monthly. A prize was given each time to the owner of the fullest box. We organized film days and the sale of stamps.

The living spirit of the activities of the Jewish National Fund was Yaakov Asher Rabinowich. The activists included Asher Epshteyn, Yosef Kaplan, Gedalia Epshteyn, Meir Guber (Mizrachi), Shmerkowich (Revisionists), and — to differentiate between the dead and the living — Shmuel Mogilnesky-Magli, Zeev Rushkin, Yosef Egolnik, Efraim

Gamerman, Yudel Sokolovsky (Hashomer Hatzair), Elka Rubinowich (Hashomer Hatzair), and others. Also active was Nybursky, my teacher in the Tarbut Hebrew School, and, may he live long, Klicki. The latter served for several years in the Jewish National Fund Central Campaign in general, and in Zionist activities in the city in particular, and he would organize literary evenings, questions and answers on Zionist and general topics that were full of content. There was positive competition between the youth of the Hashomer Hatzair and the Revisionist youth. In truth, we should note regarding this competition that the former had the upper hand with regard to Jewish National Fund activity. Even those townsfolk who were absent from the town all year as students of the seminaries or other schools in Warsaw, Vilna and other places would work with double effort for the Jewish National Fund when they returned to town for the major vacation. Among the activists who were journalists were the brothers David-Noach of blessed memory, and to differentiate between the dead and the living, Meir Sokolovsky, who were students of the seminary prior to this, and later served as teachers.

{128}

Keren HaYesod was also not neglected in our city. The living spirit behind it was Michel Egolnik. He was assisted in his work by Yudel Slutitzky (Yudel Zeidke's) who was one of the simple folk, a tradesman who was very busy, but dedicated with heart and soul to the Zionist idea and the Keren HaYesod. Shlomo Jezernitzky was also active. Dr. Yatom, Shmuel Magli, and others were very active in this realm.

We will return now to the Fund of Redemption [3]. We already pointed out above that Yaakov Asher Rabinowich was one of those most active for this fund. He did not act as a member of a specific party, but rather as an independent activist, a general Zionist, and a person who was acceptable to everybody. He would also visit the weddings of the Orthodox, even of those who were philosophically distant from Zionism, and would collect money for the Jewish National Fund during the celebration. He would also come to the synagogues in which many people were opponents of Zionism, and place a collection plate there on the eve of Yom Kippur. For who would be able to stop him from being there and collecting donations for this holy aim?

{127}

Jewish National Fund (Keren Kayemet) Brigade in Ruzhany

**Translator's note: date on photo is 9 Iyar 5688 / 1928.**

The two standing at the top: Yona Epshteyn, Baskha Levinov.

First row, standing right to left: Nachum Alperstein, Moshe Lissobitsky, David Alperstein, Yisrael Belkin, – , Shifra Zazhvir, Chinka Gerbolcki, Aryeh Pitkovsky, Nechama Bashin, – , Chabula Zakheim, Yosef Kaplan, Rachel Chwojnik, Todel Slutzky, Batya Ett (Reiner), Sonia Kaplinsky, Yitzchak Nybursky, Dovka Halpern.

Second row: David Podrevsky, Ethel Vygodesky, Isser Klebensky, Rivka Wynitsky, Malka Segal, Avner Ziskind, Rachel Lissobitsky, Hinda Ditkovsky, Malka Sokolovsky, Chinka Chwojnik, Fruma Gustovsky, Sonia Rizkin, Rivka Shapira, Itka Kaplan, Yentel Podrevsky.

Third row: Hinda Klebensky, Yosef Egolnik, Duba Chwojnik, Zeev Rushkin, Yaakov Asher Rabinowich, the teacher Klicki, Yaakov-Asher Epshteyn, Byulopolski, Rachel Brazovsky, Dvora Skliravitz, Yudel Ditkovsky, Gedalia Epshteyn, Liba Chomsky, Chantsha Bialos.

Fourth row: Leibel Skolnik, Sonia Kolodany, Sonia Itzkowich, Aharon, Rivka Pitkovsky, Libka Chwojnik, Zlata Brouda, Chaim Isser Abramovich, Leibel Rizkin.

The two lying down: Sonia Levenbok, Roza Egolnik

## The Market for the Jewish National Fund

There were many activities that were conducted by the Ruzhany citizens for the benefit of the fund, but we must point out one activity that surprised them all — the market ("bazaar") that was conducted for the benefit of our fund. We worked on the preparations for about half a year. All of the women of the town donated to this activity, giving sheets, tablecloths, and the like. Mrs. Leah Lerman of blessed memory excelled among the active women. She was active, and urged others to activity.

The women baked many cakes as the time of the market approached. The market was set up in the large hall of the movie theater. Booths were set up, and in each booth there were different types of merchandise for sale. The booths were decorated with rugs and other decorations.

The Polish intelligentsia was also invited to the opening. They appeared, headed by the Polish mayor, who greeted the endeavor for which the market was created with warm words.

The market was open for five days, until all of the residents of Ruzhany and the two nearby agricultural settlements visited it. Many residents from the nearby cities, including Slonim, Kosova, and other places, arrived. We collected 1,000 Polish zloty, which was a large sum according to the values of that times. We gave over the money with the request to inscribe Mr. Yitzchak Grynbaum in the Golden Book of the Jewish National Fund.

Not only did the market raise a large sum of money, but it also provided spiritual sustenance. Each morning of the five days was dedicated to discussions and lectures for the children of the private cheders and the Talmud Torah, who came with their teachers and principal Avigdor Michel Goldberg, and for the students of the Tarbut Hebrew School with their teachers and principal. Each evening of the five days was dedicated to presentations on the Land of Israel for the adults.

The preparations for the market and the market itself strengthened the will of the members for additional work for the Jewish National Fund, and the army of workers grew.

Shmuel Magli

{129}

## The General Zionist Organization

The General Zionist Organization in the city mainly included members of Al Hamishmar, which was founded by Yitzchak Grynbaum. It served as the spiritual and organizational patron of all of the Zionist youth organizations in the town, and supported their activities. Its active members Michel Egolnik, Mogilensky, Dr. Yatom and others, together with Meir Guber of Mizrachi organized Oneg Shabbat evenings in the hall that was located in the home of Yaakov Asher Epshteyn. These evenings attracted large numbers of people from the town during the winter months of 1924-1925.

The General Zionist Organization conducted broad publicity activities for the national funds. In 1928, on the occasion of the visit of Mr. Hertzfeld — a visit that turned into a holiday for the town — the Jewish National Fund Brigade organized an enthusiastic reception for the guest, with representatives from all of the organizations: General Zionists, the Jewish National Fund Brigade, Hashomer Hatzair, and Hechalutz. The guest spoke in the Great Synagogue on the Sabbath. A banquet took place in his honor on Saturday night. He was registered in the Golden Book as a token of appreciation.

The General Zionists were active in the area of Zionist work, communal activism, and work for Hebrew Culture. They were most active in the communal area at the time of elections for the Polish Sejm and the Zionist Congresses. Of course, their path was not always paved in roses, and at times they even suffered from disappointment and disillusionment under the oppressive hand of the enemy. For example, at the time of the Sejm elections in 1926, Mr. Mogilensky and the rest the members of the election committee suffered beatings from a member of the Sanacza (Pilsudski's party) who took control of the ballot box and exchanged all of the ballots with ballots of his party.

{131}

The crowning accomplishment of the activities of the General Zionists was their cultural work, which expressed itself with the establishment of the Tarbut Hebrew School, which maintained itself with their support.

A farewell party to the Magli family as they make aliya to the Land of Israel

**Standing right to left: Yosef Kaplan, –, –, Yonah Epshteyn, Efraim Gamerman, –, Berl Ett, –, Yaakov Asher Rabinowich.**

**Standing: Roza Kaplinsky, Necha Foksman, Marishka Skliravitz, –, Sonia Limon.**

**Sitting: Fania Skliravitz, Shmuel Magli, his wife, Moshel Skliravitz (standing), Dr. Yatom.}**

{130}

**Hashomer Hatzair at its inception**

First row, standing right to left: Oska Kagan, Chatza Berman, Isser Klebensky.

Second row: Zeev Rushkin, Todel Slutzky, David Levinov, Nachum Alperstein, Avraham Karpelewich, Leibel Skolnik, Zeev Brezticki, Eliahu Leviatan, Yisrael Epshteyn, –, Moshe Kamenmostki (Geshuri).

Third row: group heads: Yosef Leviatan, Moshe L. Eisenstein, Yosef Abramovich (head of the brigade), Shasa Pines (his vice), Yosef Egolnik, Zeidel Lerman.

Fourth row: Leizer Kfitz, Asher Kolishevsky, Itzel Limon, Leibel Rizkin, Moshe Leib Shipitzsky, Chaim Pines, Moshe Lissobitsky, David Alperstein, Mendel Slutzky.

Fifth row: Leibel Krashinsky, Gedalia Epshteyn, Aharon Pitkovsky, Moshel Itzkowich.

## The Hashomer Hatzair Movement in Ruzhany

Hashomer Hatzair at a camp under the leadership of Yosef Abramovich, Ruzhany, 5684 (1924)

**Translator's note: the caption on the photo indicates that it is lunchtime at the camp.**

The Hashomer Hatzair movement, which began as a non-factional Zionist scouting organization, arose in Galicia after the First World War, and spread throughout Poland. It reached the towns of Pulsia.

Hashomer Hatzair was founded in Ruzhany by Yosef Abramovich, who had learned scouting from the brothers Yaakov and Eliezer Shapira, the heads of the Slonim chapter.

The youth of Ruzhany accepted this scouting movement with enthusiasm. Many joined its ranks and fulfilled all of their obligatory duties with love and dedication. There was a great innovation inherent in this movement, for it was a manifestation of a blend of Zionism and independent Jewish thought.

{132}

How proud was my heart during those days. I regarded myself as one of the young soldiers of the Hebrew nation that was rising to life. In organization ranks, with orders issued in Hebrew, calisthenics, appointing of heads of groups, divisions and brigades, the command to stand at attention issued by the second-in-command Leibel Ziskind at the time that the head of the roll call Yosef Abramovich arrived, awakened us and summoned us to new life.

Our uniforms resembled those of the Shomrim of the Galilee, whose names went before them. Echoes of stories and legends of the Hashomer in the Land reached us, brought joy to our hearts, and brightened our souls in the gray corners of the Exile. They restored our hearts and instilled faith in us. We knew that nights awaited for us in the Land, consisting of the paths of the praised Hashomer.

I will always remember the day when the brigades of the chapter marched on a major parade through the outskirts of the town, self-assured and filled with hope, on their way to the forest on Lag BaOmer or another day of gathering. I will never forget those evenings when we sat around the bonfire at dusk singing with an intimate voice, full of longing:

"Without you, oh Galilee, what am I and who am I? Galilee, Galilee, you are indeed my only one."

Then we were raised up on the wings of imagination, moving to the Land of the Fathers, as if sitting around a bonfire in the Galilee, the cradle of Hashomer, and participating in the building and guarding of our Homeland. These were moments of happiness, which did not end when the bonfire was extinguished and we returned home. Rather, they were hidden in the heart as a keepsake, and never ceased to whisper the hope until it was fulfilled when I made aliya to build up and guard the homeland.

Meir Sokolovsky

## Hashomer Hatzair Renews its Activities

We aroused Hashomer Hatzair to renewed activity in 1926. The instigators were Yudel Sokolovsky, Elka Rubinowich, Yona Epshteyn, Chaim Sapir and Mordechai Katz. During the years of my activity, I succeeded in rising from a simple member to the head of a group, division and brigade. I even reached the level of chapter head. Our activities were many and broad. We would gather for activities twice a week on weekdays, and also on Friday night and Saturday. However, the headquarters were open as well on the other days of the week.

During any free time, the members would come to the headquarters of Hashomer Hatzair to simply spend time with friends.

We did great things. We studied Hebrew, Hebrew History, Zionism, facts about the Land, as well as political economics. We learned about the classes and their wars from Zaks' book, and we learned women's history and Socialism from Babel. The newspapers of Hashomer Hatzair also gave us a great deal of educational material. Despite the fact that they were hard to understand, I spent hours upon hours reading the newspapers of Hashomer Hatzair with Hebrew and vernacular dictionaries opening and closing in succession in order to figure out the meaning of the "high" words that are not understood. I also participated in gatherings that imparted leadership material to us, such as: The educational gathering in accordance with Freud, conducted by Zohar, and others.

Emissaries would come to us from the central leadership, bringing joy to our spirits. This was Yechiel Grynberg, who, even though he was not in the Land, said that he knew it like his five fingers. This was not only boasting, for he had researched it with all its details, just as all of us were immersed in a competition to learn about the Land through stories and emissaries from the Land, until it seemed to all of us that we had seen it with our eyes — both it and all that had happened therein. With our imaginations, we looked at its variegated landscapes, and felt all of its changes. Even the short Feivel Gezbah, whose power was with his mouth, would visit us frequently. We learned no small amount from him as well.

{133}

However, these were not considered by us to be the primary visitors. We had a stronger spiritual connection with the chapter from the closest city to us, Slonim. Emissaries, and regular, heartwarming visitors would come to us from there. A Hassidic spirit pulsated in them and would rest upon us as well.

Nybursky, a teacher of the Tarbut Hebrew School, helped us a great deal. He dedicated several hours a day to group leadership. He would also participate in our activities in Hechalutz, the organization in which our members joined after graduatiing from our movement in order to learn independence and prepare themselves for aliya and life among the builders of the Land. We collected many donations as members of the Jewish National Fund Brigade in the town. We worked with enthusiasm, in order to lay the groundwork for the time when the Land would be able to receive us as we go on aliya to settle there.

From Elka Rubinowich-Enis

**A group of Hashomer Hatzair**

First row, standing right to left: Yocheved Wilensky, Esther Epshteyn, Duba Skliravitz.

Second row: Sonia Michnovsky-Sokolovsky, Hinda Klebensky, Esther Chwojnik, Fania Stein.

Third row: Sheindel Epshteyn, Ethel Sokolovsky, Roza Michnovsky.

{134}

**Hashomer Hatzair brigade**

**First row, standing right to left: Shlomo Dovkin, Tuchman, —, Yehudit Epshteyn, —, Shifra Foksman, Yaakov Rabinowich, Chaya Itzkowich, —.**

**Second row: Moshe Babich, Hinda, Nechama Kaplan, —, Dina Pomerantz, Yenta Zlotner, Karpelewich.**

**Third row: —, Kimerman, Zavel Tuchman, Sheindel Epshteyn, —, —.**

**Fourth row: Roza Michnovsky, Fishel Gerbolcki, Teibel Berman, Yisrael Foksman, Ethel Sokolovsky, —, Hinda Babich.**

Hashomer Hatzair – Beit Alfa group for older youths

First row, standing right to left: –, Epshteyn, –, Yosef Epshteyn, Rudetsky, Shimon Sokolovsky, –.

Second row: Shifra Foksman, Itsha Gamerman, Naomi Pitkovsky, Zavel Tuchman, Sonia Ivan, –, –.

Third row: Maya Pines, Vichna Shemes, Yaakov Rabinowich, Dina Pomerantz.

{135}

A group of Hashomer Hatzair in Ruzhany, 3 Cheshvan 5690 / 1929

Standing next to the wall on top, in the first row: Zavel Tuchman, Esther Epshteyn, —, —.

Standing next to the wall on top in the additional row: Yaakov Rubinowich, Itsha Gamerman, Rudetsky, Alperstein, —.

Standing next to the wall in an additional row, one lower: Sheindel Joselwicz, Pitkovsky, Sarah Gamerman, Feitsha Lev, Sheindel Ett.

In the long row, standing right to left: –, –, –, –, David Pitkovsky, Esther Shemes, Pitkovsky, –, –, David Rubinowich, –, –, Feigel Pripstein, Liba Zemach, –, Berl Ett, Tzadok Skolnik, –, Rivka Pitkovsky.

Sitting in the long row: Noach Gvurin, Shlomka Gaselewich, Yona Epshteyn, Efraim Gamerman, Yitzchak Nybursky, –, –, Yudel Sokolovsky, Elka Rubinowich, –, –.

Lower row, sitting: Zerach Chwojnik, Chana Epshteyn, Rachel Egolnik, –, –, Sarah Foksman, Pinka Tserbiticki, –, daughter of Shlomka Sokolovsky, Dina Pomerantz.

{136}

Their spirit, as well as ours, was the spirit of scouting. We were like them. This was not like the Hashomer Hatzair in Warsaw, where political tones began to overtake their scouting ideals. On the other hand, the Hatzofeh newspaper of Hashomer Hatzair was enjoyed by both us and the group from Slonim. On its front cover there was a picture, drawn by his hand, of a scout blowing a trumpet and an erected tent. Its content was scouting, and its language and style were simple and understandable.

We did not suffice ourselves with a tent drawn on the front page of Hatzofeh, for we erected actual tents in the joint summer camps with our Slonim friends. Their pleasant memory is well etched in our hearts.

We did a great deal for the youths of the town. We gathered them around the concept of the Land of Israel. We distanced them from assimilation and the "clubs" that were opened for them in the Polish schools. We brought the various classes of the town and its suburbs closer to each other. The children of the street, the Jewish children studying in the Polish school, and the students of the Tarbut Hebrew school mingled together and became one group, members of the same nation. The spirit of idealistic actualization pervaded. There was a great deal of activity in various arenas. We did no small amount in the theatrical arena. At times, we put on a performance for the adults with great success, and reaped praise. We would spend evenings in discussions of various topics. The debates and the stories transported us to the Land that was being built up. At the end of the discussion, the members would burst forth in song. The song was sublime, rising up and piercing the heavens.

## Beitar

In 1928, the Beitar organization was established in Ruzhany. Its strength was lesser than the Hashomer Hatzair Zionist Organization. Yitzchak Jezernicki (Shamir) was among the organizers of Beitar in the town. In the "Moment" daily newspaper, number 245 from 1934, the head of Beitar in Ruzhany writes something that tells us about the town council in Ruzhany as well as the Beitar Zionist youth organization:

"Here, the founding meeting of the magistrat (town council) took place. Mr. P. Krojelski (a gentile) was elected as the mayor, and Avraham Limon (a Jew) was elected as the vice mayor. The representatives were Father Spartanski and Yaakov Kaplan (a Jew).

The local Beitar was preparing to shortly celebrate its sixth year of existing. The program will include a gathering, a parade, etc."

Since no further details about the activities of Beitar were given to us from any member of the organization despite us asking them, we must suffice ourselves with the small amount written above.

{137}

## My Native Town

The image of my dear native town Ruzhany is constantly etched in my memory, and stands as living before my eyes. I cannot give a full description of the fullness of life that was lived in my quiet, beloved town, in which my cradle stood. However, I will attempt to draw forth from the abyss of forgetfulness some details of the life of the youth of the town from the years 1929-1933.

## The Bund

As far as my memory serves me, the youth had a strong desire for social and political activity. From among the political parties, the Bund had great influence during the first period. They did not have a hall or headquarters for their gatherings and activities. For the most part, their gatherings took place in the Y. L. Peretz "Di Yidishe Bibliotek" library, which was located on the second floor of the home of Rivka Rabinowich. Otherwise, they would gather under the open skies on the road to Slonim, not far from the Christian cemetery.

## The Communists

Several Communist youths and students who came from outside had influence on the youth of the town. At times, this aroused a fierce battle, and vibrant debates took place about various world outlooks and dreams of a better future. Many of the youth followed the propaganda, and were caught in the net of provocation. One bright day in August 1934, several of them were captured and led to jail in chains.

## Hechalutz

A great deal of Zionist and social activity took place in the ranks of the youth who were members of Hechalutz and Hashomer Hatzair. Hechalutz was a strong organization in town. Until 1929, the meeting place at the home of Sheina Pitkovsky on Blizonoj Street was at its disposal, and from there it moved to the home of Yona Epshteyn. The meeting place was always bustling with members. It was always like a boiling cauldron, with stormy debates taking place within the house. Hechalutz would often organize celebrations at the Tarbut School, with the proceeds going towards the Jewish National fund.

## Hashomer Hatzair

The members of Hashomer Hatzair had the lion's share of the Zionist activity. This was the strongest organization in town, and bore the mark of a scouting organization. The head of the chapter, Yudel Sokolovsky, along with Elka Rabinowich conducted the work of Hashomer Hatzair in Ruzhany. Both of them are in Israel today. The roles of Chaim Sapir, David Rabinowich and Dinale Pomerantz were also significant. The three of them perished in the terrible Holocaust. May their memories be blessed forever.

The importance of Hashomer Hatzair in the town was great. The members of the Hashomer Hatzair movement passed through all the educational ranks from cubs to older members. They would then go on hachshara, having been imbued with dedication to the national idea and the true Zionist scouting spirit. The work for the Jewish National Fund, including the collection of monthly donations via the blue box, was one of the special tasks which Hashomer Hatzair took on.

Decades have now passed since then, and more than a decade has passed since the terrible Holocaust brought destruction upon my dear birthplace, but I will never forget it. Its precious image, spices with green upon a spring landscape, will remain with me forever.

Rivka Zilberberg (Pitkovsky)

## Educational Institutions

{138}

### Educational Institutions in the Town

New winds began to blow through the town before the First World War. The cheder partially gave way to the modern cheder, and the latter — to formal schools.

### Gorodskowaya-Ucziliszyca (The Civic School)

The first of them was the civic school, Gorodskowaya-Ucziliszyca that was originally designated for the gentile children, although many Jewish children attended. A student did not gain a great deal of knowledge from this school, for its course of study consisted merely of two classes of high school. It had great value, however, for the Ruzhany youth found in it a source for general knowledge. Thanks to it, a group of intellectual youth arose according to the concepts of the times.

### The Kinderheim

Second to it was the Kinderheim elementary school, which opened during the German occupation during the time of the First World War. Its teachers were Moszkowski, Rizkin, and others [4]. The language of teaching was double: Yiddish and German. The value of this school was great, for aside from knowledge the children also received lunch, which they were very much in need of at that time. This was a great form of support for the hungry, like bread and Torah in one place [5].

### Progymnaszja

During the early days of the era of transfer of government from the German occupation to Polish rule, a school name Progymnaszja was founded in Ruzhany. Its first teachers were the Beizer brothers and the Berman brothers. This school existed for only one year. It was then closed by the Polish government due to its using of the Russian Language for its language of teaching.

### The Powszechna

The era of the penetration of the Polish Language to the residents began in those days. The authorities opened the Powszechna Polish school. Jewish children did register for this school, but their numbers were small despite the good conditions of this school, including a good building, free tuition, etc.

## The Yiddish School

The Yiddish circles established the Yiddish Weltliche School during those days. The language of education was Yiddish. Hebrew was only taught as a language. It is important to note that this Yiddish school was not anti-Zionist despite the fact that the majority of the board members were Bundists. This was due to the fact that one of the enthusiastic supporters of this school was a member of Poale Zion, who had great influence. Thanks to him, this school did not embark on an anti-Zionist track. This educational institution was founded in the year 1920. It was headed by a dedicated leadership committee, which obtained the large sum of money needed to maintain it. It was led by Yaakov Kaplan during its first years of existence. He was considered to be one of the good teachers. His students remember very well his literature classes, when he would read a section from the writings of Sholom Aleichem or another writer and would literally bring him to life with his words. Since he was an actor by nature, he would imbue the classroom with the atmosphere appropriate for the section that he was reading.

{139}

## The School of the Rabinowich Family

The Rabinowich family obtained special rights for establishing a progressive Hebrew School. They established a four-grade Hebrew school for beginners, and conducted it according to the modern teaching approach, including illustration and song. The teacher Bila, who was the wife and assistant of her husband, the educator Eliezer, excelled not only in her dedication to her role as an educator but also in her pleasant voice. The sounds of Torah and song burst forth together from the windows of this school.

## The Tarbut Hebrew School

The Hebrew Tarbut School, founded in 1922, earned an honorable place in the town. This school was a source of Zionist influence in Ruzhany. The students were mainly children of the wealthy and well to-do, and therefore it had a stronger foundation than the other local schools. One of these young people who attended this school will tell about it.

From E. Leviatan

## The Tarbut School in Ruzhany

The crowning achievement of educational creativity in the town was the Tarbut Hebrew School that was founded in Ruzhany during the 1922-1923 school year. Many of the students from the Yiddish public school, from the Talmud Torah and the cheders transferred to this Hebrew school immediately after its founding. Parents and children faithful to the Zionist idea, preparing for the time of aliya and complete actualization, gathered around this school. Those residents of the town with Zionist sensitivities found Hebrew and Zionist education to be a source of comfort in the present and hope for the future. The parents of the children, upon whom fate had determined that they would live in the Diaspora under an inimical and oppressive government and withstand a difficult struggle for existence, hoped that their children would succeed in going abroad to freedom and building their lives in the Land of Israel. Of course, these parents hoped that if luck would favor them, they would join their children in the future and become rooted in the Land with their assistance. These parents maintained their faith in this educational institution throughout all the years and struggled for its existence during the years of economic depression. The school continued to exist until the outbreak of the Second World War.

## The School Trustees

The following people were among the founders and primary supporters of the school: Michel Egolnik, Yaakov Pitkovsky, Anshel Krolinski, Shlomo Jezernitzky, Berl Chwojnik, Shmerkovitz, Shmuel Mogilensky, Dr. Yatom and others. The first principal of this institution was David Nir, who was sent by the Tarbut headquarters in Warsaw.

The following teachers are also among the faithful and dedicated supporters of the school: Rabinowich, Bloch, Komarovsky, and Sheina Mirl Skolnik — a gifted teacher who was incidentally a native of our town. Due to their dedication to the school, these teachers refused to leave it. Even though their salary might be late in coming, they maintained their guard in the continued existence of this national institution that was dear to them.

{140}

The Tarbut Hebrew School in Ruzhany

**Bottom row, sitting from right to left:** Yaakov Berkowich, Chaim Epshteyn, Shimon Turn, Zeidel Lerman, Zeev Rushkin, secretary of the school, Zeev Brezticki, David-Noach Sokolovsky, Rivka Bashin, Moshe Wishnivsky, Akiva Pitkovsky.

**Next row up, sitting:** Nechama Bashin, Asher Kolishevsky, Lekibel Rizkin, Leibel Skolnik, Avraham Itzkowich, Chinka Grabolsky, Nachum Alperstein, the principal David Noyer, Roza Egolnik, Malka Segal, the teacher Sheina-Mirel Skolnik, Sonia Levenbok, Yosef Egolnik, Meir Sokolovsky, Dvora Shekel-Ravich, Merke Ozernicki.

**Next row up, sitting:** the teacher Schwartz, Mendel Slutzky, Shmuel Rubinowich, Gedalia Epshteyn, Tzvi Zakheim, Peshka Abramovich, Moshe Kamenmostki (Geshuri), Yitzchak Limon, Efraim Rubins, Roza Kaplinsky, Sonia Itzkowich, Keila Letzky, Frida Pines, a girl from a nearby town, David Pitkovsky.

{141}

The students whose parents were unable to pay the tuition fees for their students were very dedicated. They would make up part or all of their tuition by giving private lessons or carrying out various jobs, even though they had to do their homework during that time.

## Disturbances by the Government

It was not only the search for financial sources for support of this private national institution that made the task difficult, but also the attitude of the Polish authorities who looked unfavorably in general at any Hebrew educational institution and attempted to disrupt it — and it was not hard to find ways to do this. On one occasion the government did not certify the principal who was recommended by the institution with the pretext that his certificate of authorization had not been shown to them. On another occasion they found that the building designated for the school was unstable and dangerous to the students. However, all of these iniquities were covered by the love of the activists for the institution. They brought the certificate of authorization of one of the teachers of the institution to the Polish authorities, who then certified her properly as a principal, despite the fact that a man who had been chosen for this purpose by the Tarbut headquarters actually served in this role. They also found a way to avoid the decree of an unstable building.

The Tarbut School in Ruzhany was a high school. However, for various reasons, the Polish authorities certified it only as an elementary school. A tumult arose in the institution every time the government inspectors appeared. They quickly carried the Latin textbooks up to the attic, for these books would serve as proof that the school was teaching as a high school despite the lack of recognition by the regime for such. Obviously, all of the teaching was conducted on an elementary school level as long as the inspector was visiting the institution. As soon as the inspector left, the regular order resumed and the institution resumed its functioning as a high school.

## Achievements of Hebrew Education

The efforts for modern Hebrew education were not in vain. The school imparted the knowledge of Hebrew language and literature to its hundreds of students. When residents of the town made aliya, it was like coming home, for they already knew the language and way of life.

The Hebrew school instilled the love of the Land of Israel into the hearts of the younger generation, which became a source of comfort for them during the most difficult moments of their lives and laid the foundation for their strong love of their homeland. With awe and love, they donated to the funds for the redemption of their native Land. At times, the children donated to the Jewish National Fund the few coins that were given to them to purchase a second breakfast. I remember how my sister Ethel's face shone with the news that she was the first in her class to fill the stamp book of the Jewish National Fund.

## Performances of the School

The Hebrew school imparted a nationalistic hue to the life in the town with its Hebrew performances on days of national pride such as the 11th of Adar and on the national holidays such as Chanuka. The performances of the Tarbut School were an important event in the town. Many months were dedicated the preparations for each play. Much effort was dedicated to rehearsals and preparations of costumes. The teachers gave of their time for this effort after teaching their regular classes in school. The rehearsals took place in the home of the teacher, with only the final ones taking place in the school. The performance itself took place in the large hall of the movie theater, which was filled to the brim. Since the hall could not accommodate everyone who came, the performances were repeated. The performances were a topic of conversation for weeks and months following. There was a variety of performances. Some were on Biblical themes such as "David and Goliath" and others were general such as "The Dolls" in which my wife also participated. There were others as well. The impression was so great that after the play, she was escorted by hand to her waiting parents. She was not the only one who enjoyed great success. The income from these performances was not small. It partially covered the school's deficit, and raised the opinion of this educational institution in the eyes of everybody.

{142}

## Graduates of this School

Most of the students of the school belonged to the Zionist youth movements. They spent some of their evenings after school in discussions and debates about their future life in the Land. The echoes of Hebrew song and dance rose up into the air of the town. The teachers of the institution supported the partnership between the school and the youth organizations. Some also dedicated their time and efforts to these organizations.

In summary: The school performances, the demonstrations of the youth organizations, the gatherings to promote the idea of a return to Zion instilled a Hebrew-Zionist content to the life of the town and a spiritual, nationalistic splendor to the holidays and festivals. The Hebrew language and national songs echoed not only between the walls of the educational institution and the halls of the youth movements, but also in the streets of the city. The national vision and aspiration for actualization pulsated in the hearts.

**A class from the Tarbut School in Ruzhany**

**First row, standing right to left:** the teachers Tzipora Fagin, Stopnicki (Nitzkin's sister), Yitzchak Nybursky, Sokolovsky.

**Second row:** —, Itzel Einstein, Ethel Sokolovsky, Rubinstein, the teacher Diker, Moshel Berman, Elka, Mordechai Ginzburg, the principal Rozin.

**Third row:** Pesha Blobitsky, Itzel Krolinsky, Sonia Michinovsky-Sokolovsky, Duba Skloiravitz, Moshel Babich, Esther Chwojnik.

**Fourth row:** Kalin Nowik from Liskova, Sheindel Epshteyn, Epshteyn.

{143}

Many of the graduates of the Tarbut School later filled important roles in life and carried them out in the best way possible. A few of these graduates, myself included, entered the field of Hebrew education. From this school, we went on to seminaries in Warsaw, Vilna and Grodno. After completing our studies, we dedicated ourselves to the education of the next generation in the Diaspora and later on in the Land (for those of us who succeeded in making aliya). As teachers and educators, we impart to our students the same positive values that we learned in the atmosphere of our town, the town of holy people, and in the atmosphere of our nationalistic Hebrew School where we learned the spirit of Torah, service and good deeds through the dedication of our own teachers. Above all, the aspiration for national actualization pulsated in Ruzhany during our day, and is our guiding light in our life path.

Meir Sokolovsky

## The Talmud Torah Institution in Ruzhany

### During the last years before the Second World War

The immigrants arrived in the land, and those remaining in Ruzhany continued to live in the darkness of exile. The desire of the masses for aliya could not be actualized due to the locked gates. With no recourse, they continued to weave their Hebrew and national life to the extent possible in their town. However, the times changed progressively for the worse. Of all the cultural institutions in town, the Talmud Torah suffered particularly, since most of its students were from poor families. The teachers' council of this six-grade educational institution writes the following in its letter of the 14th of Adar, 5695 (1935) [6].

"To our dear, honorable townsfolk such as Mr. Abba Leviatan, warm greetings."

"The times have changed. Other times have arrived. Until now, America sustained us, but today we turn to you, the Ruzhany natives in the Land of Israel. Of course you know about the terrible economic situation of the natives of our town, almost all of whom lack a source of livelihood. How worse is the situation of the Talmud Torah educational institution, where approximately 160 Jewish children study, the children of the poorest familles of our townsfolk. Our honorable trustee Mr. Alter Brzenicki, who made aliya, can describe our difficult situation to you with his own mouth. We have heard that you are conducting a collection on our behalf. Try to make it successful, for if not, our institution will be closed. The merit of the students studying Torah should stand in favor of all of those who are occupied in the provision of this assistance. May they enjoy long life, health, and livelihood. May it be G-d's will that we all come together speedily on soil of our Holy Land. Amen.

With blessings of Zion,

The teachers' committee of the Talmud Torah of Ruzhany:

Eliezer Chaim Karelitz, Zelig Rizkin, Chaim Zerach Rotstein, Aharon Yaakov Pitkovsky.

In the name of the trustees: Meir Guber"

{144}

The collection took place and a sum of money was sent, a portion of which was to provide support for the Talmud Torah, and another portion as an addition to the Maot Chittin fund.

Letters of thanks for the money that was sent from time to time from the Land to Ruzhany were received in 5695 and 5696. The final letter states:

"The sum that was received from America, from the Land of Israel, and from here (that is, from the residents of Ruzhany themselves) was distributed (as Maot Chittin) among 197 needy familles, consisting of 692 individuals.

We are signing with feelings of honor and blessing; that our ears should hear and both our and your eyes should witness bountiful happiness and wealth, peace and contentment, and the building and broadening of our Holy Land. Let no more breaches and cries be heard from our holy areas. This is a prayer from your friends, and includes all of Israel.

Meir Guber, Zeev Shereshrevski, Yaakov Meir Epshteyn."

## David Miller

David Miller studied in the Talmud Torah and Yeshiva of Ruzhany during his youth. Like all other Yeshiva students, he took his meals from the householders on a rotation basis. He always remembered this rotation. From the time he became wealthy in America (oil was discovered on his land), he would donate large sums of money to feed the Yeshiva students. In his will, he left a certain percentage of his yearly income for the Talmud Torah of Ruzhany. May his memory be blessed.

{145}

# Charitable and Benevolent Institutions

## Charitable Institutions in Ruzhany During the 19th Century

### The Hospital

Ruzhany was ahead of all other towns of the region in the arena of communal activism and charitable institutions. A hospital already existed in 1875. As is described in *Halevanon* 1875 (8), it was burned down along with other buildings during the large fire of that year. The following is written there:

"All people who were bitter, afflicted or suffering found refuge in the hospital. There, they would be given balm, bandages and all of their requirements until they would be able to arise from their bed. The upholders of this institution are the two important men who are as prominent as crown jewels — the wealthy, intelligent brothers whose names should be glorified from generation to generation. The first one is the Gaon Rabbi Yechiel Michel, and the second is his younger brother who helps him, Yerucham Fishel Pines. This building was also destroyed. Now, who will have mercy on the sick, take them in, and bandage their wounds?"

We do not know when the hospital in Ruzhany was rebuilt. However, the concern for the sick and suffering did not cease in the city, and in 1833, the Linat Tzedek organization was founded, as is described in *"Hamelitz"* issue 20 from that year:

### Linat Tzedek

"From Ruzhany in the Grodno District, Mr. E. Y. Wallach praises the people of his city who founded the 'Linat Tzedek' Organization, to provide people to stay over at the home of any ill person, may G-d protect us, with two shifts per night. Wealthy people of the city are numbered among them, and all of them stood on their guard equally. The set-up is very honorable, and it is appropriate for such an organization to exist in every holy community."

### The Hospital is Rebuilt

In *Hamelitz* 1893 (43), Yitzchak Meir Gerber writes about the hospital being rebuilt in Ruzhany and also serving as an infirmary:

"The hospital in the city is built magnificently in a large building at the edge of the city. Its doors, windows and even floors are covered with lacquer and wax to give them a splendid, sparkling appearance.

Two physicians, one Jewish and the other Christian, visit this hospital daily, each taking his turn. A person would support the sick person and turn him over on his sickbed. He would bring the medicine from the pharmacy, feed him and give him drink. The poor people of the city who could not afford to bring a physician to their homes would come there to ask for the advice of the physicians without having to pay a fee. They would also be given sufficient medicine at no cost. A garden was planted in the yard of this building, from which a pleasant aroma wafted through the windows, restoring the soul of the sick people. Convalescents would go there daily to enjoy the clear air from between the branches..."

{146}

About eight years later, M. Shereshbasker writes the following in *Hatzefira* 1901 (230) about the situation of the hospital:

"The hospital is among the most effective of the benevolent institutions. It was designed with intelligence and set up for the well-being of the sick people. Its twelve rooms are large and spacious. There is a special room for storage and preparation of all types of medication. Large trees surround the building from the outside. Regular, expert physicians visit the sick people daily. The institution is supported by the donations of its regular members as well as private donations. We hope that the philanthropists of our community will donate of their money for the benefit of the institution over and above their set donations, so the directors can have the means to prevent shortages, and so that the institution can be the pride of our community."

## Charitable Institutions in Ruzhany During the 20th Century

Shmuel Magli writes the following about the medical situation in the town during the subsequent years.

"I arrived in Ruzhany in 1911. The only pharmacy in the city was owned by a Christian. There were two medical professionals ("feldschers" in the vernacular): Libitshke and Eizik. There were a few medicine shops there: of Eizik Kaplinski, of Notke, and of Moshke Shamit. All of the townsfolk visited the feldschers since there was no physician [7], and they purchased medicines from the medicine shop, since the pharmacy was owned by a Christian who related to them in an inimical manner.

At that time, there was a committee for the visiting of the sick (Bikur Cholim) in the town, which provided food and medication for the sick. Shimon the shochet, Shmuel Leib, Bilais, and David-Noach

Pines were members of this committee. I summoned the aforementioned committee to a meeting in the pharmacy that I purchased from the Christian, and we decided to bring a physician to the town. There was a good physician in Byten named Dr. Rozenblit. I traveled there and influenced him. He agreed to settle in our town. How splendid was his appearance as he passed through the streets of the town on a horse-drawn wagon, hastening to visit the sick in their homes or to go the hospital in order to tend to those laid up there. He spent three years in the town, and then left. Dr. Burshechivski and Dr. Gurewich followed after him. However, the First World War broke out, the physicians were drafted, and we were left without physicians. However, there was no need for such at that time, for we did not have anything to eat, and the people got better... in any case from their illnesses."

**Dr. Aharon Aran (Chwojnik)**

## Medical Activity After the First World War

In 1922, after the First World War, Dr. Aryeh Aran (Chwojnik) a Ruzhany native, came to town after completing his medical degree at the university in Geneva, Switzerland. He remained in Ruzhany for half a year and then made aliya. However, he did no small amount of work in the town during that brief period. During his time, there was no other physician in the city aside from Kamintzky, whose value as a physician was not great.

{147}

Medical assistance was given at that time to the local sick people who were poor through the Magen David Adom, which was set up instead of Linat Tzedek. Dr. Aran came and founded the Taz, which gave legitimate medicine to those in need. Through his effort, a physician named Dr. Yatom was brought to the city. The hospital was reopened, and its successful activities were renewed.

**A movie day for the Magen David Adom**

**First row, standing right to left:** Aharon Lanzbitsky, Leibel Ziskind, Yosef Abramovich, Heshel Gezbah, Sonia Leviatan, Zeidel Rushkin, Yoshka Shipiatzky, Chwojnik, Moshka Guldis.

**Second row:** Ahuva Leviatan, Ahuva Chwojnik, Zeev Ziskind, Simcha Rozenschein, Shipiatzky, Duba Chwojnik-Ziskind.

## The Summer Camps for Children

The natives of Ruzhany did a great deal in the area of medical institutions, but the crowning achievements of the aforementioned activities were the summer camps for children that were set up in the town after the First World War for every child who was in need of convalescence after an illness, due to bodily weakness, due to low body weight, etc. In the camp that was conducted in rented houses that were located in the forests a few kilometers from Ruzhany, the children in need of convalescence enjoyed the fresh air, plentiful food, and spending their free time at pleasant activities. Various group games were organized, plays were prepared, etc. Of course, they were under expert supervision the entire time.

{148}

**Activists of the hospital in Ruzhany**

First row, standing right to left: Yaakov Kaplan, Turn, —, Feigel Shapira, Roza Pines, the wife of Yaakov Asher Epshteyn.

Second row: Necha Shemshinowich, the wife of Shmuel Mogilevsky, — Aharon Gamerman, Leibel Chwojnik.

Third row: Mordechai Karpelewich, Shimon the shochet, Dr. Yatom, Dr. Aryeh Chwojnik, Avigdor Michel Goldberg, Shmuel Leib the shoemaker.

Lying: Epshteyn, Simcha Rozenschein.

Wealthy parents provided the money required for this, and the Taz organization covered a portion of the budget. A special annual movie day brought in donations for this cause. Finally, the dramatic circle would organize parties, the income of which was dedicated to the setting up of camps, so that no child lacking the means for convalescence would be unable to attend the camp. These camps were open primarily during the long annual vacation each year until 1939, the year of the outbreak of the Second World War. In the latter years before that war, a special building was put up for those camps instead of the rented houses that had been used until that time. This new building was erected in the Bliznawi Forest. Its equipment was new and of the finest quality. This building served as an example for all, and was a topic of conversation in all of the neighboring towns.

## Other Institutions

It was not only medical and social institutions that were founded and conducted in Ruzhany. There were also many other charitable and mutual assistance organizations there. There was a charitable fund, a committee for bread for the poor, and the large people's bank that earned an honorable place in the bank center in Warsaw, all significantly helped the townsfolk to maintain their stand during the years of economic depression and government attacks on their commercial status, etc.

## Those Who Faithfully Occupy Themselves in Communal Affairs

Naftali Kantorowich tells that all of the aforementioned institutions were run by people who occupied themselves faithfully in communal affairs. "Many of the aforementioned communal activists were from among the workers and tradesmen. In many cases, the dedication of these communal activists transcended all bounds, and their deeds are etched in the memory forever. It is appropriate to mention here not only Yona the shoemaker about whom we have written above, but about another 'Rabbi Yochanan Sandlar' [8], who was Yaakov Michel Lev, an active member of the leadership of most of the institutions. It is appopriate to tell here about one of his deeds, about which he often retold:

{149}

It was the days of the major vacation. The children were convalescing in the camp in the forest. Yaakov Michel Lev was working at his shoemaker's table. Through the window in his room, he saw that the skies were darkening. He left his work implements, removed his apron, quietly left his house and set out for the camp. The man walked five kilometers by foot in order to be sure that the children had gone into the houses.

Such were the dedicated activists that we had in our town, and such people stood at the helm of our communal and cultural institutions in our old home of Ruzhany [9]. These activists are no longer alive. The Holocaust overtook them all and killed them. However, their spirit remains alive within us forever. Upon us, the survivors, rests the holy obligation to tell our young children about their important work, so that they will be educated in the light of their deeds. Honor to their memories."

By Meir Sokolovsky

**TRANSLATOR'S FOOTNOTES**

1. The Fourth Aliya is the wave of immigration to Palestine from 1924 - 1929. During its latter period, Arab riots took place in Palestine.

2. A Hachshara kibbutz near Kobrin.

3. The main purpose of the Jewish National Fund at that time was to purchase land in Israel for Jewish settlement.

4. There is a footnote in the text here: See above, "The Kinderheim".

5. I.e. This is an idiomatic expression, meaning that the school provided both educational and physical benefits.

6. The date is Purim.

7. A feldscher is not a licensed physician, but rather an "old time barber-surgeon", according to the Weinreich dictionary.

8.. A Talmudic sage whose name means 'shoemaker'.

9. There is a footnote in the text here, as follows: This sincere communal activity also influenced the younger generation, and many of the girls of our town, including my wife who is a Ruzhany native would go around from door to door every Friday to collect challas for the poor of the town. Of course, the director of this activity was Yaakov Michel Lev the shoemaker.

{150}

## Second World War and the Holocaust

### Nineteen Days of the German-Polish War, and Russian Jurisdiction in Ruzhany

At the outbreak of the war between Germany and Poland, the dread of the approaching Nazi enemy fell upon the Jews. Their fear increased with the rapid advent of the Germans. Then we found out in Ruzhany that the enemy was approaching Brest-Litovsk. Something like this had never been heard of before — that such large areas were conquered in such a short time. Everyone was wondering how it could be that the Germans succeeded in crossing hundreds of kilometers of enemy territory within a few days? How did they penetrate so deeply into the warring country with the clap of one hand? And when the news later arrived that the Germans had reached the nearby city of Pruzhany with six tanks, the youth of Ruzhany fled to Batun on their route to Russia. Leibel Babicz (Moshe's brother) came after those who were fleeing, riding on a bicycle, and told them that the Germans had retreated, and that White Russia all the way to Brisk, including Ruzhany, will belong to Russia.

The youth returned. Gentiles from the village of Bereznica, who were known as Communists, immediately arrived to Ruzhany armed and organized the guarding of the city. The Poles fled.

On September 17, we waited impatiently for the arrival of the Russians. We went out to greet them with flowers in our hands. We were informed of the approach of the Russians from the nearby town of Slonim. There was great joy when their first tank arrived. Everyone wished each other "Mazel Tov."

The new guard began. The Russian police and post office were housed in Sobol's two-story house. Through them, the young Communists ran the civic affairs. These included David Rabinowich, who was the director of the sawmill and flower mill of Pines; and Chaikel Wissotzky (the son of Simcha the hat maker) who became the director of the hide factory. Yaakov Meir Maruchnik, a tanner from the "Other Side of the River" Lane, who was not previously known at all as a Communist activist, became one of the most active members in the Communist movement after that time. Obviously, when the Communist rule began, he was appointed by the government as a representative to the Minsk Soviet.

During the first days of Russian rule, disarray fell upon the city. Several of the wealthy people and merchants of the city, including Noach Pines and his family, Chaim Turn and his family, and Yekutiel

Sherman were deported to Siberia. Difficult life began in the city itself. The shops, which still remained open for a brief time, closed. As well, the independent tradesmen were not able to maintain their stand, and were forced to join one of the cooperative groups and receive the wages of a worker. For the most part, the workers remained without work. I, for example, worked for the tailor Chaim Kimerman. They joined him to the tailors' cooperative group, for he had a machine, but I, as the employee, was not accepted for the reason that I did not have a machine, so I was let go from my work.

I was forced to work in the forest. When I did not have work in the city, I suspected that they would send me out [1] from my city to another work place. The door could have opened at any moment, and one of the young Communist workers — David Rabinowich, Chaikel Wissotzky, the Kaganowicz brothers, and Sheindel Joselwicz — could come to inform me that I must travel to work in such and such a place that is outside our city. This indeed happened. Once I was sent to dig a ditch near Kobrin where the Russians had demanded workers. The young activists in the city fulfilled their request, as usual. I was very happy when I returned home, for a person's food supply was more secure in his home, where he had stockpiled stuff beforehand.

{151}

Therefore, I made efforts to obtain work in the city, so that I could remain there. I worked at digging mortar and other jobs, as is written, "with mortar and bricks," so that I would not be sent outside the bounds of the city.

It was difficult to obtain bread. In order to do so, one had to get up in the night and stand in line in order to be among the first to receive the kilogram of bread. People wasted a great deal of time standing in the lineup. There were those who put their allotment away and then stood in line once more to receive an additional kilogram, for what would a person not do to sustain himself and his family? People also received clothing by standing in line for a long time. People even stood in line to obtain liquor, even those people who did not use it for drinking, but rather for selling. The vodka was received for a cheap price and later sold for an inflated price, which of course lightened the budget of the person.

On April 23, two months before the outbreak of the war between Germany and Russia, the Russians drafted people from the 1918-1919 age cohort. The draftees from Ruzhany at that time included: me, Yosef Lev, the son of Yaakov Michel Lev the shoemaker (today in the Land); b) Moshe Babich (today in the Land); c) Moshe Foksman the grandson of Chasha Malka's (today in the Land); d) Itsha Yosha

Brazovsky the son of Rafael the Kotlier. He was killed in an accident in Poland while riding on his bicycle after the war; e) Yitzchak Gamerman, who went missing, apparently killed during the war; f) Yaakov Slonimsky the grandson of Leibitshka the doctor (today in America). However, the Russians did not draft everyone of that cohort, for those they did not trust were not called up and were "exempt." Among those were Moshe Karlinski the son of the formerly wealthy man Anshel, and others. After a short time, the following people were also drafted: g) Moshe Berman the son of Shlomi Stier's (today in Leningrad); h) Bulia Krolitzky the son of Simcha the Brukirer (the paver).

I left the city when I was drafted, and I was far away from everything that took place there and was decreed against it from that time

From Moshe Lev (the son of Yaakov Michel Lev)

## Echoes in Writing

With the entry of the Russians, weeks and months of getting accustomed to the new living conditions ensued. The merchants whose stores were liquidated and closed remained without a staff of bread[2]. Many other people of the city were also left without livelihood. Both groups looked for work so that they could sustain themselves. They transferred from job to job because they could not get used to difficult work conditions due to their older age, or because a job that they had started with had ended, and they had to look for another. In most cases, the salary was insufficient for livelihood. Roza Michnovsky [3] writes:

{152}

"I only earned 180 rubles as a teacher, and this only met my needs with difficulty. Father worked and only earned 150 rubles."

How did Roza suddenly become a teacher during the Russian era? We learn this and many other things from those days from the letters of David-Noach Sokolovsky [4]. His letter of May 14, 1940 states:

"We did not suffer from the retreat of the Polish army. Shimon [5] returned from the army. Father is working. We are healthy, earning money, and satisfied. The Germans did not reach us. Today we feel ourselves calm and secure under the protection of the mighty Red Army and in our great homeland the U.S.S.R. I organized the school in the town. Ethel and Michla [6] are taking a short course that will enable them to be teachers. Roza is with them as well. They receive stipends that enable them to study and complete the course."

**Roza Michnovsky**

He tells in his letter of September 9, 1940:

"Ethel and Roza are already working as teachers in the village of Krupa, and Michla in the village of Polonsk."

However, David-Noach did not live in the city for a long time, as is described in his letter of September 22, 1940:

"I already do not live in the town, but rather in a village called Milkhovich, a distance of 14 kilometers from Ruzhany. I come to town once a week on the "outing" day." (This is what Sunday was called, which was a day off for everyone regardless of religion and nationality.)

From this letter we learn that the Jewish Sabbath did not exist as a rest day for the Jews during the Russian era. It was not only the Sabbath that disappeared from the horizon. Even before this, the

Tarbut Hebrew School had disappeared. We read about this in a letter from David-Noach on November 2, 1940:

"It was good for Miriam [7], for she completed her year with excellence, despite the abnormal conditions. She was studying in the sixth grade in the gymnasium, and was forced to change her language of study three times in a brief period. At first she studied in the Tarbut Hebrew Gymnasium, where the language of instruction was Hebrew. When it was closed by the government, she was forced to transfer to a Polish gymnasium, with the national language being the language of instruction. From there, she transferred to a Belorussian high school, with Belorussian as the language of instruction.

The letter of January 13, 1941, tells that Miriamka was not disappointed, and completed her studies with excellence.

David-Noach's wanderings had not yet finished, and he tells in his letter of February 27, 1941:

"I am studying the German Language in the Pod-Institut in Bialystock. When I finish this upper level school, I will be able to teach German in secondary schools. Write to me at the Ruzhany address, for my own address is not permanent, as you have found out. For some time, I was situated in my city, then they suddenly transferred me to a village, and now I am in the large city of Bialystock. By the time you answer me, I may very well be in some other place."

{153}

With these last words, and in another sentence in one of his last letters: "Oh would it be that we will see the end of the war, and be able to see each other or at least hear good news from each other." — we can see that he suspected in his heart what might come. Indeed, these things suddenly came more than we could have suspected, and far more than we or they could even describe.

Meir Sokolovsky

## In Ruzhany During the Time of the Nazis

In July 1941, two weeks after the invasion of the Germans and their entry to the areas of White Russia, I, Chana Kirstein — a native of Kalusz — and my husband Julian Kirstein arrived in Ruzhany. We had come from Volkovisk. At the outbreak of the Second World War in 1939, we fled from Kalusz to Volkovisk, and now, with the entry of the Germans, we moved to Ruzhany.

During the first days of the German-Russian war, the Germans heavily bombed Volkovisk. Most of the houses of the Jewish quarter there went up in flames, and we did not have any place to live. My husband took a map in his hands and said, "Since the city of Ruzhany is located a distance of 50 kilometers from Volkovisk, and has no train station, it will be quieter there. Aside from this, we have acquaintances there, the members of the Miller family from Kutno. At a time of difficulty, it is good to be together with close people." We packed our few belongings and moved to Ruzhany.

**Heda Chana Kirstein**

## The First Victims

About ten days after we arrived in the town, the first victims fell, including my husband and the teacher David-Noach Sokolovsky, another acquaintance from Kalusz, where he had worked for ten years as a teacher. It took place like this: My husband, David-Noach Sokolovsky, Mr. Miller and I were in the house of Mottel Zazhvir, working on political matters. Among other things, we talked about the ghetto that the Germans wanted to set up in the town in the near future. It was twilight. We suddenly heard noise on the street. We went out in order to hurry home. According to the decree of the German government, we had to be closed into our houses before dark, a time when a Jew was not allowed to be found on the streets. We saw Germans on the streets, who ordered us to run to the Great Synagogue. I wanted to run along with my husband, but the Germans did not allow it, and commanded me to go home, promising me that my husband would return immediately. The Germans rounded up approximately 1,000 men next to the synagogue. Indeed, Jews were not gathered from every street. Zazhvir, for example, who did not go outside, remained in his house. The Germans placed the men who were gathered together into rows, with their faces toward the wall of the synagogue

{154}

and pointed machine guns at them from behind. The men thought that their end had come. The fear of death fell upon them. The Germans approached the men who were standing and asked them their professions. Those who mentioned that they were tailors, bakers, or other tradesmen were asked to remain in place. My husband who said that he was an electrician, David-Noach Sokolovsky who said that he was a teacher, Yaakov Kaplan who said he was a bank official, and other members of the intelligentsia whose names I do not know, approximately 15 in number, were ordered to board a vehicle that transported them to an unknown place. They were taken at nightfall. The heart predicted bad things.

The Germans informed the Judenrat that there is a possibility to redeem the prisoners for a specific sum of silver and gold. I removed my ring and gave it over. As a refugee, I had no other gold. Other people gave over their silver and gold, and the Germans obtained more than they had demanded. However, we did not see our loved ones again.

I decided to go and search for my husband in the fields, villages and forests, to find him alive or dead. The teachers Ethel and Michla Sokolovsky, David-Noach's sisters, wanted to join me, but their mother told them that her heart was telling her that David-Noach, her dear son, was no longer among the living, so why should she lose them as well? I went out alone despite the mortal danger on the route. I reached as far as Pushcha Bilobiska, and to 20 kilometers beyond Slonim. I searched, but for naught. The gentiles said that the Germans took the fifteen outside the town, shot them and buried them.

## Fear and Oppression

The fear and oppression grew continuously, even though we sensed such even before. A few days before the murder of my husband, a German came to our house and asked my mother, who was peering from the window, whether there was a Jew present. My mother was astounded, and did not know how to act. If she said that there was not, and they entered and found one, they would kill him without doubt. She answered the Germans, "Yes... Yes..." The Germans commanded that he be brought out. My husband went out to the Germans, and they took him to work. When my husband returned from work healthy and whole, we were very happy, for a Jew was forfeit, and his life was hanging by a hook at any second.

**From right to left, standing: Michla, David-Noach and Ethel. Sitting: Miriamka Sokolovsky.**

I said that my mother was peering out the window. Why? Because with our great oppression and broken hearts, we waited for a miracle from Heaven that might bring the Nazi nightmare to an end. At night, when we sat imprisoned in our houses, gathered in our corners, our minds were filled with only one thought: would it be that the night would pass, and we will get up in the morning with a different face on the world, and that the dread of the Nazis would disappear. We would lift up the curtains a bit from the windows and peer outside to see what was transpiring on the street. When we saw a German approaching, looking sad, we would be comforted that apparently they had suffered a defeat, and our salvation was very near.

{155}

## Various Decrees

However, the salvation was far off from us, and the oppression and degradation that began at the moment of the entry of the Germans to the town continually increased. I was absent from the town during the first weeks of Nazi rule, but the Ruzhany residents told me that various decrees were imposed on the Jews immediately upon the entry of the Germans. First of all, every Jew was obligated to fasten a yellow band on his clothing; it was forbidden for a Jew to walk on the sidewalk — he must set his path in the middle of the street along with the animals; every Jew had to remove his hat before a German; and other such decrees.

## Judenrat

Immediately after their entry, the Germans appointed a Judenrat from amongst the community notables. Among others, members included Shlomo Jezrenisky. Some of the members of the Judenrat served as guarantors who would receive harsh punishments if the decrees of the Germans were not carried out in full. The Judenrat appointed Jewish policemen, whose job was to carry out the decrees of the German regime and the requests of the Judenrat. The headquarters of the Judenrat was in the Great Synagogue.

## Forced Labor

One of the tasks of the Judenrat was to find people for forced labor on a daily basis. The workers received only a piece of bread in payment. The men worked at gardening, paving roads, and other such jobs. The women cleaned the floors of the houses of the Germans and washed their linens. Despite the difficulty of the work, people went willingly, for they received a meager piece of bread for their work.

## Torments

After the proclamation of these first commands, the Germans gathered the Jews in the town marketplace — as was told to me by Ruzhany natives — men, women and children, and placed them in lines. The Germans mocked them, poured water on them, and commanded several Jews to dance before them. The gentiles stood around and laughed at the straits of the Jews. Many of the Jews were beaten with murderous blows for no fault at all. Thus began the first days of physical and spiritual oppression, which did not let up for one moment. The cheders and schools were closed by the Germans as soon as they took control. The spiritual decline, which led to physical neglect, began immediately after they came.

All of this took place in the first weeks, before I came to Ruzhany. Daily and hourly torments disturbed the calm of the Jews. However, the murderous acts had yet to start. About ten days after we arrived in the town, the terrible murder of 15 city notables and refugees took place. Before the wound of the disappearance of these people had healed, a new terrible blow was perpetrated against the population of the city. Several Jews were imprisoned as apparent Communists, including Sara Gamerman, who was indeed secretary of the district committee during the Russian era. A monetary fine was again imposed in order to free the prisoners. Once again, the required sum was collected, but once again our brothers and children did not return to us. They never returned. The mourning and grief grew. The feeling that we were imprisoned without an exit oppressed us endlessly.

{156}

The fear was so great that we were afraid to go to the synagogue on Yom Kippur lest the murderers take the opportunity to surround the synagogue and kill us. Only a small number of people endangered themselves to attend the synagogue despite everything. Most of the people went out to work.

## The Ghetto

The establishment of the ghetto, about which our dear ones talked on the day of their and our tragedy, was created a short time after their deaths. We were locked into a narrow ghetto, in which there were a small number of houses. Its eastern boundary ran from the house of the Tuchman family until the Kanal Stream. There were only four houses along this boundary. To the west of this boundary, the ghetto only included the Shulhauf. Most of the other Jewish houses were given to gentiles and Germans. This tiny area of the narrow ghetto housed the thousands of Jews of the town along with the refugees.

The crowding was terrible. For example, the Tuchman house, which consisted of two small rooms and a dark kitchen, housed four families: 1) the Tuchman family consisting of a mother and her daughter Gisha. (Mrs. Tuchman's son Moshe was not with us. He was taken to work in a certain area and was not in the town when we were later removed from Ruzhany). 2) My mother and I. 3) Moshka Goldin (he later died in the bunkers of Volkovisk). 4) Miller and his wife.

We maintained the hygiene despite the crowding. We drew water for washing as well as drinking from the wells.

## Obtaining Food Provisions

Man does live by water alone. Food is also required. From where can food be obtained, if we were forbidden to leave the ghetto to purchase food? What did they do? Some people snuck out secretly to purchase food. There was no fence around the ghetto. A Jew was forbidden from buying meat and butter. If a German saw a Jewish child eating a piece of bread and butter, he would ask the child where he lived. When the child innocently responded to the question, the German would enter the house of the parents of the child and beat the parents soundly. The parents would later recite Birchat Hagomel [8] since the German was satisfied with only beatings. A gentile was permitted to bring foodstuffs for sale outside the bounds of the ghetto. However, the gentiles acted craftily and snuck the food into the ghetto in order to sell. Of course, they received full value for every provision, and when the money ran out they were given the equivalent of money in the form of clothing and other objects.

The Jewish settlements near Ruzhany remained in existence, and they greatly eased the situation. I worked for some time in the settlement of Konstantinova. We received potatoes and other vegetables from the farmers of the settlements.

I also obtained wood for heating. How? The gentiles would bring the wood mainly to Germans, and they gave some of the wood to Ida Kaplan, the daughter of Yaakov, who had been murdered. How was Ida able to do this? She was a laundress for them. She gave some of the wood that she received to me. Despite everything, it would have been possible to manage somehow. In some manner, it was possible to work and remain alive, had the Germans not later taken us out of the town to the bunkers in Volkovisk and from there to the ovens.

{157}

## Work

Everyone obtained some sort of work. Gisha Tuchman was a weaver, who created very fine items. She had plenty of work, but in return all she received was bread and marmalade. This meager food was insufficient to sustain the body in a state of proper health, and therefore her work quota declined.

The shoemakers and tailors had plenty of work. The Germans needed various types of clothes to be sewn for themselves. Often, a German would demand from some tradesman or another that they give preference to his order over the order of another German. Yaakov Pitkovsky the harness maker had plenty of work, as did the other tradesmen. The Germans also employed people at the hide factory in the town. The Germans exported the lions' share of its products to Germany, but they kept a portion locally for the needs of the Germans of the town.

## The Life of the Jews Becomes Cheap

The life of the Jews became wanton. There were no bounds to the torment and degradation. Once a German entered the home of Shlomka and Ethel [9] Pitkovsky. When he saw their pretty eldest daughter, he desired her and attempted to take her. He threatened that if she did not go with him, he will kill the entire family. The girl raised a loud cry. The cries were heard in the ghetto. Fear and trembling took hold of everyone, but they could not offer help. We were lacking in means. A miracle happened in that the German became startled from the outcry and left her alone.

A Jewish refugee living in the town was working as a translator for the Germans. This refugee kept his distance from the Jews, and even educated his son as a gentile. One day, the Germans hanged this refugee in the middle of the marketplace before everyone. Apparently, this translator knew too much. Thus, this person who distanced himself from his nation gained nothing from such.

## Punitive Fines

The Germans would impose various punitive fines (contributions) upon the Jews of the town. They demanded that the Jews give them beds, bedding, closets, clothing, kitchen utensils, and tableware. When winter came, the Judenrat received a command to provide fine, clean blankets. The district policemen were sent out to bring what was demanded, but a Jew would get out of giving over the little that he still possessed by sending the policeman to his Jewish neighbor who was apparently more wealthy than he. Thus, disputes broke out between the Jewish policeman on one side, and their neighbors on the other. In such a manner, the Germans fomented strife among brothers, and this internal strife further degraded us. Finally, we were forced to give over what was demanded, for if the Judenrat did not fulfill the demands of the Germans, the members of the Judenrat, the Jewish police and the Jews themselves would be held accountable.

{158}

Aside from the official punitive fines, the Germans did not hold back from demanding additional money from the Jews, for who told them what to do? Often, a German would take a Jew out of his house, bring him to the German's house, and order him to do various jobs without any payment at all. On the contrary, he would also give the Jew an appropriate beating accompanied by a false charge, as if the Jew was responsible for the war. And he, the "accursed Jew" was the prime cause for Germans having to wander off afar.

Once I met a German on the road, and he called me to work for him. I went, for what choice was there? The German told me to clean a slaughtered fowl. I did my job and took comfort that I might receive a small piece of meat in exchange for my work. When I gave the German the cleaned goose, he demanded that I clean it more. I worked once again. Then he told me to cut it up, for he wished to send the goose to his family in Germany. I did as he asked. However, he fell upon me with curses: "You stupid, accursed, dirty Jewess, you cut it up too much. How can this get there in this manner?" I was happy that I left healthy and whole, albeit without payment.

## Pillage in the Houses of the Town

Once again, they expelled us all from our houses to the meadow (Voyan) that was behind the bathhouse. Even the gentiles were expelled from their houses this time. This public tribulation was a sort of half comfort. If we were together as Jews and gentiles, the matter is not all that bad. As both groups stood together, the Germans passed through the houses of the Jews and the gentiles and stole everything that they could. They found almost nothing in the houses of the Jews. Therefore, they stole from the houses of the gentiles, which had no small amount of pillaged Jewish property. With all this, the Jews were punished once again. The gentiles accused them of bringing the tribulation of the pillage onto them as well. For example, the house of the gentile Botkovich was full of all sorts of good things, for his daughter was the friend of the German mayor (Amst Kommissar). When this gentile returned from his field and discovered that his treasures had been pillaged, he blamed Ida Kaplan, the daughter of Yaakov, who had been murdered, for causing the plunder of his home.

How? That day, she did the laundry in a German home, who was delayed in going out to the field on account of her. She, the neighbor of Botkovich, directed the Germans to his house. Therefore, he threatened to kill her and her entire family, mother along with children. Ida and her brother wept, fell before his feet, pleaded, and swore that Ida was innocent of any wrongdoing. The Germans themselves knew how to get into every home. The sight was terrifying. The life of the Jews was forfeit from the time that the Germans entered, and every gentile could murder them. Were it not for the fact that this Botkovich received his entire fortune back with the help of his daughter, who was the friend of the German mayor, who knows what the fate of the Kaplan family might have been.

## Washerwomen

As mentioned, this Ida Kaplan earned her bread from washing the linens of the Germans. At times, she also included me in this work. Once, we went after work to bring the washed laundry to the house of a German. He came out quickly and in confusion, as he ordered us to flee for our lives, for a guest captain was inside the house. This captain had gotten angry and asked, "How come there are so many Jews wandering about here? In Minsk, they have already liquidated all of them." We fled, of course without receiving a piece of brown bread with marmalade in payment. We were happy that we had escaped from death.

{159}

## We Wanted to Go Out to the Forest

It was April 1942. The frightful Nazi rule had already lasted for three-quarters of a year. Springtime arrived, but the winds of death hovered over us. Gisha Tuchman, Ethel and Michla Sokolovsky, and I along with other young men and women decided to go out and join the partisans in the forests. Luck had it that, at that time, two youths from Slonim reached us in a state of great perplexity. They told us that they had fled from their city in which the Germans had murdered most of the Jews, and were setting out to the forests in order to join the partisans. However, it became clear that we had gone from the skillet to the frying pan. The forest was swarming with hungry and naked Russian soldiers, who were no less dangerous than the Germans themselves. They would attack every person entering the forest, pillaging everything from them, stripping them of their clothes, and taking their lives as well. There was a double danger for women, for they did not hold back from rape. (These Russian soldiers were unable to leave the forests and surrender to the Germans, for the

Germans were murdering them by the hundreds and thousands.) The two youths did not return to the forest, but rather remained in Ruzhany. The mother of the Sokolovsky girls, who was not pleased with them going out to the forest on account of the danger, was very happy that this was canceled.

## The Words of Warning of a German

Germans would often come to our house to have their watches fixed by Moshka Goldin the watchmaker. One Friday, as the Tuchman mother and my mother were lighting the Sabbath candles in a corner of the room so that they would not be seen outside, a German entered with his head down. We were astounded at his appearance. He opened his mouth and said, "Hitler, Hitler! How far have you gone with your evil deeds? A great deal of culpability rests upon you and your conscience! The blood of the Jews of Slonim who had been taken out and murdered this morning in their pajamas, shouts until the hearts of the heaven. Flee, oh Jews, hide in hiding places, and save yourselves." We said to ourselves that the bad spirit of this bearer of tidings was due to a defeat that the Germans had suffered, and therefore he is telling us these stories of atrocities, so that we would not rejoice.

However, a Ruzhany girl who had fled from Slonim, and a few other people who had come out of the pits into which they were tossed after the shootings, and had by chance not been injured and were able to escape after the German murderers left, confirmed the atrocities.

We prepared a hiding place. We constructed a double wall in our wood storage shed in our yard. This would be our hiding place when we would be "taken out to be killed" (the "aktion"). However, we did not have a chance to use it, for when a decree was issued shortly thereafter that all of the Jews would be taken out from the town to work camps, there was no reason to remain in the hiding place, where we would be found and murdered.

Relative calm pervaded in the summer of 1942, before we were taken out of the town. We did not realize that this was the calm before the storm. The Germans then permitted us to purchase foodstuffs and prepare them for the approaching winter, our second winter under the Nazi yoke. I prepared potatoes in the cellar, as well as butter in a pot for my mother. However, I did not have any meat. I did not realize that we were preparing this for the murderers.

## The Day of Deportation

The terrible day of November 2, 1942, arrived. During the entire previous night, the bicycles of the Germans buzzed around in the darkness of the silent night as usual. We, who were closed into the houses all night, were unable to sleep this time, for our hearts prophesied ill tidings. Masses of Germans swarmed around the city. Polish policemen helped them. At dawn, the Judenrat was informed that all of the Jews must gather immediately in the meadow (Voyan) behind the bathhouse. Everyone must take only a bundle of clothing. Every person should also take his silver, gold and jewelry, if he has such left, for they will be not returning to their homes, but rather going to a labor camp. The bundles must be placed in the wagons that the farmers had provided in accordance with the command of the Germans. The children will be transported in the wagons as well. The adults will walk on foot. Many did not believe that their destination was a work camp, and did not take anything. Everyone thought about escaping. The edict stated that if one person of a family is missing, those remaining would be shot. People streamed across the meadow. With perplexed eyes, they parted from their houses and their native town in which they, their parents, and many preceding generations first saw the light of the world. Women screamed. Children cried. A few went along quietly. Along the way, I wanted to commit suicide. A German who saw me called out to me, "You are crazy, you are going to a work camp."

{160}

Our eyes looked upon the houses of worship that stood silently. Sonia Ivan the seamstress, who married the refugee Fuchs of Kalusz during the time of Russian rule, approached the great synagogue, and left her eight-week old child there saying, "Perhaps someone will come and take him, and he will live." I told her to take the child now, but she refused.

In the morning, the meadow was full. The children were tossed onto the wagons. Babies were also tossed on them. Everything became one heap. The danger of suffocation existed for many children. When one mother approached to remove her baby from the heap and place it in a more comfortable place, she was shot dead on the spot.

## On the Way

The order was given, and the caravan moved along the dirt road of approximately 50 kilometers long that led from Ruzhany to Volkovisk. Immediately with the first steps, a woman who was limping and was not able to keep up with the required speed was shot. The armed

Germans rode on horses, and the people were forced almost to run. Whoever stumbled during the brisk walk was shot on the spot.

It was an unbearably hot day. The dust that was raised by the footsteps of thousands of people marching on the dirt path was choking to the dry throats. We licked aluminum pots in order to cool our burning lips. It was no wonder that many children, particularly those who were 7 - 8 years of age, jumped from the wagons and attempted to moisten their dry lips when they saw a river or even some sort of sewage pit. The Germans mowed them down with machine guns. The gentiles related that the route was strewn with corpses. Many mothers who were moving along separately from their children did not know at all that their children had been murdered. The Germans behaved as wild beasts. They became angry and shot mercilessly at the smallest infractions. Everything was in order to instill their fear!

Along the way, a Polish policeman shouted to us, "Escape! They are taking you to slaughter!" We did not believe him. We continued on in a group. It was perhaps better and safer together. We were afraid to take one step to the side. It is hard for me today to believe this. Whoever has not experienced this cannot understand it.

The fear was very great. A person was not a person. At the sight of every house, everyone thought: "I was unable to remain in that house." Next to every pit, everyone thought, "I was unable to disappear there." The youth comforted themselves, "We are young, they will take us to work."

{161}

We reached Podroisk toward the evening. There we stopped to spend the night on the street. We met with our brethren in tribulation, the natives of Liskova. Bonfires were lit around us all night, so that we would not escape in the dark. Here was given the one and only chance for mothers to nurse their children. A slice of bread was distributed to each person.

The next day, we continued on our terrifying journey until we reached Volkovisk. We were placed in bunkers. Along the way to the bunkers, the mother of Tuchman found comfort in reading letters from her son in the Land.

## In the Bunkers in Volkovisk

Each family began to gather together once we were brought into the camp of bunkers. Mothers searched for their Moshele, Shlomole, Rivkele and Miriamke. Only then did they find out how many of them were lost along the way. Heartrending weeping shook up the air of the earth.

Here was a Ruzhany native with a baby in his arms. His wife had been murdered in the concentration area in the meadow when she tried to straighten the seat of that baby. He approached a German and asked him to shoot the baby, saying, "His mother has been killed, and I have no milk for him. Shoot him." The so-called "merciful" German fulfilled the request of the poor father and shot the baby. I stood there and wept bitterly. This took place before my eyes. The father remained alive, because he had three other young children and how could he leave them alone?

The hot day passed. Evening came. The cold worsened. A heavy dew covered the ground upon which we rested all night.

The next day, members of the Kaplan family and another family were brought by car from Ruzhany. They had hidden behind a double wall that they had set up in their houses, and did not leave Ruzhany together with us. The Germans found them, and brought them to us, after administering deathly beatings to them. They made the young and old stand together for the entire day without food. Their appearance was terrifying and their suffering was immeasurable.

The hunger began to leave its mark. Gisha had a gold watch. Her mother did not want her to sell it, but she sold it for a piece of bread. She gave us also a piece of the small slice.

I remained with the people of Ruzhany for only two nights. Then I transferred to the bunkers of the people of Volkovisk, where I found my sister who had married Salomon the watchmaker from Volkovisk.

The Germans misled us with false promises that they would keep us alive. A doctor came to check if there were any people who were healthy and fit for work. A few of us thought that we would be transferred to arms factories in Germany. Our only thought was: to live, to live! We clung to the thread of life with our remaining strength.

## Hunger

The hunger and torment was great. The eyes came out of their sockets. The feet swelled. Children did not pay attention to their mothers and fathers. Fathers did not pay attention to their children. Some mothers showed signs of concern for their children. It is hard to describe the torment of hunger.

The Germans brought a wagon full of potatoes to the bunker camp. Many stormed the wagon in order to grab a raw potato. The Germans shot them, and the entire area around the wagon was covered with corpses. The Germans brought a second wagon that day. The storming and the shooting repeated themselves. The same scene took place the following day. The Germans brought these wagons deliberately and murdered many people.

{162}

Many people reached the end of their strength. One old man was lying above us — we slept on platforms three high — who no longer had the strength to get down. He urinated on us the entire time until he expired. He lay there dead, and a foul stench came to our nose. There is no movie film that is able to describe the atrocities that we endured. The bathroom was designated for both men and women. From a moral perspective, we were trampled to the dust. We ceased being human beings. Thus did the murderers oppress us more than their killing.

## Taking Out to the Ovens

One night, the Germans took out the Ruzhany natives from their bunkers. They walked as shadows in the dark. Frightful cries reached us. Were they thus being taken to Germany for work?

We almost died of hunger. Men went out to work and brought a beet or a loaf of bread back with them. The man who returned peeled the beet, and many people gathered around him to gather the pieces of peel. It was hard to grab them. Many hands competed for a piece of beet peel. They did not take us women out to work, only the men. The hunger was too difficult to bear, and did not give me any rest. I had to leave the camp in order to save myself from death by hunger. I had to bring something for my starving mother. I removed the pants of a dead man, dressed up as a man, and went out with the crowd of thousands of men going to work. Along the way, my hair stuck out from my hat. The men recognized that I was a woman and advised me to escape. Otherwise, I would be shot immediately by the Germans who were accompanying us to work. Along the way, we passed an alleyway. I snuck out from the row of marchers and entered the alleyway without the Germans noticing. I approached the house of a gentile woman who took me in. From then, I lived as a Christian woman.

Chana Kirshstein

## I Passed Through Ruzhany During the Days of the Nazis

I left Slonim at the end of July 1942 on my way to the environs of Volkovisk, Bialystock, etc. We heard that the Germans had not yet harmed the Jews in those areas. We explained to ourselves that these areas were annexed to the Deutche Reich (Germany), so they avoided a general annihilation of Jews there. The situation in Slonim, Baranovich, etc., which were included in the occupation zone of White Russia ("*Gebeits Komisariat Veiss Rotenien*"), was different. There was a border with toll collectors ("Tzol-amt") between the sectors.

During the months of July - August 1942, the era of smuggling across the border began. It was conducted by Christian guides, mainly young men and women. They would come from Slonim, and for a price of 30-40 dollars per head, they would transfer small groups of three or four Jews from Slonim to Ruzhany, the first town across the border. Jews who were apparently saved from the depths of the area of the Reich went from Ruzhany to the direction of Volkovisk and Bialystock. Those who were primarily concerned with transferring them were the members of the Ruzhany Judenrat.

{163}

## Along the Way from Slonim to Ruzhany

I set out in a group of four people being guided by a young gentile who walked a certain distance from us. It was evening when we left Slonim. We removed our yellow patches. We went along twisted routes through fields and gardens. We crossed the road that leads to Ruzhany after we made sure that nobody was traveling on it, and that there was no danger for us to walk on it for a few seconds. We again walked through routes that were not real routes, through forests, fields, and hidden paths. We crossed the border in the darkness of the night without sensing it, and were now in the sector of the Third Reich.

Toward morning, we reached the farm of a farmer who was among the group of smugglers. We sat locked up in his barn until the following evening. In the darkness of the second night, we continued along our way following the gentile woman, who appeared again and took us to Ruzhany.

I arrived in town in the early morning hours. Rain was pouring down, literally a flood. We got wet until the bones. Streams of water came down from our clothes. We blessed the rain with a heart full of joy; for thanks to it, we did not meet one living being along the way, either on the way to the town or in the town itself. This is indeed what we wanted! The gentile brought us to the house of a Jew, and then she immediately disappeared.

We knocked on the door of the house whose residents knew about our arrival from before. We rested in this house until the morning. At dawn, we dispersed, each of us going to a different house.

## Two Days in the Town

I remained in Ruzhany for two days. During this time, we sent our request to the people of the Judenrat, who concerned themselves with putting us up, finding food, and most important, providing documents and means of transportation so that we could move on in the direction of Volkovisk-Bialystock. Indeed, within 24 hours we had the personal documents, signed by the German commander of the city. These documents permitted each of us to reside in Bialystock, and to move along the roads in that direction. Armed with these documents, we boarded two wagons hitched with the horses of local farmers, and we left Ruzhany in the light of the day, openly and before everybody. We arrived in Bialystock in peace.

Thus did I find myself in Ruzhany for 48 hours during my wanderings in 1942. (We went from the skillet to the frying pan, even though we did not know that from the outset.) Of course, I did not see much of it, since we were not permitted to move about in a free manner, so that we would not arouse suspicion about the many refugees there. However, something remains in my memory from those two days. First and foremost, the deep impression of mutual assistance that was given to the many refugees with the full cooperation of the Judenrat members remains etched in my mind. I should note further that the assistance was given with great risk and self-sacrifice, and in the most effective manner. These were deeds done with a lofty spirit to give assistance to one's persecuted brethren without any payment and without any bounds. May this be remembered positively for them. The disparagement of all the Judenrats is not just. This Judenrat operated honestly and with dedication, without any equal. I did not pay even one cent for my document, for I did not even have such. Not only this, but furthermore, I received everything for free, without payment, as if it was owed to me. To the best of my knowledge, the natives of Ruzhany acted in this manner to every persecuted brother, and at times with great personal risk. The matter was well organized, with widespread participation of the broader community who opened their hearts and homes to a tormented brother. I spent the two nights in two houses. This was done so as to hide me well, and keep me away from any bad eye. I felt at all times that I was welcomed with open arms and with a warm Jewish heart.

{164}

## Something of the Lives of the Jews During the German Era

The Jews in Ruzhany were forced to live in special houses, so that they would not share a roof with Christians; however, their freedom of movement was not taken from them.

The Judenrat in Ruzhany organized the sending of the men to work according to the daily quotas as demanded by the work office of the German authorities. The Jews worked at backbreaking labor both in the city and in the forests.

The members of the Judenrat fulfilled all of the demands of the Germans, including the taxes and fines (contributions) that were imposed upon them. They provided the Germans furniture, clothing, linens, hides, and all sorts of other things that the government demanded with their various and strange desires.

However, to this time, the hand of annihilation did not reach the Jews of Ruzhany or the other cities that had been annexed to the Deutsches Reich. However, the frightening tidings of Job that the refugees of Slonim and its region brought with them about the general annihilation of all the Jews of White Russia (Veis Rutenien) instilled their fear and dread upon the Jews of Ruzhany, who crowded into their homes with the constant fear of "what will the day bring?" The terrible nightmare of the slaughter of the Jews across the border drove away the calm of the Jews of Ruzhany. The only thought that granted a ray of hope into the hearts and did not let them give up completely was that such a mass slaughter beyond all legality would not take place in the areas included in the Deutsches Reich, for the world would not be silent at such news.

However, the enemy did not think that way. The enemy had various ways to murder the Jews. The turn of the residents of those sectors that had been annexed to the Deutsches Reich had now come. A new way of executing the diabolical plan of murdering the Jews down to the last one appeared once again.

## The Deportation

Until November 2, 1942, there was no sign of impending change with respect to the Jews of the Reich. However, early in the morning of that day, about 20,000 Jews were suddenly taken out of their homes: men, women, and children from the cities of Volkovisk, Ruzhany,

Mosty, Prozowa, Piesk, Swisloch, Izabelin, and the rest of the nearby towns. They were concentrated into bunkers in one of the suburbs of Volkovisk. How did this transpire?

Early in the morning of that day, the German authorities ordered the Jews to gather in one place in each town, so that they would be transported to Volkovisk, and from there to work camps in another place. The execution of this edict was given over to the government of each city. If the fate of the Jews of all the towns of the district was evil and bitter, both as they were being rounded up in their towns and as they were marching to Volkovisk, a frightful journey — the fate of the Jews of Ruzhany was sevenfold more evil and bitter. From the first day a terrible fright fell upon them.

{165}

The men of the German government accused them falsely as they were being rounded up in the city, and tortured them along the long route. Those who fell behind were cruelly beaten and also shot. Neither food or water was given to them. The babies particularly suffered. They cried from hunger and thirst, and the parents were not given the opportunity to feed them or give them something to drink.

## In the Bunkers of Volkovisk

The Jews of Ruzhany drank the poison cup completely. Those who succeeded in completing the frightful journey were housed in bunkers that were called "The Ruzhany Bunkers". These bunkers were the smallest, most crowded, and worst of the bunkers. Even though it was a time of heavy rains, and the nights were the cold, frozen nights of the beginning of the winter, hundreds of Jews were forced to remain outside under the cover of the heavens, for the bunkers could not accommodate everyone. To our misfortune, the offices of the camp commanders were next to the bunkers of the Ruzhany residents, and they were always supervising us — of course, not for positive reasons.

20,000 people were sent to structures, with up to 500 people in each bunker. There were three layers of boards along one side, and each person found a place for rest and sleep. Of course, the crowding was great even when lying on one side. The sleep was not sleep, and the rest was not rest.

The Jews lived in stifling conditions of filth, hunger and thirst, with the fear of death hovering before their eyes: men and women, elderly and children, pregnant and nursing women, healthy and ill people, strong and weak, youth and children — all of them mixed together in heaps of bodies, under the staff of the camp commandant and his soldiers. They were waiting moment by moment for the bitter end. Hundreds already met their deaths during the first days of these living conditions. The death rate in the Ruzhany bunkers was especially large. There were days when the death rate reached 20 people in one day. These bunkers also housed the largest number of sick people.

The first transport of food — bread and potatoes — was brought only after three days in the wagons. The crowds, crazed with hunger, attacked the wagons in order to get a few potatoes outside the line. The camp guards opened fire on them. Despite the fact that people died or were wounded as a result, these stormings repeated themselves on the following days. The daily ration was ¼ kilogram of bread and a plate of soup. Not everyone received even this meager ration.

The issue of heating, necessary for some warmth, was very difficult. Many were beaten and a few were even shot for every attempt to remove boards from the fence.

## Daily Life in the Bunkers

The residents of the bunkers suffered unparalleled suffering at every moment and every hour. Who among us can imagine 24 hours in the bunkers? It was still dark outside when the day in the camp began. The workers lined up in the yard at an early hour. The women searched for means to warm a bit of water for the children. There was great motion near the outhouses. The internal toilet in each bunker was designated for the use of the children and elderly only, and anyone able to go outside was not to use them. The situation outside was no better. This was a large stable with room for 20 people. Two lines were formed, one for men and one for women. After each group of men, a group of women entered, and this repeated itself. A lad said to the women, "Women, go in together with the men. Don't be embarrassed. Either way, they will toss us into one grave…"

{166}

Each person made some sort of order in the bunkers after the night. Then, they scattered, some to fetch water, and some to stand in line for the rotting bread. In one bunker, dozens of groups of Jews gathered for communal prayer. The rabbis decreed a public fast, recited Selichot (penitential prayers), worshiped fervently, and recited Avinu Malkeinu verse by verse. "Bring us salvation shortly" — the prayer leader wept out loud, and everyone answered after him. When he reached "act on behalf of the suckling babes," and "on behalf of the schoolchildren" — the voices pierced the heavens. The Jews stood there, sinking in the mud, in the semi-darkness, some wearing tallis and tefillin — if he had made sure to take them at the last minute — and some without, turned into themselves and knocking from the depths of despair on the Gates of Mercy with their last strength.

Tzirka appeared in the bunkers a few times a day. He was a quiet, deliberate, cunning and cynical German murderer. He took apparent interest in the sick and in their care, and promised them that the situation would be much better in the new camp to which they would be sent...

The workers returned from their work toward evening. One would be carrying a block of wood, another some onions or beets that he had managed to obtain, and the third a piece of bread that he managed to obtain from a farmer. Everyone entered the bunkers immediately after dark. Everyone lit up their corner to the best of their ability. One burned some pinewood, and another was astute enough to use a chemical kerosene solution and some straw as fuel. Everyone stared at the lights, and it took a long time until everyone settled down for the night, lying on the side (there was no room to lie any other way). A Jew in the corner recited Psalms to the light of a burning chip of wood, while another recited Shema aloud. A Jewess talked to herself incessantly. A young, tormented women rocked her young sick baby, singing incessantly for three days in a row, with a trembling, heartrending voice: "I want home". Others had not yet finished the hunt for lice. An asthmatic breathed heavily and coarsely, groaning, unable to find a place for his sick body.

When I woke up in the middle of the night, I had the impression that the picture had not changed at all. Sleep did not pervade in the bunker, but rather a form of paralysis. Here and there, the recital of Shema could still be heard. The Jew continued to swallow the verses of Psalms. The groans of the sick Jew could still be heard. And the withered, young mother continued to rock her child and sing the same song, "I want home..."

The first illnesses, of the stomach and intestines, spread very quickly. Later, the lice appeared, and as a result, a typhus epidemic broke out. The people of Ruzhany did not reach that stage, for before that time they were removed from their bunkers to be annihilated.

The people of Ruzhany had the rights of being first in everything, until the end. They were the first to suffer the great suffering of the journey to Volkovisk, the first to suffer from any action of the camp directors against the Jews, and the first for the bitter end. Their removal from the camp of Volkovisk took place in the darkness of night. The next day, the rest of the camp residents discovered that the people of Ruzhany were no longer among them. Three days later, the camp directors demanded several dozen workers to clean up the empty bunkers. The frightening scene unfolded before their eyes — a mixture of utensils, rags, torn and worn out bedding, various scattered kitchen utensils, food remnants, holy objects, here a book, there a picture, here a purse, there a letter. Among all of these heaps was the body of an old man, an old woman, and a sick person who were unable to participate in the final march. They died slow deaths, and only after the Germans were certain that the last of them was no longer alive did the Germans command several dozens of young people to open the bunkers and clean them. There is nobody alive today who can serve as an eyewitness to the removal, the transport, and the extermination of these people. The awful picture that unfolded before the eyes of the workers who were cleaning the bunkers can only receive some expression in the suffering of those sentenced to death, who had to still traverse vast distances and suffer additional new torments until their last moment.

{167}

The same fate awaited all the residents of the camp, whether they were taken out of the bunkers early, or after weeks or months. However, the Ruzhany bunkers had already given expression to the atrocities of the worst kind, and remain etched in the mind of each of us who saw the people of Ruzhany during their last days in the Volkovisk camp.

The suffering of the Ruzhany people is etched in my mind much more than that of those who were taken out to be murdered in crowds or groups in other cities. Those people saw their bitter end a few hours before they were shot. This was not the case with the thousands who were taken from their towns to the bunkers of Volkovisk, whose death throes lasted for weeks and months with torments every minute, every hour, day by day and night by night. They felt their deaths approaching through libels, degradation, hunger, and the suffering of family members whose fate had been sealed and whose annihilation was at hand. You would see them in terrible death throes, and you would be unable to save yourselves or them. The agony of the parents was especially great at the sight of their young children, who could have looked forward to long lives were it not for the enemy that strangled them and closed off all gates of salvation.

Dr. Noach Kaplinsky

## Echoes

The picture stands as if alive next to my eyes, and shakes up my soul. The Nazi command that they must leave their houses and native city and set out on a long journey struck the Ruzhany natives like thunder on a clear day. They must walk 50 kilometers from Ruzhany to Volkovisk — them, their wives, elders and children.

## At the Meadow

A crowd of people, mourning and with their heads covered [10], stood in the meadow of the town. Heartrending sounds of crying babies rise up to the air. They do not understand the nightmare that is overtaking them. The crying of the children congeals the blood. These children grew up before their time and understood very well the fate awaiting them. Before they saw the light, the light of the world was extinguished before them. The hearts of the parents were bursting. The eyes of many were dripping tears, and the tears were frozen in the eyes of others. They knew that their fate had been sealed, and that they did not care that they would be in this impure world for less time, but with respect to their children who had not yet lived their lives — who will save them from this certain fate that was overtaking them at the dawn of their lives? Therefore, their hearts were grieving. The gaze of their eyes looked around, but without refuge. Tens, hundreds of soldiers and policemen, armed from head to toe, surrounded them. Behind the wall of steel was an inimical world.

{168}

Here was a new command. The children will go on the journey separately from their parents. The hands of the children were pulled by force from the hands of their parents who were holding them as their last support, and were taken from them. Babies were taken by force from the arms of their mothers who were cradling them, and tossed onto the wagon. The young child had to go himself on the route to the abyss. Begging and pleading did not help. The screaming and the fainting were for naught.

## Along the Way

The command was given, and the caravan set out. They dragged along for an entire day. Their minds clouded over, their knees buckled, their feet stumbled, but there was no rest or respite. Everyone who stumbled was destined for death. A bullet would put an end to his life. There was nobody to bury him. The dead person would remain as a trampled corpse on the road, and would be destined for food for the birds of the sky and beasts of the forest. For fear of death, people summoned their last strength so as not to stumble behind, but the elderly and weak were unable to keep up. Despite their strong will, their strength abated. A cold sweat covered their entire bodies. They felt the bitterness of death approaching. They fell into the hands of the murderers, who were following on their heels like hunting dogs, and there was no escaping them. With the recital of Shema, they gave up their pure souls. They closed their eyes, facing heavenward with a silent cry and a demand for justice. They demand justice from Heaven: For what reason and why were the hands of the righteous and pure given into the hands of evildoers, the likes of which have not been seen by the face of the sun since the day G-d created the heavens and the earth.

The babies cried bitterly. They wanted to be with their mothers. The babies screamed loudly. They were starving. They were thirsty. The way was long, the hours passed by, and the day almost ended. The parents were not given permission to give food or drink to their children. Suddenly, a screaming mother burst forward toward her children. She was at the threshold of despair and madness. A father also ran toward his child, speaking words of craziness. They were attacked from behind with cruel fury. Wounded and bleeding, they wailed and set out on their way, away from their children. Those who were not sobered from these deathly blows and attempted to approach the wagon of the children despite everything, were killed by shots. Sheindel Epstein, the daughter of Alter the smith, ran to her two-year-old son. A bullet hit her and killed her. The Heavens were mute and the world was all silent.

The eyes of the children saw and were shocked. The screams and the muteness were intertwined. Who can describe the depth of the pain in words? Some children ran to their parents despite the command of death. Starving babies expired without anyone to help.

The journey lasted for two days. During this time, the mothers were given only one opportunity to be with their children and give them some food. The members of the Ruzhany community, including my father, mother, brothers and sisters, went on this tortuous journey for two days. They are all holy and pure, like the entire community of Ruzhany. They were beloved and pleasant in their lives and were not separated in their deaths [11]. Many Jews who stumbled were shot along the way and remained strewn in the fields. Who knows if someone from my own family died in this manner. Perhaps those who died were better off than those who continued along the way.

{169}

## In the Bunkers

The fate of those who remained alive was evil and bitter. When they arrived in Volkovisk, the survivors of the town of Ruzhany were housed in eight small bunkers at the edge of the camp. People from other towns were housed in other bunkers. However, the thousands of Jews who came from Ruzhany were not able to fit into these eight cramped Sodomic shelters that were designated for them. Hundreds were simply forced to remain outside. The days of snow and cold were beginning. These days were deliberately chosen by the enemy to crush the spirit of the victims and to annihilate them.

Food was not given, and the hunger left its mark. There was no water for washing. The few wells in the camp were barely sufficient in order to assuage the thirst of the masses of people — 20,000 people from Volkovisk and other towns. The filth spread. The faces of the people changed so much after a few days that nobody could recognize each other.

The hunger increased, and when a strong, well-guarded wagon with potatoes entered the camp, the wagon was broken by the people who attempted to grab raw potatoes. The S.S. men shot them. People fell victim, but others continued to trample over the corpses and to run to the wagon, without taking heed of the danger.

Illnesses broke out in the camp, and there was no medication. It is obvious that many people died on a daily basis. The death rate of the Ruzhany natives was especially great. The number of sick people increased day by day. People looked like shadows. Who can describe the agony of the parents when they saw their children dying of hunger before their eyes, with the diseases wreaking havoc, and nobody to save them? Who can imagine the torment of the children upon watching their parents die, leaving them orphaned and alone in this dark world?

## The Extermination

An edict was issued that the natives of the town — the men, their wives, and children — must pack their belongings to prepare for a transport to work camps in Germany. They were to be ready that very night. At dawn, with a freezing temperature of minus 20 degrees and a strong snowstorm, the men, women, and children, dragged themselves along partly barefoot and wearing worn out clothing. The crying and wailing reached to the heavens. They were chased out of the bunkers with murderous blows from rubber batons falling upon their heads and bodies. They were allowed to take only one small bundle. It was clear that this train ride was not to work camps, as the Germans had misled them the entire time, but rather to a place from which people do not return alive. The Ruzhany natives were the first to go on this extermination transport. People of the other towns were transported later, at intervals of a few days. All of them perished in the ovens of Treblinka. Not one native of Ruzhany remains as an eyewitness to the final torture in the death camp or in the oven camp of Treblinka [12].

{170}

I was not among them. Only the echoes of the agonies of my family, my townsfolk, and the natives of the towns and holy communities of Poland and other European lands reached me. I do not know who fell on the route from a bullet of the murderers, who perished by hunger and disease in the bunkers, and who was burnt alive in the ovens [13]. I had left the Diaspora years before this. I did not find peace in walking on foreign land. I succeeded in outsmarting the British government who opened up the gates of the Land only to a few, and I made aliya to the Land. I hoped to see my family among us after some time. Some of them tried to make aliya in order to later bring their families, but they did not receive permission. The foreign government guarded the gates of the Land, which were almost locked. They remained locked even when the Holocaust came. The nations of the Land stood aside. The survivors fell on the roads without a place of refuge, for their Land was locked and in the hands of strangers.

By Meir Sokolovsky

## Everything Precious to Me...

Everything that is so precious to me, in darkness

Was dragged to the wagon,

Only it remains — an insipid game —

The memory.


I am imprisoned in a muddy well — the wailing

A person

Next to blood

I...

By Shmuel Rabinovich

## In the German Captivity

Zàlman Roznitzky, the son of Itshe Nathan and the grandson of Shimon Nathan of the flourmill, tells:

"During the time of the Second World War, on September 20, 1939, I fell into German captivity in the forests of Kompanow near Warsaw. I was sent to Landsdorf along with the Polish captives, and from there to Amr on the French border. I was held in that camp until August 1940. Then the Germans concentrated all the Jewish prisoners who originated in the Russian-Eastern sector of Poland and brought the to Gorlice. From there, they were transported to Lublin in January 1941. There, the Germans set up a hangar for the S.S. men in Lublin. Other Ruzhany natives were together with me there: Yaakov Rabinowich (the son of Beilka), Nota Rotner (the son of the lessee who lived in the courtyard of the synagogue), Moshe Lewin (from a Pawlowa family), Yitzchak Levenbok (from a Konstantinova family), Berl Rodtzky (the son of Eliahu the smith who lived near the market), Shlomo (Einstein's son-in-law), Rafael Movshowitz (the grandson of Yehuda Leib the shoemaker, the son of the sister of Fishel Karpelewich), Moshel Adef (the son of Yaakov Asher the "fisher" from Hagoszczenecz), Michel Pintlewich (the husband of Hinda Ogolnik, who later died of typhus in Lublin), Eliezer Kanetzpolsi (the son-in-law of Eisenstein the Torah reader, Gittel's husband).

{171}

In Lipova Camp 7 in Lublin, there were thousands of Jewish soldiers from the Polish army, who were natives of the eastern-Russian sector of Poland. They housed us in horse stables, which were turned into some form of bunks. We suffered greatly in that camp. We lived from the munificence of the Lublin Judenrat for a brief period. We had nothing with which to cover ourselves. There was complete want. The packages that arrived from home, from Ruzhany, saved us.

From the month of July 1941 and onward, we built Majdanek. Once, during the construction, I was driving with an S.S. man, who boasted to me that the Majdanek Camp would occupy the entire vast area of forests around, for it must house all of the Jews and the population of Moscow.

We were sent to work in various places. Only I remained to work in the hangar. I was one of its first builders. We set up the hangar in the airfield.

Ninety percent of the camp inmates took ill with typhus. The sick people were transferred to the hospital in Lublin that was set up in one of the synagogues. I also took ill and was hospitalized. When I returned to the camp after the illness, a selektion took place. The weak people were sent to the Majdanek Camp, which had been built by us. I was removed from the transport and returned to my workplace in the center of Lublin "Trupwirtshafts Lager Der Waffen S.S. Garten Strasse." I was very weak. When I recovered, the Germans took me out to work, and I was the only Jew who went about almost free. I had connections with the previous camp. I supported the camp residents. There were 6,000 people there, including 2,000 women whose jobs were to sort the clothing of the Jews who had been sent to Majdanek.

The Germans brought about 1,500 Jews to the camp next to the airport, including the following Ruzhany natives who had moved to Bialystock: Betzalel Podrevsky, Avrahamel Limon, and Aber Liverant. The Germans sent the families of these people directly to the furnaces of Majdanek. The wife of Zalman, the son of Dov Levenbok, who was also brought to Bialystock, was among the 2,000 women working at sorting the clothing.

The Germans maintained the aforementioned 6,000 people in the camp until November 2, 1943. On November 3, not one Jew was left in the camp next to the airport, in Majdanek or Lublin. The Germans murdered 18,400 Jews in the three camps during those days. Testimony from a reliable source exists regarding this.

In June 1944, I fled from my workplace to the fields and hid. I was afraid of people. I slept among the stocks of grain. I obtained food from farmers by threats. After great suffering, I was liberated by the advancing Russians.

In January 1946, I moved from Lublin to Krakow. In June of that year, I moved with my cousins Shimon and Nachum to Frankfurt am Main in Germany. From there I made aliya to the Land. I arrived in August 30, 1949. I returned home, to my homeland.

From Zalman Rozanitzky

## What Happened To Me When I Returned Home

When I was freed from the Red Army in 1945, I moved back home to Ruzhany. I was in a very nervous and edgy state. When I arrived to within a kilometer of the town, I descended from the car and continued on by foot. It was twilight. It began to get dark as I arrived at the entrance. One of the civilian policemen stopped me and asked me, "Who are you!" After a few moments of silence, I requested that he bring me before his commander. As I was walking, the thought popped into my mind: my great-grandfather, my grandfather, my father, and I had all been born in this place. I had spent my childhood years there, and now they are asking me, "Who are you?!"

{172}

After checking my documents, the head of the civilian police expressed his sympathy with my grief, with the grief of the town in which not one survivor of my family or of the entire town remained, and the grief of a member of the Jewish nation who was bereaved of his brethren throughout all of Europe. I left the police station. Where should I go? Darkness fell, and a deathly silence fell over the town. Not a person could be seen. Everything had been turned into ruins. I turned to the side lanes of the gentiles, where the houses were still standing. I knocked on the door of one of the gentiles who had been a former neighbor. He was very surprised when he saw me. He could not understand that a Jew from our town had survived. From his mouth, I learned of the bitter fate of my family and of all my brothers or sisters who lived in our town.

The next day I was informed that two Jews who had survived the German slaughter lived in the town. They fought in the partisan units in the forests of Ruzhany. One was Shmuel Bliznansky, the son-in-law of the former tanner Aharke Gamerman. The other was Chaim David, the son of Berl Shepes of the new Jewish settlement of Pavlova.

Deathly silence pervaded in the town. I did not see a solitary person walking alone on the burnt, barely recognizable streets. I walked along, afraid of my own shadow. I passed by the burnt schools. A short time ago, they stood on their foundations, and many Jewish students streamed to them daily, with lively chatter on their mouths and joyful song on their lips. The childishness. My eyes saw what was there, and mass destruction had fallen on everything. Is such a thing possible? From the scattered ruins, it was as if the voices of our young children rose up: Take revenge upon our spilled blood — Revenge!

I approached the synagogue courtyard, the Shulhauf. I remember the motion in the mornings in my town. The Jews with their tallises under their shoulders were going to worship. The pleasant chant of Gemara rose up from the Talmud Torah through the entire synagogue courtyard. Now it is silent, silent as a grave. Everything turned to ruin. Only the Great Synagogue remains standing alone, as if immersed in deep mourning. It was weeping for its worshippers who were no more. It was as if echoes could be heard from inside: "G-d is a G-d of vengeance, G-d of vengeance appear, rise up the Judge of the earth, pay back the arrogant" [14]. Where is the G-d of vengeance who will take revenge for our pure blood that was spilled?

The next day, I visited the desecrated grave of the martyrs in the cemetery. Crushed and broken in body, embarrassed and humiliated in spirit, I left my home, the home of several centuries, my town Ruzhany.

Naftali Kantorowich

## Yaakov Meir Maruchnik

Yaakov Meir Maruchnik amazed the residents of the town twice:

When the Russians entered Ruzhany, they appointed a committee to oversee local matters. Yaakov Meir was on the committee. What did he have to do with them? — the Jews asked each other — the rest of the members of the committee were known as being friendly with the Russians, but Yaakov Meir Maruchnik, the modest man who was never involved in communal matters, what was he doing here?

{173}

After some time, Yaakov Meir became once again a topic of conversation within the Ruzhany community. In the announcement on the main streets, the name of Yaakov Meir Maruchnik was announced as the district representative to the national council of White Russia. Yaakov Meir was among the chief speakers in a public meeting in the town square (an area between rows of stores) in honor of the annexation of Pulsia to White Russia.

The residents of the town knew little about this quiet man who lived in the far-off "Across the River" Lane. He never stood out as a communal figure or as a man of society. He always belonged to "those small people" who went about their affairs discreetly without disturbing the community by their presence.

The tanners who worked together with Yaakov Meir in the tannery knew of his honesty, his diligence, and his readiness to always come to the assistance of his fellow. He himself was satisfied with little, but he always stood his ground on any matter related to the rights of the working person. Therefore, his friends saw him as fitting to be their trusted representative in professional matters.

The people closest to him knew him as a pleasant person with fine traits and a developed sense of humor. His only weakness was books, which he studied constantly. Of course, he enjoyed acquiring any book that he liked, and his library continued to grow, to the great amazement of his friends.

Yaakov Meir did not get involved in political matters. He was distant from any participation in party debates, and was known as a person who does not get involved in such matters. He was always levelheaded in friendly conversations, but those who knew him from up close said that he would express clear Communist opinions. He was a devotee of progressive literature, and would describe an interesting Russian book from time to time, but always in a non-confrontational or nonjudgmental manner.

When Yaakov Meir Maruchnik became known as a member of the city leadership who fulfilled his role faithfully as a communal representative who was acceptable to the people, the Communists in the town began to spread rumors that Yaakov Meir had always been a secret Communist, and that only few people knew and were in contact with him about this.

**Yaakov Meir Maruchnik**

The people of Ruzhany felt that this Communist activity was an involvement in foreign streams. Many said that they knew that Yaakov Meir had no connection to Communism, but was rather a man of the people, who saw in his new role a mission to help the Jewish residents in a time of trouble. They also said that Yaakov Meir continued to worship every morning.

Yaakov Meir Maruchnik did not speak about himself, and nobody knew if these rumors were true. The only thing known without doubt was that his ear was open to everyone who turned to him, and he always tried to come to the assistance of the local residents.

{174}

When the Russians left the city, many Communist activists left with them. Yaakov Meir Maruchnik remained. He met his death at the first slaughter that took place when the Nazi murderers entered the town.

By Naftali Kantorowich

## In Memory of the Martyrs of Ruzhany

I came to Ruzhany after the Russian conquest, when they kicked out the Nazis. I found two Jews alive there. To their good fortune, they escaped from the hands of the Nazis and lived as partisans in the forests. They returned to their town only after the Russian conquest, and they settled there. One is Chaim David the son of Dov Sobolsky, who escaped from the Volkovisk bunkers. He prepared to steal across the border and arrive in the Land, but later changed his mind and decided to go to his sister in Russia. The second was Shmuel Bliznansky. He did not want to receive me, and the gentiles who worked with him said that he does not feel well. He had apparently taken to drink in order to forget the terrifying atrocities.

Ruzhany was the only town in which nobody remained who was able to tell about what happened to its Jews [15]. The testimony of Dr. Noach Kaplinsky, who escaped from Slonim, where they had liquidated the Jews, and arrived in Volkovisk via Ruzhany, is reliable. He was received pleasantly by the Jews of Ruzhany. The Jews of Ruzhany provided him with papers so that he could continue on his journey. As an eyewitness during the days that he remained in the town, he realized that the situation of the Jews was better there than in other places. However, after he left there, he did not hear anything further of them until they were brought to Volkovisk. Dr. Reznik says that the deportation to Volkovisk began on November 2, 1942. The gentiles from Podroisk claim that approximately 500 Jews died on the route to Volkovisk, but they were apparently exaggerating. In Volkovisk, the Jews from Ruzhany were accommodated in the worst bunkers, and suffered unparalleled hunger. They were deported to Treblinka on November 28, 1942. Many victims fell on the short route from the bunkers to the train.

I was surprised that, unlike the Jews of other towns, the Jews of Ruzhany did not go out to the forests. The gentile Mabroznicki told me (these gentiles, who were Communists, were also the policemen and heads of the city, and had a delegate to the Moscow council. The Jew Yaakov Chaim Maruchnik was appointed to the Minsk council in 1939 at the age of 42.), that on the final day before the deportation, eight Jewish youths organized themselves in order to penetrate the partisan camp in the forests of the region, Gustovski was among them. These lads had arms, leather clothing, and money. The gentile brought them to a hill and told them that they would reach the partisan guard in the Boyalshtshina Forest after they cross the river. The Jews remained on the hill until dawn and did not cross the river, but rather returned and joined their brethren who were being taken from the city. Was it the fear of the partisans, who during the early period did not accept Jews into their service, but rather liquidated them, that impeded them? Or perhaps they misled themselves into believing that the Jews were indeed being taken to a labor camp, as the Germans said? Who knows? There were those who believed the latter and brought their property to a gentile acquaintance, asking him to hide the property until their return. My family did so.

{175}

Thirty-six Jews were hidden in the town of Zarela, including the Klibansky family. After all of the Jews were taken out, the gentiles of the nearby village of Molochky said, "Shall we leave them alive?" They came, killed them, and left them in the field. After a few days, they said, "We will go cover them with dirt, lest an epidemic break out." When they began to cover them, Roza, the live daughter of Klibansky jumped out from atop the body of her mother, with wild screams wafting through the air. She attempted to flee, and a gentile chased after her for four kilometers and then killed her. Thus did a gentile woman tell me as I was conversing with her on a sidewalk on the street. She added, "Do not be silent about this gentile, pay him back what he deserves." However, my feeling was that this gentile woman said this because she had not reached an agreement with that gentile about an equitable distribution of the loot.

The gentile Kosmovsky told me, "I am the only one who did not touch the loot. Even the clergy, both Pravoslavic and Catholic, are not clean from this sin. I did not receive anything..." According to his story, the Russians had previously burnt his house, and during the German era he did not have a house into which he would have been able to amass the loot.

My favorite neighbor, Mazurko, had a nine-year-old son Stach. I had a seven-year-old son. This neighbor was one of the many who transported the Jewish children to Volkovisk on their wagons. My son was transported on Mazurko's wagon. Mazurko himself told me this. There were bushes along the side of the road to Volkovisk. My son asked him, "Let me hide among the bushes, and when you return, take me as a son, and I will be Stach's friend." The gentile did not heed his request. I asked him, "Why did you not fulfill his request?" The gentile looked at me as if he did not understand my words! And before this, he was considered as one of the righteous gentiles. From amongst all the gentiles that benefited from my mill, not one of them helped me during my time of distress. He was the only one who would bring me flour for Passover; and his heart had also turned on him, and he did not take heed of the request of my son and did not understand my question. This is the point to which things had reached!

Yaakov Shimshoni

During the Memorial to Martyrs of Ruzhany on January 4, 1954.

## The Beloved and the Pleasant

I went to Poland in the summer of 1938 to visit my family in my hometown of Ruzhany. I had long conversations with my parents, my brothers, my sisters, my friends, and the Jews of other towns — my brethren and fellows of my nation. Who would have believed that this was our last meeting? Who would have believed that the Holocaust was standing just behind the wall?

The residents of the town in general, and the members of my entire family in particular, stand before my eyes as if alive.

My mother, Chana the daughter of David Noach Rozenfeld of Porozovo, stemmed from a rabbinical family. My grandfather was a great scholar who taught Torah to all the lads who were not able to go to the Volozhin Yeshiva and drink of the wells of that Torah source. My mother's entire aim was to see to it that her children would be great in Torah — first through the cheders and the Talmud Torah, and later through the Tarbut Hebrew School. She withheld bread from her mouth and ours, and did not sew clothing for herself or for us if she did not first have the money to pay tuition. She brought her children to the level of knowledge so that they would be educators in Israel.

My father Yitzchak-Izak, the son of Reizl and Efraim, loved labor, just as his muscular, work-loving father who worked all his days, and was active and vibrant until his eighties. All his days, my father toiled to earn a livelihood so as to provide bread for the increasing number of children in his house. My father also loved to serve as the prayer leader and Torah reader in the synagogue. The tune that he would always sing of the weekly portion at home before the Sabbath or the festival still resonates in my ears to this day.

{176}

My brother David-Noach worked in teaching. He devoted the lion's share of his meager salary to support our parents, leaving for himself only a small amount to sustain himself modestly, saying that he is in debt to his parents who raised him, educated him, and brought him to that point.

My two younger brothers were Yaakov and Shimon. The latter, who was a member of Hashomer Hatzair in our town, reached the age of 20 and served in the Polish Army. This army was overrun by the Nazi troops, and Shimon returned home. He suffered the same fate as the entire family and community.

My sisters Ethel and Michla, who had now come of age, began teaching at the time that the Russians entered the town. They taught in the villages that were near the town. When the Germans entered, their fate was known from the outset.

יצחק אייזיק סוקולובסקי,
אשתו חנה
ובת הזקונים שלהם מרימ'קה

**Yitzchak-Izak Sokolovsky, his wife Chana, and their youngest daughter Miriamke.**

Dear Miriamke, the youngest daughter of our family, who had superb talents and excelled in her studies much more than her brothers and sisters, was unable to complete her studies in the gymnasium on account of the German invasion. When the Germans invaded, all of the studies of the Jewish children ceased, and their fate was sealed.

You all wanted to make aliya, and were unable to do so. The Mandate government locked the doors of the country with seven bolts. My efforts did not succeed for my brother David-Noach, who would have been able to make aliya for a student like me; and for my brother Shimon, who could have been accepted to Mikve-Yisrael, or the rest. Who could have imagined that the Holocaust, which was unparalleled in all of world history, was about to begin? After hellish torture, you were all turned into dust by the impure Nazis. The fate of this family was the same as that of all the families of Ruzhany. They were beloved and dear in their lives, and were not separated in their deaths [11].

All generations who issue from us should recall this forever. That which the German Nazis did to us should never be forgotten. We will always do great things in the Land, as if all of those holy martyrs are standing beside us and assisting us. Their spirit will be guarded with us forever.

Meir Sokolovsky

# In Memory of Those Who Made Aliya, Worked, and Are No More

{177}

**Avraham Yitzchak Chwojnik and his wife Sara Henia of Blessed Memory**

Success shined for Avraham Yitzchak Chwojnik, the son of Fishel and son-in-law of Leizer the tanner, and he became wealthy. He did not keep his wealth for himself as the wealthy are wont to do, but rather tried to support charitable institutions. He especially concerned himself with providing heating wood and candles for the Mauer Beis Midrash, so as to provide light and heat for the Torah students. He also concerned himself with the repair of that Beis Midrash.

His wife Sarah Henia was his assistant in those matters. Approximately 40 Yeshiva students would dine at his table. She had a large pot in which she prepared food for them. Similarly, he supported the poor of the city.

When Sarah Henia came to the Land thanks to her son Dr. Aryeh Aran, who was the pioneer of the family and later brought almost all of the family to the Land, she continued her charitable deeds here. She had a special place in the Carmel Market, where she stood and collected donations for the needy. People immediately recognized the woman and her ways, and happily gave her their donations. She was one of the founders of the "Lone Senior's Home" on 9 Avoda Street in Tel Aviv. She remained faithful in her deeds until her final day.

From Dr. Aryeh Oren (Chwojnik)

{178}

## Rabbi Zeev Wolf the son of Rabbi Yitzchak Yaakov (Samsonowich) of blessed memory

**Rabbi Zeev Wolf Samsonowich**

Rabbi Zeev Wolf of blessed memory of Ruzhany was the scion of the wide-branched Mirkin family. He was a man of great action, respected by his fellowman, upright, and fearing Heaven.

He was educated in the lap of Torah, as were most of the Jews of the town. When he grew up, he had a family of seven children. Nevertheless, he always found sufficient time to study Midrash, Ein-Yaakov and Mishna on a daily basis. He dedicated himself to communal affairs despite the difficulties of earning a livelihood. He was an active member of the Talmud Torah committee after Reb David, one of the heads of the Chevrat Mishnayot, one of those concerned with the livelihood of poor scholars, and one of those who hosted poor guests on Sabbaths. Similarly, he was an active member of most communal institutions. Every Friday, he would volunteer to walk around the city and declare the closing of the shops on time. Despite the suffering of his life, he was always cheerful and content with his lot.

His hand was open to anyone who asked. He would walk among the poor of the city and offer help. He would distribute charitable loans, and would never be exacting about the timeframe of payment. At times, he suffered from losses, but he accepted everything with love.

After the death of his wife and after the great fire, when his sons left him and traveled to America, Rev Zeev did not follow after them. However, he left his beloved Ruzhany and turned his steps to home, to his true home, to the Holy Land, to Jerusalem, the desire of his heart. He spent his final days there, and died on the 13 of Cheshvan, 5674.

In Jerusalem, as in the Diaspora, he dedicated himself all his days to the study of Torah, Mishna, and Midrash. His good name was etched on the marble tablet in the Great Synagogue of Meah Shearim as one of the founders of its Chevra Mishnayot.

He lived under meager means in the Land. He satisfied himself with meager bread and small portions of water despite the large sums of money that his sons sent him from America, for he distributed most of the money he received to his friends and to poor scholars. He accepted everything with love until the day of his death, and his motto was "this too is for good."

Eliahu Landsberg

## Leibel Ziskind of blessed memory

Leibel Ziskind, the son of Moshe the smith (Jubiler), was one of the younger activists in our town. He threw himself into communal activity with great energy and drive. Within a short period, he attained an honorable place in the leadership of the Jewish institutions of the town. These were townsfolk who had studied Torah from the best teachers of the city, read a great deal of books, and amassed knowledge and secular education through self study. These youths of the town, saturated with Jewish tradition, a Zionist tendency and sublime social idealism, gave their full energy to the youth movements in the city, to Zionist activity, and to the dissemination of culture and progress. However, these youths were unable to remain in their town. The place had become too constricted for them. With the passage of time, they grew "wings," spread them, and wandered far off, some on Hachsharah and aliya, and others to the far reaches of the world.

{179}

Already in cheder, Leibel excelled as an activist. When he grew up, he was among the organizers of the "Zelbsts-Bildungs-Farein" (Autodicactic Organization). When it disbanded and the "Herzlia Zionist Youth Movement" arose, Leibel became involved in cultural activity there as well. He was the one who led the communal singing at Friday night parties. His voice was sweet, and the main thing was that he knew how to choose the fitting song (along with Sonia Leviatan, may she live long, who is married to Baruch Moskowitz, who also excelled in pleasant song). He entertained those at the party and the residents of the neighborhood with his rendition of the Sabbath hymns and songs of Zion.

In the interim, years passed. The kids grew into goats. The time came to move from publicity activities to actualization. Leibel joined Hechalutz. "Until this time, we preached nicely," he declared at the founding meeting of the Chalutz organization in Ruzhany, "The time has come that we now fulfill nicely." For reasons not related to himself, he was unable to immediately fulfill that which he preached. He moved to work in Bialystock. After he married Dova Chwojnik, the young couple moved to live in Volkovisk. He continued his communal activity in his new places, and did not cut off his connections with Hechalutz. Even though he became entrenched economically in Volkovisk, he did not give up on his life's desire. His face was always turned toward the Land of Israel. When the opportunity arose, he quickly liquidated his business and made aliya at the end of 1933, filled with energy and hope for the desired future.

לייבל זיסקינד

### Leibel Ziskind

"I finally arrived home," he said to us during our first meeting. Indeed, Leibel felt himself as a veteran of the Land from his first day. All difficulties in becoming accustomed to the new place, all difficulties in arranging work, the crowded living quarters — he accepted everything as natural, as a necessity, without complaint. Even though he endured several difficult years, he remained calm in his soul and content with his lot.

He stopped busying himself with communal affairs in the Land. He avidly followed anything that was taking place in the settlement, he came to meetings and lectures, but he always remained as an onlooker from the side. His friends who knew Leibel from the era of his activism in the Diaspora often attempted to pull him into the circle of communal life. However, he continued to refuse, saying:

"My wife and I are actualizing Zionism by our very being here. We are faithful to the Workers' Movement in that we live off the toil of our hands and eat our bread from the sweat of our brow — there are better and more talented people than me for communal activity."

This upright man left us at a young age. He was 36 years old when he died. His memory will be preserved by anyone who knew him.

Yosef Abramowich

{180}

## Nachum Alperstein of blessed memory

I do not want to wax greatly in praise, but it seems to me that I would not exaggerate if I say that there was nobody who knew him who did not love him. That is, literally love him!

This love accompanied him throughout his life, and somewhat eased his difficult life. Worries of livelihood troubled his parents, and Nachum was forced to begin to bear the yoke of livelihood when he completed the Tarbut School. He worked in brick manufacturing, and later in the forest.

Unlike his friends, he did not suffice himself with preaching about labor and promising to fulfill such only in the Land. He was one of the first of our friends who joined Hechalutz in 1926. He went out to Hachsharah in Michlin, and when that Hachsharah Kibbutz disbanded, he did not give up on his aspirations. When a new awakening came after the disturbances of 5689 (1929) and a Hechalutz chapter was founded in Ruzhany, he was among the first to go out to Hachsharah. This was in May 1930. Within a few days, he succeeded in endearing himself to all the members of the Kibbutz. Even the workers and the gentiles held him in esteem on account of his serious attitude toward work.

When Hershel Pinsky of blessed memory came after about half a year to certify people for aliya with only three certificates in his sack for the Kibbutz of more than 50 members who had been waiting for their certification for more than a year, Nachum was the first to obtain a certificate, even though he had not yet attained "tenure."

Nachum made aliya to the Land and once again demonstrated his serious and dedicated attitude to work. The tribulations of absorption were not difficult for him. He knew the language, and therefore immediately entered into the "Hasadeh" group of Mikve Yisrael graduates in Rishon Letzion. After a few weeks, he already competed in digging deep pits with the veteran diggers. In the harsh winter of 1932-33, when the lack of work in the Moshava was at its peak due to the estrangement of the farmers to the Hebrew worker, Nachum was one of the few who worked in an orchard. He received a higher salary than the others. With a piece of bread and slice of halvah for the entire day, he went out to backbreaking work with a hoe as he competed with dozens of Arabs who attempted to tire him out and peg him as an unsuccessful person in the eyes of the orchard keeper. However, his stubbornness stood in his stead, and he did not fall behind them. He returned to his tent-home broken and weakened. However a complaint never came to his lips, for he realized that there is no replacement for him. There was always pleasant smile on his lips.

With the hope that he would be able to help his parents and have his sisters make aliya, he left the kibbutz and moved to Tel Aviv. There too, he endured all the tribulations of an intermittent building worker.

After he got married, he succeeded in entering the Lebanon ice cooperative. Although he evaded the nightmare of unemployment, anyone who has attempted the backbreaking work of ice delivery knows what it is about. Getting up in the middle of the night and climbing stairs all day is not one of the easiest things.

I cannot refrain from mentioning an additional thing — his sweet voice and love of song and cantorial music. He sang in the workers' choir for a long time.

Ten years ago, he underwent a successful operation in his throat due to a malignant tumor. All he lost was his voice. For a long time, he was presented as an example at every medical convention, where his persistence was lauded, thanks to which his voice returned, to his joy and the joy of those close to him.

However, this time, his luck ran out. He suddenly took ill. He was taken to the hospital and operated on successfully. Then the tragedy came suddenly. He was only 46 years old when he died.

Dear Nachum, the clods of earth of our Land, into which you exerted so much sweat, are dear to you. Your friends and acquaintances will remember you forever. May your memory be blessed.

Zeev Rushkin

## TRANSLATOR'S FOOTNOTES

1. There is a footnote in the text on page 150 — but there is no marker in the text: The son of Yaakov Michel Lev. As can be seen from the next page, this applies to the author of the article.

2. See Leviticus 26:26.

3. There is a footnote in the text here as follows: the sister of my wife Sonia.

4. There is a footnote in the text here as follows: my older brother.

5. There is a footnote in the text here as follows: my younger brother.

6. There is a footnote in the text here as follows: my two older sisters.

7. There is a footnote in the text here as follows: my younger sister, the youngest of our family.

8. A blessing recited upon delivery from danger or recovery from a serious illness.

9. There is a footnote in the text here: My cousin — the editor.

10. The head covered refers to a token of mourning, taken from the story in the Book of Esther where Haman returns to his home "mourning and with his head covered."

11. From David's elegy to Saul and Jonathan, II Kings, 1:23.

12. There is a long footnote in the text here, as follows: In the article "In Hell, in Treblinka" by Vasily Grosman, published in the Moscow publication "International Literature, German Pages" 1945 (5), a great deal is told about this death camp.

All of the residents of the bunkers of Volkovisk were transported by train to Treblinka. They were told that they were going to the main train station, from where they would be taken to work camps. After they entered the pit of the station, they discovered that they had been misled. A feeling of helplessness oppressed them, since they saw that they were being taken to an area fenced in by barbed wire and concrete, with many Nazis standing there with machine guns and shooting. They were forced to strip. Naked, and with an increasing feeling of helplessness, the men were prodded on by the butts of the rifles of the S.S. men and the trained dogs that bit their naked skin and tore them apart limb by limb — into rooms that were then sealed shout. They died by asphyxiation from gas that flowed into the rooms.

For a period of 13 months, 396 days, trains full of Jews arrived from all corners of Poland, White Russia, Germany, Czechoslovakia, Bulgaria, and Bessarabia. Approximately 3 million Jews found their death there.

13. The above footnote, from a source written in 1945, is not numerically accurate. Also, throughout this article, there is a reference to being killed in the ovens. This is a common statement — although the truth was, as written in the footnote above, that the people were killed in the gas chambers and then burnt in the crematoria.

14. Psalms 94:1.

15. There is a footnote in the text here as follows: When this article was given over, we did not yet know about the testimony of Chana Kirshstein.

{181}

# The Organization of Ruzhany Natives

## Dr. Aryeh Aran (Chwojnik)

He was born in Ruzhany. He completed medical school in Geneva, Switzerland. He continued his studies in Zurich. He worked in Vienna, Paris, and America. He was already active as a member of Poale Zion in Switzerland in 1915. He organized the "Taz" and the hospital in Ruzhany. He made aliya in 1922, and set up the "Histadrut Shechenim" (Organization of Neighbors) and "Shchhunat Hashchenim" (Neighborhood of Neighbors) here. He served as a member of the Tel Aviv city council for six years. He set up the "Hachlama" convalescent home in Ramat Gan. Today he continues to work as an ear, nose and throat specialist in Tel Aviv.

## Abba Leviatan

He was a native of Ruzhany, and one of the pillars of communal activity there. He served as the gabbai of the Great Synagogue for 20 years (1901-1921). He was a founder of the Volunteer Firefighters in the town, and one of its heads until he made aliya to the Land in 1924. He was the head of the militia during the change of regime.

Many accompanied him as he left Ruzhany. Abba Chwojnik asked him, "Many have made aliya, without many accompanying them. How did you merit?" Abba Leviatan answered him, "I belonged to everyone — and everyone to me. I worked with the government authorities and with the police for the benefit of anyone who was in need of such."

## Shmuel Magli (Mogilenski)

He was the owner of the pharmacy in Ruzhany from 1911 to 1932, the year he made aliya. He was an active member of the Zionist organization of Ruzhany, an activist with the Keren Kayemet LeYisrael, and other organizations. He owned a farm and orchard in Raanana until 1945. Today, he owns a pharmacy in Tel Aviv.

ועד ארגון עולי רוז'ינוי

בשורה הראשונה — מימין לשמאל עומדים: יודל סוקולובסקי, אלישע שמשוני, רוזה יובילר (פינס), אפרים גמרמן, רפאל קרליץ.
בשורה השניה: יוסף אברמוביץ, שמואל מגלי, ד"ר אריה ארן, אבא לויתן.
בשורה השלישית: זאב רושקין אלקה אינס (רובינוביץ), מאיר סוקולובסקי.

**The Organization of Ruzhany Natives**

First Row, right to left, standing: Yudel Sokolovsky, Elisha Shimshoni, Roza Jubiler (Pines), Efraim Gamerman, Rafael Karelitz.
Second Row: Yosef Abramowich, Shmuel Magli, Dr. Aryeh Aran, Abba Leviatan.
Third Row: Zeev Rushkin, Elka Ines (Rubinowich), Meir Sokolovsky.}

{182}

## Roza Jubiler-Pines

She was a native of Ruzhany. She completed her medical studies in Leningrad in 1918. She then completed additional studies in London and Berlin. In 1922, she returned to Poland and worked as an eye doctor. When Hitler ascended to government in 1933, she made aliya and works here in medicine.

## Yaakov Shimshoni

He was one of the intelligentsia youth of Ruzhany. He studied Torah from the best teachers in town, and also mastered general education in the Real School of Slonim. He was considered to be an honorable person, even though he conducted himself modestly and spent his time studying. He owned the largest flour mill in town. After the region was conquered by Soviet Russia in 1939, he left the town and remained in Russia. He returned to Ruzhany after the downfall of the Nazis and saw it in its full destruction. He made aliya to the Land and today is a librarian in the Kaduri agricultural school.

## Yosef Abramowich

He was a native of Ruzhany. He was the son of Meir Hirsch and Shitel-Chana. He studied in Ruzhany with the best teachers. He continued in the gymnasium in Slonim and university in Warsaw. He made aliya to the land in 1933. He worked as a teacher for many years. After the founding of the state, he became a supervisor in the Ministry of Education and Culture. He was active in the area of physical education and sport, and published several books on these topics.

## Elisha Shimshoni

He was a native of Ruzhany, the son of Nachum and Miriam (Rogov). He studied in cheders, and was known as an excellent student. He made aliya along with his parents, brothers and sisters. He worked at various jobs during the early years. He traveled to Germany and completed his studies in engineering. As an expert engineer in statics and building, he erected rows of large houses in Tel Aviv and its environs. Today he is active as a responsible engineer in The Union of Kibbutzim.

## Meir Sokolovsky

He was a native of Ruzhany, the son of Yitzchak-Izak and Chana (nee Rosenfeld). He studied in the Tarbut Hebrew School in Ruzhany. He continued and completed his course of studies in the Poznansky government seminary for Hebrew teachers in Warsaw. He worked as a teacher in Poland. He made aliya at his first opportunity, in 1934. He completed additional studies at the Hebrew University of Jerusalem and worked in the capital as a building worker, and in the Sharon as an agricultural worker. In 1935, he was again called to teaching. From that time on, he worked as a teacher. With the arrival of the large wave of aliya after the War of Independence, he directed the school in the Gelilot transit camp. Today he is the principal of a government school in Tel Aviv.

{183}

## Zeev Rushkin

He was a native of Ruzhany. He studied in the Tarbut Hebrew School. He continued his studies in the Yavneh School in Lodz. He was active in the youth organizations and dedicated to the funds. He was active in Hechalutz. He completed his Hachsharah in Janow and made aliya to the Land in 1931. He lived for two years in a field camp in Rishon LeZion. He then moved to Tel Aviv and worked in building. Today, he is a driver and a partner in the Beit Hamischar.

## Yudel Sokolovsky

He is a native of Ruzhany. He studied in the Tarbut Hebrew School. He was the head of the Hashomer Hatzair chapter in the town from 1926 to 1932, the year of his aliya. He worked in the orchards of Petach Tikva. He studied agriculture in Italy in 1934-1935. Today, he is the director of the Yatur touring company.

## Elka Rubinowich-Ines

She was the daughter of a family of teachers in Ruzhany. She studied in the Tarbut Hebrew School. She was one of the heads of the Hashomer Hatzair chapter in the town from 1926-1932, the year of her aliya. She was a member of the Nes Ziona Hashomer Hatzair Kibbutz for some time. She worked in paving roads, building, and agriculture. She completed her studies in the Halpern seminary. She was one of the first residents of Givat Rambam.

## Rafael Gamerman

He was a native of Ruzhany, the son of Aharon and Alta (the daughter of Avigdor Michel Goldberg). He studied in the Tarbut Hebrew School, and was a member of Hashomer Hatzair in the town, and active for the funds. He made aliya to the Land in 1934. He lives in Tel Aviv, and works as an accountant. He serves as the volunteer secretary of the Gemilut Chasadim fund of the Organization of Ruzhany Natives.

## Rafael Karlits

Rafael (Zeidel) Karlits the son of Eliezer Chaim was born in Kosow Polski in 1912. He moved to Pavlova near Ruzhany. For all the time, he studied and was educated in the Tarbut Hebrew School in Ruzhany. He made aliya in 1932. He studied plumbing. He suffered no small amount. Today he is the owner of a private business for installation needs.

## Yitzchak Einstein

יצחק אינשטין

### Yitzchak Einstein

He was a native of Ruzhany. He studied in the Tarbut Hebrew School. During the Russian occupation in 1942, he served as the accountant for the city bank. After the tribulations of various camps, he arrived in Israel. Today he is an official of the audit office in the country.

{184}

## Our Families [1]

### The Family of Michael Egolnik

Michael, the son of Avraham Moshe, was an intelligent man, who was also concerned with the education of other townsfolk. He was one of the founders of the Tarbut Hebrew Gymnasium, to which he dedicated a great deal of his time, and one of the activists of the Keren HaYesod in Ruzhany. He was an astute communal activist, with generous traits. His primary desire was to make aliya to the Land, but did not succeed in doing so.

His wife Freda, the daughter of Meir Moshe, was very dedicated to her family, and always concerned herself with the education of her children.

### The Family of Abba Chwojnik

Chaitsha and Abba Chwojnik.

Abba the son of Chaim David and Beila Chwojnik was the owner of the tannery on Milner Street next the Zlawa River. He was a gabbai of the Ever Hanahar synagogue, and a prayer leader. He was the chief activist of the Chevra Kadisha (burial society). He was active for the Keren HaYesod. His wife Chaitsha (nee Roschowsky) loved giving discreet charitable gifts to those in need.

{185}

## The Family of Yosef Michnovsky

**Yosef Michnovsky and his children Bluma and Getzel. His wife Yehudit (Itka) Michnovsky**

Yosef, the son of Moshe-Yaakov and Chana Bunia Michnovsky, was a father who did everything in order to provide food for his children. He was a quiet, scholarly man, but modest and discreet. He would divide the hours of his workday between his store in town and studying a chapter of Talmud.

His wife Itka (Yehudit) was a modest, kindhearted woman. She was a loving and dedicated mother to her children with all strands of her soul.

They aspired to make aliya to the land, but they perished in the Holocaust before they could do so.

## The Family of Eliezer Rubinowich

אליעזר רוביניביץ' ואשתו בילקה

**Eliezer Rubinowich and his wife Bielka**

The modest image of Eliezer Rubinowich, who was dedicated to teaching, without doubt lives in the hearts of many of our townsfolk. He attempted to introduce new methodologies in the study of reading and arithmetic. He taught geography and nature with the help of stories. He colored the long school day of his students by reading sections of marvelous literature with artistic talent. He educated us, his children, in the spirit of the Haskala and labor. How great was his joy when his eldest son Shmuel was certified to make aliya through Hechalutz. He also encouraged me, his only daughter, to make aliya and study agriculture. In the recesses of his soul he harbored the hope that the day would come when he would join us and spend the rest of his days as a farmer in Israel. However, fate did not have it thus.

My mother Bielka the Teacher was a goodhearted woman who empathized with the suffering of her fellowman. The daughters of people whose luck was hard received an education in her school with no fees.

{186}

The great tribulations of raising children did not pass over our house. My brother David, the pride of the children, was taken in by Communism. When he was 17 years old he was sentenced to four-and-a-half years of imprisonment. He fulfilled his sentence in the infamous Brisk fortress. (His brilliant speech that he gave at the time of his trial was disseminated in booklet form throughout Poland.) When our city was conquered by the Russians, David rose to greatness. Nevertheless, the authority and the honor did not remove him from his levelheadedness. As in the days of degradation and torment in prison, during his days of greatness he remained strong in spirit and clean of hands, all the way until the bitter end. How did he perish? News arrived that he met his end during the bombing of a bridge during the Nazi rule. Another version states that he was a partisan leader, and was murdered by a gentile partisan on account of his Jewishness a few days before the liberation.

דוד, יעקב ויוסף רובינוביץ'

**David, Yaakov and Yosef Rubinowich**

My brother Yaakov, the third son, was loved and well accepted by his many friends and buddies. He was a member of Hashomer Hatzair, served in the Polish army, and fell into Nazi captivity along with other Polish soldiers. He was imprisoned in a camp in Lublin where he perished.

My brother Yosef, the youngest child, was more talented than the other children. He received a scholarship during the Russian era. He shared the bitter fate of our parents and perished along with the rest of our townsfolk, while still young and tender.

## Yekutiel Sherman

יקותיאל שרמן

**Yekutiel Sherman.**

He was one of the young activists in Ruzhany. He was a very talented man, of great action. Prior to the world war, he was the head of the firefighters in the town, a member of the town council representing the workers, and a member of the directorship of the Kultur Farein and the Peretz Library. With the entrance of the Russians to the town, he was deported to Siberia where he died in 1942 in the city of Kyzyl-Yurt. His wife Peshka (nee Lerman) was a member and talented actress in the dramatic club. She perished in Ruzhany along with their two children.

{187}

## The Family of Moshe Itzkowich

The Itzkowich family and their relatives after the marriage of Chaya Abramowich to Leibel Dumovsky

The photo includes the young activists of Ruzhany in the latter period, including: Yekutiel Sherman, and Shimon Turn — a teacher and activist (who was taken out to be killed by the Russians when they entered the town).

Standing in the row on top: Epstein the daughter of Zidel, Klebensky, Dumovsky, Maruchnik, Dumovsky, Kuklicha, Dumovsky, Maruchnik.

Second row: Yekutiel (died in Kutels) holding his son, Dumovsky, Lipovsky, Gershon, Pia, Wilensky, Lerman the daughter of Leib, Klebensky. On the side, the brother-in-law of Fuksman.

Third row sitting: Dumovsky couple, Shlomo, his wife, and child with his daughter-in-law Abramowich. Meir-Hirsch and Shitel-Chana.

Fourth row: Libe Lerman, Klebensky, Lerman, Wilensky, Shimon Urn, Abramowich — 2 female guests.

Dvora Itzkowich writes the following, among other things:

My father Moshe Itzkowich was an intelligent, practical Jew. He was known in our town as "Moshe the Schwartzer" (Moshe the Black), and owned a large haberdashery business. Only the nearby business of Stein was larger.

My mother Rivka was a quiet, modest, goodhearted woman who loved her corner. She left this world before the clouds had darkened the skies.

My older sister Chaya, wise and upright, raised a fine family of five children. They all perished during the Holocaust. My second sister Hadassah, diligent and full of life, established a wonderful family. She had two children. The evil hand murdered them. My youngest sister Sonia, refined and modest, had to take care of the household, consisting of my father and a brother, after mother's death, while she was still young. Later she built her home with Yechezkel. The storm uprooted her with her young child in her arms.

My dear brother Avrahamel, where are you? You walked among us like an upright tree. You studied in the Tarbut Hebrew School, and I dreamed that we would see each other in Israel. You would come, build up, and be built. Then the storm came and uprooted the tall tree. When? How? Where?

{188}

## Where are They?

I wish to utter a great, bitter scream until the heavens and earth shake. But the years passed, and the earth did not shake from the slaughter of millions. People continue in their lives, and I also continue here. The command of life is to live, and to life. In your deaths, you commanded us about life. However, the heart bursts from grief. The soul is tormented. My dear ones, where are you? I, the daughter and sister, am the remaining survivor from a large Jewish family that was cut off from the earth by the cruel hand. The monster of the 20th century wiped all that was dear to me off the face of the earth.

I am a brand plucked from the flames, who was saved by chance from the terrible fate of my family. Perhaps fate wanted me to live so that there would be somebody to remember the beloved, dear souls, so that somebody would remain to bear the hatred of the despicable nation who murdered millions of my brethren and had no mercy on the elderly or children. The heart bleeds. The tears have dried. However, the deep grief rests in the heart. What became of my father's household? Where are you, my dear ones? Where are you, oh community of Ruzhany? Where are you, Jewish communities?

## The Breznitzky Family

ליבע ברזניצקי     אלתר ברזניצקי

**Alter Breznitzky and Liba Breznitzky**

דוד-בנימין ברזניצקי

**David-Binyamin Breznitzky**

Moshe (Alter) Breznitzky was born in Ruzhany in 1887 to his father David the son of Leib and his mother Liba, a G-d fearing woman who was dedicated to her fellowman. He was educated in Yeshivot, and was knowledgeable in Torah. He served as the gabbai of the Mauer Beis Midrash, was a member of the Chevra Shas (Mishna study group), an activist in the Chevra Kadisha (burial society), and active on behalf of Keren HaYesod. He made aliya in 1934 and settled in Ramat Gan. He was an active member of the organization of Ruzhany natives, and a gabbai in the Tiferet Bachurim Synagogue in Ramat Gan. He taught classes at the Chevra Mishnayot. He merited to see the laying of the cornerstone of the expanded Tiferet Bachurim Synagogue, on behalf of which he worked, but he did not merit to see it fully built, for he died on the 20th of Nissan 5714 (1954).

{189}

His son David Breznitzky, may G-d avenge his blood, was born in Ruzhany in 1920. He studied in the Tarbut Hebrew School. He made aliya along with his parents, brothers and sisters in 1934. He was a quiet lad, refined and admired by people. On the 18th of Tevet 5706 (1946), as he was traveling through Tel Aviv at midnight at the corner of Maza Street and Petach Tikva Road on the way to his home in Ramat Gan, he was arrested by British policemen from Sharona and was beaten to death. (This was the time of the underground Irgun actions against the Mandate government.)

To differentiate between the dead and the living, there is Hadassah Breznitzky, a good women, loved by people, and an exemplary, dedicated mother. After her beloved husband was cruelly beaten to death, she fled from her place of living and settled near her daughter in Tel Aviv.

יד הדסה ברזניצקי

**Hadassah Breznitzky**

## Yocheved Sokolovsky

יוכבד סוקולובסקי

**Yocheved Sokolovsky**

Her husband passed away before his time, and she concerned herself with her family's livelihood. Her busy workday was divided between her store in the town and the Dutch cheese factory in the village of Yundilovichi. She succeeded in making aliya to the Land along with most of her family, and continued with her diligence in searching for sources of livelihood for her family. She also did not keep back from performing good deeds, such as collecting donations for the Yeshiva of Rabbi Podolsky, working for Hachnasat Kalla (support of poor brides), and others.

## Yitzchak Rudetsky

He was a native of Ruzhany. He studied in cheders, in the Yeshiva, and on his own. He was a flour merchant, but he dedicated his free time to attending classes in the Gershonowich Beis Midrash in the town. He made aliya to the Land. He lived in Afula and was active in communal affairs there. He was the founder of the charitable fund among other things.

## Those Who Fell in the War of Independence

{190}

**Eliezer Orkin of blessed memory**

**Eliezer Orkin**

Eliezer was born to Miriam and Zalman Orkin in Ekron on 10 Tammuz 5689 (1929). His father Zalman was the son of Hinda Liba and Reb Yisrael Chaim Orkin, and the grandson of Reb Tzvi Orkin, who was among the first eleven settlers who founded Ekron in the year 5645 (1885) after making aliya from Ruzhany. His mother Miriam was the daughter of Tauba and Chaim Ruchmis (Hinda Liba Orkin and Tauba Ruchmis were daughters of Chaya Tzipora and Reb Zalman Mendel Ruhzansky "The lessee"). Miriam made aliya from Ruzhany in 1927 and married her relative Zalman in Ekron.

Eliezer was their firstborn son. His parents continued in the long-standing traditions of their forbears and occupied themselves in farming. Eliezer was educated in agriculture from his childhood. The difficult economic situation of the family forced Eliezer to bear the burden of livelihood along with his parents from a young age. At the ages of eight and nine, one could see him as a thin child, wearing a threadbare coat, going out even on rainy days to take the cows to pasture kilometers away from the settlement. During the summer, one could find this lad among the rows of cucumbers or tomato bushes, and the like.

It was not only the economic pressure that made him into a farmer. There was another, deeper reason, which was primary. Eliezer was born with farmer's blood coursing through his veins. He was born to be connected to the field, the garden, and the barn, or as Mr. Krause, the director of his school (Mikve Yisrael) once said: "Oh, he was born in a furrow."

He completed public school in Ekron in the year 5703 (1943), and naturally continued his studies in Mikve Yisrael (the same school in which his father graduated in the first graduating class). Here, Eliezer turned to studies more than to his home, and he was successful. He studied in a theoretical manner all those things that he loved, and in which he had been occupied with even before his studies in the agricultural school.

Eliezer concluded his studies in Mikve Yisrael as a member of the 26th graduating class in the year 5706 (1946). Again, in a natural way, he went out to fulfill his duty to the state (without being legally obligated to do so, since the law of military service was only passed later, in 5709 / 1949). He enlisted in the Palmach despite his young age, for he was 17 years old. His training took place in Givat. Even there, he devoted his primary attention to the innovations and development of agriculture. Eliezer, with the "plow" in his nose, was to go out to a commander's course with the first people of the Palmach. The fact that he was accustomed to field conditions from his youth helped him in that course, and he developed into an exemplary fighter and field man.

{191}

At the end of the course, the Hebrew insurgence movement set out to its first large-scale activities. This was in summer of 5707 (1947), when the largest Haapala ship, "Exodus from Europe in 5707" arrived. The ship was brought to the entry of Haifa, and the immigrants who were refugees of the sword saw the Land from afar, and "their eyes pined and saw, but they had no power to save themselves." With force, through the use of tear gas, clubs and live fire, the British transferred the immigrants to three ships and sent them back to Hamburg, Germany. Three of the immigrants were killed during the transfer, and several were injured. The anger was great. The Jewish settlement was shaken up. The spirits of the pre-state fighters demanded action. Then it was decided to bomb the radar that was located on Mt. Carmel in Haifa, which helped the British, who were following after our refugees, to expose and hunt the Haapala ships and send them back to Cyprus or Germany. The best of the men were chosen from amongst the Palmach training camps, Eliezer among them. One of our fighters fell during the radar attack — Eliezer. He was wounded as they were retreating from the radar after carrying out the action. His friends wanted to carry him with them, but the wounded Eliezer understood that they were liable to be killed if they were to remain in the area for longer than necessary. He asked them to take his revolver from him and to give his regards to his family and friends. He remained alone, bleeding on the slopes of Mt. Carmel.

For fear of ambush, the British did not enter until the morning. They brought Eliezer to the government hospital in the morning. Even there they did not leave him, but began to wear him down with questioning. Despite his wounds and pain in his last moments, Eliezer did not reveal anything to them. He told them that he was from Ekron and not Givat (they could have traced down the action in Givat, but not Ekron). Eliezer died during the questioning.

Eliezer, the sabra of sabras, set out to react to and protest the torment and oppression perpetrated against his brethren, the remnants of European Jewry, refugees from the greatest and cruelest slaughter in history. Eliezer the "plower" did not go out to kill after he was shaken up by the cruelty with which his brethren were treated. Rather, he set out proudly to sound the alarm and warning that we cannot accept such injustice quietly. He fell in his battle.

He was buried in Ekron on the 4th of Av, 5707 (1947)

By Yisrael Orkin

## Mordechai Orkin of blessed memory

He was born in Gedera on 22 Tevet, 5667 (January 8, 1907) to his parents Tzvi and Chana. After concluding his studies in the Herzlia Gymnasium in Tel Aviv, he worked on his father's farm, and later as the director of the warehouse for citrus packing products for several companies. During the final seven years of his life, he worked as a leading official in the Hadassah Hospital on Mt. Scopus in Jerusalem. He was always active in the Hagana. In his Moshav, and during the time he worked at Hadassah, he took various courses, and then directed the group of workers. Immediately after November 29, 1947, he would spent his nights on guard duty in the building, until he fell while on guard duty at the hospital on 27 Adar II, 5708 (April 7, 1948). He left behind a wife and two children. His daughter was born three months after his death. His legacy included a collection of poems.

{192}

## Shmuel Rubinowich (Haramati) of blessed memory

**Shmuel Rubinowich (Haramati)**

He was born in Ruzhany, Poland on 9 Tevet, 5671 (January 9, 1911) to his parents Eliezer and Bilha. During his childhood, he studied Hebrew, Bible and even Russian from his father, who was a teacher. Later, he studied in the Tarbut Gymnasium, where he excelled in his high level of knowledge, and astonished all who knew him with his brilliant talents. He joined Hashomer Hatzair at the age of 15. At the age of 18, he moved to Hechalutz, and went out to the Shacharia Hachsharah Kibbutz. He made aliya in March 1931 with a group of Shacharia members, and joined the Hakovesh Kibbutz in Kfar Saba. This was the time of the "conquest of work" [2] in the Moshava, and he worked as an agriculturalist in Pardesia, and later in the orchards of his farm in Ramat Hakovesh until his last day. He volunteered for guard duty in 1942, and served on the coast guard. At the end of the war in 1945, he returned to the farm, and to his work in the orchard.

With the bustle of the variegated life in the bustling Kibbutz, he liked to be alone. He was alert to everything that took place, attentive and concerned about everything that transpired on the farm, in the country, and the wide world, daring and independent in his judgments on life and the society, on literature and various cultural events. He was interested in conversation with his workmates. During the evenings, Shmuel kept apart from the group, and was alone with himself "under the broom tree," under the shade of poetry. He delved deeply into modern Hebrew poetry, poetry of the middle ages, and modern Russian poetry. At times, he expressed the thoughts of his soul in writing.

He hated all formalities and shrank from all harsh words — he forged his expressions from his heart, and drew them from the depths of his soul — from ancient languages, from a language that had not become parched and had still preserved its early strength. He would search for fundamentals, and take hold of opinions in their first incarnation, while the realities of the present situation evaded him.

Some of his poems were published in "Maala," "Davar," "Mishmar," "Derech Hapoel," "Gilionot," and "Mibifnim." The rest were found in manuscript form in his legacy.

On May 14, 1948, the day of the fierce attack on Ramat Hakovesh, Shmuel was on guard at a front guard post, and he was wounded by a bullet that penetrated the post. He died of his wounds the next day, on 6 Iyar, 5708 (May 15, 1948). He was buried among the victims of the battle of Ramat Hakovesh — in a plot of land in the orchard in which he had worked throughout all his years at the Kibbutz.

By Elka Ines (Rubinowich)

{193}

## The Jewish Body

This is the ancient body, it is the book
Which was written by the hand of the treacherous times,
It is the phoenix that arose from the ashes,
Supreme over our earth.

It rose up in the smoke of the conflagration,
It was hidden in the crevices of the mist;
It was sold in the marketplaces of Europe
With the label, "Soap of the Jews."

But it grew from the wondrous ground...
It arose from the ashes of the burnt body,
It broke through the siege and the prison
It took hold and blossomed in its land.

Not the spirit - the body is the book
Of books. Its ancient verses
Even the chapters of Jezreel and Chefer
Are newly engraved on its pages.

Shmuel Rubinowich

## Malachi Moskowich of blessed memory

מלאכי מושקוביץ'

**Malachi Moskowich**

He was born in Tel Aviv on the 13th of Shvat 5789 (January 31, 1929) to his mother Sonia of the Leviathan family of Ruzhany and his father Baruch Moskowich.

He graduated from the Nes Ziona public school in Tel Aviv. He then studied in the Herzlia High School in Tel Aviv, from which he graduated in the year 5707 (1947).

He was unaffiliated with any faction. He was a member of the older scouts in Tel Aviv. He was a leader in the Chg'm in the high school. He was an athlete. In the year 5707, he received the "Shtam" Cup for his sporting competitions in high school.

He aspired to become a mechanical engineer, and wished to continue his studies in the aircraft building. His favorite subjects were mathematics, physics, and geography.

He was a member of the Irgun for 15 years. Happy and very emotional, he once quietly told me, "Father, tonight, I am invited to be sworn into the Irgun trainees, and from this day, I will begin to fulfill my role as a member of the ranks, and to take an active role in the defense of our Land."

He was a good friend, dedicated to the idea, always prepared to help, to the point where he earned a special note in his report card in public school, "He is loved by all his friends." He was also dear to his teachers, especially in the Herzlia High School.

After the conclusion of his studies in High School, he went with his friends to Hachsharah in Kibbutz Dafna. He had energy and was self-assured. His friends told me that he would encourage them during the most difficult exercises. He excelled as a first aid leader in the battlefield. In any place where he exerted his leadership, he immediately endeared himself to everybody.

{194}

As far as I know, he participated in the battle of Kfar Szold, was injured in his thigh, went to a hospital in Tiberias, and recovered. He made the rounds along the borders of Syria and Lebanon, and, along with his friends, set plans to bombard the bridges over the borders. He participated in the conquest of Tiberias. He would appear in the most dangerous places during the time of the battles, and claim, "I am a lucky person, and nothing will happen to me." He believed in himself too much. According to his friends, he participated in all of the battles of the Upper Galilee.

Eight days before he fell, he was able to come home for a brief furlough. He was full of life and joy, and was proud that his parents were participating in the battle of independence along with him. He said to his mother, "Don't worry, everything will be good. Every mother must be prepared for the worst possible situation. Do not weep for me. Be proud of your son, he will not disappoint you." They wanted to set him up as a guide in the city, but he refused, saying, "I will not leave my friends to fight without me." When he set out he said, "Mother, we will establish the state, and I will return home to you whole and healthy."

He did not disappoint in his death, just as he did not disappoint in his brief life. He fulfilled his desire and gave his life on the 11th of Nissan 5708 (April 20, 1948), as he was hastening to save his wounded friend in the heat of the battle near Mivtzar Koach (Nebi Yosha) in the Upper Galilee, despite the warning of his commander.

We parents are left with good memories of him, and the great anguish in the heart. However, we are proud of him that he did not embarrass us, that he fulfilled the role that was placed upon him until the bitter end.

May his memory be blessed forever within us.

His father, Baruch Moskowich

## Tuvia Kushnir of blessed memory

Tuvia Kushnir was born in Jerusalem on 2 Cheshvan, 5683 (October 12, 1922) to his mother Esther, a Ruzhany native, the daughter of Yekutiel the "Linik," the rope maker, and his father Shimon. His parents were veteran farmers, and pioneers of the Second Aliya.

Tuvia grew up and studied in Kfar Yechezkel. His parents had a farm there. When he graduated elementary school there, he moved on to high school, where he displayed exceptional interest in biology and botany. He conducted various scientific experiments, including grafting and crossbreeding, etc. From his astute observations, he invented important theories. During his many tours throughout the Land, he discovered various species and types of plants that had not yet been known in the Land. With the passage of time, he developed comprehensive knowledge regarding all areas of plant life in the Land, and in botany in general.

He moved to Jerusalem, completed high school and entered university. He studied biology, and during his first two years, he astounded his teachers with his broad knowledge. His independent research aroused the admiration of expert professionals. His ideas and discoveries in biology left a great deal of work for the researchers after his death. He entered military service with the recognition that during the time of the war for the existence of the nation and the Land there was no other choice, despite the fact that he greatly regretted "the loss of time." Even while he was living in an army base, he studied between one military action and the next. He participated in many actions for the defense of Jerusalem, and fell with the 35 who were hastening to the aid of the besieged Gush Etzion on the 5th of Shvat 5708 (January 16, 1948). He was buried in Kfar Etzion, and his body was transferred from there along with the remainder of the fallen of the Gush to Mount Herzl on the 25th of Cheshvan 5710 (November 17, 1949).

{195}

## Yoel Segal of blessed memory

Yoel, the son of Yaakov and Pesha (the daughter of Shmerel the baker from Ruzhany), participated in the battles of the War of Independence in the mountains of Jerusalem, where he fell. Despite the searches conducted by his parents, his bones were not found, and he was not brought to burial. May his memory be a blessing.

The Guber Family

Mordechai, the father of the brothers Efraim and Tzvi Guber of blessed memory, wrote to me:

"My father, Tzvi Guber, was a native of Ruzhany, and a resident of this city for most of his life. At the time of his old age, he moved to live in Horodok and was known there as Hershel Ruzhinauer.

I was born in Horodok, but my father sent me to study in the Yeshiva in Ruzhany, between the years 1903-1906. I studied Torah with Rabbi Avraham Shkolnik (who was later an elder of the town) and with Rabbi Shabtai. I took my meals on a rotation basis with the relatives of my father. These were the years of communal ferment in Ruzhany. I absorbed the atmosphere of the town. The impression of those years influenced me throughout my life."

During the latter years, Mordechai Guber and his wife Rivka led the inexperienced residents of Chevel Lachish, who were beginning to settle this new tract of land. During these days, Mordechai and Rivka Guber gave over their farm to the defense fund.

Mordechai was also elected as the chairman of the civic council of Chevel Lachish.

This family was known for the fact that two of its sons gave their lives for the defense of the homeland during the War of Independence.

This family was discreet in its deeds, diligent with its agricultural farm, and dedicated to the proper education of its sons. The way of the fathers was a sign for the children. The fathers also often enlisted to any vital settlement activity and actual military endeavors. One can learn about the children as well as the parents from the following articles about the sons that fell.

Meir Sokolovsky

## Efraim Guber of blessed memory

אפרים גובר

**Efraim Guber**

He was born in Rechovot on 4 Kislev 5688 (November 28, 1927) to his parents Mordechai and Rivka. He concluded public school at the age of 12. The father went out to direct the young Moshav in one of the valleys, and Efraim joined the work of the farm. "My father has not been at home for a year and a half... There was nobody to help my mother somewhat, and she was buckling under the yoke. Out of necessity, I remained at home, while all of my friends were continuing on with their studies." He had dreams of continuing his studies when his father would return home; but in the meantime, the Second World War broke out. The institutions were calling upon the Jewish settlement to volunteer for the British Army. "If I was of army age, I would have immediately enlisted... We can acquire the Land of Israel only by giving it our blood and fighting for its freedom." When the father was rejected from the army due to his age and health, he expressed his opinion that they were obligated to donate a quarter of their income for the families of the soldiers in exchange. The father accepted his opinion, and signed up to this.

{196}

The mother found no rest. Her brothers and sisters were brought there, to the conflagrations and disgrace. "Is it possible that we can have an ideal Jewish home today, when the entire House of Israel is engulfed in flames?" When she passed through a street with her son and saw a proclamation summoning women to volunteer, "We turn to you in every place of your work — in the fields, factories, offices, house, and wherever you are," she would ask her son, "What is your opinion? To whom is this proclamation directed?" "To you, Mother," the lad would respond. He, along his father, would take upon themselves the responsibility for the home, the farm, the ten-year-old brother and the three-year-old sister, even though he was only 14 years old at the time. He would then point out, with contentment, "I know that if there were to be a draft of women, my mother would certainly be among the first to enlist."

Later, when the mother was in the army, he encouraged the father to move from an assistant farm to a full-fledged farm in the Moshav of Kfar Warburg. He was burdened with the yoke of building the farm. After two years of the mother's army service had passed, he asked her to return home, for he was already able to take her place, even though he was only 15 ½ years old. "Now you must return to the farm, and I will go out to the arms. I do not want Mother to protect me anymore." The mother understood the soul of her son and responded immediately to his summons. Under her influence, he first entered guard duty and practice service. After nine months, he enlisted in the army, disguised as someone older than his age, with the approval of his parents. Later he served in the Hebrew Brigade, fought against the Nazis on the European front, met Holocaust survivors there, worked among them, and helped with their illegal immigration. When he returned from the army in 1946, he was active in matters of defense of the Land. He helped the aliya into the first eleven points in the Negev. He participated in the smuggling in of the illegal immigrants from the Shabtai Luzinsky ship at Chof Nitzanim. He blended in with them, was deported with them to Cyprus, worked there among the refugees, and returned to the Land.

At the beginning of 1947 he participated in actions in the Negev as a unit commander. During the defense of Tirat Shalom from the Iraqi bands who fortified themselves in Kafr Kubiba, he remained in order to provide cover for his friends after he ordered them to retreat because their ammunition had run out. At that time he was hit by a bullet, and he fell. This took place on the 15th of Adar II, 5708 (March 26, 1948), when he was only 20 years and 4 months old. Excerpts of his diary and letters were included in Sefer Haachim that was published in 5710 (1950) by the Moshavim Movement Publishers and Massada.

## Tzvi Guber of blessed memory

He was born in Kfar Warburg on 29 Iyar 5691 (May 16, 1931) to his parents Mordechai and Rivka, who were residents of the village. He was the younger brother of Efraim, who had influence on him in becoming rooted to the earth. He graduated the school in the village. Like his brother, he became involved in farming at a young age, and loved it. His poetic soul was exposed from his childhood. It found expression in articles, letters, and attempts at poetry. The War of Independence found him attentive and tense, and he was only 16 ½ years old then. The death of his brother Efraim affected him greatly. He swore over his grave to follow in his path, and he fulfilled that oath. After the death of his brother, he immediately set out along with all of the people of the village to the division of military assistance that guarded those who manned the battlefronts in the areas of Kfar Warburg. When the situation grew more serious, he entered into service in the Palmach. After a long and desperate battle next Cholikiat (Chalatz), where not more than 30 lads held their stand in the face of the larger armed Egyptian forces, he provided cover for the division at the only mortar thrower, and he fell there. This took place on 1 Tammuz, 5708 (July 8, 1948).

{197}

צבי גובר

**Tzvi Guber**

From this era of his final days, a few creations regarding action and sacrifice were left behind: "Dror" (Liberty) (poem), "Mother" (a poem in prose) dedicated to his mother and all mothers who lost their sons in battle, "Shirat Hakever" (the Song of the Grave), and "Nesher" (Eagle). Only after a year were his bones found, and he was brought to eternal rest in the military cemetery in Kfar Warburg, in a common grave with his brother Efraim. This carried out his will as written in one of his letters, "If I too fall — bury me next to Efraim. Next to him, I was never afraid, and I will never be afraid." A common marble gravestone unites the two graves. The inscription is as follows, "Beloved and pleasant in their lives, they were not separated in their deaths."

The Moshav of new immigrants of Holocaust survivors next to Kfar Warburg was called "Kfar Achim" (The village of the brothers) in memory of the two brothers. The writings of the brothers were collected into <u>Sefer Haachim</u> (The Book of Brothers) that was published in 5710 (1950) by the Moshav Movement Publishers and Massada.

## Dror (Liberty) [3]


My brethren, the sacrifice of the nations and the ramp of their altar,

Based upon bereavement and your warm blood —

Will straighten a whipped back, will raise a lowered head,

The copper skies were shaken up with shouts of "Heidad!"

The children of a scattered and wandering nations, "The refuse of the dwellers of earth"

The prey of every scoundrel, persecuted by man and G-d, —

Believe in tomorrow, for us it is a day of light!

In the night, thunderously raise up the banner of liberty!

Despite the foolish calm and the false hopes,

The night is still long, the battle is still cruel!...


From the bowels of the earth that is sated with the flesh of the children,

The breast of the suckling child and the abundance of victims;

The ashes of the furnaces — where, in endless agony,

For its name — hell shudders and the rock is horrified,

Our myriads became dust and ashes.

From "living cisterns", from the darkness of the grave


{198}

A terrible, strangling, gurgling sound can still be heard there,

The echoes of the terrifying cries ascending from the depths;

From the mouth of the "human soap" made from the flesh of children and mothers

To wash the blood stains from the hands of their murderers:

From the kidneys of the graves, from the depths of every pit,

Skeletons burning in pitch will sing out in freedom!


We too have a homeland in the wide world,

A haven for a broken back, a refuge and warm home,

Small — but ours! Outside of it there is no place

For a nation that has been rejected and persecuted from beneath the heavens!

Wild, overpowering storms howl,

We will not stumble backward; there is a hymn in our mouth: freedom!

Who is afraid of death? A son whose mother and father have been slaughtered?

The daughter of a slaughtered mother? The father of a child who has been burnt:

Brothers! Strengthen yourselves along the way, prepare for battle!

Every gift — is minimized! Every sacrifice is not great!

We will not fear even if our blood flows over,

Why would we be afraid to fall?

To fall — will fill the world!

Oh, sons of freedom, straighten your backs, sound a song of praise!

Fortunate is your generation that merited such from amongst the sixty generations!

You are freemen on your soil, your homeland,

Strong as a mighty rock, as free as a tempest!

Your heart strengthens me, Mother! It is good, warm, full of glory

To you we take an oath: We will never betray you!

Take heed: mountain to mountain, valley to valley will say,

Waterfall to waterfall, sea to sea will storm,

Depth to depth will shout out, crag to crag will thunder:

You are freemen here, freemen here, a nation!

Tzvi Guber
July 28, 1948

**TRANSLATOR'S FOOTNOTES**

1. There is a footnote in the text here, as follows: In keeping with our announcement at the memorial meeting of last year that every Ruzhany native is welcome to provide us with information and details about their families in order to publish in the book; we are publishing those notes which the families provided us. It is unfortunate that not many people responded to our announcement, and it is not our fault that this chapter is not complete.

2. According to the Alcalai dictionary, this is a "term used to describe efforts of early Jewish immigrants to do work not generally done in the Diaspora, or done by non-Jews in Palestine."

3. There is a footnote in the text here, as follows: His final poem, written when he went out to the Palmach.

## "Amal is Geven a Shtetl"

### Ruzhinoy as I Remember

Once There Was A Shtetl

Joseph Abramovitsch

Translated by Lillian Olshansky

Dyed is my garment in wine that is bloody;

I trod in the winepress and – all by myself!

The winepress is full, and I am but one;

I called on the nations, but nobody came!

"From Isaiah" – I. L. Peretz

This book of Ruzhnoy was written and published in Hebrew. The publishers of the book, which must serve as a tombstone for the destroyed shtetl, wanted to remain faithful to the old custom of the Jewish communities of conducting the town business in traditional Hebrew. Also, Israel today has the largest number of Ruzhnoyer who still have vivid memories of the shtetl and still live with these memories; and only the Israel Ruzhnoyer Society was in a position to publish such a book. It is, therefore, no wonder that this book appears in the language of Israel. As a memorial, however, this book would not be true to itself, if it had completely muted the language in which the shtetl lived, worked and was annihilated. We place this written gravestone in memory of our loved ones who were murdered as a result of not having come to Israel. In so doing, we must remember the language of our fathers and mothers, the language in which they said their farewells to us with tears and blessings when we left the shtetl. In remembrance of the mother tongue of our shtetl we are, therefore, writing this additional chapter in Yiddish.

Because of limited space we can only give a general overview of Ruzhnoy and her institutions as she remains in our memories.

**Ruzhnoy As We Remember It**

Ruzhnoy was a shtetl like all other shtetlach of its kind in Poland and White Russia, settled for many generations between fields and woods, near hills with birch trees, near a river with a wooden bridge and swampy meadows, an old and settled shtetl, that had a history of hundreds of years behind her, and that had already renewed her appearance several times.

After every great disaster she replaced her low thatch-roofed houses with brick houses with red roof tiles; from time to time paved the main streets with large stones; renovated the porches, white-washed the chimneys, and appeared young and brave again.

Ruzhnoy had a large market with two double circles of shops. Near them were two churches with tall steeples and large church yards which contained the priests' houses, surrounded by trees, with their servants and vicious dogs.

From the marketplace the shtetl branched out on all sides, and spread out over a large area with its streets and alleys.

The longest streets were the two main streets - Schloss Gass [Castle Street] and Vilner Gass [Vilna Street].

They were considered more important because of their larger houses and their genteel occupants, because of the factories that used to be there, and because they were authentically Jewish streets.

Schloss Gass – the name is self-evident – recalled a street with a historical palace, in which Polish magnates lived and ruled. It is true that most of the palace was burned down during the First World War, however, the surviving portion looked imposing and gave the shtetl a special importance. The canal stream that quietly snaked through the shtetl imparted much charm to the Schloss Gass. Cutting across Schloss Gass and then Milner Gass [Mill Street], the stream flowed gently over the meadows and emptied into the Ruzhnoyer River.

Milner Gass was named for a large water mill (crafted in an Asian style) that once stood at the end of the street, near the river. The street had two-storied brick houses, and further on were large tanneries and leather workshops that were a source of pride.

Saturday evening, when everyone used to go out to promenade, Milner Gass was crowded with people dressed up in their Sabbath clothes, strolling back and forth.

A little to one side, as if it especially wanted to separate itself from the world, was the Ruzhnoyer synagogue courtyard.

Between small wooden houses, on a wide unfenced plaza, stood three buildings close together. The tallest of these was the "Big Synagogue," a tall, white-painted building, with tall narrow windows and a half-round tin roof.

The synagogue occupied the place of honor and lent beauty to the whole courtyard with its old aristocratic appearance.

Near the synagogue stood the prayer house, with its thick gray walls, where the rabbi and his assistant prayed, and which was always filled with worshippers from the Talmud Society and the Mishnah Society.

A little to one side stood another prayer house where the craftsmen worshipped. They could not allow themselves time for too much conversation during prayers and readings; between afternoon and morning prayers they had to be satisfied with studying a short section, or to simply say a few chapters of the Book of Psalms before they got back to work.

Not far from these three buildings were two more prayer houses which considered themselves part of the synagogue courtyard: the two-story Agudah Bet Midrash in which there was a place for Sabbath hospitality and for a yeshivah, and the Talmud Torah which also had a regular minyan.

Besides the prayer houses of the synagogue court, Ruzhnoy also possessed various small synagogues in other parts of the town.

The side streets of Ruzhnoy had nothing to be ashamed of in their appearance. It is true they were not all paved, but this allowed them to have large yards fenced in with wooden rails and pickets.

The houses here were smaller, but the gardens and orchards were large.

In the summer time the small houses were almost completely drenched in green. A little less cozy was the Gentile section.

There one was always aware of the mixed smells of fresh hay and rotten manure and garbage.

From the stalls and yards one could hear cries of the domestic animals and the barking of dogs.

The town was laid out in a broad valley between the low Slonim hills on one side and the distant Volkovysk hills on the other; and the naked, half-burned, mysterious palace looked down on all of this from the Castle Hill.

## Life and Livelihood

Ruzhnoy had a Jewish community of several thousand souls, which had led its distinctive life over hundreds of years, side by side with a Gentile population that was always alien, separate and, for the most part, hostile.

The Jewish life in Ruzhnoy went along on its own well-trodden path - not concerning itself with what the Gentiles intended and did - without fear, secure and proud, as if it were not the Gentiles but actually they, the Jews, who controlled everything and everyone. With a sort of scorn and indifference they lived their modest lives, did what they had to and what was allowed, in order to support a family in dignity, to study Torah, do good deeds, and be virtuous Jews before God and in the eyes of the world.

As did all the Jews in the area, most of the Ruzhnoyer Jews made a living from trade and handicrafts. There was a time when Ruzhnoy had great weaving and spinning factories and great tanneries.

The Ruzhnoyer woolen blankets, the thick and thin pelts, had a market in the larger world. At that time, Ruzhnoy had its Jewish proletarians who subsisted only on their daily wages.

There were Jewish weavers, spinners, spool winders, Jewish wet and and dry tanners. After the First World War, during the time of the Polish rule, all the factories were liquidated and many Ruzhnoyer wandered overseas to seek a livelihood in the big world.

In more recent times, the Jews lived off their small stores and artisan workshops. Some of them traded with landowners, leasing a mill, having a monopoly on whiskey. Those who had expertise in forest and wood trade were middlemen and brokers of forests. They set upsawmills and built distilleries for extracting tar and turpentine from the wood.

Market days and the large fairs were an important source of income for the Ruzhnoyer. Peasants flocked in from the surrounding villages. Butchers and horse-traders came from the nearby towns. Dealers came to buy fox fur, pig hair, dried mushrooms and berries, and all kinds of different merchandise.

Ruzhnoy also had Jewish farm workers. There were two Jewish villages near the shtetl (the "old" and the "new" colonies), with Jewish peasants who pursued a rural agriculture, working and living like the Gentile peasants in the area.

Members of these villages were among the founders of the early Jewish colonies in Israel. A number emigrated to Argentina and settled there in similar agricultural communities.

Most of them, however, remained in the Ruzhnoyercolonies as farmers.

The two colonies (their official names were Pavlava and Constantinova) were founded in 1850.

Tsar Nicholas I, at that time, allowed a number of Jewish families to settle in villages and work as farmers. Thirty families settled in Pavlava and fifteen in Constantinova. Every family received a plot of ground.

## Ancestry and Heritage

Every shtetl has its history and legends that are told and written about in the town chronicles, memorialized on parchment and on the gravestones in the cemetery. Ruzhnoy had its own rich past and lineage and took great pride in its martyrs.

The place of honor in Ruzhnoy's page in history is given over to the "Martyrs of Ruzhnoy."

This is the story of a blood-libel that took place in Ruzhnoy three hundred years ago, shortly after Chmielnitzki's times.

A Gentile boy who had been stabbed was thrown into the cellar of a Jewish house by Jew-hating Gentiles. They blamed the Jews, whom they accused of killing the boy in order to use his blood in baking matzos. It was then decreed that all the Jews of Ruzhnoy should be put to death. Two young men, named Israel and Tuvieh, sacrificed themselves and surrendered to the hangman. The entire story with all the details of their martyrdom was described in the book *Daas Hakedoshim*.

Since then, a special prayer was said in the Ruzhnoyer synagogues every Rosh Hashonah in remembrance of the martyred men.

Ruzhnoy was also proud of its rabbis. Well-known rabbis, who became famous for their innovations in the rabbinical literature, sat on the Ruzhnoyer rabbinical council. Among them was Rabbi Jonathan Bar Joseph, author of *The Salvation of Israel*, printed in Frankfurt in 1720, a valuable book with an astronomical explanation of mystical events.

Rabbi Itzhak Isaac Chaver was the author of several books.

Rabbi Mordechai Gimpel Jaffee was one of the first rabbis to involve himself in an organization that encouraged aliyah of farmers to Israel. He helped lead a group of Jewish peasants from the Ruzhnoyer colonies to Israel, and he himself settled in Jerusalem.

Among the last rabbis in Ruzhnoy was Rabbi Shabbtai Wallach, who was very active and involved. He happened to be an uncle of Litvinov.

The large yeshivahs were an important part of Ruzhnoy's heritage. They were supported by the wealthy Piness and Chvonik families. Many young men were attracted to Ruzhnoy's yeshivahs from other towns.

These "yeshivah bocherim" [students] were assisted by Ruzhnoyer proprietors and landlords who supplied them with "teg" [meals provided at certain houses on given days of the week], and with lodging at an inn.

A separate page would record Ruzhnoy's idealists, its wealthy benefactors, and its ordinary people who did a great deal for charity and good deeds.

They used to talk about one woman who anonymously distributed her rich husband's money among the sick and needy. David the teacher, a Jew who himself lived in poverty, used to cajole money from rich people and give it to poor Jews and Christians. Laybe-Vash, a wealthy Jew, gave away most of his fortune secretly, as anonymous gifts. Others included Jakov Limun, Nyomele the butcher, and more.

Ruzhnoy's heritage included a whole series of devoted community workers who were active in the town proper and later became famous in the Jewish world at large. Foremost among them was Yechiel Michel Piness, one of the delegates to the First Zionist Congress.

In 1878 he liquidated his businesses and settled in Israel, where he was active in various communal activities.

In later years there was Aaron Libeshitsky, who was a Hebrew teacher and writer, and a composer of children's songs and stories.

Zelig Shereshevsky (Sher) was a labor activist in Ruzhnoy and one of the founders of "Zionist – Socialists." He spent a long time in prison for political activities. In America, as of this day [1957], Shereshevsky is active in the Workmen's Circle and is one of the popular columnists in the newspaper, "The Forward."

Melech Epstein, the son of the teacher Shmuel Chaim Eppletreger, was to become a well-known labor leader in America. He began his political activities in the Labor Zionist circles and later became one of the leaders of the Yiddishist circles in Warsaw. He came to America as a political émigré. At first he was involved in Zionism, but eventually went over to the Communist Party and was editor of the communist newspaper "Freiheit" for many years.

Moishe Limun was one of the first Zionist activists in the shtetl. He was active in the student circles in Kharkov where he became well - known as a gifted speaker. Returning to Poland, he was selected to be a member of the Central Committee of the Zionist organization, and for a long time was chairman of the Zionist organization in Lodz.

Dr. Laibl Chvonick, a son of the famous wealthy family, left his home and moved to Israel where he was involved with the workers' movement. Disregarding his large medical practice, he always found time for many varied community activities.

Mendke Chvonick was an outstanding chess player. As chessmaster from Israel he took part in some international chess tournaments. He also had a top role in the Israeli teachers' association.

Ruzhnoy played a role in the history of the Jewish labor movement. In 1878 a weavers' strike broke out in Ruzhnoy at the Piness factory. It quickly escalated into a general strike of all the workshops in the town. In the Tsarist times of that day, striking was a heroic feat. The manufacturers moved heaven and earth to break the "Bundists," but they accomplished nothing. The workers did not give in and they won the strike.

In the final years before the destruction of the Jewish community, Ruzhnoy produced young community leaders who continued the idealistic traditions of the earlier generations. These young people were involved either with charitable institutions or were active in political parties. Most of them devoted themselves whole-heartedly to the Zionist cause in the organizations "Hashomer-Hatzeir" and "Hachalutz." But also, the opponents of Zionism, the youths of communist camps, did their work in accordance with their sincere convictions, and more than one of them languished in prison for many years because of their ideals.

## The Communal Life

The legal affairs in Ruzhnoy were conducted for many years in the traditional manner. The rich men of the town, the trustees of the synagogue, together with several community leaders, were obliged, for the sake of good deeds, to concern themselves with the appropriate financial means to be able to support a rabbi and an assistant, a cantor, and ritual slaughterers. They also needed to provide for a bathhouse with a kosher "mikve" [ritual bath], a school for poor children ["Talmud Torah"], a Sabbath shelter for poor travelers and other necessary services. The needed funds came from the tax on kosher meat and from selling "aliyehs" [call to read from the Torah].

Also, money was collected for Passover meals for the poor and for marrying of orphans and other poor girls by the community, as a philanthropic service. In addition, pledges and donations were received from good and pious Jews who gave openly and knowingly.

After the First World War the community relations in the town changed greatly. A new generation of community leaders arose who developed a number of economic and cultural institutions that could have served as models for the adjacent towns. Among the developments were the Consumers' Union, organized by the dentist, Papermaker, during wartime, in order to cultivate the unused fields in the area; the Tanners' Cooperative, a voluntary production association of tanneries; the Food Cooperative, where the members were able to buy various kinds of merchandise at cost price; the Free Loan Society and the People's Banks, which served as low-interest credit organizations for the shopkeepers and craftsmen. A successful children's colony house was run in the nearby forest.

On an intellectual level were the cultural institutions. The older generation used to tell about an underground education circle that existed in Ruzhnoy even before Tsarist times. The tanners and weavers used to gather together on Slonim Hill to read illegal socialist literature.

In later years Ruzhnoy could boast of the Self-Education Society, the Young Zionists (Hertzliah), and the Peretz Library. In addition, the shtetl had a beautiful choir, a drama group, and an "Oneg-Shabbes" circle. The frequent readings, the literary evenings and the political lectures always drew many listeners.

A beautiful chapter in Ruzhnoy's history points with pride to its school system. It was said that Ruzhnoy was especially lucky in having good teachers in the Talmud Torah and its private "chedorim" [religious schools]. The Ruzhnoyer Yeshivah also had a good reputation.

Ruzhnoy was one of the first towns to introduce secular schools. Nearly fifty years ago Ruzhnoy already had a kindergarten: Baylke Rabinovitch was the first in the area to found a kindergarten for four- to five-year-old children. The "Children's Home" during the time of the German occupation (1915-1917) was in itself a successful test in combining learning with handicrafts; and it conducted a children's club and a school kitchen. A new spirit in the town brought in the Jewish secular public school in 1921. This popular way of learning, the steady contact with parents, and the fact that the basic language was Yiddish, attracted a large parents' group from among the working people and made the school into an important cultural center in the town. A year after the establishment of the Jewish school, the Hebrew school was started, and it became very successful in a short time.

The prosperous elements and the Zionist circles saw in the Hebrew school the best means of eliminating the "left" leanings that had grown in the town during that time. Also, the Hebrew school was blessed with devoted teachers, and thanks to them, the Zionist activity was strengthened. Most of the membership of the Zionist youth organization was recruited from among the Hebrew students.

Ruzhnoy was able to organize self-defense groups that could handle pogroms very effectively. It taught the hooligans that the Jews in the town were not defenseless. The first self-defense group was organized in 1905 by the Tanners' Union; and the Ruzhnoyer volunteer firemen (led by Abba Levitan) chased the rabble-rousing pogromists out of town more than once.

During the time of the Poles, the Gentiles knew that a well-organized self-defense group existed in the town. The Polish troublemakers were taught a lesson when they got the notion to "entertain" themselves in the town: Ephraim Gustavsky, Chaim-Isser Abramovitsch and other Jewish young men made the Poles understand that the Jews did not rely on the Polish police to defend them.

In the Claws of the Nazis

It's burning! Dear brothers, it's burning!

Alas, our poor unfortunate shtetl is burning!

Angry, raging winds

Tearing, breaking and blowing,

Fan the wild flames ever strongly.

Everything around us is already burning.

"It's Burning" – Mordechai Gevirtig

Ruzhnoyer Jews shared the bitter fate of all the Jews in Poland. In November of 1942 they were ruthlessly torn away from their homes and sent out on a road of agony to the gas ovens of Treblinka.

In Ruzhnoy the Nazi beasts succeeded in achieving their devilish plan completely. Not a remnant remained of the Ruzhnoyer Jews who found themselves in the town under the German occupation. Only two people have been located until now, who went through the Nazi hell, and, with the Ruzhnoyer, lived through the suffering and anguish of that horrible time. The two are:

CHANA KIRSHTEIN, a woman from Kalish who, in 1939, fled with her husband, JULIAN, from their city, Kalish. In their wanderings they happened to come to Ruzhnoy, and there they met their bitter fate. Julian Kirshtein was shot in Ruzhnoy by the Germans – part of the first group to be killed. His wife, Chana, remained in Ruzhnoy, and in November 1942 was taken to Volkovysk in order to be transported to an extermination camp. Arriving in Volkovysk, Chana Kirshtein succeeded in escaping to the Aryan side and, disguising herself as a Gentile, she was able to stay alive.

DR. NOAH KAPLINSKI, a young doctor from Slonim, went through the great slaughter, when the Germans, together with Ukrainian bands, murdered all the Jews in the Slonim ghetto. Dr. Kaplinski fled from Slonim in July 1942; he wanted to steal through Ruzhnoy at night to Volkovysk, and from there get to Bialystok. In Slonim they used to say - relates Dr. Kaplinski – that in Ruzhnoy and Volkovysk the Germans would not kill all the Jews, because these towns together with the entire Bialystok quarter were allocated to the German Reich, while Slonim and Baronovitch belonged to the Russian sector, to White Russia.

Dr. Kaplinski and several other Jews from Slonim smuggled themselves into Ruzhnoy with the help of Gentile guides. They were sheltered for two days by Ruzhnoyer Jews, then wandered further toward Volkovysk. Dr. Kaplinski tells that during the two days in Ruzhnoy they felt as if they were in paradise, having seen with their own eyes what happened in Slonim. They knew what was taking place in other towns, and, therefore, they were very uneasy about the calm of the people in Ruzhnoy. They were treated well in the town, given food and drink. The Judenrat [Jewish Council] provided them with false papers as Bialystokers, all done gratis in order to help. With those papers they departed for Volkovysk free as birds.

Several months later, Dr. Kaplinski met up with the Ruzhnoyers once again. This time he saw them broken, suffering, starving, in the Volkovysk barracks.

We will now briefly include what the individual witnesses narrated at a memorial gathering of Ruzhnoyer that took place in Tel-Aviv.

Chana Kirshtein's story:

## The First Victims

"Ten days have passed that we have been under the occupation. The Jews go about under great tension, but they are quiet. Everyone occupies himself with his usual work. They carefully observe all the injunctions. Jews are not allowed to walk on the sidewalk but must walk in the middle of the street; you must take your hat off to every German; after sunset a Jew is not allowed out of doors. Everyone is behind closed doors; they sit in the dark or behind thickly covered windows.

One evening, when the Jews were hurrying home, the Germans suddenly started pulling men from the streets and houses and took them to the synagogue courtyard. After a short time they brought in nearly 1,000 men. The place was surrounded by armed Germans, all standing facing the synagogue and behind them were soldiers with machine guns. The Germans then chose 15 men, mostly intellectuals, put them into trucks and took them off in an unknown direction. Later on it was learned that they had all been shot.

Among the first victims were Jacob Kaplan, David Noah Sokolovski, Julian Kirshtein." Chana Kirshtein does not remember who the others were.

## Pressure in the Ghetto

"The Nazi noose became tighter and tighter around the neck. The restrictions became worse and worse. The Jews were forced to wear the yellow symbol of shame [yellow star]. The Judenrat had to supply more and more workers for forced labor. At every step the Jews were insulted and beaten. New arrests took place and the Germans demanded ransom to free the prisoners. The Jews gathered their money together and gave up their wedding rings. But the Germans never kept their promise. They took the gold and those arrested never came back.

"The ghetto that the Germans allotted to the Jews was so small that two or three families occupied one small room. The Germans and local Gentiles stole the Jews' belongings. Seldom did a Gentile show compassion; most of them helped the Germans in their horrible deeds. There were Gentiles who smuggled food into the ghetto, but they did it only for money. Every piece of bread had to be paid for with something of value.

The Germans took pains to create discord among the Jews. They would bait one against another, force one to inform against another. From day to day, the Jews were pressured and humiliated more and more, and became more exhausted and starved. They were helpless and defeated, not knowing where help would come from."

## Their Last Days

"The night of the first to the second of November 1942, the Jews in the shtetl did not sleep. All night long they heard the clatter of the motorcycles, the noise of movement, yells from the German soldiers and Polish policemen – there was a feeling that something was about to happen.

At dawn the emissaries from the Judenrat came and gave notice that all Jews, from children to adults, must gather on the meadow near the bath. Each one was allowed to take along a small bag of belongings, and the things of value that they owned, as they would not be returning to Ruzhnoy.

All the men with their wives and children would ostensibly be taken to a work camp. The order stated that if one member of a family was missing, the entire family would be shot.

"In the morning it appeared as if everyone was going to a funeral. From every corner Jews were on their way to the place of assembly. Men carried bundles, women held children's hands. Some cried silently, others lamented aloud. Many walked slowly with bowed heads, with empty hands and with a deathlike detachment.

At the assembly place the Germans were waiting, armed with automatic guns and vicious dogs. The adults were lined up in rows; the small children were thrown into wagons belonging to the Gentiles. The checking, the counting and the lining up of the people were accompanied by blows from the heavy blackjacks, barking of dogs and shooting. A mother, who tried to go to her child, who was in a wagon, was shot on the spot.

"The living funeral went on its way. The armed Germans were mounted on horses, and they constantly hurried the Jews on foot to go faster. Those who stopped were beaten murderously, and if one fell and was not able to go on he was shot right then and there. The road - a sandy, difficult road - led to Volkovysk. The day was also blazing hot; seldom was it so hot in November. Exhausted and thirsty, they went forth with their last bit of strength. The Germans behaved like wild animals. They shot for every little thing. The entire route was sown with dead bodies. Very many were shot near water wells. The Germans shot anyone running to get a drink. The languishing children did not think about this and dozens of them met their deaths licking water from the puddles.

"On the third of November the half-conscious Ruzhnoyer arrived in Volkovysk. The mothers looked around and saw that the children were missing. Every family was only now able to realize which of their members were missing. In Volkovysk the people from Ruzhnoy were packed like cattle into dark, earthen barracks, that appeared worse than pigsties, and here they had to wait to be sent to a 'work camp'..."

In the Volkovysk memorial book, which was published in New York by Dr. Einhorn, there is this description of the last days of the Ruzhnoyer in the Volkovysk barracks:

"The Ruzhnoyer Jews occupied the bunkers opposite the Volkovyskers. They took up a block of eight small bunkers. Their quarters were far worse than those of the Volkovysker Jews. The two thousand Ruzhnoyer Jews could not all fit into the bunkers at night, because there was not enough room for all of them on the planks, and many of them had to remain outside. If the death rate of the camp as a whole was high, it was even higher among the Ruzhnoyer Jews. Now, near the transports, they were the first to go to the fire.

"At the designated time, two o'clock at night, the Gestapo appeared in the camp and began to drive the Ruzhnoyer Jews out of their bunkers. Under a hail of blows and gunshots in the air, they were driven out together to one spot not far from the camp. There they were lined up in rows and were closely guarded.

When the required number was fulfilled, they were led to the freight cars that stood in the open field. They were forced into the cars and the train started to move in the direction of the center of Volkovysk. That day the temperature had dropped to twenty degrees and there was a terrible snowstorm. The cries and screams of the people truly split the heavens.

That was the first transport from the Volkovysk bunker.

"By morning the entire Ruzhnoyer block was emptied and the entrance to the camp was locked. Only on the third day did they assign around a hundred young men to 'clean up the block.' Among the bundles of rags and various other things, they discovered several dozen stiffened corpses of the sick and weak Jews who were unable to make the trip on the transport. The Germans had allowed them a slow death, and only when they had all died did the Germans order the block cleaned."

What goes on in the shtetl after the war no one knows. At the end of 1945, two Ruzhnoyer Jews, returning from Russia, visited the shtetl. The two people are: YANKEL SHAMSHANOVITCH (Yankel Vitzes) and NAFTALI KANTOROVITZ (Naftalke der Garber). The town was almost all burned down. Only the Gentile side streets were untouched. The single Jewish building left standing intact was the big Synagogue. The two visitors could not stay in the town very long; they felt as if they were in a graveyard. The Gentiles looked at them with suspicion mixed with fear, as if they were asking: What are these ghosts doing here?

In the town at that time there were actually two young men, the only ones who survived in the forest – SHMUEL BLISNOSKI, Arke Gomerman's son-in-law, and CHAIM DAVID SAVULSKI, Berl Shepes' son, from the new colony. Shmuel is the only one who remained in the town, and Chaim David later went to his sister in Russia.

Ruzhnoy no longer exists. The little Jewish shtetl of Ruzhnoy has been erased from the world. On the map of western White Russia there is a small black dot, marked with the word "Ruzhany," but that no longer has any connection with Ruzhnoy.

Ruzhany today is a small half-burned Gentile town. The Gentiles have lot of open space there. They can build new houses on the foundations and mounds of ash from the burned-down Jewish houses.

They are now actually moving from the "Pig Street" to the Castle Street. They carry heavy bags, they take along their possessions – the down pillows, the copper pots and the porcelain dishes, ladles, glass goblets, brass lamps, silver candlesticks and other such articles, that they now have in abundance.

The youth of Ruzhany, the young Gentile men and women, have never seen a Jew. The old people do not want to remember the Jews any more; they want to forget them forever.

They have already knocked down the long fence of the old Jewish Cemetery, they have spread out on all sides the gravestones dating back hundreds of years, they have chopped down the trees, plowed up all the graves…but there remains standing, in the middle of the town, a pale, orphaned building – the Jewish "Big Synagogue."

She stands, as a solitary, vindictive figure, waiting for God.

## In Memory of Our Martyrs

{212}

This town, in which a Jewish tradition had been woven for many centuries; where thousands of Hebrews lived a pleasant family life, a life of modesty and discreteness; where they faithfully occupied themselves with communal affairs, lived lives of dedication to the community and the individual; where tens of generations of Jewish people created a fine Jewish communal life — was wiped out and is no longer.

Who would have thought that this generation of pure Jews, pious people and doers of charitable deeds among them, good Jews who were involved with Torah and the way of the world, would be trampled by the heavy, impure foot of despicable people of the Nazi nation?

Who would have thought that the pioneering youth who were prevented from aliya only by the locked gates of the Land, the vibrant and lively youth, young and pleasant, believing in the rebirth of the nation and awaiting the possibility of fulfilling the aspirations pulsating in their hearts, would be wiped out as if they never existed?

Who would have imagined that the breath of the young religious school children, which rose through the air of our town since time immemorial, would be silenced, and the Torah teachers of those children would disappear from under G-d's skies?

Who would have imagined that the babies, who had just begun to see the light of the world, would be murdered in such a cruel manner by the impure people; and that their world would darken even before they could comprehend the low level to which the Nazi murderers had fallen?

Who could have thought that the approximately 4,000 Jews of the town — men, women, and children, people of upright paths and spiritual value — would go up in smoke in the ovens of Treblinka and be turned to ashes.

Nobody from our town had ever seen such melancholy atrocities, that no mortal could have conceived of from the outset. To this day, it is hard for me to believe that such things took place in the annals of the world.

Flourishing and vibrant, completely and lovingly dedicated to the care of its cultural, educational and social-communal institutions, with the sounds of Torah emanating from the windows of its Talmud

Torah, Beis Midrashes and schools — I still see the town in the eyes of my spirit.

The bitter reality is that the town no longer exists, its residents have turned to ashes and are no more, and that only a few remnants remain — those of its residents who left the town before the advent of the Nazi Holocaust.

These residents had seen the light of the day in the town, grew up there, and attained their Jewish and human consciousness there. They left, and brought its good name afar. Many of them succeeded in arriving at the safe shores of their homeland, where they are continuing to weave the tapestry of Jewish Ruzhany in their historic homeland, interlocked with the new spirit of our land.

The rest of its thousands of residents who lived in the town until the outbreak of the Second World War, are no longer. Physical and spiritual torture, and a cruel death was their lot.

However, it was as if the spirits of the souls of the martyrs of Ruzhany as well as the martyrs of the rest of the communities of the Diaspora of Poland and other Diaspora countries were standing with us during the War of Independence. They are giving us, the survivors of the Diaspora and the natives of the land, strength and power to stand up with splendor, might and glory in the spirit that pulsates within us, the few against the many, leading to the independence of Israel, and "Giving the glory instead of ashes" [1], as is stated in the words of the prophet Isaiah (chapter 61, verse 3).

The Editor

{228}

## List of Ruzhany Natives Living in Israel

| | |
|---|---|
| Abolitz (Pines) Malka; Aryeh, his wife Shulamit (Mahala); Chana | Tel Aviv |
| Avner (Rizkin) her husband Moshe; Tziona, Oded | Haifa |
| Abramowich Yosef, his wife Tova; Alexander, his wife Ayala; Nili | Tel Aviv |
| Egolnik Yosef, his wife Ahuva; Michael, Moshe Gila | Tel Aviv |
| Oren (Chwojnik) Aryeh-Leib, his wife Roza (Pines); Matityahu, his wife Rachel (Szliowsky); Eitan; Eliezer, his wife Ruth (Zagagi); Ran | Tel Aviv |
| Oren (Chwojnik) Yosef, his wife Yehudit; 2 daughters | Tel Aviv |
| Oren (Chwojnik) Yosef, Menachem, his wife Esther; Yona, his wife Miriam (Lipnik) | Tel Aviv |
| Achituv (Levinov) Batya; Chaya, Yael | Ramat Gan |
| Ivan Dov; his wife Liba | Tel Aviv |
| Izakson (Chwojnik) Chana, her husband Shmuel-Nechemia; Sara, her husband Gidon Yafet; Tzipora | Ramat Gan |
| Ines (Rubinowich) Elka, her husband Yerucham; Ofra, David | Givataim |
| Einstein Yitzchak, his wife Sara (Izkovich); Yoel, Rachel | Tel Aviv |
| Itzkowich Dvora, her husband Mordechai Gutman; Rivka, Chaim, Yifat | |
| Itzkowich Yaakov, his wife Gita (Kaplan); Pnina, her husband Yisrael Gelfand; Yuval, Atalia, Shaul | Haifa |
| Itzkowich Meir, his wife Tzvia; Amnon | Tel Aviv |
| Aloni Yocheved (Lebenbok), her husband Moshe; Ezra, Pinchas, Pnina | Givataim |
| Alfer (Kaplinsky) Sheina; Malka, Bilha, Dova, Rachel | Tel Aviv |
| Alperstein Dina (Dinerman); Aviva, Ruchama, Yosef | Tel Aviv |
| Anoch (Mirkin) Blyuma; Chana, her husband Moshe Rappaport; a son and daughter; Ruth | Ramat Gan |
| Epstein Tzvi, his wife Ahuva (Tzemach) Yafa, Moshe | Tel Aviv |
| Epstein Tzipora (Leb), her husband Tzvi; Yehuda, Galila | Tel Aviv |
| Epstein Sara-Chana | Tel Aviv |
| Artzi (Ditkovsky) Fruma, her husband Mordechai; Chaim, Galila | Holon |
| Arkin (Ruchmas) Miriam, her husband Zalman; Ami, Achiezer | Ekron |
| Erlich (Epstein) Leah; Miriam | Ramat Gan |
| | |

| | |
|---|---|
| Babitz Menachem, his wife Chaya | Haifa |
| Babitz Moshe, his wife Chaya | Haifa |
| Babitz Pnina | Tel Aviv |
| Bulgatz Tzvi, Lehavot, Chaviva | |
| Bornstein Smadar (Sara Chwojnik) her husband Eliezer; Vered | Tel Aviv |
| Bursi Chana (Pinman); Miriam Rutman; 2 children; Binyamin | Tel Aviv |
| Bursi (Garber) Shimon, his wife Rachel; Yitzchak, Shmuel | Tel Aviv |
| Blumberg Abba, his wife Charna; Yosef, his wife Sara; Yehudit, Shulamit<br>Sara Taziani; Betzalel, Yehudit | Tel Aviv |
| Brauda Yona, her husband Nachum; 2 children | Tel Aviv |
| Brona Leah | Afula |
| Brauda Sonia | Tel Aviv |
| Bashin Nathan, his wife Naomi; Sara, Nechama | Jerusalem |
| Breznitzky Hadassah | Ramat Gan |
| Breznitzky Aryeh, his wife Sara; Nina, Leora | Tel Aviv |
| Breznitzky Chaim, his wife Rivka; Ram, David | Ramat Gan |
| Bryn Gisian (Rudetsky), her husband Nachman; Tzvia, Shai, China | Afula |
| | |
| Gvurin David, his wife Shchora; Tzvi, Amiram | Ramat Gan |
| {229} | |
| Guber Mordechai and his wife | |
| Gur-Aryeh (Peres) Miriam, her husband Nachman | Kfar Haroeh |
| Gishura Avuva (Kamnimostky); Moshe, his wife Esther (Grabolski); Rafael, Dror | Rishon Letzion |
| Giladi (Klitzky) Rivka, her husband Yaakov; Dov | Haifa |
| Giladi (Bialobitzky) Sara | Haifa |
| Gamerman Efraim, his wife Yaffa (Ivan); Varda, Naomi | Tel Aviv |
| Gamerman Pinchas and his wife | Tel Aviv-Jaffa |
| Garber Blyuma | Tel Aviv |
| Gardovchik Reuven, his wife Fania; Tzvi, Leon | Hadera |
| Grynfeld Genia (Meirovich) | |
| | |
| Duvshani (Krupnik) Chava, her husband Yosef; Shlomi and his wife Hadassah; 2 daughters (Nitza); Geula Machtiger, her husband Reuven; Yael, | Kiryat Shalem |
| Dobkin Yosef; Shlomo; Karpel-Natan and his wife. 2 children | Raanana |

| | |
|---|---|
| Dobkin Sara (Sokolovsky), her husband Shmuel; Chaim, Miriam | Tel Aviv |
| Dlogolansky (Pomerantz) Esther, her husband Nathan; Carmela, Sara, Yaakov, Chaya | Petach Tivka |
| Hoffman (Ziskindovich) and her husband; Leah, Zehava, | Tel Aviv |
| Hornik (Shapira) Rivka and her husband | Ramat Gan |
| Heller (Pines) Malka, her husband Yisrael; Chana, her husband Yochanan Posner; Tzipora, Geula | Tel Aviv |
| Wolk Chana (Shpiler), her husband Meir; 2 children | |
| Weingarten Gisia (Roditzki), her husband Mordechai; Rachel | Jerusalem |
| Weinstein Yaakov, his wife Mina; Yitzchak | Petach Tikva |
| Wolodinsky Elihan | Ramat Gan |
| Witkin (Molchadsky) Malka | Jerusalem |
| Zilberberg (Pitkovsky) Rivka, her husband Yeshayahu; Asher, Shmaryahu, Yair | Tel Aviv |
| Zoltkovsky (Pitkovsky) Rivka, her husband Chaim | Givataim |
| Ziskind (Chwojnik) Dova; Ruth | Tel Aviv |
| Zlotner Moshe, his wife Ira; Bilha, Eliezer, Sheina-Liba | Haifa |
| Zmochovsky Chana; Shmuel, his wife Leah; Yona, Chemda, Ruth | Jerusalem |
| Zandman Rivka (Bashin); Yaakov, Chaya | Jerusalem |
| Zaklad (Levina) Sonia | Ramat Gan |
| Zakheim Naftali, his wife Rachel (Roditzky); Yehoshua, Dalia | Kfar Yechezkel |
| Zakheim Michael, his wife Tzipora;<br>a) Gilada Givata, his wife Tzvi; Naava, Eliezer<br>b) Yechiela Lev, her husband Elia; Ran, Edna | Haifa |
| Chwojnik Avraham, his wife Esther; Matityahu, Daniela. His sister Rachel | Tel Aviv |
| Chwojnik Baruch, his wife Tatiana; Naomi, her husband Naftali Gurwitz; Dror, Eitan | Tel Aviv |
| Chwojnik Zerach and his wife; Chaim, Avner, Shlomo | |
| Chwojnik Chaim-David, his wife Shulamit; Ami, Tzvia | Kfar Menachem |
| Chwojnik — the widow of Fishel (Petia); 2 children | |
| Chover (Chwojnik) Esther, her husband Yaakov; Gad, Chaviva, and Avi | Beit Guvrin |

| | |
|---|---|
| Chwojnik Rachel; Leah | Tel Aviv |
| Chasid (Ziskindovich) Chaya and her husband: Moshe, Bilha, Shulamit, Leah, Aryeh | Givataim |
| Chaikin Gershon and his wife; and daughter | Tel Aviv |
| | |
| Timinski Zerach, his brother Yaakov | Tel Aviv |
| Trabgoda (Epstein) Miriam, her husband Yosef; Dalia, Chaim-Dov | Tel Aviv |
| Turn Chaim, his wife Chava; Esther Bloshtik and her husband: Binyamin | Haifa |
| | |
| Jubiler (Pines) Shoshana | Tel Aviv |
| Joselovich (Shamshonowich) Sara, her husband Emmanuel; Miriam, Chava, Yair (Miriam is married to Tzchovoy; Nuni; Chava and her husband) | Ramat Gan |
| Cohan Shama (the granddaughter of Chaim Zalman Weinstein) | Kiryat Bialystock |
| Yaakovi (Pitkovsky) Rivka, her husband Shmuel; Shmuel Gilai | Haifa |
| Jakobson Yitzchak | Ramat Gan |
| Yatom Dr. Yaakov Shulamit, Shoshana | Mikve Yisrael |
| | |
| Kochavi (Shkolnik) Yona | |
| Kaspi (Shipiatzky) Bilha, her husband Yaakov; Chaya, Ami | Cheroot |
| {230} | |
| Lev Yosef, his wife Leah; Zahava, Tovia | Tel Aviv |
| Lebenbok Yitzchak | Tel Aviv |
| Lebenbok Noach | Tel Aviv |
| Lubinov (Krupnik) Freda, her husband Moshe; Sara Harchol, her husband Eliahu; Yiftach.<br>Chasia, her husband Ofir Meir; David, Chaim | Kfar Tabor |
| Levin Shmuel, his wife Miriam; Tzipora, Avraham | Lod |
| Lutker Raaya, her husband Asher Snapir; Oded, Nota | Beit Dagan |
| Leviatan Abba, his wife Sara-Rivka; Ahuva — the widow of Klinzweig; Elana, Zeev.<br>Yitzchak, his wife Rachel (Chwojnik); Naomi | Tel Aviv |
| Eliahu, his wife Rachel; Roni Gidon | Tel Aviv |
| Luria Yehuda, his wife Zelda, Aryeh, Dov | Tel Aviv |
| Levi (Shamshonowich) Dvora, her husband Isadore; Miriam | Tel Aviv |
| Lyuboshitzky Betzalel, his wife Gittel; Rafael, Galila; his mother Yehudit — the widow of Aharon | Haifa |

| | |
|---|---|
| Liskovsky (Lebovitz) Bilha, her husband Yehoshua; Tova Weinstock, her husband Nathan; Nuriel-Shalom | Tel Aviv |
| Lipovsky | Rechovot |
| Landsberg Eliahu and his wife; Bilha | Tel Aviv |
| Liskovsky Dov, his wife Yaffa (Janowitz); Zehava, Yehudit | Tel Aviv |
| Lerman Tzvihis grandchildren Chazon Nurit, Chanoch | Tel Aviv |
| | |
| Meirovich Shlomo | Tel Aviv |
| Magli (Mogilinski) Shmuel, his wife Sheina; Malka; Yisrael, his wife Emma (Shatz); Shachar, Yael, Uri | Tel Aviv |
| Molchodsky Mordechai | Kfar Saba |
| Moritz (Sokolovsky) Yehudit, her husband Moshe, Mordechai | Tel Aviv |
| Moskowich (Leviatan) Sonia, her husband Baruch; Amalia Strikovsky, her husband Tovia; Niva | Tel Aviv |
| Mirman Yehudit (Sokolovsky), her husband Yitzchak; Moshe, Rachel | Shefayim |
| Mirkin Meir | Jerusalem |
| Meller Yehudit, her husband Chaim; Shulamit, Amitzur, Miriam | Ekron |
| Meller Rivka, her husband Yosef; Tzipora, Noga, Esther | Bitzron |
| Mrochnik Nathan, his wife Rachel | Petach Tikva |
| | |
| Nir (Sobolsky) Esther, Haifa | |
| | |
| Soytitzky Moshe, his wife Ita (Babich); Simcha, his wife Miriam; Shoshana, Reuven; Berl, his wife Chana; Malka. Leah, her husband Berl Pashnitzky; Eliakim, Chaim | Haifa |
| Solominsky Chavaka | Rechovot |
| Solitarnik Chana; Rachel (Shereshevsky) | |
| Sokolovsky Avigdor, his wife Chaya; Pesha-Leah, her husband Yoel Solnik; Yoram; Chanoch, Reuven | Holon |
| Sokolovsky David, his wife Bilha; Revue, Pesia, Meir | Ramat Gan |
| Sokolovsky Yocheved; Yehuda, his wife Sonia; Mordechai, Reuven | Tel Aviv |
| Sokolovsky Meir, his wife Sonia (Michenobski); Elana, Ayala, Yehudit | Tel Aviv |
| Siduransky Yosefa; Todza, his wife Genia; Yehoshua, Lilia; Necha, her husband Herman Bankrot; Yehudia. Malka, her husband Yona; 2 girls | Kiryat Bialystock |
| Sirkis Yehudit (Garbolski), her husband Yosef; Aryeh, Bruria, | Petach |

| | |
|---|---|
| Zlata | Tikva |
| Senderovich Fruma (Gostovski), her husband Moshe; Sara | Holon |
| Snobski Rachel (Gerber) and her husband; Shmuel, Moshe Daniela | Tel Aviv |
| | |
| Polik Mordechai | Jerusalem |
| Foxman Yisrael, his wife Malka; Nechama, Shifra | Kiryat Chaim |
| Pitkovsky David, his wife Sara; Gidon, Amnon | Haifa |
| Pitkovsky Akiva, his wife Nina; Dov | Haifa |
| Finman Necha | Tel Aviv |
| Pines Dvora; Roza | Tel Aviv |
| Pines Dan, his wife Fania; Kupai, his wife Chana; a daughter; Ronit | Tel Aviv |
| Pines Sonia; Chaim-Shimon, his wife Chava; Eliahu-Akiva, Yehuda; Aryeh, his wife Yaffa; Avihu, Shai | Tel Aviv |
| Pekarsky (Egolnik) Chana, her husband Moshe: Rina | |
| {231} | |
| (continued) her husband Eliahu; Reider; Orna, Amos, Michal | Cheroot |
| Privolsky Basha (Mruchnik) her husband Yisrael; Yaakov, Yitzchak | Holon |
| Friedlander (Shereshevsky) Yehudit, her husband Ben Zion; Pazut; Tamar and her husband: Boaz.<br>Perlman (Klebensky) Hinda, her husband Aryeh; Eitan, Tziona | Haifa |
| | |
| Kwozcki (Sokolovsky) Malka, her husband Shlomo; Tova, her husband Shmuel Pines; Yaakov, Miriam | Tel Aviv |
| Kushnir Esther; David | |
| Kaplan Chana (Breznitzky), her husband Yeshayahu; Adi, Aliza, Ahuva | Tel Aviv |
| Kolcki Lili — widow of Yaakov; Nadia | Haifa |
| Kliniod Pesha (Abramowich), her husband Yosef; Menachem, Yair | Tel Aviv |
| Kleiner Hadassah (Rabinovich) | Nachalat Yitzchak |
| Krupnik David, his wife Rachel Inker; Chaya, her husband Yaakov Hoffman; Ditza, a boy.<br>Sarah; Tzipora, her husband Simcha Weiss; a daughter, Ahuva, Chasia, Tzvi | Zichron Yaakov |
| Karlin Sheina (Chaikin); 2 sons | Tel Aviv |

| | |
|---|---|
| Kaplinski Yitzchak, his wife Dvora; Tamar, Chuma | Tel Aviv |
| Karlinski Chaim; his wife Chava Pines; Leah | |
| Karpelovich Yosef, his wife Betty; Meir | Hadar-Yosef |
| | |
| Radzominsky (Padwa) | Ramat Gan |
| Rubinstein (Jozelovsky) Dvora | Ramat Gan |
| Rodler (Inker) Rashka | Tel Aviv |
| Roditzki Yitzchak | Afula |
| Ruzansky Avraham | Tel Aviv |
| Rotstein Yitzchak, his wife Lyuba; Miriam, Hinda, Moshe-Chaim | Beit Yehoshua |
| Rushkin Zeev, his wife Sarah; Edna, Tzvia, Rachel | Tel Aviv |
| Rushkin — widow of Yaakov; 2 children | Tel Aviv |
| Roznitzky Zalman, his wife Sonia; Yitzchak, Yaakov | Tel Aviv |
| Roznitzky Nachum | Chadera |
| Roznitzky Shimon | Haifa |
| Reiner (Ett) Chasia; Yisrael, Shmuel, Malachi | Raanana |
| Rechtshendler (Mazur) Chava, her husband Feivel; Leah | Haifa |
| Rafaeli (Pines) Freda; Nima, Ruth, Rafael | Tel Aviv |
| Rappaport Dvora (Garber) her husband Aryeh; Yoram, Yitzchak | Zichron Yaakov |
| | |
| Shadmi Shachna the son of Mosheke (Berman) | Kibbutz Ayalon |
| Shiva (Shemesh) Esther, her husband Dov; Gilad | Kibbutz Ayalon |
| Shamir (Jezranicky) Yitzchak, his wife Sara; Yair, Gilada | Tel Aviv |
| Shimshony Yaakov, his wife Chaya | Kaduri |
| Shimshony Meir, his wife Sarah Liberman; Miriam, her husband Yosef Ostov; Ron, Naava; Tzvi, and his wife | Ramat Gan |
| Shimshony Esther-Leah — the widow of Shimon (Beizer); Zeev, his wife Anita; Lili. | |
| Shimshony Elisha, his wife Leah; Arnon, Nachum | Tel Aviv |
| Shapira Elisheva (Shimshony), her husband Moshe, Yardena, Hella, Dorit | Jerusalem |
| Shipiancky Moshe | Ramat Gan |
| Stein Zlata (Broida); a daughter | Tel Aviv |
| Sherobsky (Ziskindovich), her husband Aharon; Tzvi | Moshav Nechalim |

{232}

## List of Liskova Natives Living in Israel

| | |
|---|---|
| Sarah Leah Shimshony (Liberman), 2 children | Ramat Gan |
| Zehava Liberman and her husband; 2 children | Rechovot |
| Yehudit Cohen (Liberman) and her husband; 2 children | Tel Aviv |
| Chemda Milberg (Liberman); 2 sons | Tel Aviv |
| Chana Liberman | Tel Aviv |
| Shimon Liberman | Tel Aviv |
| Runik Binyamin | Tel Aviv |
| Yona Rotstein (Reznik) | Tel Aviv |
| Chasia Eisenberg (Roznik) | Tel Aviv |
| Yekutiel Krebchok | Hadera |
| Yosef Krebchok | Tel Aviv |
| Zelig Krebchok | Bat Yam |
| Moshe Krebchok | Haifa |
| Rasha Sheintel (Krebchok) | Kiryat Chaim |
| Yosef Pomerantz | Holon |
| Yisrael Pomerantz | Holon |
| Yona Reznik | Tel Aviv |
| Yaakov Reznik | Tel Aviv |
| Dvora Reznik | Tel Aviv |
| Brina Reznik | Tel Aviv |
| Avraham Wolfowich | Tel Aviv |
| Chaya Krebchok | Hadera |
| Ezriel Broshi | Tel Aviv |
| Moshe Brestowitzky | Tel Aviv |
| Pesach Bendetowich | Holon |
| Yona Brochnesky | Kibbutz Lehavot Chaviva |
| Yehuda Muziricky | Holon |
| Pesia Bocher (Mazericky) | Holon |
| Yosef Mazericky | Tel Aviv |

| Yafa Bocher | Tel Aviv |
| Sonia Rozman (nee Guthelf) | Kiryat Chaim |

**TRANSLATOR'S FOOTNOTES**

1. The Hebrew words used here for 'glory' and 'ashes' consist of the same three letters, in different order.

# Martyrs of Ruzhany - List Expanded from Names in Original Book

| Key: | | | m=male<br>f=female | U=Unmarried<br>M=Married<br>W=Widow | |
|---|---|---|---|---|---|
| **Family name** | **First name(s)** | **Maiden name** | **Sex** | **Marital** | **Father's** |
| ABRAMOVICH | Chaim Issar | | m | U | Meir Hirsch |
| ABRAMOVICH | Meir Hirsch Sheitel | | m | M | |
| ABRAMOVICH | Chanah | | f | M | |
| ABRAMOVSKI | Dov | | m | M | |
| ABRAMOVSKI | Rachel | | f | M | |
| ADEF | Bashka | | f | M | |
| ADEF | Mashkah | | f | U | Yacov Asher |
| ADEF | Moshe | | m | U | Yacov Asher |
| ADEF | Yacov Asher | | m | M | |
| ALPER | Avraham Shlomo | | m | M | |
| ALPER | Razel Markah | | f | M | |
| ALPERSTEIN | David | | m | U | Yosef |
| ALPERSTEIN | Ethel | | f | M | |
| ALPERSTEIN | Hindah | | f | U | Yosef |
| ALPERSTEIN | Teivela | | f | U | Yosef |
| ALPERSTEIN | unknown | | f | W | |
| ALPERSTEIN | Yosef | | m | M | |
| ANISH | Aharon | | m | U | Moshe |
| ANISH | Devorah | | f | M | |
| ANISH | Gittel | | f | U | Yosef |
| ANISH | Heshel | | m | U | Moshe |
| ANISH | Leah | | f | U | Moshe |
| ANISH | Moshe | | m | M | Berel |
| ANISH | Mottel | | m | U | Yosef |
| ANISH | Rachel | | f | M | |
| ANISH | Sarah | | f | W | |
| ANISH | Yakutiel | | m | U | Moshe |
| ANISH | Yosef | | m | M | Berel |
| APELTERG | David | | m | U | |
| APELTERG | Rachel | LISSOBITSKY | f | M | Neta |
| APELTERG | unknown | | m | M | |
| BABICH | Avraham | | m | U | Avraham |
| BABICH | Avraham Lieb | | m | M | |
| BABICH | Chaim | | m | U | |
| BABICH | Chanah Sarah | | f | M | |
| BABICH | Eliezer | | m | U | |
| BABICH | Esther | | f | W | |
| BABICH | Feigel | | f | U | |
| BABICH | Feigel | | f | U | Avraham |
| BABICH | Herschel | | m | U | |

# Martyrs of Ruzhany - List Expanded from Names in Original Book

| Key: | | | m=male<br>f=female | U=Unmarried<br>M=Married<br>W=Widow | |
|---|---|---|---|---|---|
| **Family name** | **First name(s)** | **Maiden name** | **Sex** | **Marital** | **Father's** |
| BABICH | Liba | | f | M | |
| BABICH | Menachem | | m | U | Avraham |
| BABICH | Miriam | | f | U | |
| BABICH | Moshekeh | | m | M | |
| BABICH | Polia | | m | M | Leib |
| BABICH | Reishel | | f | M | |
| BABICH | unknown | | f | M | |
| BABICH | unknown | | f | M | |
| BABICH | unknown | | f | W | |
| BABICH | Velvel | | m | M | |
| BABICH | Yosef | | m | M | Shmuel Yehudaleh |
| BABICH | Zvi | | m | U | Avraham |
| BABITZ | Sarah | RUHZNITSKY | f | M | |
| BABITZ | Yitzchak | | m | M | |
| BARON | Alta | | f | M | |
| BARON | Biliah | | f | M | |
| BARON | Leah | | f | U | Yitzchak |
| BARON | Mara | | f | U | Mordechai |
| BARON | Mordechai | | m | M | |
| BARON | Yacov | | m | U | Mordechai |
| BARON | Yenta | | f | U | Mordechai |
| BARON | Yitzchak | | m | M | |
| BASHIN | Sprinza | | f | W | |
| BASKIN | Avraham | | m | M | |
| BASKIN | Hasha | | f | M | |
| BASS | Shlomo | | m | U | Chaim |
| BASS | unknown | GISHELVICH | f | W | |
| BAUM | Matlia | | f | M | |
| BAUM | Shimshon | | m | M | |
| BAYR | Bliume | | f | W | |
| BAYR | Elka | | f | U | Abba |
| BAYR | Moshe | | m | M | Abba |
| BAYR | Mottel | | m | M | Abba |
| BAYR | Mottel | | m | U | Abba |
| BAYR | Shmuel | | m | M | |
| BAYR | unknown | | f | M | |
| BAYR | unknown | | f | M | |
| BAYR | unknown | | m | M | Abba |
| BAYR | unknown | | f | M | |
| BAYR | unknown | | f | M | |

# Martyrs of Ruzhany - List Expanded from Names in Original Book

| Key: | | | m=male<br>f=female | U=Unmarried<br>M=Married<br>W=Widow | |
|---|---|---|---|---|---|
| **Family name** | **First name(s)** | **Maiden name** | **Sex** | **Marital** | **Father's** |
| BAYR | unknown | | m | M | Shmuel |
| BAYR | unknown | | f | M | |
| BAYR | unknown | | f | U | Abba |
| BAYR | Yehudit | | f | U | Shmuel |
| BECKEROWICH | Moshe | | m | U | Eliezer |
| BECKEROWICH | Rachel | MARUCHNIK | f | W | Yechezkel |
| BECKEROWICH | Raphael | | m | U | Eliezer |
| BECKEROWICH | Yosef | | m | U | Eliezer |
| BELKIN | Henya | | f | | |
| BERET | Benyamin | | m | M | |
| BERET | Henya | SHERESHEVSKY | f | M | Ze'ev |
| BERET | Ida | | f | U | Benyamin |
| BERKOWICH | Eliahu | | m | U | |
| BERKOWICH | Roza | | f | U | |
| BERKOWICH | Shyndel | | f | U | |
| BERKOWICH | Sonyia | | f | W | |
| BERKOWICH | Yitzchak | | m | U | |
| BERMAN | Benyamin | | m | M | |
| BERMAN | David | | m | M | |
| BERMAN | Mordechai | | m | M | |
| BERMAN | Moshe | | m | M | |
| BERMAN | Naomi | | f | U | Benyamin |
| BERMAN | Rashka | | f | M | |
| BERMAN | Razel | | f | W | |
| BERMAN | unknown | | f | M | |
| BERMAN | unknown | | f | M | |
| BERMAN | unknown | | f | M | |
| BERMAN | unknown | | f | M | |
| BERMAN | Yehoshua | | m | M | David |
| BIALOS | Dovidel | | m | U | |
| BIALOS | Feigel | | f | U | |
| BIALOS | Leibka | | f | M | |
| BIALOS | Yisroel | | m | M | |
| BIALOS | Yitzchak | | m | U | |
| BIALOVICKI | Chaim | | m | M | |
| BIALOVICKI | Chanah | | f | U | Yisroel |
| BIALOVICKI | Hasakah | | f | U | Yisroel |
| BIALOVICKI | Hirsch | | m | M | Yisroel |
| BIALOVICKI | Mendel | | f | | |
| BIALOVICKI | Sheinah Gittel | EPSHTEYN | f | M | Alter |
| BIALOVICKI | Sheine Gittel | | f | M | |

# Martyrs of Ruzhany - List Expanded from Names in Original Book

| Key: | | | m=male<br>f=female | U=Unmarried<br>M=Married<br>W=Widow | |
|---|---|---|---|---|---|
| Family name | First name(s) | Maiden name | Sex | Marital | Father's |
| BIALOVICKI | Shifra | | f | M | |
| BIALOVICKI | Tema | | f | M | |
| BIALOVICKI | Yisroel | | m | M | |
| BLUGATCH | Avraham | | m | M | |
| BLUGATCH | Benyamin | | m | M | |
| BLUGATCH | Chaim | | m | M | Benyamin |
| BLUGATCH | Charne | | f | M | |
| BLUGATCH | Eliezer | | m | U | Benyamin |
| BLUGATCH | Esther | | f | W | |
| BLUGATCH | Itcha | | m | U | Moshe |
| BLUGATCH | Leibel | | m | M | |
| BLUGATCH | Leibka | | f | U | Moshe |
| BLUGATCH | Moshe | | m | M | |
| BLUGATCH | Moshekeh | | m | U | |
| BLUGATCH | Reiza | | f | M | |
| BLUGATCH | Rivkah | | f | U | |
| BLUGATCH | Sheine | | f | U | Yitzchak |
| BLUGATCH | Sheine Raska | | f | M | |
| BLUGATCH | unknown | | f | M | |
| BLUGATCH | unknown | | f | M | |
| BLUGATCH | unknown | | f | M | |
| BLUGATCH | unknown | | f | M | |
| BLUGATCH | unknown | | m | U | Moshe |
| BLUGATCH | Yitzchak | | m | M | |
| BLUGATCH | Yitzchak | | m | M | |
| BLUGATCH | Zlota | | f | U | Yitzchak |
| BRAZOVSKY | Chaim | | m | M | |
| BRAZOVSKY | Itcha Yosha | | m | M | Raphael |
| BRAZOVSKY | Pesha | BRESTOWICKI | f | M | |
| BRAZOVSKY | Raphael | | m | M | |
| BRAZOVSKY | Tiva | | f | M | |
| BRAZOVSKY | Yocha | | f | M | |
| BRECKNER | unknown | BAUM | f | M | |
| BRECKNER | Zidel | | m | M | |
| BRESCHNESKY | Bashkah | | f | M | |
| BRESCHNESKY | Issar | | m | M | |
| BRESLIN | Peshka | | f | U | |
| BRESLIN | Razel | | f | W | |
| BRESLIN | Shimshon | | m | U | |
| BRESTOWICKI | Barouch | | m | M | |
| BRESTOWICKI | Berel | | m | M | |

# Martyrs of Ruzhany - List Expanded from Names in Original Book

| Key: | | | m=male<br>f=female | U=Unmarried<br>M=Married<br>W=Widow | |
|---|---|---|---|---|---|
| **Family name** | **First name(s)** | **Maiden name** | **Sex** | **Marital** | **Father's** |
| BRESTOWICKI | Ovadiah | | m | M | |
| BRESTOWICKI | Peshka | | f | M | |
| BRESTOWICKI | Rivkah | SCOLNIK | f | M | |
| BRESTOWICKI | Tiva | | f | W | |
| BRESTOWICKI | unknown | | m | M | |
| BRESTOWICKI | unknown | | f | M | |
| BRESTOWICKI | unknown | | f | M | |
| BRESTOWICKI | unknown | | f | M | |
| BRESTOWICKI | Velvel | | m | U | |
| BRESTOWICKI | Yisroel | | m | M | |
| BROUDA | David | | m | M | |
| BROUDA | Noach | | m | M | |
| BROUDA | Rachel | | f | W | |
| BROUDA | Teivel | | f | M | |
| BROUDA | unknown | | f | M | |
| BRURMAN | Peshka | WILENSKY | f | W | Moshe Reuven |
| BULGATZ | David Noach | | m | M | |
| BULGATZ | Shifra | KFITS | f | M | Schana |
| BUROVSKY | Baracha | | f | M | |
| BUROVSKY | Moshe | | m | M | |
| BURSTYN | Shabtayel | | m | M | |
| BURSTYN | Sonyia | ROTHSTYN | f | M | Chaim Zerach |
| BURSTYN | unknown | | f | U | Shabtayel |
| BURSTYN | Yacov | | m | U | Shabtayel |
| CHARDAK | Esther | | f | M | |
| CHARDAK | unknown | | m | M | |
| CHAZAN | Banish | | m | U | Heshel |
| CHAZAN | Eliezer | | m | U | Heshel |
| CHAZAN | Feigel | | f | U | Heshel |
| CHAZAN | Heshel | | m | M | |
| CHAZAN | Pitcha | | f | M | |
| CHAZAN | Zvi | | m | U | Heshel |
| CHEIKEN | Avraham | | m | M | |
| CHEIKEN | Myrl | | f | M | |
| CHERNIKHOV | Akivah | | m | M | |
| CHERNIKHOV | Avraham | | m | U | |
| CHERNIKHOV | Avraham Yitzchak | | m | U | Akiva |
| CHERNIKHOV | Esther | | f | U | |
| CHERNIKHOV | Henya | | f | U | Akiva |
| CHERNIKHOV | Hindah | | f | U | |
| CHERNIKHOV | Rachel | | f | U | |

# Martyrs of Ruzhany - List Expanded from Names in Original Book

| Key: | | | m=male<br>f=female | U=Unmarried<br>M=Married<br>W=Widow | |
|---|---|---|---|---|---|
| **Family name** | **First name(s)** | **Maiden name** | **Sex** | **Marital** | **Father's** |
| CHERNIKHOV | Reishel | | f | M | |
| CHERNIKHOV | Sarah | | f | M | |
| CHERNIKHOV | unknown | | m | U | Akiva |
| CHERNIKHOV | unknown | | m | U | Akiva |
| CHERNIKHOV | Yeshiahu | | m | U | |
| CHERNIKHOV | Zvia | | f | U | |
| CHOMSKY | Chava | | f | M | |
| CHOMSKY | Shmuel | | m | M | |
| CHROITISKI | Chanah | | f | M | |
| CHROITISKI | Heinke | | f | U | Mordechai Yehudaleh |
| CHROITISKI | Mordechai Yehudaleh | | m | M | |
| CHROITISKI | Shlomokeh | | m | U | Mordechai Yehudaleh |
| CHWOJNIK | Abba | | m | M | |
| CHWOJNIK | Aviva | | f | U | Yitzchak |
| CHWOJNIK | Chaim David | | m | U | |
| CHWOJNIK | Chayacha | | f | M | |
| CHWOJNIK | Fishel | | m | U | Yitzchak |
| CHWOJNIK | Fishel | | m | U | |
| CHWOJNIK | Mottel | | m | U | Yitzchak |
| CHWOJNIK | Peshka | | f | M | |
| CHWOJNIK | Roza | | f | M | |
| CHWOJNIK | unknown | | m | U | Yitzchak |
| CHWOJNIK | Yitzchak | | m | M | |
| DAVIDSON | Sarah | | f | W | |
| DERCHINSKY | Aharon | | m | M | |
| DERCHINSKY | unknown | | f | M | |
| DERCHINSKY | unknown | | f | W | |
| DITKOVSKY | Chaim | | m | M | Zvi |
| DITKOVSKY | Chaya | | f | M | |
| DITKOVSKY | Freida | | f | M | |
| DITKOVSKY | Moshe | | m | U | Chaim |
| DITKOVSKY | Peretz | | m | U | Yehudah |
| DITKOVSKY | Rachel | | f | U | Chaim |
| DITKOVSKY | Reuven | | m | U | Yehudah |
| DITKOVSKY | Yehuda | | m | M | Zvi |
| DITKOVSKY | Zvi | | m | W | |
| DUBINSKY | Berel | | m | M | |
| DUBINSKY | unknown | | f | M | |
| DUBRIN | Chaim | | m | U | Shmuel |
| DUBRIN | Miriam | | f | U | Shmuel |

# Martyrs of Ruzhany - List Expanded from Names in Original Book

| Key: | | | m=male<br>f=female | U=Unmarried<br>M=Married<br>W=Widow | |
|---|---|---|---|---|---|
| **Family name** | **First name(s)** | **Maiden name** | **Sex** | **Marital** | **Father's** |
| DUBRIN | Shmuel | | m | M | |
| DUBRIN | unknown | | f | M | |
| DUBROVSKY | Chaya | | f | M | |
| DUBROVSKY | Elka | | f | U | Neche |
| DUBROVSKY | Libka | | f | | Neche |
| DUBROVSKY | Neche | | m | M | |
| DUBROVSKY | Schwarzel | | m | | Neche |
| DUMOVSKY | Chaya | ABRAMOVICH | f | M | Meir Hirsch |
| DUMOVSKY | Leib | | m | M | |
| DUMOVSKY | Shlomo | | m | M | |
| DUMOVSKY | unknown | | f | M | |
| DUMOVSKY | Yisroel | | m | U | Leib |
| EBB | Chaim | | m | M | |
| EBB | Freida | | f | M | |
| EDELSTEIN | Aharon Hilel | | m | M | Yosef |
| EDELSTEIN | Asher | | m | M | Yosef |
| EDELSTEIN | Chaya | | f | M | |
| EDELSTEIN | Feigel | | f | M | |
| EDELSTEIN | Golda | | f | M | |
| EDELSTEIN | Hinkah | SHIPITZSKI | f | M | |
| EDELSTEIN | Mordechai | | m | M | Yosef |
| EDELSTEIN | Mordechai | | m | M | |
| EDELSTEIN | Moshe | | m | M | Yosef |
| EDELSTEIN | Sarah | | f | M | |
| EDELSTEIN | Sarah | | f | M | |
| EDELSTEIN | Yosef | | m | M | |
| EGOLNIK | David Noach | | m | M | |
| EGOLNIK | Esther Riva | | f | W | |
| EGOLNIK | Freida Yenta | | f | W | |
| EGOLNIK | Moshe | | m | U | Michael |
| EGOLNIK | Rachel | | f | U | Michael |
| EGOLNIK | Roza | | f | U | Michael |
| EGOLNIK | Zipah | | f | M | |
| EGOLNIK | Zipkah | SLONIMCHIK | f | | |
| EINSTEIN | Brynne | | f | U | Yoel |
| EINSTEIN | Chaim | | m | U | Yoel |
| EINSTEIN | Chasia | | f | U | Yoel |
| EINSTEIN | Chaya | | f | M | |
| EINSTEIN | Itcha Meir | | m | M | Yoel |
| EINSTEIN | Rachel | | f | M | |
| EINSTEIN | Shimon | | m | M | Yoel |

# Martyrs of Ruzhany - List Expanded from Names in Original Book

| Key: | | | m=male<br>f=female | U=Unmarried<br>M=Married<br>W=Widow | |
|---|---|---|---|---|---|
| Family name | First name(s) | Maiden name | Sex | Marital | Father's |
| EINSTEIN | unknown | | f | M | |
| EINSTEIN | Yehoshua | | m | M | |
| EINSTEIN | Yoel | | m | M | Yehoshua |
| EISENSTEIN | Brynne | | f | U | Chaim Wolf |
| EISENSTEIN | Chaim Wolf | | m | M | |
| EISENSTEIN | Moshe | | m | M | Chaim Wolf |
| EISENSTEIN | Pesalah | | f | M | |
| EISENSTEIN | Sheinah | | f | U | Chaim Wolf |
| EISENSTEIN | unknown | | f | M | |
| EISENSTEIN | Yacov | | m | U | Chaim Wolf |
| ELBERG | Miriam | | f | U | Shmuel |
| ELBERG | Moshe | | m | U | Shmuel |
| ELBERG | Rachel | SAMSONOWICH | f | M | |
| ELBERG | Shabtay | | m | U | Shmuel |
| ELBERG | Shmuel | | m | M | |
| ELBERG | Yitzchak | | m | U | Shmuel |
| EPSHTEYN | Alter | | m | M | |
| EPSHTEYN | Alter | | m | M | |
| EPSHTEYN | Alter | | m | M | Moshe Aharon |
| EPSHTEYN | Alter | | m | M | |
| EPSHTEYN | Arim | | m | M | |
| EPSHTEYN | Avraham | | m | U | Chaim Berel |
| EPSHTEYN | Barouch | | m | M | |
| EPSHTEYN | Benyamin | | m | M | |
| EPSHTEYN | Biliah Myrel | | f | M | |
| EPSHTEYN | Buba | ORLINSKY | f | M | Hazkal |
| EPSHTEYN | Chaim | | m | M | |
| EPSHTEYN | Chaim | | m | U | |
| EPSHTEYN | Chaim | | m | M | Yacov Reuven |
| EPSHTEYN | Chaim Berel | | m | M | |
| EPSHTEYN | Chanah | | f | W | |
| EPSHTEYN | Chanah | | f | U | Yedidiah |
| EPSHTEYN | Charne | | f | U | Alter |
| EPSHTEYN | Chava | | f | M | |
| EPSHTEYN | Chavaleh | | f | U | |
| EPSHTEYN | Chaya | | f | M | |
| EPSHTEYN | Chaya | | f | M | |
| EPSHTEYN | Chaya Peskeh | ALPERSTYN | f | M | |
| EPSHTEYN | Dyna | | f | M | |
| EPSHTEYN | Eliezer | | m | U | Yedidiah |
| EPSHTEYN | Esther | | f | M | |

# Martyrs of Ruzhany - List Expanded from Names in Original Book

| Key: | | | m=male<br>f=female | U=Unmarried<br>M=Married<br>W=Widow | |
|---|---|---|---|---|---|
| **Family name** | **First name(s)** | **Maiden name** | **Sex** | **Marital** | **Father's** |
| EPSHTEYN | Ethel | | f | M | |
| EPSHTEYN | Fruma | EDELSTEIN | f | M | Mordechai |
| EPSHTEYN | Gadaliah | | m | M | Barouch |
| EPSHTEYN | Gadaliah | | m | U | Chaim Berel |
| EPSHTEYN | Hazkal | | m | M | Yacov Reuven |
| EPSHTEYN | Henyala | | f | U | Chaim Berel |
| EPSHTEYN | Leah | | f | M | |
| EPSHTEYN | Leah | | f | U | Mordechai Yacov |
| EPSHTEYN | Leibchik | | m | | Mordechai Yacov |
| EPSHTEYN | Leibel | | m | U | Barouch |
| EPSHTEYN | Lifcze | | f | U | Yedidiah |
| EPSHTEYN | Meir | | m | M | Mordechai Yacov |
| EPSHTEYN | Meir Zundel | | m | U | Barouch |
| EPSHTEYN | Michalia | | f | M | |
| EPSHTEYN | Mondja | | f | M | |
| EPSHTEYN | Mordechai Yacov | | m | M | |
| EPSHTEYN | Moshekeh | | m | M | Simcha Yosef |
| EPSHTEYN | Myrl | | f | M | |
| EPSHTEYN | Naomi | | f | U | Yom-tov |
| EPSHTEYN | Nechama | | f | M | |
| EPSHTEYN | Perlah | | f | U | |
| EPSHTEYN | Pesach | | m | U | Yedidiah |
| EPSHTEYN | Rachel | | f | U | Yedidiah |
| EPSHTEYN | Reuven | | m | M | |
| EPSHTEYN | Rivkah | | f | M | |
| EPSHTEYN | Roza | | f | U | Alter |
| EPSHTEYN | Sarah | | f | U | |
| EPSHTEYN | Sarah Bilia | | f | M | |
| EPSHTEYN | Sarkah | | f | W | |
| EPSHTEYN | Shmuel | | m | U | Alter |
| EPSHTEYN | Sonyia | | f | U | Yedidiah |
| EPSHTEYN | Sonyia | | f | M | |
| EPSHTEYN | unknown | | | | Yedidiah |
| EPSHTEYN | unknown | | | | Yedidiah |
| EPSHTEYN | unknown | | f | M | |
| EPSHTEYN | unknown | | f | M | |
| EPSHTEYN | unknown | | f | M | |
| EPSHTEYN | Yacov Asher | | m | M | |
| EPSHTEYN | Yacov Reuven | | m | M | |
| EPSHTEYN | Yedidyah | | m | M | |
| EPSHTEYN | Yehudit | | f | U | Yedidiah |

# Martyrs of Ruzhany - List Expanded from Names in Original Book

| Key: | | | m=male | U=Unmarried | |
|---|---|---|---|---|---|
| | | | f=female | M=Married | |
| | | | | W=Widow | |
| Family name | First name(s) | Maiden name | Sex | Marital | Father's |
| EPSHTEYN | Yitzchak | | m | M | |
| EPSHTEYN | Yoel | | m | M | Yacov Reuven |
| EPSHTEYN | Yom-Tov | | m | M | Yacov Asher |
| EPSHTEYN | Yosef | | m | U | Yedidiah |
| EPSHTEYN | Zila | | f | M | |
| EPSHTEYN | Zissel | | m | U | Arim |
| EPSHTEYN | Zusha | | m | | Alter |
| ETT | Devorah | | f | M | |
| ETT | Dov | | m | U | Shmuel Lezer |
| ETT | Malkah | | f | W | |
| ETT | Michael | | m | M | |
| ETT | Moshe Berel | | m | M | |
| ETT | Rachel Leah | | f | M | |
| ETT | unknown | | f | M | |
| ETT | Velvel | | m | M | Moshe Berel |
| ETT | Yafa | | f | U | Shmuel Lezer |
| FARBER | Hirsch | | m | M | Moshe |
| FARBER | Moshe | | m | M | |
| FARBER | Sander | | m | M | Moshe |
| FARBER | unknown | | f | M | |
| FARBERMAN | Avraham | | m | M | |
| FARBERMAN | Fruma | | f | M | |
| FARBERMAN | Sarah | | f | U | Avraham |
| FARDER | Mara | | f | M | |
| FARDER | Velvel | | m | M | |
| FELDMAN | Pesha Leah | RUCHAMIS | f | M | Tuvia |
| FELDMAN | Ze'ev | | m | M | |
| FINEBERG | Avremh | | m | U | Mordechai |
| FINEBERG | Basaha | | m | M | Mordechai |
| FINEBERG | Feivel | | m | U | Mordechai |
| FINEBERG | Mordechai | | m | M | |
| FINEBERG | Shlomo | | m | U | Mordechai |
| FINEBERG | unknown | | f | M | |
| FINEBERG | unknown | | m | U | Mordechai |
| FINEBERG | Yehudaleh | | f | M | |
| FINEMAN | Mordechai Yonah | | m | M | |
| FINEMAN | Rachel | | f | M | |
| FINKEL | Chasia | | f | M | |
| FINKEL | Manya | | m | M | |
| FINKEL | Maya | | f | M | |
| FINKEL | Moshekeh | | m | M | Yacov |

# Martyrs of Ruzhany - List Expanded from Names in Original Book

| Key: | | | m=male<br>f=female | U=Unmarried<br>M=Married<br>W=Widow | |
|---|---|---|---|---|---|
| **Family name** | **First name(s)** | **Maiden name** | **Sex** | **Marital** | **Father's** |
| FINKEL | Sonyia | | f | M | Zalman |
| FINKEL | unknown | | f | M | |
| FINKEL | unknown | | f | M | |
| FINKEL | unknown | | f | M | |
| FINKEL | Yacov | | m | M | |
| FINKEL | Zalman | | m | M | |
| FINKEL | Zvi | | m | M | Zalman |
| FOKSMAN | Aharon Mordechai | | m | M | |
| FOKSMAN | Avraham Lipa | | m | M | |
| FOKSMAN | Avraham Meir | | m | M | |
| FOKSMAN | Brynne | | f | M | |
| FOKSMAN | Chanah | | f | M | |
| FOKSMAN | Chanoch | | m | U | Aharon Mordechai |
| FOKSMAN | Feigel | | f | U | Shmuel |
| FOKSMAN | Hasha Malkah | | f | M | |
| FOKSMAN | Levy | | m | M | Aharon Mordechai |
| FOKSMAN | Mordechai | | m | M | |
| FOKSMAN | Moshe | | m | U | Mordechai |
| FOKSMAN | Moshe | | m | U | |
| FOKSMAN | Moshe Meir | | m | M | |
| FOKSMAN | Neche | | f | M | |
| FOKSMAN | Rachel | | f | M | |
| FOKSMAN | Reuven | | m | U | |
| FOKSMAN | Sarah | | f | M | |
| FOKSMAN | Sheine | | f | U | Shmuel |
| FOKSMAN | Shmuel | | m | U | Aharon Mordechai |
| FOKSMAN | Shmuel | | m | M | |
| FOKSMAN | unknown | | f | M | |
| FOKSMAN | unknown | | f | M | |
| FOKSMAN | unknown | | m | U | Mordechai |
| FOKSMAN | unknown | | f | M | |
| FOKSMAN | Yakutiel | | m | U | Mordechai |
| FOKSMAN | Zelig | | m | M | |
| FREEDMAN | Rachel | | f | M | |
| FREEDMAN | Yehudaleh | | m | M | |
| FUCHS | Maklish | | m | M | |
| FUCHS | Sonyia | | f | M | Yitzchak |
| FUCHSMAN | Rachel | GOLDSTYN | f | M | Moshe Avraham |
| FUCHSMAN | Yacov Meir | | m | M | |

# Martyrs of Ruzhany - List Expanded from Names in Original Book

| Key: | | | m=male<br>f=female | U=Unmarried<br>M=Married<br>W=Widow | |
|---|---|---|---|---|---|
| **Family name** | **First name(s)** | **Maiden name** | **Sex** | **Marital** | **Father's** |
| FURMAN | Dov | | m | U | Yechezkel |
| FURMAN | Leibale | | f | U | Yechezkel |
| FURMAN | Peshka | | f | M | |
| FURMAN | Yacov | | m | U | Yechezkel |
| FURMAN | Yeihezkel | | m | M | |
| GALINCKI | Bilka | | f | M | |
| GALINCKI | Chaim | | m | M | |
| GAMERMAN | David | | m | U | Eliahu |
| GAMERMAN | David | | m | U | Eliahu |
| GAMERMAN | Duba | | f | M | |
| GAMERMAN | Eliahu | | m | M | |
| GAMERMAN | Eliahu | | m | M | |
| GAMERMAN | Ephraim | | m | U | Eliahu |
| GAMERMAN | Ephraim | | m | U | Eliahu |
| GAMERMAN | Herschel | | m | M | |
| GAMERMAN | Pesha | | f | U | Eliahu |
| GAMERMAN | Pesha | | f | M | |
| GAMERMAN | Sarah | | f | U | Eliahu |
| GAMERMAN | Yitzchak | | m | M | Eliahu |
| GAMERMAN | Zelda | | f | M | |
| GAMERMAN | Zelda | | f | M | |
| GEBZAH | Heshel | | m | M | Shlomo |
| GEBZAH | Shlomo | | m | M | |
| GEBZAH | unknown | | f | M | |
| GEBZAH | Zvia | | f | M | |
| GERBER | Liba | | f | W | |
| GERBOLCKI | Arieh Lieb | | f | M | |
| GERBOLCKI | Avremh | | m | U | Yacov |
| GERBOLCKI | Chanania | | m | U | Yacov |
| GERBOLCKI | Etka | | f | M | |
| GERBOLCKI | Etka | | f | M | |
| GERBOLCKI | Fishel | | m | U | Yacov |
| GERBOLCKI | Golda | ORLINSKY | f | M | Hazkal |
| GERBOLCKI | Liba | GUBER | m | M | Alter |
| GERBOLCKI | Ozer | | m | U | Yacov |
| GERBOLCKI | Perlah | | f | U | Yacov |
| GERBOLCKI | Yacov | | m | M | |
| GERBOLCKI | Yacov | | m | M | |
| GERBOLCKI | Yehoshua | | m | M | |
| GERSHTYN | unknown | | m | M | |
| GERSHUNY | Foigel | | m | M | |

# Martyrs of Ruzhany - List Expanded from Names in Original Book

| Key: | | | m=male<br>f=female | U=Unmarried<br>M=Married<br>W=Widow | |
|---|---|---|---|---|---|
| Family name | First name(s) | Maiden name | Sex | Marital | Father's |
| GERSHUNY | unknown | | f | M | |
| GLUZONOWICH | Meir | | m | U | |
| GLUZONOWICH | unknown | | f | W | |
| GOLDBERG | Araka | | m | M | |
| GOLDBERG | unknown | | f | M | |
| GOLDBERG | unknown | | m | M | |
| GOLDBLATT | Hasha | | f | U | Yerachmiel |
| GOLDBLATT | Herschel | | m | M | |
| GOLDBLATT | Shmerl | | m | M | |
| GOLDBLATT | unknown | | f | M | |
| GOLDBLATT | unknown | | f | M | |
| GOLDBLATT | unknown | | f | U | Yerachmiel |
| GOLDBLATT | Yerachmiel | | m | W | |
| GOLDBLATT | Zaffa | | f | U | Yerachmiel |
| GOLDSTYN | Meir | | m | U | Moshe Avraham |
| GOLDSTYN | Moshe | | m | U | Noach |
| GOLDSTYN | Moshe Avraham | | m | M | |
| GOLDSTYN | Noach | | m | M | Moshe Avraham |
| GOLDSTYN | Roza | | f | M | |
| GOLDSTYN | unknown | | f | U | Noach |
| GOLDSTYN | Yehudit | | f | M | |
| GOLDYN | Batya | | f | U | Mordechai |
| GOLDYN | Chava | | f | M | |
| GOLDYN | Mordechai | | m | M | |
| GOLDYN | Moshe | | m | M | |
| GOLDYN | unknown | | f | M | |
| GOLDYN | Yacov | | m | M | Mordechai |
| GOLDYN | Yehudit | | f | M | |
| GRAMERMAN | Duba | KAPLINSKY | f | M | Moshe |
| GRENGAS | Avigdor | | m | M | |
| GRENGAS | Esther | | f | M | |
| GUBER | Alter | | m | M | |
| GUBER | Berel | | m | M | |
| GUBER | Chanah | | f | M | |
| GUBER | Elka | | f | M | |
| GUBER | Itka | | f | U | Berel |
| GUBER | Malkah | | f | U | Berel |
| GUBER | Meir | | m | M | |
| GUBER | Meir | | m | M | |
| GUBER | Rasha | | f | W | |

# Martyrs of Ruzhany - List Expanded from Names in Original Book

| Key: | | | m=male<br>f=female | U=Unmarried<br>M=Married<br>W=Widow | |
|---|---|---|---|---|---|
| **Family name** | **First name(s)** | **Maiden name** | **Sex** | **Marital** | **Father's** |
| GUBER | unknown | | f | M | |
| GUBER | unknown | | f | M | |
| GUBER | Yitzchak | | m | U | Berel |
| GULDIS | Alta | GUBER | f | M | |
| GULDIS | David | | m | M | |
| GULDIS | Shabtay Musha | | m | U | Yehoshua |
| GULDIS | unknown | | f | M | |
| GULDIS | Yehoshua | | m | M | |
| GUSTOVCKI | Aharon | | m | M | |
| GUSTOVCKI | Eliahu | | m | M | Zvi |
| GUSTOVCKI | Ephraim | | m | M | |
| GUSTOVCKI | Feigel | MARUCHNIK | f | M | Yechezkel |
| GUSTOVCKI | Heinke | | f | U | Zvi |
| GUSTOVCKI | Hindah | | f | U | |
| GUSTOVCKI | Meir | | m | M | |
| GUSTOVCKI | Moshe | | m | M | |
| GUSTOVCKI | Moshe Hirsch | | m | U | Ephraim |
| GUSTOVCKI | Mosheleh | | m | U | Zvi |
| GUSTOVCKI | Sonyia | KOLODANY | f | M | |
| GUSTOVCKI | unknown | | f | M | |
| GUSTOVCKI | Yitzchak | | m | M | |
| GUSTOVCKI | Yoel | | m | M | |
| GUSTOVCKI | Zipah | | f | M | |
| GUSTOVCKI | Zvi | | m | W | |
| GVURIN | Chava | | f | U | Yisroel |
| GVURIN | Leah | | f | M | |
| GVURIN | Shimon | | m | M | |
| GVURIN | Sulia | | f | M | |
| GVURIN | Yisroel | | m | M | Zvi |
| GVURIN | Zvi | | m | W | |
| HIRSCHENHORN | Moshe | | m | M | |
| HIRSCHENHORN | Nechama | | f | U | Moshe |
| HIRSCHENHORN | Roza | | f | M | |
| HIRSCHENHORN | Shmuel | | m | U | Moshe |
| ILLEWICKI | Aharon | | m | M | |
| ILLEWICKI | Duba | GERBER | f | M | |
| ILLEWICKI | Yitzchak | | m | U | Aharon |
| INKER | Chanah Sarah | SELMAN | f | M | Tunia |
| INKER | Eidel | | f | | Shmuel |
| INKER | Reuven | | m | | Shmuel |

# Martyrs of Ruzhany - List Expanded from Names in Original Book

| Key: | | | m=male<br>f=female | U=Unmarried<br>M=Married<br>W=Widow | |
|---|---|---|---|---|---|
| Family name | First name(s) | Maiden name | Sex | Marital | Father's |
| INKER | Shmuel | | m | M | |
| INKER | Tuvia | | m | | Shmuel |
| INKER | unknown | | f | M | |
| INKER | Zvi | | m | M | |
| ITZKOWICH | Avraham | | m | U | Moshe |
| ITZKOWICH | Bat Sheva | | f | W | |
| ITZKOWICH | Moshe | | m | W | |
| ITZKOWICH | Yitzchak | | m | U | Eliahu |
| IVAN | Chanah | | f | W | |
| JAKIMOVSKY | Moshe | | m | M | |
| JAKIMOVSKY | Roza | ROZENSTYN | f | M | |
| JANKELOWICZ | Eliezer | | m | M | |
| JANKELOWICZ | Herschel | | m | M | Eliezer |
| JANKELOWICZ | unknown | | f | M | |
| JANKELOWICZ | unknown | | f | M | |
| JEZRENITSKY | Ezra | | m | M | |
| JEZRENITSKY | Freida | | f | M | |
| JEZRENITSKY | Miriam Nachum | | f | M | |
| JEZRENITSKY | Pesach | | m | M | |
| JEZRENITSKY | Perel | | f | M | |
| JEZRENITSKY | Shlomo | | m | M | |
| JOSELWICZ | Baracha | | f | U | Yosef |
| JOSELWICZ | Dwashke | | f | M | |
| JOSELWICZ | Nechama | | f | U | Yosef |
| JOSELWICZ | unknown | | f | U | Yosef |
| JOSELWICZ | Yosef | | m | M | |
| JUZHLOVSKY | Elka | EDELSTEIN | f | M | Mordechai |
| JUZHLOVSKY | Yitzchak | | m | M | |
| KAGNESKY | Avraham | | m | M | |
| KAGNESKY | Avraham | | m | U | Berel Leib |
| KAGNESKY | Berel Lieb | | m | M | |
| KAGNESKY | Chanah | | f | U | Noach |
| KAGNESKY | Herschel | | m | U | Berel Leib |
| KAGNESKY | Noach | | m | M | |
| KAGNESKY | Reishel | | f | M | |
| KAGNESKY | Rivkah | | f | M | |
| KAGNESKY | Roza | | f | U | Berel Leib |
| KAGNESKY | Shmuel | | m | M | Noach |
| KAGNESKY | Sima | | f | M | |
| KAGNESKY | unknown | | f | M | |

# Martyrs of Ruzhany - List Expanded from Names in Original Book

| Key: | | | m=male<br>f=female | U=Unmarried<br>M=Married<br>W=Widow | |
|---|---|---|---|---|---|
| **Family name** | **First name(s)** | **Maiden name** | **Sex** | **Marital** | **Father's** |
| KAGNESKY | unknown | | f | M | |
| KAGNESKY | unknown | | f | M | |
| KAGNESKY | unknown | | m | M | |
| KAGNESKY | Vichne | | f | | Avraham |
| KAGNESKY | Yosef | | m | M | Avraham |
| KAGNESKY | Yosef | | m | M | Berel Leib |
| KAGNESKY | Zipkah | | f | M | Noach |
| KAGNITSKY | Aharala | | m | U | Yacov Hirsch |
| KAGNITSKY | Razel | | f | M | |
| KAGNITSKY | Yacov Hirsch | | m | M | |
| KAMENTSKY | unknown | | m | | |
| KAMENTSKY | unknown | | f | | |
| KAMINER | unknown | | f | W | |
| KAMINTSKY | Duba | | f | M | |
| KAMINTSKY | Heinke | | f | U | Pinchas |
| KAMINTSKY | Huma | | f | U | Pinchas |
| KAMINTSKY | Pinchas | | m | M | |
| KANNOWITS | Mottel | | m | U | |
| KANNOWITS | Sheine Bliume | | f | M | |
| KANNOWITS | Yehuda | | m | U | |
| KANTOROWITS | Chanah | | f | U | Yisroel |
| KANTOROWITS | Duba | | f | M | |
| KANTOROWITS | Naftali | | m | U | Yisroel |
| KANTOROWITS | Shimon | | m | U | Yisroel |
| KANTOROWITS | Tiva | | f | | Yisroel |
| KANTOROWITS | unknown | | f | M | |
| KANTOROWITS | unknown | | f | U | Yisroel |
| KANTOROWITS | Yisroel | | m | M | |
| KANTOROWITS | Yitzchak | | m | U | Yisroel |
| KANTSPOLSKY | Eliezer | | m | M | |
| KANTSPOLSKY | Gittel | EISENSTEIN | f | M | Chaim Wolf |
| KANTSPOLSKY | Rivkah | | f | U | Yacov |
| KANTSPOLSKY | unknown | | f | M | |
| KANTSPOLSKY | Yacov | | m | M | |
| KAPLAN | Avraham | | m | U | Moshe |
| KAPLAN | Baracha | | f | M | |
| KAPLAN | Daliah | | f | U | Moshe |
| KAPLAN | Duba | | f | U | Reuven |
| KAPLAN | Herzel | | m | M | |
| KAPLAN | Isachar | | m | M | Reuven |
| KAPLAN | Kaylia | | f | M | |

# Martyrs of Ruzhany - List Expanded from Names in Original Book

| Key: | | | m=male<br>f=female | U=Unmarried<br>M=Married<br>W=Widow | |
|---|---|---|---|---|---|
| Family name | First name(s) | Maiden name | Sex | Marital | Father's |
| KAPLAN | Leah | | f | M | |
| KAPLAN | Milia | | f | M | |
| KAPLAN | Minia | | f | M | |
| KAPLAN | Moshe | | m | M | |
| KAPLAN | Moshe | | m | M | |
| KAPLAN | Nechama | | f | U | Yosef |
| KAPLAN | Razel | SOKOLOVSKY | f | M | Yitzchak Reuven |
| KAPLAN | Reuven | | m | M | |
| KAPLAN | Roza | KAPLINSKY | f | M | Moshe |
| KAPLAN | Roza | | f | M | |
| KAPLAN | Sarah | | f | M | |
| KAPLAN | Saraleh | | f | U | Yosef |
| KAPLAN | Tzirel | | f | M | |
| KAPLAN | unknown | | f | M | |
| KAPLAN | unknown | | f | M | |
| KAPLAN | Yacov | | m | M | |
| KAPLAN | Yeshi'ika | | m | U | Kaylia |
| KAPLAN | Yosef | | m | M | |
| KAPLAN | Yosef | | m | M | Moshe |
| KAPLAN | Zidel | | m | M | |
| KAPLINSKY | Eliahu | | m | M | |
| KAPLINSKY | Huma | | f | M | |
| KAPLINSKY | Itka | CHEBOINIK | f | M | |
| KAPLINSKY | Miriam | | f | U | Eliahu |
| KAPLINSKY | Moshe | | m | M | |
| KAPLINSKY | Shlomo | | m | U | Moshe |
| KAPLINSKY | Zvi | | m | U | Eliahu |
| KARLITS | Berel | | m | M | |
| KARLITS | Malkah | BRESLIN | f | M | |
| KARLITS | Mosheleh | | m | U | Berel |
| KARLITS | Mottel | | m | U | Berel |
| KARLITSKY | Alter | | m | M | |
| KARLITSKY | Chaim | | m | M | Alter |
| KARLITSKY | Henya | | f | M | |
| KARLITSKY | Moshe | | m | M | Alter |
| KARLITSKY | Rivkah | | f | M | |
| KARLITSKY | Simcha | | m | M | Alter |
| KARLITSKY | unknown | | f | M | |
| KARLITSKY | unknown | | f | M | |
| KARLITSKY | unknown | | f | M | |
| KARLITSKY | Velvel | | m | M | Alter |

# Martyrs of Ruzhany - List Expanded from Names in Original Book

| Key: | | | m=male<br>f=female | U=Unmarried<br>M=Married<br>W=Widow | |
|---|---|---|---|---|---|
| **Family name** | **First name(s)** | **Maiden name** | **Sex** | **Marital** | **Father's** |
| KARLITSKY | Yedidyah | | m | M | Alter |
| KARPEL | Yehudit | | f | U | Meir |
| KARPELEWICH | Azriel | | m | M | Yehudah Leib |
| KARPELEWICH | Bashkah | | f | M | |
| KARPELEWICH | Fishel | | m | M | Yehudah Leib |
| KARPELEWICH | Hazkal | | m | M | |
| KARPELEWICH | Karina | | f | M | |
| KARPELEWICH | Meir | | m | M | |
| KARPELEWICH | Melech | | m | U | Meir |
| KARPELEWICH | Moshekeh | | m | M | Yehudah Leib |
| KARPELEWICH | Raphael | | m | M | Yehudah Leib |
| KARPELEWICH | Razel | | f | M | |
| KARPELEWICH | Sheine | | f | M | |
| KARPELEWICH | unknown | | f | M | |
| KARPELEWICH | unknown | | f | M | |
| KARPELEWICH | unknown | | f | M | |
| KARPELEWICH | unknown | | f | M | |
| KARPELEWICH | unknown | | f | U | Yehudah Leib |
| KARPELEWICH | unknown | | f | U | Yehudah Leib |
| KARPELEWICH | Vichne | | f | M | |
| KARPELEWICH | Yehuda Lieb | | m | M | |
| KARPELEWICH | Zvi | | m | U | Meir |
| KATOCK | unknown | | f | M | |
| KATOCK | unknown | | f | U | Yoshka |
| KATOCK | Yonah | | m | | Yoshka |
| KATZ | Liba | | f | M | |
| KATZ | Moshe | | m | M | |
| KATZ | Tuvia | | f | M | |
| KATZ | unknown | | m | M | Moshe |
| KATZIN | Banish | | m | M | |
| KATZIN | Barouch | | m | U | Rasha |
| KATZIN | Hindah | | f | M | |
| KATZIN | Hirsch | | m | M | |
| KATZIN | Mendel | | m | M | Rasha |
| KATZIN | Rasha | | f | | |
| KATZIN | Shmuel | | m | U | Rasha |
| KATZIN | unknown | | f | M | |
| KATZIN | unknown | | f | M | |
| KATZIN | unknown | | f | M | |
| KATZIN | Zvi | | m | U | Rasha |
| KATZMAN | Avraham | | m | M | |

# Martyrs of Ruzhany - List Expanded from Names in Original Book

| Key: | | | m=male<br>f=female | U=Unmarried<br>M=Married<br>W=Widow | |
|---|---|---|---|---|---|
| Family name | First name(s) | Maiden name | Sex | Marital | Father's |
| KATZMAN | Chanacha | SHERESHEVSKY | f | M | Ze'ev |
| KATZMAN | Rachel | | f | U | Avraham |
| KATZMAN | Rivkah | | f | U | Avraham |
| KEN | Moshe | | m | M | |
| KEN | Yachne | | f | M | |
| KENZIPOR | Chanah | MIZHBOVSKY | f | M | |
| KENZIPOR | Chanah | | f | M | |
| KENZIPOR | Mottel | | m | M | |
| KFITS | David Lieb | | m | M | |
| KFITS | Esther | | f | U | |
| KFITS | Herschel | | m | U | |
| KFITS | Miriam | | f | U | |
| KFITS | Noach | | m | M | Schana |
| KFITS | Perel | | f | M | |
| KFITS | Schana | | m | M | |
| KFITS | unknown | | f | M | |
| KFITS | unknown | | f | M | |
| KFITS | unknown | | f | M | |
| KIMELMAN | Barouch | | m | U | Chaim |
| KIMELMAN | Chaim | | m | M | |
| KIMELMAN | Mara | | f | M | |
| KLEBENSKY | Esther | | f | M | |
| KLEBENSKY | Esther | | f | M | |
| KLEBENSKY | Gittel | | f | M | |
| KLEBENSKY | Issar | | m | M | |
| KLEBENSKY | Liova | | f | U | Moshe Eliahu |
| KLEBENSKY | Moshe Eliahu | | m | M | |
| KLEBENSKY | Rachel | BASHIN | f | M | |
| KLEBENSKY | Rachel | | f | M | |
| KLEBENSKY | Roza | | f | U | Moshe Eliahu |
| KLEBENSKY | unknown | | f | M | |
| KLEBENSKY | Yitzchak | | m | M | |
| KLICKA | Benyamin | | m | M | |
| KLICKA | Devorah | | f | M | |
| KLICKA | unknown | | f | M | |
| KOLIA | Esther | | f | M | |
| KOLIA | Mendel | | m | M | |
| KOLODANY | Feigel | | f | M | |
| KONITZA | Brynne | | f | U | Moshe |
| KONITZA | Chaya | ITZKOWICH | f | M | Moshe |
| KONITZA | Eliahu | | m | M | |

# Martyrs of Ruzhany - List Expanded from Names in Original Book

| Key: | | | m=male<br>f=female | U=Unmarried<br>M=Married<br>W=Widow | |
|---|---|---|---|---|---|
| Family name | First name(s) | Maiden name | Sex | Marital | Father's |
| KONITZA | Eliezer | | m | M | |
| KONITZA | Ephraim | | m | M | |
| KONITZA | Freida | | f | U | Eliahu |
| KONITZA | Frumkah | | f | U | Moshe |
| KONITZA | Golda | | f | U | Yoshka |
| KONITZA | Golda | | f | U | Shalom |
| KONITZA | Leah | | f | M | |
| KONITZA | Minia | | f | U | Shalom |
| KONITZA | Moshe | | m | U | Eliahu |
| KONITZA | Reuven | | m | U | Ephraim |
| KONITZA | Rivkah | | f | U | Moshe |
| KONITZA | Ryna | | f | M | |
| KONITZA | Shalom | | m | M | |
| KONITZA | unknown | | f | U | Moshe |
| KONITZA | unknown | | f | M | |
| KONITZA | unknown | | f | M | |
| KONITZA | Vichne | | f | U | Yoshka |
| KONITZA | Vichne | | f | U | Eliahu |
| KONITZA | Vichne | | f | U | Shalom |
| KONITZA | Yacov | | m | U | Eliahu |
| KONITZA | Yehudaleh | | m | U | Eliahu |
| KONITZA | Yehudit | | f | U | Yoshka |
| KONITZA | Yoshka | | m | M | |
| KOSOVSKY | Chaim Mordechai | | m | M | |
| KOSOVSKY | Gittel | | f | M | |
| KOSOVSKY | Mita | | f | M | |
| KOSOVSKY | Nissan | | m | M | |
| KOSOVSKY | unknown | | f | M | |
| KOVNESKY | Berel | | m | M | |
| KOVNESKY | Chanan | | m | M | |
| KOVNESKY | Chava | | f | U | Chanan |
| KOVNESKY | Mottel | | m | U | Shmuel |
| KOVNESKY | Reikleh | | f | M | |
| KOVNESKY | Shmuel | | m | M | |
| KOVNESKY | Tiva | | f | M | |
| KOVNESKY | Yenta | | f | M | |
| KOZNITSKY | Bashka | | f | M | |
| KOZNITSKY | Feigel | | f | U | Gershon |
| KOZNITSKY | Gershon | | m | M | |
| KOZNITSKY | Shimon | | m | U | Gershon |
| KOZNITSKY | Shyndel | | f | U | Gershon |

# Martyrs of Ruzhany - List Expanded from Names in Original Book

| Key: | | | m=male<br>f=female | U=Unmarried<br>M=Married<br>W=Widow | |
|---|---|---|---|---|---|
| Family name | First name(s) | Maiden name | Sex | Marital | Father's |
| KOZNITSKY | Yitzchak | | m | U | Gershon |
| KRABCHUK | Celia | | f | M | |
| KRABCHUK | Leah | | f | | |
| KRABCHUK | Leah | | f | M | |
| KRABCHUK | Shlomo | | m | M | |
| KRABCHUK | Shmuel Chaim | | m | M | |
| KRASHINSKY | Chanah Liba | | f | M | |
| KRASHINSKY | Chaya Sarah | | f | M | |
| KRASHINSKY | Leibel | | f | M | |
| KRASHINSKY | Tuvia | | m | M | |
| KRASHINSKY | unknown | | m | M | |
| KRASHINSKY | unknown | | f | U | |
| KRINSKY | Chayaka | | f | U | |
| KRINSKY | Masha | SHLUTZKI | f | M | |
| KRINSKY | Moshe | | m | U | |
| KRINSKY | Moshe Yehudaleh | | m | U | |
| KRINSKY | unknown | | m | M | |
| KRINSKY | unknown | | f | M | |
| KRINSKY | Yehuda | | m | M | |
| KRINSKY | Yehudaleh | | m | M | |
| KRINSKY | Yonah | | m | U | |
| KRINSKY | Yosef | | m | U | |
| KROLINSKY | Anschel | | m | M | |
| KROLINSKY | Chanah | | f | M | |
| KROLINSKY | Duba | | f | U | Anschel |
| KROLINSKY | Mosheleh | | m | U | Anschel |
| KROLINSKY | Yentel | | f | U | Anschel |
| KROLITSKY | Ethel | | f | M | Yehudaleh |
| KROLITSKY | Ethel | | f | M | |
| KROLITSKY | Freida | | f | M | |
| KROLITSKY | Mordechai | | m | M | |
| LANZBITSKY | Aharon | | m | U | |
| LANZBITSKY | Berel | | m | U | |
| LANZBITSKY | Leah | ROTHSTYN | f | M | Chaim Zerach |
| LANZBITSKY | Leibel | | m | U | Mottel |
| LANZBITSKY | Lia | | f | M | |
| LANZBITSKY | Mottel | | m | M | |
| LANZBITSKY | Mottel | | m | M | |
| LANZBITSKY | Rivkah | | f | M | |
| LANZBITSKY | unknown | | f | U | Mottel |
| LEBITSKY | Devorah | KOVNESKY | f | M | Shmuel |

# Martyrs of Ruzhany - List Expanded from Names in Original Book

| Key: | | | m=male<br>f=female | U=Unmarried<br>M=Married<br>W=Widow | |
|---|---|---|---|---|---|
| **Family name** | **First name(s)** | **Maiden name** | **Sex** | **Marital** | **Father's** |
| LEBITSKY | Mottel | | m | U | Zelig |
| LEBITSKY | Zelig | | m | M | |
| LERMAN | Sarah | | f | U | |
| LERMAN | unknown | | f | M | |
| LERMAN | Zidel | | m | M | |
| LEV | Avraham | | m | U | Yacov Michael |
| LEV | Moshe | | m | U | Yacov Michael |
| LEV | Rivkah | | f | U | Yacov Michael |
| LEV | Sarah | | f | U | Yacov Michael |
| LEV | Yacov Michael | | m | M | |
| LEV | Zipah | | f | M | |
| LEVENBOK | Bandet | | m | U | |
| LEVENBOK | Benyamin | | m | U | Hirsch |
| LEVENBOK | Etka | | f | M | |
| LEVENBOK | Hirsch | | m | M | |
| LEVENBOK | Humkah | | f | U | Hirsch |
| LEVENBOK | Leahkah | | f | U | Hirsch |
| LEVENBOK | Meir | | m | M | |
| LEVENBOK | Rivkah | | f | M | |
| LEVENBOK | unknown | | f | U | Hirsch |
| LEVENBOK | unknown | | f | W | |
| LEVENBOK | Yacov | | m | U | |
| LEVENKOV | Perel | ANISH | f | M | Berel |
| LEVINOV | Chanah | | f | M | |
| LEVINOV | Chaya | | f | U | |
| LEVINOV | Chaya Sarah | | f | U | |
| LEVINOV | David | | m | U | |
| LEVINOV | Devorah | | f | M | |
| LEVINOV | Eliahu | | m | U | |
| LEVINOV | Fruma Leah | | f | W | |
| LEVINOV | Moshe | | m | M | |
| LEVINOV | Moshe | | m | M | |
| LEVINOV | Nechamkah | | f | M | |
| LEVINOV | Shamai | | m | M | |
| LEVITAN | Berel | | m | M | Moshe Chaim |
| LEVITAN | Malkah | | f | M | |
| LEVITAN | Moshe Chaim | | m | M | |
| LEVITAN | Shlomo | | m | U | Yom-tov |
| LEVITAN | unknown | | f | M | |
| LEVITAN | unknown | | f | M | |
| LEVITAN | Yenta | | f | M | |

# Martyrs of Ruzhany - List Expanded from Names in Original Book

| Key: | | | m=male<br>f=female | U=Unmarried<br>M=Married<br>W=Widow | |
|---|---|---|---|---|---|
| Family name | First name(s) | Maiden name | Sex | Marital | Father's |

| Family name | First name(s) | Maiden name | Sex | Marital | Father's |
|---|---|---|---|---|---|
| LEVITAN | Yitzchak | | m | U | Moshe Chaim |
| LEVITAN | Yom-Tov | | m | M | |
| LEVITAN | Yosef | | m | M | Moshe Chaim |
| LEVITSKY | Biliah | | f | M | |
| LEVITSKY | Mordechai | | m | M | |
| LEVITSKY | Peshka | BABICH | f | M | Shmuel Yehudaleh |
| LEVITSKY | unknown | | m | M | |
| LEVITSKY | unknown | | f | M | |
| LEVITSKY | Yacov | | m | M | Mordechai |
| LEVITSKY | Zvia | | f | U | Mordechai |
| LEVKOVSKY | Sheine | | f | M | |
| LEVKOVSKY | Yacov Zalman | | m | M | |
| LIBERANT | Avraham (Aber) | | m | | |
| LIBERMAN | Chaim | | m | U | Yeshi'ika |
| LIBERMAN | Chanah | | f | M | |
| LIBERMAN | Hasha | BASKIN | f | M | Yeshi'ika |
| LIBERMAN | Moshekeh | | m | | Yitzchak |
| LIBERMAN | Moshekeh | | m | | Yeshi'ika |
| LIBERMAN | Mottel | | m | M | Yeshi'ika |
| LIBERMAN | Shmerl | | m | U | Yitzchak |
| LIBERMAN | Shmerl | | m | M | Yeshi'ika |
| LIBERMAN | Shmuel | | m | M | Yitzchak |
| LIBERMAN | Simcha | | m | U | Yitzchak |
| LIBERMAN | unknown | | f | M | |
| LIBERMAN | unknown | | f | M | |
| LIBERMAN | unknown | | f | M | |
| LIBERMAN | unknown | | f | M | |
| LIBERMAN | Yeshi'ika | | m | M | |
| LIBERMAN | Yitzchak | | m | M | |
| LIBERMAN | Zafnia | | m | U | Yeshi'ika |
| LIMON | Avraham | | m | M | |
| LIMON | Benyamin | | m | M | |
| LIMON | Leibel | | m | M | |
| LIMON | Miriam | | f | M | |
| LIMON | Reuchama | | f | M | |
| LIMON | Reuchama | SHERESHEVSKY | f | M | Ze'ev |
| LIMON | Shmuel | | m | U | Avraham |
| LIMON | Shmuel | | m | U | Leibel |
| LIMON | Sonyia | | f | M | |
| LIMON | Yacov | | m | U | Avraham |

# Martyrs of Ruzhany - List Expanded from Names in Original Book

| Key: | | | m=male<br>f=female | U=Unmarried<br>M=Married<br>W=Widow | |
|---|---|---|---|---|---|
| Family name | First name(s) | Maiden name | Sex | Marital | Father's |
| LIPSHITZ | Alter | | m | U | |
| LIPSTOCKI | Faya | | f | M | |
| LIPSTOCKI | Gershon | | m | M | |
| LISSKOVSKY | Arieh | | m | M | |
| LISSKOVSKY | Berel | | m | M | |
| LISSKOVSKY | Gadaliah | | m | M | Moshe |
| LISSKOVSKY | Miriam | | f | M | |
| LISSKOVSKY | Moshe Chaim | | m | M | |
| LISSKOVSKY | unknown | | f | M | |
| LISSKOVSKY | unknown | | f | U | Yacov |
| LISSKOVSKY | unknown | | f | M | |
| LISSKOVSKY | unknown | | f | M | |
| LISSKOVSKY | unknown | | m | U | Leib |
| LISSKOVSKY | unknown | | f | M | |
| LISSKOVSKY | unknown | | f | M | |
| LISSKOVSKY | unknown | | f | M | |
| LISSKOVSKY | Yacov | | m | M | |
| LISSKOVSKY | Yitzchak | | m | U | Berel |
| LISSKOVSKY | Yoceved | RUCHAMIS | f | M | Tuvia |
| LISSKOVSKY | Yosef | | m | M | Moshe |
| LISSKOVSKY | Zvi | | m | U | Yacov |
| LISSKOVSKY | Zvi | | m | M | |
| LISSOBITSKY | Bashkah | | f | M | |
| LISSOBITSKY | Gittel | | f | M | |
| LISSOBITSKY | Moshe | | m | M | Yosef |
| LISSOBITSKY | Neta | | m | M | |
| LISSOBITSKY | Sonyia | BASHIN | f | M | |
| LISSOBITSKY | unknown | | m | M | |
| LISSOBITSKY | unknown | | f | M | |
| LISSOBITSKY | Yosef | | m | U | |
| LISSOBITSKY | Yosef | | m | M | |
| LUBOSHITSKY | Aharon | | m | U | Dov Eleizer |
| LUBOSHITSKY | Dov Eliezer | | m | W | |
| LUBOSHITSKY | Moshe | | m | U | Zvi |
| LUBOSHITSKY | unknown | | f | M | |
| LUBOSHITSKY | Zvi | | m | M | Dov Eleizer |
| LURIA | Biliah | | f | M | |
| LURIA | Dov Hazkal | | m | M | |
| LURIA | Avraham | | m | U | Dov |
| LURIA | Moshe | | m | U | Dov |

# Martyrs of Ruzhany - List Expanded from Names in Original Book

| Key: | | | m=male<br>f=female | U=Unmarried<br>M=Married<br>W=Widow | |
|---|---|---|---|---|---|
| **Family name** | **First name(s)** | **Maiden name** | **Sex** | **Marital** | **Father's** |
| LURIA | Razel | | f | U | Yosef |
| LURIA | Sarah | | f | M | |
| LURIA | Sima | | f | M | |
| LURIA | Yitzchak | | m | M | |
| LURIA | Yosef | | m | M | Yitzchak |
| MARANTZ | Chaim | | m | U | David |
| MARANTZ | David | | m | M | |
| MARANTZ | Sarah | | f | M | |
| MARANTZ | unknown | | | | David |
| MARANTZ | Zvi | | m | U | David |
| MARMINSKY | Devorah | SKLIRAVITZ | f | M | |
| MARMINSKY | Esther | MELLER | f | M | |
| MARMINSKY | Moshe | | m | M | |
| MARMINSKY | Moshe | | m | M | Raphael |
| MARMINSKY | Raphael | | m | M | |
| MARMINSKY | Shlomo | | m | U | Moshe |
| MARMINSKY | unknown | | f | M | |
| MARMINSKY | Yehudaleh | | m | M | |
| MARUCHNIK | Avraham | | m | U | Yechezkel |
| MARUCHNIK | Devorah Golda | | f | M | |
| MARUCHNIK | Minka | | f | U | Yechezkel |
| MARUCHNIK | Mordechai | | m | M | |
| MARUCHNIK | Moshe | | m | U | Zadok |
| MARUCHNIK | Sarah | | f | W | |
| MARUCHNIK | Shlomokeh | | m | M | Mordechai |
| MARUCHNIK | Sulia | | f | M | |
| MARUCHNIK | unknown | | f | M | |
| MARUCHNIK | unknown | | f | M | |
| MARUCHNIK | Yacov Meir | | m | U | Zadok |
| MARUCHNIK | Yeihezkel | | m | M | |
| MARUCHNIK | Yosef | | m | U | Zadok |
| MARUCHNIK | Zalman | | m | M | Mordechai |
| MARYNNE | Chaya Sarah | | f | M | |
| MARYNNE | Moshe | | m | M | |
| MARYNNE | unknown | | f | M | |
| MARYNNE | unknown | | f | U | Moshe |
| MARYNNE | Yehuda | | m | M | Moshe |
| MARYNNE | Zvia | | f | U | Moshe |
| MASHTZNIN | Moshe Zalman | | m | M | |
| MASHTZNIN | Shmuel | | m | M | Moshe Zalman |

# Martyrs of Ruzhany - List Expanded from Names in Original Book

| Key: | | | m=male<br>f=female | U=Unmarried<br>M=Married<br>W=Widow | |
|---|---|---|---|---|---|
| **Family name** | **First name(s)** | **Maiden name** | **Sex** | **Marital** | **Father's** |
| MASHTZNIN | unknown | | f | M | |
| MASHTZNIN | Vicha | | f | M | |
| MAYEROWICH | Ethel | | f | M | |
| MAYEROWICH | Rivkah | WYNITSKY | f | M | Shmuel Aharon |
| MAYEROWICH | Shaul | | m | M | |
| MAYEROWICH | Yitzchak | | m | M | |
| MAYERSON | Eliahu | | m | M | |
| MAYERSON | Sarah | | f | W | |
| MAYERSON | Sonyia | | f | M | |
| MAYERSON | unknown | | f | U | Eliahu |
| MAYERSON | Yehuda | | m | U | Eliahu |
| MAZOR | Chaim | | m | M | |
| MAZOR | Leah | | f | M | |
| MAZOR | Yacov | | m | U | Chaim |
| MELLER | Avraham | | m | M | |
| MELLER | Ephraim | | m | M | |
| MELLER | Feigel | | f | M | |
| MELLER | Helia | | f | M | |
| MELLER | Miriam | | f | W | |
| MELLER | Nechama | | f | U | Schana Feigel |
| MELLER | Osnat | | f | U | Ephraim |
| MELLER | Schana | | m | M | |
| MELLER | unknown | | f | M | |
| MICHNOVSKY | Bliume | | f | U | Yosef |
| MICHNOVSKY | Gezel | | | | Yosef |
| MICHNOVSKY | Itka | | f | M | |
| MICHNOVSKY | Roza | | f | U | Yosef |
| MICHNOVSKY | Yosef | | m | M | |
| MILLER | Genia | | f | M | |
| MILLER | unknown | | m | M | |
| MINKOWICH | Avremh | | m | M | Berel |
| MINKOWICH | Berel | | m | M | |
| MINKOWICH | Moshe | | m | M | Berel |
| MINKOWICH | Sima | | f | M | |
| MINKOWICH | unknown | | f | M | |
| MINKOWICH | unknown | | f | M | |
| MIRKIN | Bliume | | f | M | |
| MIZHBOVSKY | Chaim | | m | M | |
| MIZHBOVSKY | Chanah | | f | M | |
| MIZHBOVSKY | Rivkah Leah | | f | W | |
| MORDECHOWITZ | Alter | | m | M | |

# Martyrs of Ruzhany - List Expanded from Names in Original Book

| Key: | | | m=male<br>f=female | U=Unmarried<br>M=Married<br>W=Widow | |
|---|---|---|---|---|---|
| Family name | First name(s) | Maiden name | Sex | Marital | Father's |
| MORDECHOWITZ | Daliahka | | f | M | |
| MORDECHOWITZ | unknown | | f | M | |
| MORDECHOWITZ | Yitzchak | | m | M | Alter |
| MOSKOVSKY | unknown | | f | M | |
| MOSKOVSKY | Yakutiel | | m | M | |
| MOVSHOWICH | Arieh Leib | | m | M | |
| MOVSHOWICH | Chanah Rozkah | EINSTEIN | f | M | Yoel |
| MOVSHOWICH | Leibka | | m | M | |
| MOVSHOWICH | Raphael | | m | U | |
| MOVSHOWICH | unknown | | f | U | |
| MOVSHOWICH | unknown | | f | U | |
| MURKAS | Sarah | | f | M | |
| MURKAS | Shimon | | m | M | |
| MURKAS | unknown | | f | U | Shimon |
| MURKAS | Zvi | | m | U | Shimon |
| NOVICK | Sarah Leah | TURN | f | M | Moshe |
| NOVIK | Sarah Leah | | f | M | |
| NOVIK | Sheine | | f | U | Yonah |
| NOVIK | unknown | | m | U | Yonah |
| NOVIK | Yonah | | m | M | |
| NOVIK | Zvi | | m | U | Yonah |
| NYBURSKY | unknown | | f | M | |
| NYBURSKY | Yitzchak | | m | M | |
| OBERSTEIN | Avraham | | f | M | |
| OBERSTEIN | unknown | | f | M | |
| ORBACH | Chanah | | f | U | Shimon Henech |
| ORBACH | Feigel | SHAPIRA | f | M | Mordechai |
| ORBACH | Shalom | | m | U | Shimon Henech |
| ORBACH | Shimshon Hanoch | | m | M | |
| ORBACH | Teivela | | f | | Shimon Henech |
| ORLINSKY | Alter | | m | M | Hazkal |
| ORLINSKY | Avraham | | m | U | Alter |
| ORLINSKY | Avraham Yeshiahu | | m | M | |
| ORLINSKY | Chanoch | | m | U | Alter |
| ORLINSKY | Hazkal | | m | W | |
| ORLINSKY | Milia | | f | M | |
| ORLINSKY | Shyndel | | f | U | Alter |
| ORLINSKY | unknown | | f | M | |
| PADAU | Arieh | | m | M | |
| PADAU | Dov | | m | U | Arieh |

# Martyrs of Ruzhany - List Expanded from Names in Original Book

| Key: | | | m=male<br>f=female | U=Unmarried<br>M=Married<br>W=Widow | |
|---|---|---|---|---|---|
| **Family name** | **First name(s)** | **Maiden name** | **Sex** | **Marital** | **Father's** |
| PADAU | Fruma | | f | U | Arieh |
| PADAU | Liba | | f | M | |
| PAIKOV | Avraham Yitzchak | | m | M | |
| PAIKOV | Esther | | f | M | |
| PAPEISH | Feivel | | m | U | Gadaliahu |
| PAPEISH | Gadaliahu | | m | M | |
| PAPEISH | Hirsch | | m | U | |
| PAPEISH | Roza | | f | U | Gadaliahu |
| PAPEISH | unknown | | f | M | |
| PEKRESKY | unknown | | m | | |
| PINES | Eliahu Akivah | | m | U | |
| PINES | Esther | | f | U | Issar |
| PINES | Feigel | | f | U | |
| PINES | Fruma | | f | M | |
| PINES | Issar | | m | M | |
| PINES | Sonyia | | f | U | |
| PINES | Yitzchak | | f | U | Issar |
| PINTALWICH | Hindah | AGOLNIK | f | M | |
| PINTALWICH | Michael | | m | M | |
| PITKOVSKY | Aharon Yacov | | m | M | |
| PITKOVSKY | Akivah | | m | U | Yacov |
| PITKOVSKY | Berel | | m | M | |
| PITKOVSKY | Bliume | | f | M | |
| PITKOVSKY | Chaim David | | m | M | Simcha |
| PITKOVSKY | Chaim Leizer | | m | M | |
| PITKOVSKY | Chava | | f | M | |
| PITKOVSKY | Chaya | | f | M | |
| PITKOVSKY | David | | m | M | Liber |
| PITKOVSKY | David | | m | M | |
| PITKOVSKY | Eliahu | | m | M | Shmuel Leib |
| PITKOVSKY | Elka | | f | U | Yisroel |
| PITKOVSKY | Elka | | f | M | |
| PITKOVSKY | Ethel | AGOLNIK | f | M | |
| PITKOVSKY | Freida Elka | | f | U | Petel |
| PITKOVSKY | Freidel | | f | M | |
| PITKOVSKY | Fruma | | f | U | Petel |
| PITKOVSKY | Herzel | | m | M | Shmuel Leib |
| PITKOVSKY | Huma | | f | M | |
| PITKOVSKY | Itka | | f | M | |
| PITKOVSKY | Leah Shosha | | f | U | |
| PITKOVSKY | Liber | | m | M | |

# Martyrs of Ruzhany - List Expanded from Names in Original Book

| Key: | | | m=male<br>f=female | U=Unmarried<br>M=Married<br>W=Widow | |
|---|---|---|---|---|---|
| **Family name** | **First name(s)** | **Maiden name** | **Sex** | **Marital** | **Father's** |
| PITKOVSKY | Liova | | f | | Shlomkeh |
| PITKOVSKY | Masha | | f | U | Shlomkeh |
| PITKOVSKY | Meir | | m | M | Shmuel Leib |
| PITKOVSKY | Miriam | | f | M | |
| PITKOVSKY | Mordechai | | m | U | Liber |
| PITKOVSKY | Mordechai | | m | M | |
| PITKOVSKY | Moshekeh | | m | M | Berel |
| PITKOVSKY | Moshekeh | | m | M | |
| PITKOVSKY | Naomi | | f | U | |
| PITKOVSKY | Pesha | | f | U | Yeshi'ika |
| PITKOVSKY | Petel | | m | M | |
| PITKOVSKY | Reuven | | m | M | |
| PITKOVSKY | Rivkah | JEZRENITSKY | f | M | Shlomo |
| PITKOVSKY | Rivkah | | f | U | Liber |
| PITKOVSKY | Sheine | | f | M | |
| PITKOVSKY | Shlomo | | m | U | Shmuel Leib |
| PITKOVSKY | Shlomokeh | | m | M | |
| PITKOVSKY | Shmuel | | m | U | Liber |
| PITKOVSKY | Shmuel Lieb | | m | W | |
| PITKOVSKY | Simcha | | m | M | |
| PITKOVSKY | Sonyia | | f | M | |
| PITKOVSKY | Sprinza | | f | U | Reuven |
| PITKOVSKY | Tzirel | | f | M | |
| PITKOVSKY | unknown | | f | M | |
| PITKOVSKY | unknown | | f | U | Moshkeh |
| PITKOVSKY | unknown | | f | M | |
| PITKOVSKY | unknown | | f | M | |
| PITKOVSKY | unknown | | f | M | |
| PITKOVSKY | unknown | | f | M | |
| PITKOVSKY | unknown | | f | M | |
| PITKOVSKY | unknown | | f | M | |
| PITKOVSKY | unknown | | f | M | |
| PITKOVSKY | Yacov | | m | M | |
| PITKOVSKY | Yacov | | m | M | |
| PITKOVSKY | Yacov | | m | U | Petel |
| PITKOVSKY | Yehudaleh | | m | M | Shmuel Leib |
| PITKOVSKY | Yeshiahke | | m | M | Shmuel Leib |
| PITKOVSKY | Yisroel | | m | M | |
| PLOTNITZKY | Feige Altah | | f | M | |
| PLOTNITZKY | Gershon | | m | M | |
| PODREVSKY | Bezalel | | m | M | |

# Martyrs of Ruzhany - List Expanded from Names in Original Book

| Key: | | | m=male | U=Unmarried | |
|---|---|---|---|---|---|
| | | | f=female | M=Married | |
| | | | | W=Widow | |
| **Family name** | **First name(s)** | **Maiden name** | **Sex** | **Marital** | **Father's** |
| PODREVSKY | David | | m | U | Meir |
| PODREVSKY | Meir | | m | M | |
| PODREVSKY | Razel | | f | M | |
| PODREVSKY | Rivkah | | f | U | Meir |
| PODREVSKY | unknown | | f | M | |
| POLIAK | Chanah | | f | M | |
| POLIAK | Moshe David | | m | M | Zidel |
| POLIAK | Rachel | | f | U | Zidel |
| POLIAK | unknown | | f | M | |
| POLIAK | Zidel | | m | M | |
| POLIK | Avraham | | m | M | |
| POLIK | Chaya | | f | M | |
| POLIK | David | | m | M | |
| POLIK | Dov | | m | U | Avraham |
| POLIK | Hindah | DITKOVSKY | f | M | Zvi |
| POLIK | Rachel | | f | U | Avraham |
| POLIK | unknown | | f | W | |
| POMERANTZ | Eliahu | | m | M | |
| POMERANTZ | Henya | | f | M | |
| POMERNITZ | Avraham | | m | U | Moshe |
| POMERNITZ | Benyamin | | m | U | Zidel |
| POMERNITZ | Bilka | ROTHSTYN | f | M | |
| POMERNITZ | Bilka | ROTHSTYN | f | M | |
| POMERNITZ | Chayka | | f | M | |
| POMERNITZ | Dyna | | f | U | Moshe |
| POMERNITZ | Leah | | f | M | |
| POMERNITZ | Milia | | f | U | Zidel |
| POMERNITZ | Mordechai | | m | M | Moshe |
| POMERNITZ | Moshe | | m | M | |
| POMERNITZ | Rivkah Leah | | f | M | |
| POMERNITZ | Tuvia | | f | U | Zidel |
| POMERNITZ | Yisroel Eliahu | | m | M | |
| POMERNITZ | Zidel | | m | M | Moshe |
| PRECHKY | Basaha Leah | | f | M | |
| PRECHKY | Yacov | | m | M | |
| PRECHOWICH | Eliahu | | m | M | |
| PRECHOWICH | Gittel | | f | M | |
| PRECHOWICH | unknown | | f | W | |
| PREPSTYN | Alta | | f | W | |
| RABINOWICH | Bilka | | f | M | |
| RABINOWICH | David | | m | M | |

# Martyrs of Ruzhany - List Expanded from Names in Original Book

| Key: | | | m=male<br>f=female | U=Unmarried<br>M=Married<br>W=Widow | |
|---|---|---|---|---|---|
| **Family name** | **First name(s)** | **Maiden name** | **Sex** | **Marital** | **Father's** |
| RABINOWICH | David | | m | M | Eliezer |
| RABINOWICH | Eliezer | | m | M | |
| RABINOWICH | Heshel | | m | M | |
| RABINOWICH | Leah'kah | | f | U | |
| RABINOWICH | Liba | | f | U | David Aharon |
| RABINOWICH | Shifra | FUCHSMAN | f | M | Mordechai |
| RABINOWICH | Shmuel | | m | U | Heshel |
| RABINOWICH | unknown | | f | M | |
| RABINOWICH | Yacov Asher | | m | U | |
| RABINOWICH | Yedidyah | | m | U | Heshel |
| RABINOWICH | Yosef | | m | U | Eliezer |
| RETNER | unknown | | f | M | |
| RETNER | Yacov | | m | M | |
| REZNIK | Malkah | SEGAL | f | M | Eliezer |
| REZNIK | Yehoshua | | m | M | |
| RIZKIN | Arieh | | m | U | Zelig |
| RIZKIN | Chaim Eliahu | | m | M | |
| RIZKIN | Esther | | f | M | |
| RIZKIN | Rachel | | f | M | |
| RIZKIN | unknown | | f | U | |
| RIZKIN | Zelig | | m | M | |
| ROSOKOVSKY | Liova | LEVITAN | f | M | Moshe Chaim |
| ROSOKOVSKY | unknown | | m | M | |
| ROTBORT | Avraham | | m | M | |
| ROTBORT | Buba | | f | M | |
| ROTBORT | Mordechai | | m | U | |
| ROTBORT | Yafa | GAMERMAN | f | M | Eliahu |
| ROTBORT | Yosef | | m | U | Avraham |
| ROTHSTYN | Aharon | | m | M | |
| ROTHSTYN | Avigdor | | m | U | Chaim Zerach |
| ROTHSTYN | Chaim Zerach | | m | M | |
| ROTHSTYN | Devorah | | f | U | Chaim Zerach |
| ROTHSTYN | Hindah | | f | M | |
| ROTHSTYN | Menachem | | m | U | Yitzchak |
| ROTHSTYN | Nechama | | f | M | |
| ROTHSTYN | Sheine | | f | M | |
| ROTHSTYN | unknown | | f | M | |
| ROZEN | Hadassah | | f | M | |
| ROZEN | Miriam | MARUCHNIK | f | M | Zadok |
| ROZEN | unknown | | m | M | |

# Martyrs of Ruzhany - List Expanded from Names in Original Book

| Key: | | | m=male<br>f=female | U=Unmarried<br>M=Married<br>W=Widow | |
|---|---|---|---|---|---|
| Family name | First name(s) | Maiden name | Sex | Marital | Father's |
| ROZEN | Zusha | | m | M | |
| ROZENSTYN | Etka | | f | M | |
| ROZENSTYN | Leibel | | m | U | |
| ROZENSTYN | Simcha | | m | M | |
| ROZENSTYN | unknown | | f | M | |
| RUBINS | Ephraim | | m | U | |
| RUBINS | Tzirel | | f | M | |
| RUCHAMIS | Avraham Yitzchak | | m | M | Tuvia |
| RUCHAMIS | Biliah Chaya | | f | M | |
| RUCHAMIS | Eliezer | | m | U | Avraham Yitzchak |
| RUCHAMIS | Mordechai Aharon | | m | M | |
| RUCHAMIS | Tuvia | | m | | |
| RUCHAMIS | unknown | | f | M | |
| RUCHAMIS | unknown | | f | M | |
| RUCHAMIS | Velvel | | m | M | Mordechai Aharon |
| RUCHAMIS | Zalman Mendel | | m | M | Tuvia |
| RUCHAMIS | Zvia | | f | M | |
| RUDETSKY | Benyamin | | m | U | Eliahu |
| RUDETSKY | Berel | | m | U | Eliahu |
| RUDETSKY | Dwasha | | f | U | Eliahu |
| RUDETSKY | Eliahu | | m | M | |
| RUDETSKY | unknown | | f | M | |
| RUDETSKY | Yacov | | m | M | Eliahu |
| RUDETSKY | Yacov | | m | | |
| RUDETSKY | Zelig | | m | U | Eliahu |
| RUHZNITSKY | Chaya | | f | M | |
| RUHZNITSKY | Max | | m | M | |
| RUHZNITSKY | Moshe | | m | U | Reuven |
| RUHZNITSKY | Shimon Natan | | m | U | |
| RUHZNITSKY | unknown | | f | W | |
| RUHZNITSKY | unknown | | f | M | |
| RUHZNITSKY | Yosef | | m | U | Reuven |
| RUSHKIN | Rachel | | f | U | Yehudah |
| RUSHKIN | Shalom | | m | U | Yehudah |
| RUSHKIN | Yenta | | f | M | |
| SABCHIK | Chanah | SLUBOTITSKY | f | W | |
| SABZIN | Arieh | | m | M | Reuven |
| SABZIN | David | | m | M | Reuven |
| SABZIN | Masha | | f | M | |

# Martyrs of Ruzhany - List Expanded from Names in Original Book

| Key: | | | m=male<br>f=female | U=Unmarried<br>M=Married<br>W=Widow | |
|---|---|---|---|---|---|
| Family name | First name(s) | Maiden name | Sex | Marital | Father's |
| SABZIN | Razan | | m | M | Reuven |
| SABZIN | Reuven | | m | M | |
| SABZIN | Simcha Rock | | m | M | Reuven |
| SABZIN | unknown | | f | M | |
| SABZIN | unknown | | f | M | |
| SABZIN | unknown | | f | M | |
| SABZIN | unknown | | f | M | |
| SAMSONOWICH | Herzel | | m | U | Shmuel |
| SAMSONOWICH | Meir | | m | U | Shmuel |
| SAMSONOWICH | Mordechai | | m | | |
| SAMSONOWICH | Moshe | | m | U | Shmuel |
| SAMSONOWICH | Tamrah | | f | W | |
| SAMSONOWICH | Vicha | | | | |
| SAMZONOWICH | unknown | | f | M | |
| SAMZONOWICH | Velvel | | m | M | |
| SAPAROWICH | Aharala | | m | U | Gezel |
| SAPAROWICH | Gezel | | m | M | |
| SAPAROWICH | Gittel | | f | M | |
| SAPAROWICH | Karpel | | m | U | Gezel |
| SAPIR | Aharon | | m | U | Shabtay |
| SAPIR | Chaim | | m | U | Shabtay |
| SAPIR | Melech | | m | U | Shabtay |
| SAPIR | Shabtay | | m | M | |
| SAPIR | Trina | | f | M | |
| SCHMIDT | Moshe | | m | M | |
| SCHMIDT | unknown | | f | M | |
| SCHMIDT | unknown | | m | M | Moshe |
| SCHMIDT | unknown | | f | M | |
| SCHWARTZ | David | | m | M | |
| SCHWARTZ | Eliezer | | m | M | |
| SCHWARTZ | Yoceved | CHEIKEN | f | M | Avraham |
| SCHWARTZBERG | unknown | | m | M | |
| SCHWARTZBERG | unknown | | f | M | |
| SEBRINSKY | Bardach Wolf | | m | M | |
| SEBRINSKY | Benyamin | | m | U | |
| SEBRINSKY | Freida | | f | M | |
| SEBRINSKY | Mosheleh | | m | U | Bardach Wolf |
| SEBRINSKY | Nachum | | m | U | |
| SEBRINSKY | unknown | PRECHOWICH | f | M | Kalman |
| SEBRINSKY | unknown | | f | U | Bardach Wolf |
| SEBRINSKY | Yitzchak | | m | U | Bardach Wolf |

# Martyrs of Ruzhany - List Expanded from Names in Original Book

| Key: | | | m=male<br>f=female | U=Unmarried<br>M=Married<br>W=Widow | |
|---|---|---|---|---|---|
| **Family name** | **First name(s)** | **Maiden name** | **Sex** | **Marital** | **Father's** |
| SEGAL | Biliah | | f | M | |
| SEGAL | Eliezer | | m | M | |
| SEGAL | Ephraim | | m | U | Eliezer |
| SELMAN | Chaim Itcha | | m | M | |
| SELMAN | Gutta | | f | U | |
| SELMAN | Hashka | | f | M | |
| SELMAN | Mendel | | m | M | |
| SELMAN | Rivkah | | f | | |
| SELMAN | Sheine Elka | | f | | |
| SELMAN | Shlomokeh | | m | M | |
| SELMAN | unknown | | f | M | |
| SELMAN | unknown | | f | M | |
| SELMAN | unknown | | f | M | |
| SELMAN | unknown | | f | W | |
| SELMAN | Yitzchak | | m | M | |
| SHAPIRA | Herschel | | m | U | Mordechai |
| SHAPIRA | Mordechai | | m | M | |
| SHAPIRA | Teivel | | f | | Mordechai |
| SHEMESH | Eliahu | | m | M | Mordechai |
| SHEMESH | Feige | | f | W | |
| SHEMESH | Leah | | f | M | |
| SHEMESH | Sarah | | f | U | Mordechai |
| SHEMESH | Vichne | | f | U | Mordechai |
| SHEMSHINOWICH | Avraham | | m | U | Moshe |
| SHEMSHINOWICH | Bashkah | | f | M | |
| SHEMSHINOWICH | David | | m | M | |
| SHEMSHINOWICH | Leibel | | m | M | |
| SHEMSHINOWICH | Moshe | | m | M | |
| SHEMSHINOWICH | Shimon | | m | U | Moshe |
| SHEMSHINOWICH | Tiva | | f | M | |
| SHEMSHINOWICH | Zipkah | | f | M | |
| SHEMSHINOWICH | Zvi | | m | U | |
| SHER | Aharon | | m | M | |
| SHER | unknown | | f | M | |
| SHERESHEVSKY | Aharon | | m | M | Puah |
| SHERESHEVSKY | Avraham | | m | M | Shabtay |
| SHERESHEVSKY | Avraham | | m | U | Puah |
| SHERESHEVSKY | Miriam | | f | M | |
| SHERESHEVSKY | Puah | | m | M | |
| SHERESHEVSKY | Shabtay | | m | M | |
| SHERESHEVSKY | Tova | | f | M | |

# Martyrs of Ruzhany - List Expanded from Names in Original Book

| Key: | | | m=male<br>f=female | U=Unmarried<br>M=Married<br>W=Widow | |
|---|---|---|---|---|---|
| **Family name** | **First name(s)** | **Maiden name** | **Sex** | **Marital** | **Father's** |
| SHERESHEVSKY | unknown | | f | M | Ze'ev |
| SHERESHEVSKY | unknown | | f | M | |
| SHERESHEVSKY | unknown | WISSOTSKY | f | M | |
| SHERESHEVSKY | Yerachmiel | | m | M | Ze'ev |
| SHERESHEVSKY | Ze'ev | | m | M | |
| SHERMAN | Biliah | | f | M | |
| SHERMAN | Feigeleh | | f | U | Peshka |
| SHERMAN | Peshka | | m | M | |
| SHERMAN | Shmuel | | m | U | Peshka |
| SHIDLOVSKY | Golda | | f | M | |
| SHIDLOVSKY | unknown | | f | M | |
| SHIDLOVSKY | unknown | | f | U | |
| SHIDLOVSKY | Yacov | | m | M | |
| SHIFRIN | Moshe | | m | M | Motta Itcha |
| SHIFRIN | Noach | | m | M | Motta Itcha |
| SHIFRIN | unknown | | f | W | |
| SHIFRIN | unknown | | f | M | |
| SHIFRIN | unknown | | f | M | |
| SHIPITZSKI | Barouch | | m | M | |
| SHIPITZSKI | Chaya Sarah | | f | M | |
| SHIPITZSKI | Chayaka | | f | M | |
| SHIPITZSKI | Freidel | | f | M | |
| SHIPITZSKI | Herzel | | m | M | |
| SHIPITZSKI | Rivkah | | f | U | Herzel |
| SHIPITZSKI | Sander | | m | U | Herzel |
| SHIPITZSKI | Sarah | | f | M | |
| SHIPITZSKI | Shlomokeh | | m | U | Yacov Berel |
| SHIPITZSKI | unknown | | f | M | |
| SHIPITZSKI | unknown | | f | M | |
| SHIPITZSKI | Yacov | | m | U | Barouch |
| SHIPITZSKI | Yacov Berel | | m | M | |
| SHIPITZSKI | Yitzchak | | m | M | |
| SHIPITZSKI | Yoel | | m | M | |
| SHIPITZSKI | Zipah Minia | | f | M | |
| SHIVITZ | Sheine | | f | M | |
| SHIVITZ | unknown | | f | U | |
| SHIVITZ | unknown | | f | U | Yehoshua |
| SHIVITZ | Yehoshua | | m | M | |
| SHLUTA | unknown | | m | M | |
| SHLUTA | unknown | | f | M | |
| SHLUTZKI | Berel | | m | M | |

# Martyrs of Ruzhany - List Expanded from Names in Original Book

| Key: | | | m=male<br>f=female | U=Unmarried<br>M=Married<br>W=Widow | |
|---|---|---|---|---|---|
| **Family name** | **First name(s)** | **Maiden name** | **Sex** | **Marital** | **Father's** |
| SHLUTZKI | Hindah | | f | M | |
| SHLUTZKI | Sarah | | f | M | |
| SHMUKLER | Chaim Yosef | | m | U | Liba |
| SHMUKLER | Liba | | m | M | |
| SHMUKLER | Michael | | m | U | Liba |
| SHMUKLER | Rivkah | | f | U | Liba |
| SHMUKLER | Sheine | | f | M | |
| SHPILLER | Chanah | | f | M | |
| SHUSTER | Malkah | EPSHTEYN | f | M | Yacov Reuven |
| SHUSTER | Malkah | | f | M | |
| SHUSTER | Sander | | m | U | Zvi |
| SHUSTER | Yenta | | f | U | Zvi |
| SHUSTER | Zvi | | m | M | |
| SKLIKAVITZ | Fania | | f | U | Gadaliah |
| SKLIKAVITZ | Gadaliah | | m | M | |
| SKLIKAVITZ | Marishka | STYN | f | M | |
| SKLIKAVITZ | Mosheleh | | m | U | Gadaliah |
| SKLIRAVITZ | Hazkal | | m | M | |
| SKLIRAVITZ | Manya | | f | M | |
| SKLIRAVITZ | Meir | | m | M | |
| SKLIRAVITZ | Sarah Bilia | | f | M | |
| SKLIRAVITZ | unknown | | f | M | |
| SKLOIRAVITZ | Barouch | | m | U | Mottel |
| SKLOIRAVITZ | Miriam | JEZRENITSKY | f | M | Shlomo |
| SKLOIRAVITZ | Mottel | | m | M | |
| SKLOIRAVITZ | Zlota | | f | U | Mottel |
| SKOLNIK | Arieh | | m | U | Yosef |
| SKOLNIK | Bashkah | KAMINTSKY | f | M | Pinchas |
| SKOLNIK | Bashkah | | f | M | |
| SKOLNIK | Buba | | f | M | |
| SKOLNIK | Chaya | | f | U | Yosef |
| SKOLNIK | Eliahu | | m | M | |
| SKOLNIK | Eliahu | | m | M | |
| SKOLNIK | Esther | | f | U | |
| SKOLNIK | Leibel | | m | U | Moshe |
| SKOLNIK | Maraka | WYNITSKY | f | M | Shmuel Aharon |
| SKOLNIK | Moshe | | m | M | |
| SKOLNIK | Shimon | | m | U | Yosef |
| SKOLNIK | Shmuel | | m | U | Yosef |
| SKOLNIK | Sima | | f | M | |
| SKOLNIK | Tehilah | | f | W | |

# Martyrs of Ruzhany - List Expanded from Names in Original Book

| Key: | | | m=male<br>f=female | U=Unmarried<br>M=Married<br>W=Widow | |
|---|---|---|---|---|---|
| Family name | First name(s) | Maiden name | Sex | Marital | Father's |
| SKOLNIK | unknown | | f | M | |
| SKOLNIK | Yitzchak | | m | M | |
| SKOLNIK | Yosef | | m | M | |
| SKOLNIK | Zadok | | m | U | Moshe |
| SLATSKY | Michael | | m | U | Shmuel |
| SLATSKY | Sarah | | f | M | |
| SLATSKY | Shmuel | | m | M | |
| SLONIMCHIK | Chaim | | m | M | |
| SLONIMCHIK | Chaya | | f | M | |
| SLONIMCHIK | Dov | | m | U | Chaim |
| SLONIMCHIK | Eidel | | m | M | Issac |
| SLONIMCHIK | Elka | | f | M | |
| SLONIMCHIK | Herschel | | m | | |
| SLONIMCHIK | Issac | | m | M | |
| SLONIMCHIK | Reuchama | | f | U | Chaim |
| SLONIMCHIK | Zelda Esther | | f | M | |
| SLONIMSKY | Chanah | | f | M | |
| SLONIMSKY | Moshe | | m | M | |
| SLONIMSKY | Zvi | | m | U | Moshe |
| SLONIMSKY | Zvia | | f | U | Moshe |
| SLONISMAKY | Devorah | | f | U | |
| SLONISMAKY | Meir | | m | U | |
| SLONISMAKY | Rivkah Devorah | | f | | |
| SLUBOTITSKY | Zissel | | f | M | |
| SLUBOTITSKY | Feige Rachel | | f | W | |
| SLUBOTITSKY | Frumkah | | f | U | |
| SLUBOTITSKY | Moshekeh | | m | M | |
| SLUBOTITSKY | unknown | | f | M | |
| SLUBOTITSKY | unknown | | f | W | |
| SLUBOTITSKY | unknown | | f | M | |
| SLUBOTITSKY | Yehudaleh | | m | M | |
| SLUBOTITSKY | Yosef | | m | M | |
| SLUBOTITSKY | Zelda | | f | U | |
| SLUCHIK | Miriam | GUSTOVCKI | f | M | Zvi |
| SLUCHIK | Noach | | m | M | |
| SLUTZKY | Chaya | | f | U | Shlomo |
| SLUTZKY | Shlomo | | m | | |
| SLUTZKY | Sonyia | | f | U | Shlomo |
| SLUTZKY | Tudel | | | | Shlomo |
| SMARKOWICH | Avraham | | m | M | Bonim |

# Martyrs of Ruzhany - List Expanded from Names in Original Book

| Key: | | | m=male | U=Unmarried | |
|---|---|---|---|---|---|
| | | | f=female | M=Married | |
| | | | | W=Widow | |
| Family name | First name(s) | Maiden name | Sex | Marital | Father's |

| Family name | First name(s) | Maiden name | Sex | Marital | Father's |
|---|---|---|---|---|---|
| SMARKOWICH | Bunim | | m | M | |
| SMARKOWICH | Gadaliah | | m | U | Bonim |
| SMARKOWICH | Ida | | f | M | |
| SMARKOWICH | Meir | | m | M | Bonim |
| SMARKOWICH | Sarah | | f | M | |
| SMARKOWICH | unknown | | f | M | |
| SMARKOWICH | unknown | | f | U | Bonim |
| SMARKOWICH | Yonah | | f | U | Bonim |
| SNEIDER | David | | m | M | |
| SNEIDER | Elem | | m | U | David |
| SNEIDER | Mottel | | m | U | David |
| SNEIDER | Razel | | f | M | |
| SNOBSKY | Ida | SLONISMAKY | f | M | |
| SNOBSKY | Yosef | | m | M | |
| SOBOL | Eliezer | | m | M | |
| SOBOL | Tema | | f | M | |
| SOKOLOVSKY | Barouch | | m | M | |
| SOKOLOVSKY | Berel | | m | U | |
| SOKOLOVSKY | Chanah | | f | M | |
| SOKOLOVSKY | Chaya | | f | M | |
| SOKOLOVSKY | Chonya | | m | M | |
| SOKOLOVSKY | David Noach | | m | U | |
| SOKOLOVSKY | Ethel | | f | U | Issac |
| SOKOLOVSKY | Heinke | BLUGATCH | f | M | Benyamin |
| SOKOLOVSKY | Issac | | m | M | |
| SOKOLOVSKY | Lipa | | m | M | |
| SOKOLOVSKY | Mashkah | | m | M | Yitzchak Reuven |
| SOKOLOVSKY | Merim | | m | M | Yitzchak Reuven |
| SOKOLOVSKY | Michalia | | f | U | Issac |
| SOKOLOVSKY | Miriam | | f | U | Issac |
| SOKOLOVSKY | Moshe | | m | M | |
| SOKOLOVSKY | Sheine | | f | M | |
| SOKOLOVSKY | Shifra | BARON | f | M | Mordechai |
| SOKOLOVSKY | Shimon | | m | U | Issac |
| SOKOLOVSKY | Shlomokeh | | m | M | |
| SOKOLOVSKY | Shmuel | | m | U | Nachman |
| SOKOLOVSKY | unknown | | f | W | |
| SOKOLOVSKY | unknown | | f | M | |
| SOKOLOVSKY | unknown | | m | M | |
| SOKOLOVSKY | unknown | | f | M | |
| SOKOLOVSKY | unknown | | f | M | |

# Martyrs of Ruzhany - List Expanded from Names in Original Book

| Key: | | | m=male<br>f=female | U=Unmarried<br>M=Married<br>W=Widow | |
|---|---|---|---|---|---|
| **Family name** | **First name(s)** | **Maiden name** | **Sex** | **Marital** | **Father's** |
| SOKOLOVSKY | unknown | | f | M | |
| SOKOLOVSKY | Velvel | | m | M | Yitzchak Reuven |
| SOKOLOVSKY | Yacov | | m | U | Issac |
| SOLTZ | Zelda | | f | W | |
| SOUROKA | Leah | | f | M | |
| SOUROKA | Yehoshua | | m | M | |
| SPITELNIK | Alter | | m | M | |
| SPITELNIK | Mushka | ANISH | f | M | Berel |
| STEIN | Fania | | f | U | Shmuel Hirsch |
| STEIN | Gittel | | f | M | |
| STEIN | Golda | | f | U | Shmuel Hirsch |
| STEIN | Sarah | | f | M | |
| STEIN | Shmuel Hirsch | | m | M | |
| STEIN | Zlota | | f | U | Shmuel Hirsch |
| SUKARNITSKY | Leibel | | m | M | |
| SUKARNITSKY | Liba | BABICH | f | M | Shmuel Yehudaleh |
| SUKENIK | Henya | SHIPITZSKI | f | M | |
| SUKENIK | Yonah | | m | M | |
| SWIATITSKY | David | | m | U | Ephraim |
| SWIATITSKY | Ephraim | | m | W | |
| SWIATITSKY | Erna | | f | U | Ephraim |
| SYDLENITSKY | Devorah | | f | M | |
| SYDLENITSKY | Shimon | | m | U | Shlomo |
| SYDLENITSKY | Shlomo | | m | M | |
| SYDRANSKY | Basha | | f | M | |
| SYDRANSKY | Eliahu | | m | M | |
| SYDRANSKY | Rachel Leah | | f | W | |
| TUCHMAN | Gisha | | m | U | |
| TUCHMAN | Henya | | f | | |
| TUCHMAN | Moshe | | m | U | |
| TUCHSCHNEIDER | Leah | | f | M | |
| TUCHSCHNEIDER | unknown | | m | M | |
| TURINSKI | Freidel | GUSTOVCKI | f | M | |
| TURINSKY | Esther | | f | U | Yacov |
| TURINSKY | Freidel | | f | M | |
| TURINSKY | Liba | | f | M | |
| TURINSKY | Mina | | f | U | Yacov |
| TURINSKY | Mottel | | m | M | |
| TURINSKY | Mottel | | m | M | |
| TURINSKY | Roza | | f | M | |

# Martyrs of Ruzhany - List Expanded from Names in Original Book

| Key: | | | m=male<br>f=female | U=Unmarried<br>M=Married<br>W=Widow | |
|---|---|---|---|---|---|
| **Family name** | **First name(s)** | **Maiden name** | **Sex** | **Marital** | **Father's** |
| TURINSKY | Shmuel | | m | M | Mottel |
| TURINSKY | unknown | | m | U | Shmuel |
| TURINSKY | Yacov | | m | M | |
| TURINSKY | Yisroel | | m | M | |
| TURINSKY | Zissele | | f | U | Shmuel |
| TURINSKY | Zvia | | f | M | |
| TURN | Chaim | | m | U | Dov Berel |
| TURN | Dov Berel | | m | M | |
| TURN | Esther | LIPSHITZ | f | M | |
| TURN | Moshe | | m | W | |
| TURN | Nissan | | m | U | Dov Berel |
| unknown | Aharon | | m | M | |
| unknown | Asher | | m | M | |
| unknown | Barouch | | m | M | |
| unknown | Bat Sheva | EPSHTEYN | f | M | |
| unknown | Bilka | BRAZOVSKY | f | M | Raphael |
| unknown | Bliumke | BLUGATCH | f | M | |
| unknown | Broda | | m | M | |
| unknown | Brynne | BARON | f | M | Mordechai |
| unknown | Chaim | | m | M | |
| unknown | Chanacha | BIALOS | f | M | |
| unknown | Chanah | | f | U | Chaim |
| unknown | Chanah | MARMINSKY | f | M | Raphael |
| unknown | Chanah | PITKOVSKY | f | M | Reuven |
| unknown | Chanah | FARBER | f | M | Moshe |
| unknown | Chasia | | f | U | |
| unknown | Chaya | VYGODESKY | f | M | Moshe |
| unknown | Chaya | KARLITSKY | f | M | Alter |
| unknown | Chayaka | SHERMAN | f | M | |
| unknown | Devorah | PITKOVSKY | f | M | Liber |
| unknown | Duba | TURN | f | M | Moshe |
| unknown | Duba | SHIPITZSKI | f | M | |
| unknown | Duba Nechama | | f | M | Avigdor |
| unknown | Eliahu | | m | M | |
| unknown | Eliezer | | m | U | Moshe |
| unknown | Esther | SOUROKA | f | M | Yehoshua |
| unknown | Esther | ZEMACH | f | M | Yacov |
| unknown | Esther | KROLITSKY | f | M | |
| unknown | Esther Neche | SNEIDER | m | M | David |
| unknown | Etka | KAPLAN | f | M | Moshe |

# Martyrs of Ruzhany - List Expanded from Names in Original Book

| Key: | | | m=male<br>f=female | U=Unmarried<br>M=Married<br>W=Widow | |
|---|---|---|---|---|---|
| **Family name** | **First name(s)** | **Maiden name** | **Sex** | **Marital** | **Father's** |
| unknown | Feige Ittka | LEVITSKY | f | M | Mordechai |
| unknown | Feigeleh | SABZIN | f | M | Reuven |
| unknown | Feivel | | m | M | |
| unknown | Frekel | | m | M | |
| unknown | Fruma Hindah | | f | M | |
| unknown | Frydel | MORDECHOWITZ | f | M | Alter |
| unknown | Frydel | PITKOVSKY | f | M | |
| unknown | Gisha | PITKOVSKY | f | M | Moshkeh |
| unknown | Gisha | PITKOVSKY | f | M | |
| unknown | Gita | PODREVSKY | f | M | Meir |
| unknown | Gittel | TURN | f | M | Moshe |
| unknown | Gittel | SCOLNIK | f | M | Moshe |
| unknown | Gutta | SELMAN | f | M | |
| unknown | Hasha | LIBERMAN | f | M | Yitzchak |
| unknown | Hazkal | | m | M | |
| unknown | Heinke | PITKOVSKY | f | M | Yacov |
| unknown | Henya | STYN | f | M | |
| unknown | Herzel | | m | M | |
| unknown | Karina Tzirel | FURMAN | f | M | |
| unknown | Leah | VYGODESKY | f | M | Moshe |
| unknown | Leah | FUCHSMAN | f | M | |
| unknown | Leah | SHIFRIN | f | M | Motta Itcha |
| unknown | Leibel | | m | M | |
| unknown | Leibel | | m | M | |
| unknown | Libaka | | f | U | |
| unknown | Libale | | f | | Chaim |
| unknown | Lifcze | | f | U | |
| unknown | Liovka | | f | U | Moshe |
| unknown | Malkah | | f | U | Frekel |
| unknown | Marishka | ZAZHVIR | f | M | |
| unknown | Masha | ORLINSKY | f | M | Avraham Yeshiahu |
| unknown | Mashkah | BAYR | f | M | Abba |
| unknown | Meir | | m | M | |
| unknown | Menedele | | m | U | Chaim |
| unknown | Menucha | SAMSONOWICH | f | | |
| unknown | Michalia | SOKOLOVSKY | f | M | Yitzchak Reuven |
| unknown | Mita | RUSHKIN | f | M | |
| unknown | Moshe | | m | M | |
| unknown | Moshe | | m | M | |
| unknown | Moshe Zvi | | m | M | |

# Martyrs of Ruzhany - List Expanded from Names in Original Book

| Key: | | | m=male<br>f=female | U=Unmarried<br>M=Married<br>W=Widow | |
|---|---|---|---|---|---|
| **Family name** | **First name(s)** | **Maiden name** | **Sex** | **Marital** | **Father's** |
| unknown | Mosheleh | | m | M | |
| unknown | Mushka | BAYR | f | M | Abba |
| unknown | Mushka | WAJNSTYN | f | M | Chaim Zalman |
| unknown | Nachum | | m | U | Shmuel |
| unknown | Naomi | PITKOVSKY | f | M | Liber |
| unknown | Naomi | EPSHTEYN | f | M | Arim |
| unknown | Natan | | m | M | |
| unknown | Nechama | LEV | f | M | Yacov Michael |
| unknown | Neche | SLONIMCHIK | f | M | Chaim |
| unknown | Perel | KOVNESKY | f | M | Shmuel |
| unknown | Pesel | ALPER | f | W | Avraham Shlomo |
| unknown | Pesha | WILENSKY | f | M | Yitzchak |
| unknown | Rachel | BRAZOVSKY | f | M | Raphael |
| unknown | Rachel | YELSKY | f | M | Moshe |
| unknown | Rachel | PITKOVSKY | f | M | Simcha |
| unknown | Rachel | SHEMESH | f | M | Mordechai |
| unknown | Rayah | KAMINER | f | M | |
| unknown | Rivkah | EPSHTEYN | f | M | |
| unknown | Rivkah | KAMINTSKY | f | M | Pinchas |
| unknown | Rivkah | SCOLNIK | f | M | Yosef |
| unknown | Rivkah | SCOLNIK | f | M | Moshe |
| unknown | Rivkah | | f | U | |
| unknown | Sarah | VYGODESKY | f | M | |
| unknown | Sarah | SLUBOTITSKY | f | M | |
| unknown | Sarah | FUCHSMAN | f | M | Aharon Mordechai |
| unknown | Sarah | | m | M | |
| unknown | Sarah Dubah | FOKSMAN | f | M | |
| unknown | Sarah Fruma | FINKEL | f | M | |
| unknown | Sarkah | SYDRANSKY | f | M | |
| unknown | Schana | | m | M | |
| unknown | Shaul | | m | M | |
| unknown | Sheine | FUCHSMAN | f | M | |
| unknown | Sheine Schitzirka | FOKSMAN | f | M | |
| unknown | Shifra | EPSHTEYN | f | M | Barouch |
| unknown | Shifra | GOLDBERG | f | M | Araka |
| unknown | Shlomo | | m | M | |
| unknown | Shmuel | | m | M | |
| unknown | Shyndel | RABINOWICH | f | M | |
| unknown | Sima | PITKOVSKY | f | M | Moshkeh |

# Martyrs of Ruzhany - List Expanded from Names in Original Book

| Key: | | | m=male<br>f=female | U=Unmarried<br>M=Married<br>W=Widow | |
|---|---|---|---|---|---|
| **Family name** | **First name(s)** | **Maiden name** | **Sex** | **Marital** | **Father's** |
| unknown | Sima | EINSTEIN | f | M | Yoel |
| unknown | Sonyia | ITZKOWICH | f | M | Moshe |
| unknown | Sonyia | MINKOWICH | m | M | Berel |
| unknown | Sonyia | PITKOVSKY | f | M | Moshkeh |
| unknown | Sonyia | KAPLINSKY | f | M | Moshe |
| unknown | Sonyia | KAPLAN | f | M | Yosef |
| unknown | Sonyia | RIZKIN | f | M | Zelig |
| unknown | Tuvia Lev | | m | M | |
| unknown | Tzirel | BAYR | f | M | Abba |
| unknown | unknown | | m | M | |
| unknown | unknown | | m | M | |
| unknown | unknown | | m | M | |
| unknown | unknown | | m | M | |
| unknown | unknown | | m | M | |
| unknown | unknown | | m | M | |
| unknown | unknown | | m | M | |
| unknown | unknown | | m | M | |
| unknown | unknown | | m | M | |
| unknown | unknown | | m | M | |
| unknown | unknown | GUBER | f | M | Alter |
| unknown | unknown | | m | M | Araka |
| unknown | unknown | | f | M | |
| unknown | unknown | | m | M | |
| unknown | unknown | | m | M | |
| unknown | unknown | | m | M | |
| unknown | unknown | | m | M | |
| unknown | unknown | | m | M | |
| unknown | unknown | ZACKHEIM | f | M | |
| unknown | unknown | | f | U | |
| unknown | unknown | | m | M | |
| unknown | unknown | | m | M | |
| unknown | unknown | | m | M | |
| unknown | unknown | JANKELOWICZ | f | M | Eliezer |
| unknown | unknown | | m | M | |
| unknown | unknown | | m | M | |
| unknown | unknown | | m | M | |
| unknown | unknown | | f | M | |
| unknown | unknown | | m | M | |
| unknown | unknown | | m | M | |
| unknown | unknown | | m | M | |
| unknown | unknown | SYDLENITSKY | f | M | Shlomo |

# Martyrs of Ruzhany - List Expanded from Names in Original Book

| Key: | | | m=male<br>f=female | U=Unmarried<br>M=Married<br>W=Widow | |
|---|---|---|---|---|---|
| **Family name** | **First name(s)** | **Maiden name** | **Sex** | **Marital** | **Father's** |
| unknown | unknown | | m | M | |
| unknown | unknown | SLONIMCHIK | f | M | Hirschel |
| unknown | unknown | | m | M | |
| unknown | unknown | | m | M | |
| unknown | unknown | | m | M | |
| unknown | unknown | | m | M | |
| unknown | unknown | | m | M | |
| unknown | unknown | | m | M | |
| unknown | unknown | | m | M | |
| unknown | unknown | | m | M | |
| unknown | unknown | | m | U | |
| unknown | unknown | | f | U | |
| unknown | unknown | | m | M | |
| unknown | unknown | | m | M | |
| unknown | unknown | | m | M | |
| unknown | unknown | | m | M | |
| unknown | unknown | PLOTNITZKY | f | M | Gershon |
| unknown | unknown | | m | M | |
| unknown | unknown | | f | M | |
| unknown | unknown | | m | M | |
| unknown | unknown | | m | M | |
| unknown | unknown | | m | M | |
| unknown | unknown | KAPLAN | f | M | Herzel |
| unknown | unknown | | m | M | |
| unknown | unknown | | m | M | |
| unknown | unknown | | m | M | |
| unknown | unknown | | f | M | |
| unknown | unknown | KAPLAN | f | M | |
| unknown | unknown | | m | M | |
| unknown | unknown | | m | M | |
| unknown | unknown | | m | M | |
| unknown | unknown | RUBINS | f | M | |
| unknown | unknown | | m | M | |
| unknown | unknown | | m | M | |
| unknown | unknown | SCHWARTZ | f | W | Eliezer |
| unknown | unknown | | f | U | Herzel |
| unknown | unknown | SCHMIDT | f | M | Moshe |
| unknown | unknown | | m | M | |
| unknown | unknown | | f | M | |
| unknown | unknown | | m | M | |
| unknown | unknown | | m | M | |

# Martyrs of Ruzhany - List Expanded from Names in Original Book

| Key: | | | m=male<br>f=female | U=Unmarried<br>M=Married<br>W=Widow | |
|---|---|---|---|---|---|
| **Family name** | **First name(s)** | **Maiden name** | **Sex** | **Marital** | **Father's** |
| unknown | unknown | | m | M | |
| unknown | unknown | | m | U | |
| unknown | Velvel | | m | M | |
| unknown | Weizel | | m | M | |
| unknown | Yachne | SHEMSHINOWICH | f | M | |
| unknown | Yeihezkel | | m | M | |
| unknown | Yenta | PODREVSKY | f | M | Meir |
| unknown | Yenta | PITKOVSKY | f | M | Simcha |
| unknown | Yeshiahke | | m | U | |
| unknown | Yitzchak | | m | M | |
| unknown | Yitzchak | | m | U | Yacov |
| unknown | Yosef | | m | M | |
| unknown | Zelda | RUDETSKY | f | M | Eliahu |
| unknown | Zelda Mendel | | m | M | Avigdor |
| VELER | Leib Eliahu | | m | M | |
| VELER | unknown | | f | M | |
| VELYN | Aharon | | m | M | Yisroel |
| VELYN | Eliahu | | m | M | Yisroel |
| VELYN | Gisha | | f | M | |
| VELYN | Mottel | | m | M | Yisroel |
| VELYN | Shalom | | m | M | Yisroel |
| VELYN | Sima | | f | M | |
| VELYN | Tuvia | | f | M | |
| VELYN | unknown | | f | M | |
| VELYN | unknown | | f | M | |
| VELYN | unknown | | f | M | |
| VELYN | Yisroel | | m | M | |
| VELYN | Yitzchak | | m | M | Yisroel |
| VYGODESKY | Charne | | f | M | |
| VYGODESKY | Ethel | | f | U | |
| VYGODESKY | Ethel | | f | U | |
| VYGODESKY | Moshe | | m | M | |
| VYGODESKY | Rava | | f | W | |
| VYGODESKY | Sarah | | f | W | |
| VYGODESKY | Yenta | | f | W | |
| WAJNBERG | Chaya | CHROITISKI | f | M | Mordechai Yehudaleh |
| WAJNBERG | Yisroel | | m | M | |
| WAJNSTYN | Chaim Zalman | | m | M | |
| WAJNSTYN | Chanah | | f | U | Moshe |
| WAJNSTYN | Hadassah | ITZKOWICH | f | M | Moshe |

# Martyrs of Ruzhany - List Expanded from Names in Original Book

| Key: | | | m=male<br>f=female | U=Unmarried<br>M=Married<br>W=Widow | |
|---|---|---|---|---|---|
| Family name | First name(s) | Maiden name | Sex | Marital | Father's |
| WAJNSTYN | Masha Feigel | | f | M | |
| WAJNSTYN | Moshe | | m | M | |
| WAJNSTYN | Reuven | | m | U | Moshe |
| WALLACH | Hadassah | | f | W | |
| WALLACH | Ittale | | m | U | Weiss |
| WALLACH | Shmaryahu | | f | U | Weiss |
| WALLACH | Yom-Tov | | f | U | Weiss |
| WEIZMANN | Yisroel | | m | M | |
| WEIZMANN | Zissel | | f | M | |
| WILENCHIK | Avraham | | m | M | |
| WILENCHIK | Libka | | f | M | |
| WILENCHIK | Moshe | | m | U | Avraham |
| WILENCHIK | Yehudaleh | | m | U | Avraham |
| WILENSKY | Chanah | | f | M | |
| WILENSKY | Kunia | | f | W | |
| WILENSKY | Yitzchak | | m | M | |
| WILENSKY | Yoceved | | f | U | Yitzchak |
| WILENSKY | Yosef | | m | U | Yitzchak |
| WISHNIVSKY | Biliah | | f | U | |
| WISHNIVSKY | Chanah | | f | U | Ephraim |
| WISHNIVSKY | Ephraim | | m | M | |
| WISHNIVSKY | Matlia | | f | W | |
| WISHNIVSKY | Sarah | | f | M | |
| WISHNIVSKY | unknown | | f | M | |
| WISHNIVSKY | Yosef | | m | U | Ephraim |
| WISSOTZKY | Heinke | PITKOVSKY | f | M | Petel |
| WISSOTZKY | Simcha | | m | M | |
| WISSOTZKY | unknown | | f | M | |
| WISSOTZKY | Yitzchak | | m | M | |
| WISSOTZKY | Yonah Shmuel | | m | U | Yitzchak |
| WYNITSKY | Aharon | | m | M | |
| WYNITSKY | Zelda | | f | M | |
| YELSKY | Malkah | | f | M | |
| YELSKY | Moshe | | m | M | |
| YELSKY | Sarah | | f | U | Moshe |
| ZACKHEIM | Avraham | | m | M | |
| ZACKHEIM | Bashkah | | f | M | |
| ZACKHEIM | Benyamin | | m | U | |
| ZACKHEIM | Berel Shlomo | | m | M | |
| ZACKHEIM | Buba | | f | | |

# Martyrs of Ruzhany - List Expanded from Names in Original Book

| Key: | | | m=male<br>f=female | U=Unmarried<br>M=Married<br>W=Widow | |
|---|---|---|---|---|---|
| Family name | First name(s) | Maiden name | Sex | Marital | Father's |
| ZACKHEIM | Chanah | | f | M | |
| ZACKHEIM | Chanania | | m | M | |
| ZACKHEIM | Chayaka | | f | M | |
| ZACKHEIM | David | | m | M | |
| ZACKHEIM | David | | m | U | |
| ZACKHEIM | Elka | | f | M | |
| ZACKHEIM | Esther | | f | U | |
| ZACKHEIM | Feigel | | f | M | |
| ZACKHEIM | Freidaka | | f | M | |
| ZACKHEIM | Karina | | f | U | Berel Shlomo |
| ZACKHEIM | Lipa | | m | M | |
| ZACKHEIM | Michael | | m | M | |
| ZACKHEIM | Mordechai | | m | M | |
| ZACKHEIM | Moshe Mordechai | | m | W | |
| ZACKHEIM | Moshekeh | | m | M | Mordechai |
| ZACKHEIM | Nissel | | m | U | |
| ZACKHEIM | Rivkah | | f | U | Berel Shlomo |
| ZACKHEIM | Sarah Yoca | | f | U | Berel Shlomo |
| ZACKHEIM | Shlomokeh | | m | M | |
| ZACKHEIM | Shmuel | | m | U | Moshe Mordechai |
| ZACKHEIM | unknown | | f | M | |
| ZACKHEIM | unknown | | f | M | |
| ZACKHEIM | unknown | | f | U | |
| ZACKHEIM | unknown | | f | M | |
| ZACKHEIM | unknown | | f | M | |
| ZAZHVIR | Mottel | | m | U | |
| ZAZHVIR | unknown | | m | M | |
| ZAZHVIR | unknown | | f | M | |
| ZAZHVIR | Zipah | | f | M | |
| ZEBLIVSKY | Eliahu | | m | M | |
| ZEBLIVSKY | Leahcheh | | f | M | |
| ZEBLIVSKY | Musha | | f | U | Eliahu |
| ZEBNITSKY | Avremh | | m | U | Petel |
| ZEBNITSKY | Chanania Chaya | | m | U | Petel |
| ZEBNITSKY | Devorah | | f | U | Petel |
| ZEBNITSKY | Matlia | | f | M | |
| ZEBNITSKY | Petel | | m | M | |
| ZEBNITSKY | Yehudit | | f | U | Petel |
| ZELBIANSKY | Avraham | | m | U | Hirschel |
| ZELBIANSKY | Herschel | | m | M | |

# Martyrs of Ruzhany - List Expanded from Names in Original Book

| Key: | | | m=male<br>f=female | U=Unmarried<br>M=Married<br>W=Widow | |
|---|---|---|---|---|---|
| Family name | First name(s) | Maiden name | Sex | Marital | Father's |
| ZELBIANSKY | Leahcheh | | f | M | |
| ZELBIANSKY | Yehudit | | f | U | Hirschel |
| ZEMACH | Elka | | f | M | |
| ZEMACH | Leibel | | m | U | Yacov |
| ZEMACH | Yacov | | m | M | |
| ZISKIND | Avner | | m | M | |
| ZISKIND | Moshe | | m | W | |
| ZISKIND | Sonyia | | f | M | |
| ZISKIND | unknown | | f | M | |
| ZISKIND | Velvel | | m | M | |
| ZISKIND | Yacov | | m | U | |
| ZLOTNER | Daniel | | m | U | Ephraim |
| ZLOTNER | Ephraim | | m | M | |
| ZLOTNER | Sheine Liba | | f | M | |
| ZLOTNER | unknown | | f | M | |
| ZLOTNER | Yacov | | m | U | Ephraim |
| ZLOTNER | Yehudit | | f | U | Ephraim |
| ZLOTNER | Yenta | | f | U | Ephraim |
| ZLOTNER | Yitzchak | | m | M | |
| ZLOTNITSKY | Chaya Yenta | | f | M | |
| ZLOTNITSKY | Simcha | | m | M | |
| ZLOTNITSKY | unknown | | f | M | |
| ZLOTNITSKY | Velvel | | m | M | Simcha |
| ZMOCHOVSKY | Bliume Delka | | f | M | |
| ZMOCHOVSKY | David | | m | U | Yisroel |
| ZMOCHOVSKY | Sarah | | f | U | Yisroel |
| ZMOCHOVSKY | Yisroel | | m | M | |
| ZUCKERMAN | Natan | | m | M | |
| ZUCKERMAN | unknown | | f | M | |
| ZUCKERMAN | unknown | | f | M | |

## Martyrs of Towns Near Ruzhany
### List Expanded from Names in Original Book

| Family name | First name(s) | Maiden name | Sex | Marital status | Father's name | Town |
|---|---|---|---|---|---|---|
| L:Liskovo | P: Pavlova | K: Konstantynowo | | | S: Kalazuby, Kolyany, Sheypyak | |
| BAYR | Avraham | | m | M | | P |
| BAYR | Rachel | SOBOLSKY | f | M | Dov | P |
| BAYR | Sarah Hasa | | f | M | | P |
| BAYR | Shlomo | | m | M | | P |
| BERNSTYN | Baracha | | f | M | | P |
| BERNSTYN | Henya | | f | U | Zundel | P |
| BERNSTYN | Zundel | | m | M | | P |
| BRUTON | Alter | | m | M | | P |
| BRUTON | Sarah Henia | | f | M | | P |
| DELOGOLANSKY | Etcha | BERKOWICH | f | M | | P |
| DELOGOLANSKY | unknown | | m | M | | P |
| DELTISKY | Avraham Yosef | | m | M | Noach Avigdor Yitzchak | P |
| DELTISKY | Pesha | RUHZANSKY | f | M | Aharon | P |
| FRYMAN | Aharon | | m | M | | P |
| FRYMAN | Chayaleh | | f | U | Aharon | P |
| FRYMAN | Rozkah | JANOWICZ | f | M | | P |
| HOFFMAN | Dov | | m | U | Yitzchak | P |
| HOFFMAN | Elka | | f | U | Yitzchak | P |
| HOFFMAN | Sheine | | f | M | | P |
| HOFFMAN | Yitzchak | | m | M | | P |
| JANOWICZ | Aharon | | m | U | Mottel | P |
| JANOWICZ | Avraham | | m | U | Mottel | P |
| JANOWICZ | Bezalel | | m | U | Mottel | P |
| JANOWICZ | Chanah | | f | M | | P |
| JANOWICZ | Freidel | | f | U | Mottel | P |
| JANOWICZ | Haika | | f | M | | P |
| JANOWICZ | Itchel | | m | | Tudros | P |
| JANOWICZ | Itka | | f | U | Tudros | P |
| JANOWICZ | Sheine | | f | M | | P |
| JANOWICZ | Shmuel | | m | U | Mottel | P |
| JANOWICZ | Tudros | | m | M | Velvel | P |
| JANOWICZ | unknown | | f | U | Tudros | P |
| JANOWICZ | Yitzchak | | m | U | Mottel | P |
| JANOWICZ | Zalman | | m | U | Tudros | P |
| KAPLAN | Eliezer | | m | M | | P |
| KAPLAN | Itka | | f | M | | P |
| KAPLAN | Shabtay | | m | M | Eliezer | P |
| KAPLAN | unknown | | f | M | | P |
| KARLITS | Brynne Liba | | f | M | | P |
| KARLITS | Eliezer Chaim | | m | M | | P |
| KARP | Hadassah | | f | M | | P |

## Martyrs of Towns Near Ruzhany
## List Expanded from Names in Original Book

| Family name | First name(s) | Maiden name | Sex | Marital status | Father's name | Town |
|---|---|---|---|---|---|---|
| L:Liskovo | P: Pavlova | K: Konstantynowo | | | S: Kalazuby, Kolyany, Sheypyak | |
| KARP | Leib | | m | M | | P |
| KOSOVSKY | Berel | | m | M | | P |
| KOSOVSKY | Shoshah Rachel | | f | U | Velvel | P |
| KOSOVSKY | unknown | | f | M | | P |
| KOSOVSKY | unknown | | f | M | | P |
| KOSOVSKY | Velvel | | m | M | | P |
| KOZAK | Chanan | | m | M | | P |
| KOZAK | Freida Leah | | f | M | | P |
| KOZAK | Freidel | | f | M | | P |
| KOZAK | unknown | | f | M | | P |
| KOZAK | Yitzchak | | m | M | | P |
| KRABCHIK | Moshekeh | | m | M | | P |
| KRABCHIK | Rachel | | f | M | | P |
| KRAVCHIK | Shmuel | | m | M | | P |
| KRAVCHIK | Shoshah | | f | M | | P |
| KRAVCHIK | unknown | | f | M | | P |
| LEVIN | Hasha | | f | U | Moshe | P |
| LEVIN | Hazkal | | m | M | | P |
| LEVIN | Leib | | m | M | | P |
| LEVIN | Leibel | | m | M | Hazkal | P |
| LEVIN | Mara | | f | U | | P |
| LEVIN | Moshe | | m | M | | P |
| LEVIN | Moshe | | m | U | | P |
| LEVIN | Mosheleh | | m | M | Hazkal | P |
| LEVIN | Pesha | KOZAK | f | M | | P |
| LEVIN | Rivkah | | f | M | | P |
| LEVIN | Sarah | | f | M | | P |
| LEVIN | Shoshah Esther | | f | M | | P |
| LEVIN | unknown | | f | M | | P |
| LEVIN | unknown | | f | M | | P |
| LEVIN | unknown | | f | M | | P |
| LEVIN | Yisroel | | m | M | Leib | P |
| LEVIN | Yosef | | m | M | | P |
| LISSKOVSKY | Chanah | | f | M | | P |
| LISSKOVSKY | Chonka | | m | M | Shmuel | P |
| LISSKOVSKY | Hamaka | | f | M | | P |
| LISSKOVSKY | Issac | | m | M | Shmuel | P |
| LISSKOVSKY | Meir | | m | M | Shmuel | P |
| LISSKOVSKY | Michalia | | f | M | | P |
| LISSKOVSKY | Mordechai | | m | M | | P |
| LISSKOVSKY | Pesha Rachel | | f | M | | P |

## Martyrs of Towns Near Ruzhany
## List Expanded from Names in Original Book

| Family name | First name(s) | Maiden name | Sex | Marital status | Father's name | Town |
|---|---|---|---|---|---|---|
| L:Liskovo | P: Pavlova | K: Konstantynowo | | | S: Kalazuby, Kolyany, Sheypyak | |
| LISSKOVSKY | Shimon | | m | M | Yacov Leib | P |
| LISSKOVSKY | Shlomo | | m | M | | P |
| LISSKOVSKY | Shmuel | | m | M | | P |
| LISSKOVSKY | Shmuel | | m | M | | P |
| LISSKOVSKY | unknown | WISSOTSKY | f | M | | P |
| LISSKOVSKY | unknown | | f | M | | P |
| LISSKOVSKY | unknown | | f | M | | P |
| LISSKOVSKY | unknown | | f | M | | P |
| LISSKOVSKY | unknown | | f | M | | P |
| LISSKOVSKY | Yacov Lieb | | m | M | | P |
| LISSKOVSKY | Yehudaleh | | m | M | | P |
| LISSKOVSKY | Yitzchak | | m | M | | P |
| MASHTZNIN | Chava | | f | U | Yacov | P |
| MASHTZNIN | Itta | | f | M | | P |
| MASHTZNIN | Mosheleh | | m | U | Yacov | P |
| MASHTZNIN | Yacov | | m | M | | P |
| MELLER | Feivel | | m | U | | P |
| MELLER | Moshekeh | | m | M | | P |
| MELLER | Nechama | | f | U | Moshkeh | P |
| MELLER | Peshka | | f | U | | P |
| MELLER | Rivkah | | f | M | | P |
| MELLER | Sheine Elka | | f | M | | P |
| MELLER | Shulamis | | f | M | | P |
| MELLER | Yakutiel | | m | U | | P |
| MELLER | Yitzchak Yacov Moshe | | m | U | Moshkeh Yitzchak | P |
| MULCHDESKY | Nathanel | | m | M | Aharon | P |
| MULCHDESKY | Rachel Leah | RUHZANSKY | f | M | | P |
| MULCHDESKY | unknown Yitzchak | | f | M | | P |
| MULCHDESKY | Aharon | | m | M | | P |
| MURDETSKY | Avraham | | m | U | Chaim | P |
| MURDETSKY | Chaim | | m | U | | P |
| MURDETSKY | Chayaka | JANOWICZ | f | M | | P |
| PERPELIOTCHIK | Sarah Rivkah | | f | M | | P |
| PITLOWICH | Edzia | | | | | P |
| PITLOWICH | Esther Razel | | f | M | | P |
| PITLOWICH | Fania | | f | U | | P |
| PITLOWICH | Shabtay | | m | U | | P |
| PITLOWICH | Shyndel | | f | U | | P |
| PRESS | Benyamin | | m | U | Chaim Berel | P |
| PRESS | Chaim Berel | | m | M | Yonah Reuven | P |

## Martyrs of Towns Near Ruzhany
## List Expanded from Names in Original Book

| Family name | First name(s) | Maiden name | Sex | Marital status | Father's name | Town |
|---|---|---|---|---|---|---|
| L:Liskovo | P: Pavlova | K: Konstantynowo | | | S: Kalazuby, Kolyany, Sheypyak | |
| PRESS | Chava | | f | M | | P |
| PRESS | Meir | | m | M | Yonah Reuven | P |
| PRESS | Rivkah | | f | M | | P |
| PRESS | Sarah Leah | | f | M | | P |
| PRESS | Tzirel | | f | M | | P |
| PRESS | Yacov Moshe | | m | M | Yonah Reuven | P |
| PRESS | Yonah Reuven | | m | M | | P |
| RECHTSHRIBER | unknown | | m | M | | P |
| RECHTSHRIBER | unknown | | f | M | | P |
| ROYTBURT | Chaya | | f | U | | P |
| ROYTBURT | Hodel | | f | U | | P |
| ROYTBURT | Mendel | | m | M | | P |
| ROYTBURT | Rivkah | | f | U | | P |
| ROYTBURT | unknown | | f | M | | P |
| ROYTBURT | unknown | | f | W | | P |
| ROZENBAUM | Esther | KARLITS | f | M | Eliezer Chaim | P |
| ROZENBAUM | Moshe | | m | M | | P |
| RUBENSTYN | Chava | | f | U | Feivel | P |
| RUBENSTYN | Feivel | | m | M | | P |
| RUBENSTYN | Herschel | | m | U | Feivel | P |
| RUBENSTYN | Leibel | | m | M | Feivel | P |
| RUBENSTYN | Malia | | f | U | Feivel | P |
| RUBENSTYN | unknown | | f | M | | P |
| RUBENSTYN | unknown | | f | M | | P |
| RUBENSTYN | unknown | | f | M | | P |
| RUBENSTYN | Yitzchak | | m | U | Feivel | P |
| RUBENSTYN | Yitzchak | | m | M | | P |
| RUBENSTYN | Zipah | | f | M | | P |
| RUHZANSKY | Chaya Rivkah | | f | W | | P |
| RUHZANSKY | Minia | | f | M | | P |
| RUHZANSKY | Noach Avigdor | | m | M | Yitzchak Aharon | P |
| RUHZANSKY | Sarah | | f | M | | P |
| RUHZANSKY | Yisroel David | | m | M | | P |
| SCHWARTZ | Rota | | f | M | | P |
| SCHWARTZ | Shabtay | | m | U | Yosef | P |
| SCHWARTZ | Yitzchak | | m | U | Yosef | P |
| SCHWARTZ | Yosef | | m | M | | P |
| SHAPIRA | David | | m | M | | P |
| SHAPIRA | Matos | | m | M | David | P |
| SHAPIRA | Pesel | | f | M | | P |
| SHAPIRA | unknown | | f | M | | P |

## Martyrs of Towns Near Ruzhany
## List Expanded from Names in Original Book

| Family name | First name(s) | Maiden name | Sex | Marital status | Father's name | Town |
|---|---|---|---|---|---|---|
| L:Liskovo | P: Pavlova | K: Konstantynowo | | | S: Kalazuby, Kolyany, Sheypyak | |
| SHERESHEVSKY | Freidel | | f | M | | P |
| SHERESHEVSKY | Nachman | | m | M | Yitzchak | P |
| SHERESHEVSKY | unknown | | f | M | | P |
| SHERESHEVSKY | Yisroel Aharon | | m | M | | P |
| SHERESHEVSKY | Yitzchak | | m | M | | P |
| SHERESHEVSKY | Zlota | | f | M | | P |
| SHULKES | Alta | | f | M | | P |
| SHULKES | Chaya | KOZAK | f | M | | P |
| SHULKES | Chaya Bilka | | f | U | | P |
| SHULKES | Eliahu | | m | M | | P |
| SHULKES | Maryna Rivkah | | f | M | | P |
| SHULKES | Michael | | m | M | | P |
| SHULKES | Moshe Aharon | | m | M | | P |
| SHULKES | unknown | | f | M | | P |
| SHULKES | unknown | | f | M | | P |
| SHULKES | Yosef | | m | U | | P |
| SLODOBNIK | Avraham | | m | M | | P |
| SLODOBNIK | Rivkah | | f | M | | P |
| SLODOBNIK | unknown | | f | M | | P |
| SOBOLSKY | Dov | | m | M | | P |
| SOBOLSKY | Eliezer | | m | M | | P |
| SOBOLSKY | Elka | | f | U | Dov | P |
| SOBOLSKY | Minia | | f | U | Dov | P |
| SOBOLSKY | Musha | | f | M | | P |
| SOBOLSKY | Shulamis | | f | U | Dov | P |
| SOBOLSKY | Tzirel | | f | U | Dov | P |
| SOBOLSKY | Yehudit | | f | M | | P |
| SPITELNIK | Chaya Sarah | | f | M | | P |
| SPITELNIK | Mushka | | f | M | | P |
| SPITELNIK | Noach Yitzchak | | m | M | | P |
| STRUBOLSKY | Yitzchak | | m | | | P |
| unknown | Avremh | | m | M | | P |
| unknown | Berel | | m | M | | P |
| unknown | Chaim | | m | M | | P |
| unknown | Chanah | SCHWARTZ | f | M | Yosef | P |
| unknown | Chanah | | f | U | Yerachmiel | P |
| unknown | Chanania | | m | U | Yisroel Aharon | P |
| unknown | Chava | LEVIN | f | M | Hazkal | P |
| unknown | Chaya Leah | KOSOVSKY | f | M | Velvel | P |
| unknown | David | | m | U | Kupitch | P |
| unknown | Eliezer | | m | U | Kupitch | P |

## Martyrs of Towns Near Ruzhany
## List Expanded from Names in Original Book

| Family name | First name(s) | Maiden name | Sex | Marital status | Father's name | Town |
|---|---|---|---|---|---|---|
| L:Liskovo | P: Pavlova | K: Konstantynowo | | | S: Kalazuby, Kolyany, Sheypyak | |
| unknown | Elka | PERPELIOTCHIK | f | M | | P |
| unknown | Esther Razel | PRESS | f | M | Yonah Reuven | P |
| unknown | Freidel | RUBENSTYN | f | M | Feivel | P |
| unknown | Freidel | JANOWICZ | f | M | | P |
| unknown | Fruma Mara | | f | U | Yisroel Aharon | P |
| unknown | Gittel | KAPLAN | f | M | Eliezer | P |
| unknown | Hadassah | LISSKOVSKY | f | M | Yacov Leib | P |
| unknown | Hashka | SCHWARTZ | f | M | Yosef | P |
| unknown | Itcha Lieb | | m | U | Yisroel Aharon | P |
| unknown | Kapitz | | m | M | | P |
| unknown | Kupitch | | m | M | | P |
| unknown | Leah | SCHWARTZ | f | M | Yosef | P |
| unknown | Leib | | m | U | | P |
| unknown | Leibel | | m | M | | P |
| unknown | Manya | STRUBOLSKY | f | M | | P |
| unknown | Mashkah | BERNSTYN | f | M | Zundel | P |
| unknown | Mashkah | SLODOBNIK | f | M | | P |
| unknown | Monya | SOBOLSKY | f | M | Eliezer | P |
| unknown | Mottel | | m | M | Velvel | P |
| unknown | Neche | KOSOVSKY | f | M | Velvel | P |
| unknown | Neche | SHULKES | f | M | | P |
| unknown | Pesha | LEVIN | f | M | | P |
| unknown | Pesha Leah | MULCHDESKY | f | M | Moshe Nataniel | P |
| unknown | Rachel | SHULKES | f | M | | P |
| unknown | Rachel | PRESS | f | M | Yonah Reuven | P |
| unknown | Rachel | | f | U | Yerachmiel | P |
| unknown | Sarah Leah | | f | U | Yerachmiel | P |
| unknown | Sarah Rivkah | KAPLAN | f | M | Eliezer | P |
| unknown | Simcha | | m | U | Yisroel Aharon | P |
| unknown | Tilka | SLODOBNIK | f | M | | P |
| unknown | unknown | RUBENSTYN | f | M | | P |
| unknown | unknown | | m | M | | P |
| unknown | unknown | | m | M | | P |
| unknown | unknown | | m | M | | P |
| unknown | unknown | | m | M | | P |
| unknown | unknown | | m | M | | P |
| unknown | unknown | | m | M | | P |
| unknown | unknown | | m | M | | P |
| unknown | unknown | | f | M | | P |
| unknown | unknown | | m | M | | P |
| unknown | unknown | | m | M | | P |

## Martyrs of Towns Near Ruzhany
## List Expanded from Names in Original Book

| Family name | First name(s) | Maiden name | Sex | Marital status | Father's name | Town |
|---|---|---|---|---|---|---|
| L:Liskovo | P: Pavlova | K: Konstantynowo | | | S: Kalazuby, Kolyany, Sheypyak | |
| unknown | unknown | | m | M | | P |
| unknown | unknown | | m | M | | P |
| unknown | unknown | | m | M | | P |
| unknown | unknown | | m | M | | P |
| unknown | unknown | | m | M | | P |
| unknown | unknown | | m | M | | P |
| unknown | unknown | LISSKOVSKY | f | M | Shmuel | P |
| unknown | unknown | LISSKOVSKY | f | M | Shmuel | P |
| unknown | Velvel | | m | M | | P |
| unknown | Yacov | | m | M | | P |
| unknown | Yehuda | | m | U | Yerachmiel | P |
| unknown | Yenta | SLODOBNIK | f | M | | P |
| unknown | Yerachmiel | | m | M | | P |
| unknown | Yisroel Aharon | | m | M | | P |
| unknown | Yitzchak | | m | U | Yerachmiel | P |
| unknown | Zipah Chaim | PRESS | f | M | Yonah Reuven | P |
| WILENSKY | Hirschleh | | m | M | | P |
| WILENSKY | Charne | | f | M | | P |
| WILENSKY | Leah | | f | M | | P |
| WILENSKY | Miriam | | f | U | Chaim Herschel | P |
| WILENSKY | Mottel | | m | U | Chaim Herschel | P |
| WILENSKY | Sheine Bliume | | f | M | | P |
| WILENSKY | Shimon | | m | M | | P |
| ANKOWICH | Berel | | m | M | | L |
| ANKOWICH | Chava | | f | M | | L |
| ANKOWICH | Hazkal | | m | U | Berel | L |
| ANKOWICH | Herschel | | m | U | Berel | L |
| ANKOWICH | Itka | | f | U | Yisroel | L |
| ANKOWICH | Mina | | f | U | Yisroel | L |
| ANKOWICH | Minia | | f | U | Berel | L |
| ANKOWICH | Perel | | f | M | | L |
| ANKOWICH | unknown | | m | U | Berel | L |
| ANKOWICH | unknown | | m | U | Berel | L |
| ANKOWICH | Yeshiahu | | m | U | Yisroel | L |
| ANKOWICH | Yisroel | | m | M | | L |
| ANKOWICH | Yisroel | | m | U | Berel | L |
| BABITZ | Gavriel | | m | M | | L |
| BABITZ | Leib | | m | M | | L |
| BABITZ | unknown | | f | M | | L |
| BABITZ | unknown | | f | M | | L |
| BECKENSTYN | Masha | | f | M | | L |

## Martyrs of Towns Near Ruzhany
## List Expanded from Names in Original Book

| Family name | First name(s) | Maiden name | Sex | Marital status | Father's name | Town |
|---|---|---|---|---|---|---|
| L:Liskovo | P: Pavlova | K: Konstantynowo | | | S: Kalazuby, Kolyany, Sheypyak | |
| BENDTOWICH | Dov | | m | U | Feivel | L |
| BENDTOWICH | Feigel | | f | U | Feivel | L |
| BENDTOWICH | Feivel | | m | M | | L |
| BENDTOWICH | Guttka | | f | M | | L |
| BENDTOWICH | Pesha | | f | U | Feivel | L |
| BERKOWICH | Feige Itta | | f | M | | L |
| BERMAN | Mordechai | | m | U | Moshe | L |
| BERMAN | Moshe | | m | M | | L |
| BERMAN | unknown | | f | M | | L |
| BLEICHER | Fishel | | m | M | | L |
| BLEICHER | Herschel | | m | U | Zalman | L |
| BLEICHER | Tuvia | | m | U | Zalman | L |
| BLEICHER | unknown | | f | M | | L |
| BLEICHER | unknown | | f | M | | L |
| BLEICHER | unknown | | f | M | | L |
| BLEICHER | Yacov | | m | M | | L |
| BLEICHER | Zalman | | m | M | | L |
| BOCHER | Yoel | | m | U | | L |
| BRUCHENASK | Hindah | | f | M | | L |
| BRUCHENASK | Yacov | | m | M | | L |
| BRUCHENASK | Yosef | | m | U | Yacov | L |
| BULGATZ | Gadaliahu | | m | U | Zadok | L |
| BULGATZ | Rachel | | f | M | | L |
| BULGATZ | Zadok | | m | M | | L |
| BUROCHOWICH | Chaim | | m | U | | L |
| BUROCHOWICH | David Herschel | | m | U | Itcha | L |
| BUROCHOWICH | Aharon | | m | M | | L |
| BUROCHOWICH | Shimon Yosef | | m | M | | L |
| BUROCHOWICH | unknown | | f | W | | L |
| BUROCHOWICH | unknown | | f | U | Itcha | L |
| BUROCHOWICH | unknown | | f | M | | L |
| BUROCHOWICH | unknown | | f | M | | L |
| BYZER | Rachel | | f | M | | L |
| BYZER | Yisroel | | m | M | | L |
| CATCHNOVSKY | Max | | m | M | | L |
| CATCHNOVSKY | Sarah Bryne | | f | M | | L |
| CHAZANSKY | Avraham | | m | M | | L |
| CHAZANSKY | Avraham | | m | M | | L |
| CHAZANSKY | Miriam | | f | M | | L |
| CHAZANSKY | Shmuel | | m | M | | L |
| CHAZANSKY | unknown | | f | M | | L |

## Martyrs of Towns Near Ruzhany
## List Expanded from Names in Original Book

| Family name | First name(s) | Maiden name | Sex | Marital status | Father's name | Town |
|---|---|---|---|---|---|---|
| L:Liskovo | P: Pavlova | K: Konstantynowo | | | S: Kalazuby, Kolyany, Sheypyak | |
| CHAZANSKY | unknown | | f | M | | L |
| CHAZANSKY | unknown | | f | M | | L |
| CHAZANSKY | Yacov | | m | M | | L |
| CHAZATZKY | Leibel | | m | U | Moshe | L |
| CHAZATZKY | Moshe | | m | M | | L |
| CHAZATZKY | Sarah | | f | M | | L |
| CHAZATZKY | Shifra | | f | M | | L |
| CHAZATZKY | Yosef | | m | M | | L |
| CHEBLOBKY | Aharon | | m | M | | L |
| CHEBLOBKY | Bliume | | f | M | | L |
| CHEBLOVSKY | Kayla | | f | M | | L |
| CHEBLOVSKY | Sarah | | f | U | Yosef | L |
| CHEBLOVSKY | Yosef | | m | M | | L |
| CHIRUM | Chaim | | m | U | Shimon | L |
| CHIRUM | Devorah | | f | M | | L |
| CHIRUM | Hodel | | m | U | Shimon | L |
| CHIRUM | Nachum | | m | U | Shimon | L |
| CHIRUM | Rasha | | f | | Shimon | L |
| CHIRUM | Shimon | | m | M | | L |
| CHIRUM | Yitzchak | | m | U | Shimon | L |
| CHWOJNIK | David | | m | M | | L |
| CHWOJNIK | Shmuel | | m | M | | L |
| CHWOJNIK | Sonyia | | f | M | | L |
| CHWOJNIK | unknown | | f | M | | L |
| CHWOJNIK | Zacharia | | m | U | Shmuel | L |
| EDELSTEIN | Barouch | | m | M | | L |
| EDELSTEIN | Barouch | | m | M | | L |
| EDELSTEIN | Esther | | f | M | | L |
| EDELSTEIN | Malkah | | f | M | | L |
| EDELSTEIN | Malvah | | f | M | | L |
| EDELSTEIN | Yehiel | | m | M | | L |
| EINSTEIN | Hasha | | f | U | Shimon | L |
| EINSTEIN | Moshe | | m | U | Shimon | L |
| EINSTEIN | Shimon | | m | M | | L |
| EINSTEIN | Yoceved | | f | M | | L |
| EISENBERG | Stifa | MORSHA | f | M | | L |
| ELMAN | Chaim | | m | M | | L |
| ELMAN | Chava | | f | U | Chaim | L |
| ELMAN | unknown | | f | M | | L |
| ELMAN | Yosefah | | f | U | Chaim | L |
| FINKELSTYN | Itka | | f | U | | L |

## Martyrs of Towns Near Ruzhany
## List Expanded from Names in Original Book

| Family name | First name(s) | Maiden name | Sex | Marital status | Father's name | Town |
|---|---|---|---|---|---|---|
| L: Liskovo | P: Pavlova | K: Konstantynowo | | | S: Kalazuby, Kolyany, Sheypyak | |
| FINKELSTYN | Shifra | | f | M | | L |
| FINKELSTYN | Shyne | | f | U | | L |
| FREEDENBERG | Feige | | f | | | L |
| FREEDENBERG | Moshe | | m | M | | L |
| FREEDENBERG | Pesach | | m | U | | L |
| FREEDENBERG | unknown | | f | M | | L |
| FREEDENBERG | Yacov | | m | U | Moshe | L |
| GAMERMAN | David | | m | U | Ovadiah | L |
| GAMERMAN | Ovadiah | | m | M | | L |
| GAMERMAN | unknown | | f | M | | L |
| GORDON | Bezalel | | m | U | Yitzchak | L |
| GORDON | Chaim | | m | U | Yitzchak | L |
| GORDON | Henya | | f | W | | L |
| GORDON | Hodel | | f | | Yitzchak | L |
| GORDON | Leibel | | m | U | Yitzchak | L |
| GORDON | Michale | | f | | Yitzchak | L |
| GORDON | Sarah | | f | U | Yitzchak | L |
| GUREWICH | Hazkal | | m | M | | L |
| GUREWICH | unknown | | f | M | | L |
| GUSTMAN | Beila | | f | M | | L |
| ILLENOWICH | Sonyia | BYZER | f | M | Yisroel | L |
| JUNGHEIT | Buba | | f | M | | L |
| JUNGHEIT | Fridrick | | m | U | | L |
| KAGAN | Devorah | | f | M | | L |
| KAGAN | Zelig | | m | M | | L |
| KANTSPOLSKY | Eliezer | | m | M | | L |
| KANTSPOLSKY | Rachel | | f | M | | L |
| KANTSPOLSKY | unknown | | m | M | | L |
| KANTSPOLSKY | unknown | | f | M | | L |
| KAPLAN | Avraham | | m | M | | L |
| KAPLAN | Chaya | | f | U | Avraham | L |
| KAPLAN | Esther | | f | M | | L |
| KAPLAN | Moshe | | m | U | Avraham | L |
| KLUCHKY | Leib | | m | M | | L |
| KLUCHKY | Rachel | | f | M | | L |
| KLUCHKY | Yitzchak | | m | U | Leib | L |
| KOGBETSKY | Avraham | | m | M | | L |
| KOGBETSKY | Benyamin | | m | M | | L |
| KOGBETSKY | Berel | | m | U | Michael | L |
| KOGBETSKY | Eliahu | | m | | | L |
| KOGBETSKY | Eliezer | | m | M | | L |

## Martyrs of Towns Near Ruzhany
## List Expanded from Names in Original Book

| Family name | First name(s) | Maiden name | Sex | Marital status | Father's name | Town |
|---|---|---|---|---|---|---|
| L:Liskovo | P: Pavlova | K: Konstantynowo | | | S: Kalazuby, Kolyany, Sheypyak | |
| KOGBETSKY | Faya | | f | M | | L |
| KOGBETSKY | Feigel | | f | U | Benyamin | L |
| KOGBETSKY | Golda | | f | M | | L |
| KOGBETSKY | Haika | | f | M | | L |
| KOGBETSKY | Leah | | f | M | | L |
| KOGBETSKY | Leibel | | m | M | | L |
| KOGBETSKY | Michael | | m | M | | L |
| KOGBETSKY | Noach | | m | U | Benyamin | L |
| KOGBETSKY | Noach | | m | U | Eliezer | L |
| KOGBETSKY | Sarah | | f | U | Benyamin | L |
| KOGBETSKY | Tuvia | | m | U | Michael | L |
| KOGBETSKY | unknown | | f | M | | L |
| KOGBETSKY | unknown | | f | U | Eliezer | L |
| KOGBETSKY | Yacov Leib | | m | M | | L |
| KOGBETSKY | Yisroel | | m | U | Eliezer | L |
| KOGBETSKY | Yosef | | m | U | Michael | L |
| KOGBETSKY | Yosef | | m | U | Benyamin | L |
| KOGBETSKY | Zlota | | f | M | | L |
| KOSOVSKY | Bliume | | f | M | | L |
| KOSOVSKY | Mendel | | m | M | | L |
| KOTSKIN | unknown | | f | W | | L |
| KOTSPOLSKY | David | | m | U | Moshe Issac | L |
| KOTSPOLSKY | Moshe Issic | | m | M | | L |
| KOTSPOLSKY | Rachel | | f | U | Moshe Issac | L |
| KOTSPOLSKY | Shyne | | f | M | | L |
| KRABCHUK | Batya | | f | | | L |
| KRABCHUK | Eliezer | | m | M | | L |
| KRABCHUK | Herschel | | m | M | | L |
| KRABCHUK | Issac | | m | U | Hirschel | L |
| KRABCHUK | Liova | | f | | Nechamia | L |
| KRABCHUK | Liova | | m | U | Eliezer | L |
| KRABCHUK | Nechamia | | m | M | | L |
| KRABCHUK | Nissan | | m | | | L |
| KRABCHUK | Pesha | | f | M | | L |
| KRABCHUK | Reuven | | m | U | Hirschel | L |
| KRABCHUK | Shmuel | | m | U | Eliezer | L |
| KRABCHUK | Shyne | | f | M | | L |
| KRABCHUK | Teiva | | f | M | | L |
| KRASHINSKY | Leib | | m | M | | L |
| KRASHINSKY | unknown | | f | M | | L |
| LAZEROVSKY | Hasha | | f | M | | L |

## Martyrs of Towns Near Ruzhany
## List Expanded from Names in Original Book

| Family name | First name(s) | Maiden name | Sex | Marital status | Father's name | Town |
|---|---|---|---|---|---|---|
| L: Liskovo | P: Pavlova | K: Konstantynowo | | | S: Kalazuby, Kolyany, Sheypyak | |
| LAZEROVSKY | Zelig | | m | M | | L |
| LEV | Avraham | | m | M | | L |
| LEV | Esther | | f | M | | L |
| LEV | Feigel | | f | | | L |
| LEV | Freidel | | f | M | | L |
| LEV | Malkah | | f | M | | L |
| LEV | Moshe | | m | U | Yehudah | L |
| LEV | Moshe | | m | M | | L |
| LEV | Pesha | | f | U | Yehudah | L |
| LEV | unknown | | m | U | Yehudah | L |
| LEV | unknown | | f | M | | L |
| LEV | Wolf | | m | M | | L |
| LEV | Yehuda | | m | M | | L |
| LEV | Yisroel | | m | U | Avraham | L |
| LEV | Yitzchak | | m | | | L |
| LEV | Zvia | | f | | | L |
| LEVIN | Liba | | f | | | L |
| LEVIN | Nechamia | | m | U | | L |
| LEVIN | Rivkah | | f | M | | L |
| LIBER | unknown | | m | M | | L |
| LIBER | unknown | | f | M | | L |
| LIBERMAN | Hasha | | f | M | | L |
| LIBERMAN | Rachel | | f | U | | L |
| MASHLIVITZ | Beila | | f | M | | L |
| MASHLIVITZ | Bina | | f | U | Yitzchak | L |
| MASHLIVITZ | Mordechai | | m | U | Yitzchak | L |
| MASHLIVITZ | Yitzchak | | m | M | | L |
| MAYERSON | Golda Feige | | f | W | | L |
| MAYERSON | Liba | | f | U | Leib | L |
| MAYERSON | Shmuel Issic | | m | U | Leib | L |
| MAYERSON | unknown | | m | U | Leib | L |
| MELITZ | Sarah | | f | U | Zidel | L |
| MELITZ | Zidel | | m | M | | L |
| MELITZ | Zvia | | f | M | | L |
| MENDELEWICH | Menucha | | f | | | L |
| MEZHERITZK | Chaim | | m | M | | L |
| MEZHERITZK | Razel | | f | | | L |
| MEZHERITZK | Sheitel | | f | | Chaim | L |
| MEZHERITZK | Sonyia | | f | M | | L |
| MEZHERITZK | Teivel | | m | | Chaim | L |
| MEZHERITZKY | Buba | | f | M | | L |

## Martyrs of Towns Near Ruzhany
## List Expanded from Names in Original Book

| Family name | First name(s) | Maiden name | Sex | Marital status | Father's name | Town |
|---|---|---|---|---|---|---|
| L:Liskovo | P: Pavlova | K: Konstantynowo | | | S: Kalazuby, Kolyany, Sheypyak | |
| MEZHERITZKY | Eliezer | | m | U | Reuven | L |
| MEZHERITZKY | Fania | | f | U | Gershon | L |
| MEZHERITZKY | Gershon | | m | M | | L |
| MEZHERITZKY | Henya | | f | U | Gershon | L |
| MEZHERITZKY | Reuven | | m | M | | L |
| MEZHERITZKY | Shulamis | | f | U | Reuven | L |
| MEZHERITZKY | Teiva | | f | M | | L |
| MICHLES | Chaim | | m | U | Yeshiahu | L |
| MICHLES | Chasia | | f | M | | L |
| MICHLES | Yenta | | f | | | L |
| MICHLES | Yeshiahu | | m | M | | L |
| MILLER | Nachum | | m | M | | L |
| MILLER | unknown | | f | M | | L |
| MORSHA | unknown | | f | M | | L |
| NOVIK | Bezalel | | m | M | | L |
| NOVIK | Chava | | f | U | Yosef | L |
| NOVIK | Dabusha | | f | | Yosef | L |
| NOVIK | Esther | | f | M | | L |
| NOVIK | Herschel | | m | M | | L |
| NOVIK | Kalman | | m | U | Yosef | L |
| NOVIK | Mordechai | | m | U | Yosef | L |
| NOVIK | Moshe | | m | U | Yosef | L |
| NOVIK | Razel | | f | M | | L |
| NOVIK | Shimshon | | m | U | Hirschel | L |
| NOVIK | unknown | | f | U | Hirschel | L |
| NOVIK | unknown | | f | M | | L |
| NOVIK | unknown | | f | M | | L |
| NOVIK | Yehuda | | m | U | Yosef | L |
| NOVIK | Yosef | | m | M | | L |
| NOVIK | Zalman | | m | U | Hirschel | L |
| NOVIK | Zvi | | m | M | | L |
| PAPEISH | Herschel | | m | M | | L |
| PAPEISH | Yana | | f | M | | L |
| PAPEISH | Yosef | | m | U | Hirschel | L |
| PERPELIOTSHUK | Eliahu | | m | U | Yosef | L |
| PERPELIOTSHUK | unknown | | f | M | | L |
| PERPELIOTSHUK | unknown | | f | U | Yosef | L |
| PERPELIOTSHUK | Yosef | | m | M | | L |
| PINTALWICH | Avraham | | m | U | Yerachmiel | L |
| PINTALWICH | Chaya Lifcze | | f | M | | L |
| PINTALWICH | Yerachmiel | | m | M | | L |

## Martyrs of Towns Near Ruzhany
## List Expanded from Names in Original Book

| Family name | First name(s) | Maiden name | Sex | Marital status | Father's name | Town |
|---|---|---|---|---|---|---|
| L:Liskovo | P: Pavlova | K: Konstantynowo | | | S: Kalazuby, Kolyany, Sheypyak | |
| PINTALWICH | Yisroel | | m | U | Yerachmiel | L |
| POGOLENSKY | Berel | | m | M | | L |
| POGOLENSKY | Chaim | | m | M | | L |
| POGOLENSKY | Chanah Feigel | | f | M | | L |
| POGOLENSKY | Heshel | | m | M | | L |
| POGOLENSKY | Musha | | f | M | | L |
| POGOLENSKY | unknown | | f | M | | L |
| POMERANTZ | Hinkah | | f | | | L |
| POMERANTZ | Leah | | f | U | | L |
| POMERANTZ | Mottel | | m | U | | L |
| POMERANTZ | Shyne | | f | M | | L |
| POMERANTZ | Tuvia | | m | M | | L |
| PRECHOWICH | Avraham | | m | U | Yosef | L |
| PRECHOWICH | unknown | | f | M | | L |
| PRECHOWICH | unknown | | f | U | Yosef | L |
| PRECHOWICH | Yosef | | m | M | | L |
| REZNIK | Bashkah | | f | | | L |
| REZNIK | Chaya | | f | M | | L |
| REZNIK | Issac | | m | U | Moshe | L |
| REZNIK | Moshe | | m | M | | L |
| REZNIK | Peitzche | | | | | L |
| REZNIK | Raphael | | m | U | Moshe | L |
| REZNIK | Rivkah | | f | | | L |
| REZNIK | Tunia | | f | M | | L |
| RIVNIK | Chaim | | m | M | | L |
| RIVNIK | unknown | | f | M | | L |
| RODNITSKY | Chava | | f | M | | L |
| RODNITSKY | Shlomo | | m | U | Yacov Hirsch | L |
| RODNITSKY | Yacov Hirsch | | m | M | | L |
| RODNITSKY | Yitzchak | | m | U | Yacov Hirsch | L |
| ROZENBERG | Esther | | f | M | | L |
| ROZENBERG | Rasha | | f | | | L |
| SAMZONOWICH | Duba | | f | M | | L |
| SAMZONOWICH | Yacov | | m | M | | L |
| SCHWARTZ | David | | m | M | | L |
| SCHWARTZ | Sarah Itta | | f | M | | L |
| SCHWARTZ | unknown | | f | M | | L |
| SCHWARTZ | Yeshiahu | | m | M | | L |
| SCHWARTZ | Zelia | | f | | | L |
| SHEIVITZ | Chaim | | m | M | | L |
| SHEIVITZ | Chanah | | f | M | | L |

## Martyrs of Towns Near Ruzhany
## List Expanded from Names in Original Book

| Family name | First name(s) | Maiden name | Sex | Marital status | Father's name | Town |
|---|---|---|---|---|---|---|
| L:Liskovo | P: Pavlova | K: Konstantynowo | | | S: Kalazuby, Kolyany, Sheypyak | |
| SHEIVITZ | Eliahu | | m | M | | L |
| SHEIVITZ | Moshe | | m | U | Zidel | L |
| SHEIVITZ | unknown | | f | M | | L |
| SHEIVITZ | unknown | | f | M | | L |
| SHEIVITZ | Wolf | | m | U | Zidel | L |
| SHEIVITZ | Zidel | | m | M | | L |
| SHILOBECHKY | Genia | | f | U | Mordechai | L |
| SHILOBECHKY | Mordechai | | m | M | | L |
| SKRIPSKY | Moshe | | m | M | | L |
| SKRIPSKY | Pesha | | f | M | | L |
| SLUTZKY | Baracha | | f | M | | L |
| SLUTZKY | unknown | | m | M | | L |
| SLUTZKY | Zidel | | m | | | L |
| STEIN | Batya | | f | M | | L |
| STEIN | unknown | | m | M | | L |
| SUIF | Brynne | | f | U | Shmuel | L |
| SUIF | Freidel | | f | M | | L |
| SUIF | Haicha | | f | M | | L |
| SUIF | Haikel | | m | M | | L |
| SUIF | Rivkah | | f | U | Shmuel | L |
| SUIF | Shmuel | | m | M | | L |
| SUIF | Shyne Itta | | f | M | | L |
| SUIF | Sonyia | | f | U | | L |
| SUKENIT | Chaya | | f | M | | L |
| SUKENIT | unknown | | m | M | | L |
| TRUMPER | Hindah | | f | M | | L |
| TRUMPER | Perel | | f | U | Ze'ev | L |
| TRUMPER | Shmuel | | m | U | Ze'ev | L |
| TRUMPER | Yosef | | m | U | Ze'ev | L |
| TRUMPER | Ze'ev | | m | M | | L |
| unknown | Dabusha | | f | M | | L |
| unknown | unknown | BERMAN | f | M | Moshe | L |
| unknown | unknown | | m | M | | L |
| unknown | Velia | | f | | | L |
| VICHNE | unknown | | f | W | | L |
| VYGODESKY | Rachel | CHAZANASKY | f | M | | L |
| WAJNSTYN | Avraham | | m | U | Barouch | L |
| WAJNSTYN | Barouch | | m | M | | L |
| WAJNSTYN | Beila | | f | M | | L |
| WAJNSTYN | Mordechai | | m | U | Barouch | L |
| WAJNSTYN | Moshe | | m | M | | L |

## Martyrs of Towns Near Ruzhany
## List Expanded from Names in Original Book

| Family name | First name(s) | Maiden name | Sex | Marital status | Father's name | Town |
| --- | --- | --- | --- | --- | --- | --- |
| L:Liskovo | P: Pavlova | K: Konstantynowo | | | S: Kalazuby, Kolyany, Sheypyak | |
| WAJNSTYN | Teiva | | f | M | | L |
| WALDMAN | Charne | BECKENSTYN | f | M | | L |
| WILENSKY | Yacov | | m | M | | L |
| WILENSKY | Yehudit | | f | M | | L |
| WOLFOWICH | Barouch | | m | U | Moshe | L |
| WOLFOWICH | Bliume | | f | U | Moshe | L |
| WOLFOWICH | Malkah | | f | M | | L |
| WOLFOWICH | Moshe | | m | M | | L |
| WOLFOWICH | Sarah | | f | U | Moshe | L |
| WOLFOWICH | Shmuel | | m | U | Moshe | L |
| YELIN | David | | m | M | | L |
| YELIN | Herschel | | m | M | | L |
| YELIN | Hinkah | | f | U | Hirschel | L |
| YELIN | Shmuel | | m | U | | L |
| YELIN | Sonyia | | f | M | | L |
| YELIN | unknown | | f | M | | L |
| ZORCHOWICH | Tema | | f | | | L |
| ZORCHOWICH | Zorach | | m | U | | L |
| ZWAJNSTYN | Abrasha | | m | M | | L |
| ZWAJNSTYN | Bunia | | f | U | Avrasha | L |
| ZWAJNSTYN | Rachel | | f | M | | L |
| ZWAJNSTYN | unknown | | m | U | Avrasha | L |
| BUKSTYN | Arieh | | m | U | Pesach | K |
| BUKSTYN | Mashkah | GERBOLCKI | f | M | Chaim Berel | K |
| BUKSTYN | Pesach | | m | M | | K |
| BUKSTYN | Yisroel | | m | U | Pesach | K |
| CHWOJNIK | Arieh Lieb | | m | U | | K |
| CHWOJNIK | Moshe | | m | U | | K |
| CHWOJNIK | Rachel | | f | M | | K |
| DINOWICH | Chava | | f | M | | K |
| DINOWICH | Schana | | m | M | | K |
| DINOWICH | unknown | | f | M | | K |
| FROUK | Berel | | m | M | | K |
| FROUK | Bilka | | f | M | | K |
| FROUK | Chanah | | f | M | | K |
| FROUK | Chaya | | f | M | | K |
| FROUK | Liba | | m | M | | K |
| FROUK | Menachem | | m | M | | K |
| FROUK | Sarah | INKER | f | M | Ephraim | K |
| FROUK | Sarah | | f | M | | K |
| FROUK | Shabtayel | | m | M | | K |

## Martyrs of Towns Near Ruzhany
## List Expanded from Names in Original Book

| Family name | First name(s) | Maiden name | Sex | Marital status | Father's name | Town |
|---|---|---|---|---|---|---|
| L:Liskovo | P: Pavlova | K: Konstantynowo | | | S: Kalazuby, Kolyany, Sheypyak | |
| FROUK | Zlotka | | f | M | Menachem | K |
| GERBOLCKI | Aharon Avraham | | m | M | | K |
| GERBOLCKI | Fischel | | m | M | | K |
| GERBOLCKI | Brynne | | f | M | | K |
| GERBOLCKI | Chaim Berel | | m | M | | K |
| GERBOLCKI | Chaim Hirsch | | m | M | | K |
| GERBOLCKI | Chaim Noach | | m | M | | K |
| GERBOLCKI | Chaya | KAGNITSKY | f | M | Shmuel Henech | K |
| GERBOLCKI | Chaya Sarah | | f | M | | K |
| GERBOLCKI | Devorah | | f | U | Chaim Berel | K |
| GERBOLCKI | Hamaka | | f | M | | K |
| GERBOLCKI | Henya | | f | M | | K |
| GERBOLCKI | Masha | | f | M | | K |
| GERBOLCKI | Razel | INKER | f | M | Ephraim | K |
| GERBOLCKI | Sarah | | f | U | Chaim Berel | K |
| GERBOLCKI | Sarah | | f | M | | K |
| GERBOLCKI | Sarah Yettel | | f | M | | K |
| GERBOLCKI | Sheine | | f | M | | K |
| GERBOLCKI | Shirka | | f | M | | K |
| GERBOLCKI | unknown | | f | M | | K |
| GERBOLCKI | Yitzchak | | m | U | Chaim Berel | K |
| GERBOLCKI | Yoel | | m | M | | K |
| GERBOLCKI | Yoel | | m | M | | K |
| GERBOLCKI | Yoel | | m | M | | K |
| GERBOLCKI | Yosef | | m | M | | K |
| GERBOLCKI | Yosef | | m | M | Chaim Berel | K |
| GERBOLCKI | Yosef | | m | M | | K |
| GINZBURG | Mordechai | | m | U | Yacov Yehoshua | K |
| GINZBURG | Pesha Yacov | | f | M | | K |
| GINZBURG | Yehoshua | | m | M | | K |
| GURSTHAL | Chaim | | m | U | Moshe | K |
| GURSTHAL | Moshe | | m | M | | K |
| GURSTHAL | Sarah Elka | | f | U | Moshe | K |
| GURSTHAL | Sheine | KAGNITSKY | f | M | Issac | K |
| ILLEWICKI | Sheine Feigel | | f | M | | K |
| ILLEWICKI | Yosef | | m | M | | K |
| INKER | Benyamin | | m | M | Ephraim | K |
| INKER | Biliah | | f | U | Ephraim | K |
| INKER | Ephraim | | m | M | | K |

## Martyrs of Towns Near Ruzhany
## List Expanded from Names in Original Book

| Family name | First name(s) | Maiden name | Sex | Marital status | Father's name | Town |
|---|---|---|---|---|---|---|
| L:Liskovo | P: Pavlova | K: Konstantynowo | | | S: Kalazuby, Kolyany, Sheypyak | |
| INKER | Esther | | f | M | | K |
| INKER | Leah | | f | M | | K |
| INKER | Leahkah | | f | M | | K |
| INKER | Rachel | | f | U | | K |
| INKER | Yacov | | m | U | Ephraim | K |
| INKER | Yitzchak | | m | M | | K |
| KAGNITSKY | Bashkah | | f | M | | K |
| KAGNITSKY | Bilka | | f | M | | K |
| KAGNITSKY | Bubcha | | f | M | | K |
| KAGNITSKY | Chaim | | m | | Mottel | K |
| KAGNITSKY | Chaya | | f | M | | K |
| KAGNITSKY | Dwashke | | f | M | | K |
| KAGNITSKY | Eidelia | | f | U | | K |
| KAGNITSKY | Eliezer | | m | U | | K |
| KAGNITSKY | Elka | | f | U | Yacov Yehoshua | K |
| KAGNITSKY | Henya | | f | M | | K |
| KAGNITSKY | Huma | | f | U | Yitzchak | K |
| KAGNITSKY | Ida | | f | U | Yitzchak | K |
| KAGNITSKY | Issac | | m | M | | K |
| KAGNITSKY | Malkah | | f | M | | K |
| KAGNITSKY | Miriam | | f | U | Yitzchak | K |
| KAGNITSKY | Mirka | | f | M | | K |
| KAGNITSKY | Mottel | | m | M | | K |
| KAGNITSKY | Shabtayel | | m | M | | K |
| KAGNITSKY | Shmuel Hanoch | | m | M | | K |
| KAGNITSKY | Sima | | f | U | Yacov Yehoshua | K |
| KAGNITSKY | unknown | | f | M | | K |
| KAGNITSKY | Yacov Yehoshua | | m | M | | K |
| KAGNITSKY | Yerachmiel | | m | U | Shmuel Henech | K |
| KAGNITSKY | Yitzchak | | m | M | Shmuel Henech | K |
| KAGNITSKY | Yitzchak | | m | M | | K |
| KAGNITSKY | Yitzchak | | m | M | Issac | K |
| KAGNITSKY | Yosef | | m | U | Yacov Yehoshua | K |
| KATOWICH | Avraham | | f | M | | K |
| KATOWICH | Fruma | | m | M | | K |
| KOZNITSKY | Gisha | | f | U | | K |
| KOZNITSKY | Michael | | m | M | | K |
| KOZNITSKY | Risha | | f | M | | K |

## Martyrs of Towns Near Ruzhany
### List Expanded from Names in Original Book

| Family name | First name(s) | Maiden name | Sex | Marital status | Father's name | Town |
|---|---|---|---|---|---|---|
| L:Liskovo | P: Pavlova | K: Konstantynowo | | | S: Kalazuby, Kolyany, Sheypyak | |
| KRABCHUK | Chaya | KAGNITSKY | f | M | Issac | K |
| KRABCHUK | Eliahu | | m | U | | K |
| KRABCHUK | Feigel | | f | M | | K |
| KRABCHUK | Freidel | | f | M | | K |
| KRABCHUK | Schana | | m | M | | K |
| KRABCHUK | Tiva | | f | | | K |
| KRABCHUK | Yitzchak | | m | U | | K |
| KRABCHUK | Zalman Berel | | m | M | | K |
| KRUPIK | Mordechai | | m | M | | K |
| KRUPIK | unknown | | f | M | | K |
| LEVENKOV | Esther | | f | U | David | K |
| LEVENKOV | Gadaliah | | m | U | David | K |
| LEVENKOV | Shyndel | | f | U | David | K |
| LEVENKOV | Yacov | | m | M | | K |
| LEVENKOV | Yitzchak | | m | U | David | K |
| LIPNIK | Issac | | m | M | | K |
| LIPNIK | unknown | | f | M | | K |
| PINSKY | Dwasha | | f | M | | K |
| PINSKY | Leibel | | m | U | Yacov | K |
| PINSKY | Shmuel | | m | U | Yacov | K |
| PINSKY | Yacov | | m | M | | K |
| POLONSKY | Avraham | | m | M | | K |
| POLONSKY | unknown | | f | M | | K |
| POMERNITZ | Avraham | | m | M | | K |
| POMERNITZ | Berel | | m | U | Avraham | K |
| POMERNITZ | Chaya | | f | M | | K |
| POMERNITZ | Hasha Liba | | f | U | Avraham | K |
| POMERNITZ | Shlomo | | m | U | Avraham | K |
| POMERNITZ | Yitzchak | | m | U | Avraham | K |
| POMERNITZ | Yoshka | | m | U | Avraham | K |
| SHIPITZSKI | Aharon | | m | M | Avraham Henech | K |
| SHIPITZSKI | Avraham | | m | U | Yehoshua | K |
| SHIPITZSKI | Avraham Hanoch | | m | M | | K |
| SHIPITZSKI | Benyamin | | m | U | Yehoshua | K |
| SHIPITZSKI | Chaya | | f | U | Yehoshua | K |
| SHIPITZSKI | Rachel | | f | M | | K |
| SHIPITZSKI | Rivkah | | f | U | Avraham Henech | K |
| SHIPITZSKI | Sarah | | f | M | | K |
| SHIPITZSKI | Yehoshua | | m | M | | K |
| SHIPITZSKI | Yocha | | f | M | | K |

## Martyrs of Towns Near Ruzhany
## List Expanded from Names in Original Book

| Family name | First name(s) | Maiden name | Sex | Marital status | Father's name | Town |
|---|---|---|---|---|---|---|
| L:Liskovo | P: Pavlova | K: Konstantynowo | | | S: Kalazuby, Kolyany, Sheypyak | |
| SOKOLOVSKY | Chaim | | m | M | | K |
| SOKOLOVSKY | Rachel | | f | M | | K |
| SYDRANSKY | Malkah | | f | M | | K |
| unknown | Chanah | FROUK | f | M | | K |
| unknown | Chanah Bilia | SOKOLOVSKY | f | M | | K |
| unknown | Chaya | LEVENKOV | f | W | Yacov | K |
| unknown | Chaya Leah | POLONSKY | f | M | | K |
| unknown | Dewoirke | SYDRANSKY | f | M | | K |
| unknown | Elka | GERBOLCKI | f | M | Yoel | K |
| unknown | Esther | CHEBOINIK | f | M | | K |
| unknown | Feige Rachel | DINOWICH | f | M | | K |
| unknown | Hamka | GERBOLCKI | f | M | | K |
| unknown | Heinke | GERBOLCKI | f | M | Yoel | K |
| unknown | Itka | | f | U | | K |
| unknown | Leah | SOKOLOVSKY | m | M | | K |
| unknown | Leah | GERBOLCKI | f | M | Chaim Hirsch | K |
| unknown | Moshe | | m | U | | K |
| unknown | Mosheleh | | m | U | | K |
| unknown | Osnat | GERBOLCKI | f | U | | K |
| unknown | Perel | LEVENKOV | f | M | Yacov | K |
| unknown | Rachel | SYDRANSKY | f | M | | K |
| unknown | Sarah | GERBOLCKI | f | M | Chaim Hirsch | K |
| unknown | Sim | | f | U | | K |
| unknown | Teivel | GERBOLCKI | f | M | Chaim Hirsch | K |
| unknown | unknown | | m | M | | K |
| unknown | unknown | | m | U | | K |
| unknown | unknown | | f | M | | K |
| unknown | unknown | | m | M | | K |
| unknown | unknown | | m | M | | K |
| unknown | unknown | | m | M | | K |
| unknown | unknown | | m | M | | K |
| unknown | unknown | | m | M | | K |
| unknown | unknown | | m | M | | K |
| unknown | unknown | | m | M | | K |
| unknown | unknown | | m | M | | K |
| unknown | unknown | | m | M | | K |
| unknown | unknown | | m | M | | K |
| unknown | unknown | | m | M | | K |
| unknown | Yakutiel | | m | U | | K |
| unknown | Yehuda | | m | U | | K |
| unknown | Yocha | KAGNITSKY | f | M | Yitzchak | K |

## Martyrs of Towns Near Ruzhany
## List Expanded from Names in Original Book

| Family name | First name(s) | Maiden name | Sex | Marital status | Father's name | Town |
|---|---|---|---|---|---|---|
| L:Liskovo | P: Pavlova | K: Konstantynowo | | | S: Kalazuby, Kolyany, Sheypyak | |
| VELER | Chaya Perel | | f | M | | K |
| VELER | Eliahu | | m | M | | K |
| VELER | Eliezer | | m | U | Eliahu | K |
| VELER | Neche | | f | U | Eliahu | K |
| VELER | Schitzirka | | f | U | Eliahu | K |
| VELER | Zvi | | m | U | Eliahu | K |
| ZEIDEL | Lev | | m | M | | K |
| ZEIDEL | Sheine | | f | M | | K |
| ZLOTNER | unknown | | f | M | | K |
| ZLOTNER | unknown | | f | M | | K |
| ZLOTNER | Yenta | | m | M | | K |
| ZLOTNER | Yosef | | m | M | | K |
| CHEMARDAY | Malkah | | f | M | | S |
| CHEMARDAY | Yisroel | | m | M | | S |
| ILLEWICKI | Alter | | m | M | | S |
| ILLEWICKI | David | | m | M | | S |
| ILLEWICKI | Henya | | f | M | | S |
| ILLEWICKI | Mordechai | | m | M | | S |
| ILLEWICKI | Rivkah | | f | M | | S |
| ILLEWICKI | unknown | | f | M | | S |
| ILLEWICKI | Yehud'l | | m | M | | S |
| ILLEWICKI | Zåvia | | f | M | | S |
| LEMPKIN | Eliahu | | m | M | | S |
| LEMPKIN | Sheine | | f | M | | S |
| LEMPKIN | unknown | | f | M | | S |
| LEMPKIN | Yosef | | m | M | Eliahu | S |
| unknown | Sonyia | ILLEWICKI | f | M | Yehudaleh | S |
| unknown | unknown | | m | M | | S |
| unknown | unknown | ILLEWICKI | f | M | David | S |
| unknown | unknown | | m | M | | S |
| FREEDENBERG | Bunia | | f | U | Yisroel | |
| FREEDENBERG | Leah | | f | M | | |
| FREEDENBERG | unknown | | f | U | Yisroel | |
| FREEDENBERG | Yisroel | | m | M | | |

# Table of Contents in Original Book

| Subject | Page |
|---|---|
| **Introduction by the Editor** | 5 |
| Schematic map of Ruzhany | 6 |
| **History:** | |
| History of the Town of Ruzhany | 7 |
| Ruzhany according to the ledgers of the council of principal communities in the State of Lithuania | 8 |
| Ruzhany according to the General Encyclopedia Orglobarnada from 1884* | 8 |
| Ruzhany according to the Jewish Encyclopedia | 8 |
| **Martyrs:** | |
| The Martyrs of Ruzhany | 10 |
| The Selicha for the Martyrs | 12 |
| Martyrs tomb | 17 |
| Descendents of the Martyrs | 17 |
| The Martyrs of Ruzhany | 18 |
| **Torah:** | |
| Cheders | 21 |
| The Teacher's Union | 22 |
| A Cheder for Girls | 23 |
| Tiferet Bachurim | 23 |
| The Yeshiva in Ruzhany | 24 |
| Various study organizations | 26 |
| Rabbis in Ruzhany | 29 |
| "Shaatnez" | 41 |
| **Labor:** | |
| The economic situation of the town | 47 |
| Lives of the weavers in Ruzhany during the 19th century | 48 |
| Families of workers in the town | 49 |
| The Labor Movement in Ruzhany in the 19th century | 50 |
| The founding of Pavlova and Konstantinova | 51 |
| **G'milut Chassadim (Benevolent Societies):** | |
| Popular idealists | 52 |
| Hadaska | 54 |
| Leib Wasz and other members of the Pines family | 56 |

| | |
|---|---|
| Yona the shoemaker | 58 |
| Nimele the butcher Bulgatz | 59 |
| Shabtai Shefem of Pavlova | 59 |

**Our Town:**

| | |
|---|---|
| Our town Ruzhinoy | 60 |
| The synagogues of Ruzhany | 62 |
| Public life in Ruzhany | 64 |
| The "Takseh" (meat tax, "Korovka") | 65 |
| From the days of my childhood in Ruzhany | 66 |

**The Fires:**

| | |
|---|---|
| The plague of fires | 68 |
| Leib "Yachid" [the only one] | 71 |
| How the fire brigade in Ruzhany was set up | 72 |
| The voluntary fire brigade in Ruzhany | 72 |
| The drills of the firefighters brigade | 73 |
| Fear of pogroms in the town in 1904 | 75 |

**The beginnings of Zionism:**

| | |
|---|---|
| "Hurry, Brothers, Hurry" written by Yechiel Michal Pines (song still sung in Israel) | 77 |
| Beginnings of Zionism in Ruzhinoy | 78 |
| Yechiel Michael Pines | 78 |
| More on the Activities of Yechiel Michel Pines | 80 |
| Passages from "The Children of My Spirit" by Y. M. Pines | 81 |
| Itta Yellin | 82 |
| Rabbi Ze'ev Wolf Shachor (black) | 82 |
| The founding of Ekron (agricultural settlement south of Tel Aviv) | 83 |
| Yearning for redemption | 85 |

**The years of agitation:**

| | |
|---|---|
| The year 1905--the political parties | 87 |
| The struggle for 12-hour work day | 87 |
| The big strike of 1910 | 88 |

**Public figures and personalities:**

| | |
|---|---|
| Lullaby | 90 |
| Aharon Libushitzky , Meir Krinsky, Zelig Sher, Melech Epshteyn , Dov Shpak Lobzowsky, Avigdor Michal Goldberg, Dr. Meir Pines, Moshe Limon | 91-95 |

**The First World War:**

| | |
|---|---|
| The Days of the First World War | 97 |
| The First Period of the German Occupation | 98 |
| From the Time of the German Occupation | 99 |
| The Forest People | 100 |
| The Big Fire | 101 |
| The Kinderheim (Children's Home) | 102 |
| The Choir | 103 |
| "Hazamir" and "Herzlia" | 104 |
| The Consum Farein (consumers' organization) | 107 |
| Between the Regimes | 108 |
| Pogroms in Ruzhinoy | 108 |

**Way of Life in the Shetl:**

| | |
|---|---|
| The libraries of Ruzhinoy | 110 |
| The library in Pavlova | 110 |
| Memories of childhood | 111 |
| Longing for Zion | 112 |
| Longing for the Land | 114 |
| Ma'ot Chitim (food fund for needy) | 115 |
| The eve of Passover in our town | 115 |

**Economic Situation:**

| | |
|---|---|
| The economic situation after the First World War | 119 |
| In Ruzhany | 119 |
| The bank in Ruzhany | 120 |

**Zionist Movements:**

| | |
|---|---|
| Hechalutz Movement in Ruzhany | 122 |
| Activities on behalf of the Jewish National Fund | 126 |
| The General Zionist Organization | 129 |
| The Hashomer Hatzair Movement in Ruzhany | 131 |
| Hashomer Hatzi'r renews its activities | 132 |
| Betar (Jabotinsky's youth movement) | 136 |
| My native town | 137 |

**Educational Institutions:**

| | |
|---|---|
| Educational institutions in the town | 138 |
| The Tarbut School in Ruzhany | 139 |
| The Talmud Torah Institution in Ruzhany | 143 |
| David Miller | 144 |

**Charitable Institutions:**

| | |
|---|---|
| In the 19th century | 145 |
| In the 20th century | 146 |

**Second World War and the Holocaust:**

| | |
|---|---|
| Nineteen Days of the German-Polish War, and Russian Jurisdiction in Ruzhany | 150 |
| Echoes in Writing | 151 |
| In Ruzhany During the Time of the Nazis | 153 |
| I Passed Through Ruzhany During the Days of the Nazis | 162 |
| Echoes | 167 |
| Poem: "Everything Precious to Me" | 170 |
| In the German Captivity | 170 |
| What Happened To Me When I Returned Home | 171 |
| Yaakov Meir Maruchnik | 172 |
| **In Memory of the Martyrs of Ruzhany** | 174 |
| The Beloved and the Pleasant | 175 |

**In Memory of Those Who Made Aliyah:**

| | |
|---|---|
| Avraham Yitzchak Chwojnik and his wife | 177 |
| Rabbi Ze'ev Wolf | 178 |
| Leibl Ziskind | 178 |
| Nachum Alperstein | 180 |
| The Organization of Ruzhany Natives | 181 |

**Our Families:**

| | |
|---|---|
| A listing & photos of some of the families | 184 |
| Those Who Fell in the War of Independence: (Israel) | |
| **Listing of many names and photos** | 190 |
| Poem: The Jewish Body | 192 |
| More names listed | 193 |
| Another poem: Liberty | 197 |

**"Amal is Geven a Stetl" - Ruzhinoy as I Remember:**

| | |
|---|---|
| Once There Was A Shtetl by Yosef Abramowich | 199 |
| In Memory of our Martyrs - Ruzhinoy and Environs | 212 |
| List of Ruzhany Natives Living in Israel | 228 |
| List of Liskova Natives Living in Israel | 232 |

# APPENDIX

## of

## Material Added That Was

## Not in the Original Yizkor Book

This appendix has been added because the editors of this translation had become aware of this new-found significant material that they thought would be of high interest to the readers of this Memorial Book. It is set aside in this appendix and prominently marked as "Not Included in the Original Yizkor Book" so that there would never be any confusion as to its source.

# My Visit to Minsk and Ruzhany, Belarus

### December 7-12, 2010

### By Tybie Abrams

## My Family's Early Days

It began with an email invitation from my nephew, Erik Seidel. He had previously played poker at a tournament in Moscow and later was invited to play in Minsk. He asked if my mother's family came from that area. I grew up hearing the tales of life in Ruzhnoi (as we called it) by my mother, who was born in 1905. Her maternal grandmother's maiden name was CHVORNIK, her grandfather was VEGOTSKY (or WIGOSKI, or as shown in the Martyrs' list as VYGODESKY). Her father was Nathan (Nusin) Levin. He came to America and joined his brother and family in Bordentown, New Jersey. He worked, moved to Trenton, and continued to send money, which they never received, as the First World War began. It took close to nine years before money reached them.

I learned of the childhood hardships Mother survived, always hungry. Many starved to death, although the German soldiers were kind enough tp give them rice, as most of these victims of war suffered from stomach ailments. Grandmother bravely somehow managed to survive and protect the three younger girls. My Mother remembered vividly the crunch of snow and the horrible Shabbos when the men came out of Shul and were shot and murdered by Cossacks. She remembered the sight of red blood splattered on white snow.

Shtetl life was very difficult as my Mother (Ruchil) remembered. One day a relative, who had money, came to visit and asked Sushe "Far vus zinen de maidlach in bet"? And Bubbe said that the girls were in bed because they were hungry and there was no food. That relative arranged for my aunt Esther to go to someone's house every day for a meal, and she brought much of it back for my Mother and Aunt Anna.

They began their trip to America twice. The first time, as the farmer's wagon proceeded on the outskirts of town, bullets flew overhead. He stopped the wagon and had my Bubbe Sushe, the girls and my Uncle Benny get off and walk back to the town. Later Benny decided to marry his Mashke, so she joined the family on the next attempt to reach Warsaw.

Once in Warsaw, Bubbe stood in line each day to get the tickets for passage. They were there about six weeks. One day a landsman met Bubbe and asked how long she'd been there. He told her that she had to BUY a place on line or she would never get to the front. She did, and succeeded. Their trip from Antwerp was long, and everyone but Mother was sick. For the first time she could have all the food she wanted, as she enjoyed everyone else's portions. They arrived at Ellis Island and a small boat came close to the ship. Zaide was on that boat and spotted his family. My Mother shouted to him "Zug eppis in English," and he said "Hello," the first English word she heard. She was sixteen, but completely lost her accent once she was in America. She was such a proud and patriotic American.

I was fascinated with the thought of a trip to the town where some generations of my family lived. I had not yet read the Yizkor Book, just relied on the history my Mother provided. Despite the sad memories Mother had, I am grateful to be able to see where she lived and where others in my family came from. I will try to see the sky and surroundings through my Mother's beautiful eyes. I will try not to think of the sad times. She had good memories of school, but never knew when the language would change from Russian to Polish and back again.

## My Trip to Minsk

My nephew Erik Seidel is a world-famous poker player and is in the Poker Hall of Fame. He travels the world. Erik was to play in a tournament at the Crown Plaza Hotel in Minsk and emailed me with an invitation to join him there. Arrangements were made. Because of Erik, I was treated with respect, attention and true caring. They anticipated my every need, even if I didn't know I had that need.

Traveling on a huge plane in the business section was the beginning of an incredible trip. The seat went all the way back into a bed. The personal screen offered movies, sports, etc. I watched two movies and with the food and attention from the staff, the seven-hour trip went quickly.

We landed in Frankfurt, and after following the signs, I reached the other terminal where my flight to Minsk would begin. It was a smaller plane and the trip was only about two hours. I received yet another kosher meal!

I was met in Minsk by Vasilley and Katya. Vasilley was with the Poker Tournament staff and Katya was my personal guide for the time I was in Belarus. Both were young and warm and concerned with my well-being. When I arrived at the hotel, Anna was there with open arms. It felt like family, and Erik wasn't even there yet! From that moment on I was treated as if I was a very special guest. Meals either appeared in my room, or plans were made for me. I had a massage, and so began my magical time in Belarus.

Katya is a Belarus citizen, Vasilley and Anna came from Moscow. Those three offered humor, companionship and constant care. They also shared their countries' history with me. I learned a lot. Belarus is a war-torn country. It was occupied by the Nazis for four years during the war. Concentration camps filled the country and there are great memorials throughout, noting and remembering the cruelty.

One of our dinners was in honor of Erik and was attended by all the Russian players and the important production people. The food was plentiful, with many choices, all of them delicious. My drink is vodka, and suddenly there appeared a vodka on the rocks. Across from me sat a man who had a full bottle in front of him. I was so impressed with his ability to drink. Their humor (when translated) was fabulous. He stood to toast Ilya, who translated for us. Ilya immediately shot back, that the man who was toasting also had an honor to be recognized--the ability to drink two glasses of vodka simultaneously. So funny. They got around to toasting everyone, and when it was my turn, I stood to acknowledge the honor and spoke about my wonderful visit. We had place cards; I sat between two women, Anna and a young woman from the production company.

I had become so accustomed to my dependence on my new companions that when I left my room to meet them for this dinner, I wandered into a huge casino that was a part of the hotel I had no idea existed. I knew that was not where I needed to be and walked out, and there, down the hall I saw Erik. I was so relieved! He walked with me to the restaurant, which I probably wouldn't have found myelf, although I had been there several times before.

## My Visit to the Minsk Jewish Center

On our schedule today, December 9. was the Minsk Jewish Center. Katya had called ahead and they were expecting us. Several one-story buildings connected, cars in the parking yard, and much snow. Our driver left us off, Katya rang the bell, and a man standing nearby directed us to the building in the back. We left our coats with a woman attendant in the coatroom area. We walked down to the basement and met Lisa. The walls were covered with pictures and maps. Many people have contacted this Jewish Center and told them about their families. Lisa asked me to do the same. I showed her the picture I had with me that was taken either in Minsk or Ruzhany. My

Grandparents, my Mother and her siblings, brothers Yirshel (Harry) and Benny, sisters Molly and Anna. My Mother was the youngest, about three years old. My Aunt Esther was not born yet. My Grandmother had lost two sons in early infancy. She vowed to G-d that if she had sons who survived, she would never kiss them on the face. To this day we kiss our children on their heads.

Since Lisa did not speak English, we spoke through Katya (interesting after spending days looking at someone's face, as I spoke to them or they spoke to me, and then waiting for the third person to translate). I spoke some Yiddish to Lisa, and she had tears in her eyes as she said to Katya, "It sounds like music to me." She had 57 close relatives, but her parents were the only survivors from two different camps.

In the translation of the book about Ruzhany, there is a description of the "arrest" of the Jews on the 2nd of November 1942, and their murder on the 28th. Lisa's account of that incident and the dates also included details about a stopping point on the way to Treblinka. The day they were "arrested," those who seemed unable to be part of the march to their death were shot. About 120 elderly were eliminated before the walk began. The rest walked. Three thousand five hundred people started that walk. On the way some died, and their bodies were abandoned where they dropped. Some who survived the walk arrived in Volkovisk. This was first built as a Russian soldiers' prison. Bunkers were carved into the walls like shelves. But there were too many Ruzhany people and there wasn't room even in the horrendous facility for all to fit in and have shelter. They had designated a special area for the Ruzhany people, but it wasn't large enough. (This Volkovisk facility was originally the stopping-off place for Jews to be gathered and then sent on to camps or some to work in Germany. But it became the last stop for those sent to Treblinka, the death camp.)

They stayed there (a more detailed description of the horrors of Volkovisk is on the Ruzhany web site) until November 22nd. The first transport began and the cattle cars were so full that the people were forced to stand tightly together. Their destination was Treblinka, where they were murdered on November 28th. The Treblinka Death Camp has a stone with the name of every village that contributed to their numbers. (NYC Public Library has the Volkovisker Yizkor Book in Yiddish and English commemorating the occupants of the bunkers.) A woman from Volkovisk was there in the bunkers when the Ruzhany people arrived and she told the story. Lisa suggested www.Bagnowka.com for additional information.

Lisa related her knowledge of Ruzhany and mentioned the blood libel case in which two rabbis were murdered. A dead Christian child had been tossed into one of their basements. Brian Zakem, the co-coordinator of the translated Ruzhany Yizkor Book is from a rabbinic family in Ruzhany (nine generations), and one of the rabbis involved was his ancestor. The horror of the treatment and murder of Jews and Jewish children becomes even more meaningful when we hear the descriptions almost first-hand and realize how this area was ravaged by the Nazis.

Treblinka had gas chambers and then the bodies were stacked like wood and burned. Right from the cattle cars the two groups were chosen. Some were sent directly to the gas chambers. They were stripped of their clothes and taken to the rooms, the gas tanks were next to the rooms. Those in the "worker group," usually young men, took the bodies from the gas chambers to be stacked and burned, or to the ovens. Then those young men were killed. There was a bakery in the camp that supplied potatoes and some sort of "bread." The people who were assigned there worked with the partisans and rescued some children and adults. One of those women rescued her sister and told the story for posterity.

Some Jews were in the camp with others. When they were separated and confined, that was called the Ghetto. The women who were strong were kept alive to sort clothes and cut hair from women. TREBLINKA was a KILLING PLACE, not a place to keep people. Some clothes were given to the Minsk Ghetto. People who needed the clothes often found garments of relatives and that was the first time they knew of the death of those relatives. The Nazis had appointed a man named Kube as governor of occupied Belarus. He went to the Opera House in Minsk with his family to find clothes which were taken from the Jews before they were gassed.

When the Jewish transport trains stopped, there were signs indicating it was a real train station. The horror was so intense that for years after the war nothing was told and much was covered up because the people couldn't bear to look at those war reminders, and the survivors did not want memories. So very little information came for many years. There is a factory now where the bunkers were located.

After the war, Soviet Russia accused survivors (not all Jews) of being spies and sent them off to Siberia. Those Jews who were forced to "work" in the camps were killed. On the internet are stories about twenty Treblinka survivors.

References to "The Pale" always mystified me. There is a map at the Jewish Museum in Minsk that draws a line around most of Belarus. For many years that was the only area where Jews could live (and it made it easier for Hitler and his minions to gather them together for murder). Hitler told his soldiers that all the areas they conquered would be theirs after the war.

Lisa said that when German visitors questioned her about hating them, she just replied that "I never was a Grandchild, that's what was taken away from me." The

Jewish Museum in Minsk would like pictures and stories about families who left the area in time to survive. (See their contact information following this.)

## My Day in Ruzhany

My nephew Erik and I spent one day, December 10, 2010 in Ruzhany. It took about three hours to reach by car from Minsk. The first place we stopped at was in front of the Mayor's office. It so happened that the Governor had come to Ruzhany to inaugurate the initial remodeling of the Palace, so the Mayor was busy with that event. However, we met a young man in front of the office building, who acted as a guide. This young man turned to me and I was surprised when he handed me a little packet wrapped in plastic and said (in Russian, translated for us by our guide from Minsk), "You should have this. It came from the house of the jeweler." It was a treasure! It is the remains of a Hebrew Pesach Haggadah. It is so fragile that I read only from the top page, the bottom is singed (by fire?) There are no front or back covers. As far as I know, Erik and I are the only descendants of Ruzhany who came for a visit. We do not know who the "jeweler" was, or the location of his house. We plan to turn the Haggadah over to a Holocaust Museum. Photos of some of the Haggadah pages follow this article. Some research by Brian Zakem has led us to believe it was printed in Vilnius, Lithuania in approximately 1922-23.

The town is surrounded by forests and after we walked through the main street, we saw where a huge market used to be. We continued through the inner streets covered with snow, to the site of the Great Synagogue and nearby Yeshiva building. We were told this was the only one left of the twelve original synagogues.

There was no identification that I felt with this being an 80% Jewish-populated shtetl. Everything was neat, few people walking, I felt neutral to the surroundings, even at the main Synagogue, whose roof it seemed would collapse with one more snowfall. The words I thought of there were "neglect" and "no one caring." A small plaque describes the year it was built. One could not feel that this was a Jewish shtetl. I could not feel emotion of any kind. We again stopped at the Municipal Building, but the Mayor was still occupied with the Governor. We then went to the Palace and were given a tour. My Mother had never mentioned this very significant part of Ruzhany. I could only think that people cared enough to restore this landmark but not concerned wiith the people who lived in Ruzhany where the Palace is located.

I was anxious to see the cemetery so that I could find names of my ancestors. The road that led to it showed a meticulously kept cemetery decorated with bright artificial flowers. The end of the road is where the snowplow left the pile of snow from the road. We had to climb over that, walk through the forest (grateful for the path the hunters made), and then came to a clearing, an open field covered with snow. There, far away, was a misshapen large "stone," and we could see two more in the distance. Most of the headstones had been removed and used by the townspeople. Suddenly I felt emotion in Ruzhany -- deep sadness at the neglect of what is left of the Jewish presence, anger that money and interest will restore "the Palace," but that this cemetery is ignored as well as the heritage of our people.

I learned that all of Belarus was occupied by the Nazis for four years. The scars remain in the many memorials erected by the Russians. There was a feeling of restraint and an artificial demeanor in Belarus. We knew that an election was coming and that was a recognition of the yoke the people endure. No one can own property in all of Belarus; the government owns all the property and the KGB is one of the largest arms of the government. Upon our return I read daily about the brutality of the post-election and the continuing arrests and government domination. How strange it is that the Russian people lived in pain under the Czars and then under Communism. It is hard to realize it is 2011 in the world, but not in Belarus, where citizens really aren't free to choose their government and continue to live in fear.

The people could not have been more pleasant or nicer to me and did not indicate their unhappiness. It is just a feeling I had even as we shopped and people were bustling and talking all around us.

The poker tournament offered a completely different environment with joviality, humor and great luxury. Typical of the government is a sports arena not far from the hotel, which was built over a Jewish cemetery! The saga of the prejudice toward my people continues. The people of Belarus suffered greatly and there were some who risked their lives for the Jews. But the evidence I saw in respecting our people on the whole seems to be contained in the Jewish Museum of Minsk.

## Looking Back

As I think back on my extraordinary trip to Belarus, a few thoughts come to mind. I never saw a stork nest! Never thought about where storks iive. I was told they live in nests very high on the trees in Belarus.

In my heart I ached for the enormity of the tragedy that befell our people during the Second World War. My presence in "The Pale," which was also home to my maternal family, cut deeply into that perception. The Nazis occupied Belarus for four years during the war. Today it still carries the scars. The houses are painted, the city of Minsk is clean and bright and orderly. But underlying all of this are the scars that country will always bear. The stark monuments attest to the horror that occurred there.

I also visited a town that had been completely destroyed. It was an incredible "monument," as a chimney was built for every house in the exact location where it had stood. An additional haunting reminder was the bell placed at the top of every chimney, and the sound of that bell filled the air in a haunting way as one after another pealed. The roof of the barn has been reconstructed. The Nazis came in and rounded everyone up, herded them into the barn and then set the barn on fire.

There is a frightening, very large figure of a man carrying a child's limp body in his arms. The story is that this man was the smithy, and that he hid in the forest until it was over, and then came back and found his son dead. Another version of this story is that some people believe he must have led the Nazis to this small village because of its isolated position. On this site are many memorials, some to the number of villages lost, some to each of the concentration camps in that area.

I was taken to visit a village that was created to show life in the 1800s. It was fascinating to see the tools and devices used during that period. For example, a bird cage in the kitchen area which was suspended from the ceiling, as a place to keep cheese; a mouse could not get to it and it kept cold in that part of the kitchen. Another device I could not identify was a pole from ceiling to floor and fairly close to the floor was a wooden ring attached to the pole. When children started to crawl they were placed in that ring and when their feet moved, they could go in a circle and still be in the same, secure place.

As a guest and proud aunt of Erik Seidel, whom they honored, I was treated as a very special person. Those memories of the caring people who watched over me will be with me forever.

I will also remember my visit to the Jewish Museum in Minsk where I learned more details about the death of the Jews of Ruzhany (I still think of it as Ruzhnoi). My day in Ruzhany was difficult because I could not picture my Mother living there. My Grandfather came to America first and before he was able to send for the rest of the family, the First World War broke out. The family remained there until after the anxiety of the war, with the lack of food or money. My Mother said she would not go back to see the town, I did that for her. There's a Castle/Fortress called the Palace referred to in the Yizkor book, which was actually owned by a nobleman who was given all the land. The village people paid rent and provided goods and services. The industries there were weaving, leather works and some other type of fabric manufacturing.

There are still European families who trace their ancestry back to that Castle, and now work has begun on reconstructing it. We happened to be there the day the Governor came to see it and we were allowed to follow him. It won't be open to the public for several months. What struck me was the interest and financial commitment to rebuilding this Castle/Fortress. This was a stark contrast to the Jewish cemetery, where headstones were removed and used by the townspeople.

I believe in fate and I believe in G-d. There remains, for the time being, a huge structure that was the largest of the twelve Ruzhany synagogues. Another snowstorm, and that roof will come crashing down into what was once a beautiful interior. At one time the Jewish population was approximately 80%. There is not a trace of Jewish presence except for that synagogue, once called "The Great Synagogue." No monuments there.

But as "fate" would have it, I was given a treasure -- the tiny Pesach Haggadah.
I hope to donate it to a Holocaust museum as the last remnant of a thriving Jewish community.

A book of remembrances, as well as the history of the Jews in Ruzhany, was written in Tel Aviv in 1956; now the translation from Hebrew is complete. I hope my story will be an addendum to the bppk as well as the Ruzhany web site, the last report to date from Ruzhany, together with the photos I took. Word came back to me that there were no winter pictures of Ruzhany. During my visit it was cold and icy, the entire area covered with snow, and the pictures I took are already on the web site.

My nephew and I are the first family members to visit our family's shtetl. It was a humbling experience. I am grateful to Erik for thinking about our heritage and enabling me to "go back." I am grateful to him for the very best trip I have ever had. with the dearest, most considerate people I ever met.

This is my rough "journal." I was given a computer and wrote home every night, although I lost a few emails and hope I have remembered enough to write this essay. Perhaps some day I will write an epilogue.

Note: for those interested in contacting the Jewish Museum in Minsk, which is attached to the Minsk Jewish Center.
  email address: jewish_museum@mail..ru
Address is:  V. Khoruzhei St-28,Minsk 220100, Belarus
                       Phone:  37517 2867961

## Information to Date about the Ruzhany Passover Haggadah

### By Brian Zakem, Co-Coordinator of the Ruzhany Yizkor Book Translation Project

The Haggadah was given to Mrs. Tybie Abrams on December 10, 2010 in Ruzhany, by a young man who acted as a guide. They were in front of the office of the Mayor, no further identification of the young man is available. He told Tybie that his father told him to make sure this religious service book for Passover should one day be given to some Jewish visitor to Ruzhany, and that it had been found in the "home of the jeweler." This remnant, approximately 60 pages, is now believed to be a Haggadah.

In the process of researching the "Ruzhany Haggadah" with the help of research librarians at the Spertus College of Judaica, Chicago, complemented by the extraordinary digging for this sacred book's facts of origin, with special thanks to Ms. Sharon Horowitz of the Library of Congress, this is what is now known about this partial document. So far, this work of "Judaica" is the only work I know about that has been uncovered from the Jewish inhabitants who lived in Ruzhany between their most probable first habitation since this privately, Sapieha family-owned market town was established in 1552 till the Jewish community's "final" demise in the Shoah, November 1942.

These pages, all of one Haggadah, consisted of an approximate total of 87 numbered pages, 13 pages of a Roman-enumerated preface incorporating at least 10 images/graphics of various sizes, beginning with its reproduced (copied) cover page from the so-called "Great Haggadah of Prague," first published in 1558. Tybie's unbound copy, a loose-paged remnant, appears to be missing about 10 pages from its preface (in the Yiddish language) and 17-plus pages of the original text.

According to the Yudelov Bibliography of Haggadot, Ms. Horowitz has to date identified four likely publishers and related information. As translated from the Hebrew these editions are listed:

1. N. Levin, Publisher, Vilna, Lithuania, 1922. Printed by I. Notes and S. Szwajiich, edited by N. Niselovits, approximate size 6-3/4 by 4 inches.
2. Second edition (same as above), 1923, same size.
3. Third edition (same as above), 1925, size increased to 9 by 6 inches.
4. Shelomoh Funk, Publisher, Vilnia, Lithuania. Printed by Express, 1931, edited by H. Niselovits, 9 by 6 inches.

It is hoped that future readers and/or dedicated researchers will aid and contact Brian **(bzakem@comcast.net)** when they discover any materials that may confirm the actual origins of this so-called "Ruzhany Haggadah."

Additional facts and narratives concerning this particular and/or related Haggadah (i.e., its contents, how marketed, etc.) may illuminate and further uncover, as part of a meaningful memorial, some Ruzhany's residents, their rich, very complex, Jewish multicultural, multiethnic and interreligious histories.

# Photos of the Ruzhany Haggadah

הגדה של פסח

## קידוש לליל א' וב' של פסח

**קַדֵּשׁ.** מען גיעסט אן דעם ערשטען כוס און דער בעל-הבית מאכט קִדּוּשׁ.

הָרֵינִי מוּכָן וּמְזוּמָן לְקַיֵּם מִצְוַת כּוֹס רִאשׁוֹן מֵאַרְבַּע כּוֹסוֹת, לְשֵׁם יִחוּד קוּדְשָׁא בְּרִיךְ הוּא וּשְׁכִינְתֵּיהּ, עַל יְדֵי הַהוּא טָמִיר וְנֶעְלָם בְּשֵׁם כָּל יִשְׂרָאֵל.

ווען עס פאלט אויס פרייטאג צונאכט הויבט מען אן פון יום הַשִּׁשִּׁי.

וַיְהִי עֶרֶב וַיְהִי בֹקֶר

יוֹם הַשִּׁשִּׁי: וַיְכֻלּוּ הַשָּׁמַיִם וְהָאָרֶץ וְכָל צְבָאָם, וַיְכַל אֱלֹהִים בַּיּוֹם הַשְּׁבִיעִי מְלַאכְתּוֹ אֲשֶׁר עָשָׂה, וַיִּשְׁבֹּת בַּיּוֹם הַשְּׁבִיעִי מִכָּל מְלַאכְתּוֹ אֲשֶׁר עָשָׂה. וַיְבָרֶךְ אֱלֹהִים אֶת יוֹם הַשְּׁבִיעִי וַיְקַדֵּשׁ אוֹתוֹ, כִּי בוֹ שָׁבַת מִכָּל מְלַאכְתּוֹ אֲשֶׁר בָּרָא אֱלֹהִים לַעֲשׂוֹת.

אין דער וואכען הויבט מען אן דא.

סַבְרִי מָרָנָן וְרַבָּנָן וְרַבּוֹתַי:

בָּרוּךְ אַתָּה יְיָ, אֱלֹהֵינוּ מֶלֶךְ הָעוֹלָם, בּוֹרֵא פְּרִי הַגָּפֶן:

בָּרוּךְ אַתָּה יְיָ, אֱלֹהֵינוּ מֶלֶךְ הָעוֹלָם, אֲשֶׁר בָּחַר בָּנוּ מִכָּל עָם וְרוֹמְמָנוּ מִכָּל לָשׁוֹן וְקִדְּשָׁנוּ בְּמִצְוֹתָיו. וַתִּתֶּן לָנוּ, יְיָ אֱלֹהֵינוּ בְּאַהֲבָה (לשבת: שַׁבָּתוֹת לִמְנוּחָה וּ) מוֹעֲדִים לְשִׂמְחָה, חַגִּים וּזְמַנִּים לְשָׂשׂוֹן אֶת יוֹם (לשבת: הַשַּׁבָּת הַזֶּה וְאֶת יוֹם)

# Appendix of Material Not included in Original Yizkor book

ביים סדר.

הגדה של פסח

רילט אָב דעם סדר מיט גרױס פֿאַראַד. די הגדה איז בײַ זײ דיעוועלבע וואָס בײַ אונז, אָבער געזאָגט ווערט זי גאַנץ אַנדערש. מען פֿערטײלט די הגדה צווישען עולם ווײַ אַ כּבוד און יעדער שטעהט אױף פֿון זײַן אָרט זאָגט מיט גרױס בּנֹה זײַן פּרק און יעצט יעדען פּסוק גלײַך איבּער אױף סאַרטיש. די שפּראַך וואָס ווערט גערעדט פֿון די בּולאַרער אידען.

אינטערעסאַנט איז, וואָס די בּולאַרער אירען טהוען אױס צו דער הגדה די שיך און בּלײַבּען זיצען אין זאָקען. די פֿרױען טהוען אפֿילו אױס די זאָקען אױך און בּלײַבּען זיצען מיט די בּאָרפֿיסע פֿיס אונטער זיך.

גאַנץ אַנדערש ווערט אָבּגעריכט דער סדר בּײַ די ספֿרדישע אידען, אין טונים, טריפּאָליס און אין תימן. די דאָזיגע אידען וואָס שטאַמען על פּי רוב פֿון די עלטעסטע אראַ- בּישע אידען מיט א שטאַרקער צומישונג פֿון די שפּאַנישע פֿערטריבּענע אידען, האָבּען אַ סך מנהגים געמײַנזאַם מיט יענע בּערג-אידען אין צענטראַל-אַזיען און אַ סך מנהגים זענען שוין אַלגעמײן ספֿרדישע. צווישען דיעזע ספֿרדיש-אַפֿריקאַנישע אידען צײלענט זיך אױס דער סדר בּײַ די טוניסער אידען, מיט זײערע אײגענעלע כּנהגים, וואָס מען געפֿינט זײ ניט בּײַ אַנדערש אידען.

אױך די טוניסער אידען פֿערזאַמלען זיך צום סדר צו אײנעם אַ אַנגעזעהענעם בּעל-הבית וואָס זיצט אױבּען-אָן בּײַ'ן טיש אױף וועלכען עס בּרענען די זילבּערנע לײַכטער און איז בּעפֿוצט מיט דער גאַנצער אָריענטאַלישער פּראַכט. דער בּעל-

פרעה אין יוסף'ס צייטען.   פרעה אין משה'ס צייטען.

משה פיטערט די שאף.

# Appendix of Material Not included in Original Yizkor book

משה אויפ'ן טייך.

הגדה של פסח ────────── 34

הָיָה תִּקַּח בְּיָדֶךָ, אֲשֶׁר תַּעֲשֶׂה בּוֹ אֶת הָאֹתוֹת. "וּבְמוֹפְתִים" – זֶה הַדָּם, כְּמָה שֶׁנֶּאֱמַר: וְנָתַתִּי מוֹפְתִים בַּשָּׁמַיִם וּבָאָרֶץ.

דָּם. וָאֵשׁ. וְתִימְרוֹת עָשָׁן.

דָּבָר אַחֵר: בְּיָד חֲזָקָה – שְׁתַּיִם. וּבִזְרוֹעַ נְטוּיָה – שְׁתַּיִם. וּבְמוֹרָא גָּדוֹל – שְׁתַּיִם. וּבְאוֹתוֹת – שְׁתַּיִם. וּבְמוֹפְתִים – שְׁתַּיִם.

אֵלּוּ עֶשֶׂר מַכּוֹת שֶׁהֵבִיא הַקָּדוֹשׁ בָּרוּךְ הוּא עַל הַמִּצְרִים בְּמִצְרַיִם, וְאֵלּוּ הֵן:

דָּם. צְפַרְדֵּעַ. כִּנִּים. עָרוֹב. דֶּבֶר. שְׁחִין. בָּרָד. אַרְבֶּה. חֹשֶׁךְ. מַכַּת בְּכוֹרוֹת:

───────────────────────────────

דבר אחר — אנ'אנדער אויסטייטשען דעם פסוק: ביד חזקה — שטארקע האנד (צוויי ווערטער) — צוויי מכות; ובזרוע נטויה — אויסגעשטרעקטער ארעם צוויי; ובמורא גדול — גרויסע שרעקן — צוויי; ובאותות — מיט צייכענס — צוויי; ובמופתים — מיט וואונדער — צוויי. דאם זענען די צעהן מכות, וואם גאט האט אנגעבראכט אויף די מצרים אין מצרים. עם הם זענען זיי:

בלוט, פרעש, פאראזיטען, א מישמאש פון שעדליכע שרצים, פעסט, הויטענצינדונג, האגעל, הייישעריקען, פינסטערניש, מכה אויף בכורים.

 הגדה של פסח.

זיך אין וואסער געשטעלט, אויף די פליגלען האָבּן
זײ די אידישע קינדערלאך אויפגעחאַפּט, הויך-הויך
האָבּן זײ זיך דאמיט אװעקגעטראגען, ביז צו די שפּי-
צן פון די הויכע פעלזען האָבּן זײ עם געבּראכט,
און דארט איבּערגעלאזט. אין זײ דארט אנם געשטהן:
פון די הארטע פעלזען האָט אָנגעהויבּן צו שטרעמען
פרישע מילך, די קינדערלאך האָבּן עם געזויגען און
ערנעהרט זיך.

און דארט אין דערהויך, וויַט-וויַט פון פסקר-
שקלאפטען מצרים, איז ערצויגען געווארען אַ פרישער
דור; אַ דור וועלכער איז געווען שטאַרק װי די פעלזען,
פריַ װי די װינדען פון פעלד, גוט און בּאַרעמהערציג
װי די מלאכים וועלכע האָבּען אויף זײ בּשוואַכט.

## Pictures of Ruzhany from the Time of World War I

The following pictures of Ruzhany are from the records of Dora Vegotsky Pitkowsky, mother of Sarah Platt, aunt of Edith Vegotsky Taylor, Co-coordinator of the Ruzhany Yizkor Project.

Michael Pitkowsky, uncle of Edith Taylor, travelled back to Ruzhany in 1913. He took an extra $100 with him in order to hire a photographer to take the photos below. They were found in the archives of his late wife, Dora Vegotsky Pitkowsky.

**View from afar**

# Appendix of Material Not included in Original Yizkor book

Synagogue in early 1900s

Synagogue in 2010

**Synagogue in 2006**

# Appendix of Material Not included in Original Yizkor book

**Bimah in Synagogue prior to World War I**

**Ark in the Synagogue**

**A Market Day**

**The Horse Market of a market day**

The market place, Rozana; Courthouse and the village church with steeple. The building on the far right is a second synagogue, not the main one.

The celebration of Polish National Holiday, May 3rd

Half of Milner Street from Sarah-Ana's building (which became a police building). The third building, Chvoinik's, became the Rozana Bank, including the second story. The street ends at Bliznoyer Street.

Schloss Street, corner building is owned by "Yankel," apparently someone Edith'a aunt knew, next to it is the slaughter house, and next to that is a house owned by Velvel Shereshevsky.

The bridge on Milner's Street and the river; lumber was transported on this river

Section of Schloss Street with bridge. There is a fire brigade building and opposite the houses is a big canal toward Isaac the butcher's son's house.

Kilbaner Street, Ruzhany

Ruzhany Theatre

Hospital, Ruzhany

Talmud Torah (Hebrew School) in Rozana

Ruzhany Pharmacy

Entry to theGrounds of the Palace of the Grand Chancellor Leu Sapieha

## Appendix of Material Not included in Original Yizkor book

**Front of the Palace of Grand Chancellor Leu Sapieha**

**Back side of the Palace of Grand Chancellor Leu Sapieha**

# Appendix of Material Not included in Original Yizkor book

# Appendix of Material Not included in Original Yizkor book

# INDEX

This Index Does Not Inclucde Pages After Page 324.

## A

Abli, 41
Abolitz, 316
Abramovich, 1, 40, 155, 177, 179, 180, 184, 188, 189, 190, 202, 211
Abramovitch, 89
**Abramovitsch**, I, 300, 308
Abramowich, Xx, 261, 265, 266, 275, 316, 321
Abramowicz, 146, 152, 157, 158
Abrams, Vii, Xxi
Achituv, 316
*Ackerfeld*, Iii, Xiii
Aleichem, 150, 151, 200
Alperstein, Xx, 179, 180, 181, 182, 184, 188, 195, 202, 261, 316
Alpert, Ii, Iii, Xiv
Amiel, 35
Anvati, 120
Aran, 211, 257, 265
Aran (Chwojnik), 210
Arkin, 316
Artzi, 316
Avi-Leah, 93
Avner, 316

## B

Babel, 191
Babich, 193, 205, 216, 320
Babicz, 215
Babitz, 317
Bachrach, 11, 23, 24
Bankrot, 320
Barzilai, 115
Bashin, 30, 149, 156, 179, 180, 184, 202, 317, 318
Bass, 151, 158
Bayr, 181
Beizer, 199, 322
Belkin, 184
Bendetowich, 323
Ben-Dror, 177
Beri'l, 120, 121, 122
Beril, 50
Berish, 44
Berkowich, 162, 202
Berl, 36
Berman, 11, 35, 37, 40, 85, 149, 153, 188, 193, 199, 205, 217, 322
Bernstein, 121
Bessin, 35
Bialik, 29, 140
Bialobitzky, 317
Bialos, 184
Bilais, 209
Blatt, Xiv
BLISNOSKI, 312
Bliznansky, 247, 251
Blobitsky, 205
Bloch, 201
Bloshtik, 319
Blumberg, 317
Bocher, 323, 324
Bornstein, 317
Botkovich, 227, 228
Brauda, 317
Brazovsky, 178, 179, 184, 217
Brestowitzky, 323
Breznitzky, 277, 278, 279, 317, 321
Brezticki, 188, 202
Brier, Xiii
Brochnesky, 323
Broida, 322
Brona, 317
Broshi, 323
Brouda, 149, 184
Bryn, 317
Brzenicki, 206
Bulgacz, 149
Bulgatz, Xviii, 85, 149, 317
Burovsky, 181
Burshechivski, 210
Bursi, 317
Byulopolski, 184

## C

Chaikin, 319, 321
Chaim Leib The Baker, 127
Charno, 139
Chasid, 319
Chazak, 27
Chazatzky, 105
Chisin, 123
Chmielnitzki, 304
Chofetz Chaim, 40
Chomsky, 184
Chover, 318
Chowjnik, 161
Chvonick, 305, 306

Chvonik, 304
Chwojnak, 145, 150
Chwojniak, 86
Chwojnik, Xx, 69, 72, 86, 90, 105, 149, 151, 152, 153, 154, 155, 157, 175, 179, 184, 192, 195, 201, 205, 211, 212, 256, 259, 264, 269, 316, 317, 318, 319
Chwojnik-Ziskind, 211
Cohan, 319
Cohen, 323
Czar Nikolai, 124
Czar Nikolai I, 73
Czar Peter I, 43

## D

Danzig, 132
David The Melamed, 75, 76
David The Teacher, 305
Davidson, 96
Diker, 205
Dinerman, 316
Ditkovsky, 149, 177, 178, 184, 316
Dlogolansky, 318
Dobkin, 317, 318
Dobrowicki, 152
Dovkin, 193
Dreyfuss, 85
Dubnow, 9, 43, 132
Dumovsky, 275
Duvshani, 317
Dzikonsky, 100

## E

Egolnik, 151, 153, 154, 157, 160, 179, 180, 181, 182, 183, 184, 186, 188, 195, 201, 202, 269, 316, 321
Einhorn, 311
Einstein, 205, 245, 268, 316
Eisenberg, 323
Eisenstadt, 11
Eisenstat, 102
Eisenstein, 161, 188, 245
Eizenstein, 89
Eliezer Ben Yehuda, 114
Epltreger, 135, 157, 163
Eppletreger, 305
Epshteyn, Xix, 107, 127, 135, 149, 152, 153, 155, 156, 162, 176, 179, 180, 181, 182, 184, 186, 187, 188, 190, 192, 193, 194, 195, 198, 202, 205, 207, 212
Epstein, 33, 99, 242, 275, 305, 316, 319
Erlich, 316
Ett, 149, 181, 187, 195, 322
Ett (Reiner), 184

## F

Fagin, 205
Fajnman, 151
Feldman, Xiii
Field, Vi, Xiii
Fine, Ii, Xiv
Fineman, 176
Finkel The Baker, 175
Finman, 321
Fitil, 30
Foksman, 187, 193, 194, 195, 216
Foxman, 321
Freud, 191
Friedland, 11, 21, 27, 51, 102
Friedlander, 321
Friedlansky, 96
Friedman, 50, 56
Frumkin, 116
Fuchs, 230
Fuksman, 275

## G

Gamerman, 175, 183, 187, 194, 195, 212, 217, 224, 247, 265, 267, 317
Garber, 317, 322
Garbolski, 320
Gardovchik, 317
Gaselewich, 195
Gashelwich, 181
Gavoha, 152
Gebzah, 107, 156
Gelber, 34
Gelfand, 316
Gelman, 121
Gerber, 32, 33, 34, 36, 152, 208, 321
Gerber (Bursky), 155
Gerbolcki, 184, 193
Gershon, 11, 275
Gevirtig, 308
Gezbah, 179, 191, 211
Gidon, 319
Gilada, 318
Giladi, 317
Ginzburg, 11, 205
Gishura, 317
Glickson, 66
Goldberg, Xix, 30, 89, 136, 137, 163, 185, 212, 267
Goldfaden, 152
Goldin, 90, 149, 225, 229
Goldyn, 153
Gomerman, 312
Gostovski, 321
Grabolski, 317

Grabolsky, 179, 180, 202
Groll, Xiii
Grosman, 263
Grynbaum, 139, 140, 185, 186
Grynberg, 191
Grynfeld, 317
Guber, 89, 176, 182, 186, 206, 207, 292, 293, 295, 296, 298, 317
Guldin, 176
Guldis, 153, 156, 182, 211
Gur-Aryeh, 317
Gurewich, 210
Gurwitz, 318
Gustavsky, 308
Gustovcki, 179, 181
Gustovski, 251
Gustovsky, 180, 184
Guthelf, 324
Gutman, 316
Gvurin, 180, 181, 195, 317

## H

Haamala, 122
Hachanski, 90
Hadaska, Xviii, 77, 78, 79, 80, 86
Hadassah, 81
Halpern, 45, 184
Heilprin, 11
Heller, 318
Herman, 37
Hertzberg, 114
Hertzfeld, 186
Hillel, 50
Hirsch, 122
Hirschhorn, Ii, Xiv
Hirshbein, 152
Hitler, 229
Hoffman, 318, 321
Hofin, 120
Hornik, 318
Horowitz, 51

## I

Ickowicz, 66
Ines, 316
Ines (Rubinowich), 265
Inker, 149, 321, 322
Itche, 37
Itzele, 33, 40
Itzkowich, 149, 161, 178, 181, 184, 188, 193, 202, 275, 316
Ivan, 194, 316, 317
Ivanov, 100
Izakson, 316
Izersky, 119
Izkovich, 316

## J

Jabotinsky, Xix
Jakobson, 319
Janowitz, 320
Javitz, 96
Jehoshaphat, 27
Jeruzolimsky, 156
Jezernicki, 197
Jezernitzky, 183, 201
Jezranicky, 322
Jezrenisky, 223
Joselovich, 319
Joselwicz, 156, 181, 195, 216
Jozelewski, 149, 151
Jozelovsky, 322
Jubiler, 265, 319
Juzhlovsky, 153

## K

Kagan, 40, 188
Kaganowicz, 216
Kamenmostki, 188, 202
Kamintsky, 105, 154
Kamintzky, 158, 211
Kamnimostky, 317
Kanetzpolsi, 245
Kantarovich, 84
KANTOROVITZ, 312
Kantorowich, 213, 248, 250
Kaplan, 89, 93, 141, 151, 152, 154, 156, 161, 162, 165, 171, 175, 176, 179, 182, 184, 187, 193, 197, 200, 212, 221, 225, 227, 228, 232, 310, 316, 321
Kaplinski, 105, 178, 209, 308, 309, 322
KAPLINSKI, 308
Kaplinsky, 179, 182, 184, 187, 202, 240, 251, 316
Karelicki, 149
Karelitz, 162, 206, 265
Karl The King Of Sweden, 12
Karlin, 321
Karlinski, 217, 322
Karlits, 162, 267
Karpelewich, 188, 193, 212, 245
Karpelovich, 322
Karpelowicz, 157
Karpels, 175
Kaspi, 319
Kassabian, Xii, Xiii
Kasten, 121
Katz, 179, 180, 190

Katzenelboigen, 41
Katzenelenboigen, 11, 12
Katzin, 91
Katzman, 107, 175, 176
Kazimierz, 12
Kazimierz II, 12
Kesler, 153
Kessler, 151
Kfitz, 188
Kimerman, 193, 216
King August II, 43
King Karl XII, 43
King Kazimierz, 24
King Stanislaw Leszczynski, 43
Kirshstein, 233, 264
Kirshtein, 308, 309, 310
KIRSHTEIN, 308
Kirstein, 219, 220
Klebensky, 181, 184, 188, 192, 275, 321
Kleiner, 321
Kletzki, 177, 178
Klibansky, 252
Klicki, 184
Kliniod, 321
Klinzweig, 319
Klitzky, 317
Kluchky, 179
Kochavi, 319
Kolcki, 321
Kolishevsky, 188, 202
Kolodany, 181, 184
Komarovsky, 201
Kosmovsky, 252
Kozak, 144
Krabczyk, 149
Krashinsky, 188
Krause, 283
Krebchok, 323
Krinski, 132, 133, 134
Krinsky, Xix, 132, 133
Krojelski, 197
Krolinski, 201
Krolinsky, 205
Krolitzky, 217
Krupeni, 30
Krupnik, 317, 319, 321
Kuklicha, 275
Kushnir, 291, 321
Kwozcki, 321

## L

Landau, Ii, Vii, Xiii
Landsberg, 258, 320
Lanzbitsky, 211
Laskowsky, 121

Laybe-Vash, 305
Leb, 175, 316
Lebenbok, 316, 319
Lebovitz, 320
Leib, 41, 176, 209
Leib "Yachid", Xviii
Leib The Carpenter, 90
Leibitshka, 217
Leizer Der Shamash, 90
Leizer The Shamash, 90
Lerman, 149, 152, 167, 175, 176, 185, 188,
   202, 274, 275, 320
Letzky, 202
Lev, 195, 213, 216, 217, 263, 318, 319
Lev The Shoemaker, 214, 216
Levenbok, 184, 202, 245, 246
Levi, 319
Leviatan, 40, 71, 85, 89, 93, 95, 105, 108,
   110, 112, 149, 154, 155, 159, 176, 188,
   200, 206, 211, 259, 264, 265, 319, 320
Leviatan-Moszkowicz, 152
Leviathan, 27, 28, 81, 86, 104, 289
Levin, 149, 319
Levina, 318
Levinov, 153, 181, 184, 188, 316
Levinson, Xiii, 139
Levitan, 308
Lewiatan, 161, 168
Lewin, 50, 121, 125, 245
Liberman, 322, 323
Libeshitsky, 305
Libitshke, 209
Liboshitzki, 90, 93
Libushitzky, Xix, 130, 132
Lilienbaum, 115
Limon, Xix, 56, 84, 138, 140, 141, 151, 153,
   187, 188, 197, 202, 246
Limun, 305
Lipovsky, 275, 320
Lipowski, 91
Liskovsky, 320
Lisovitzki, 90
Lisowicki, 166
Lissibitsky, 181
Lissobitsky, 184, 188
Lissovsky, 162
Litvinov, 67
Litwin, 77, 81, 86
Liverant, 107, 153, 246
Liwerant, 151
Lobzowsky, Xix, 135
Lubinov, 319
Luria, 95, 96, 118, 319
Lutker, 319
Lyuboshitzky, 319

## M

Mabroznicki, 251
Machtiger, 317
Magli, 183, 185, 187, 209, 265, 320
Magli (Mogilenski), 264
Mahar'al Of Prague, 42
Marminski, 168
Maruchnik, Xx, 215, 248, 249, 250, 251, 275
Mazericky, 323
Mazur, 322
Mazurko, 252
Meirovich, 317, 320
Meirowitz, 123
Melamed, 75
Meler, 121
Meller, 162, 320
Menes, 72
Michels, 175
Michenobski, 320
Michinovsky-Sokolovsky, 205
Michnovsky, 192, 193, 217, 218, 270
Michnovsky-Sokolovsky, 192
Milberg, 323
Miller, Xix, 207, 220, 225
Miller (Mronchik), 129
Mintz, 11, 72, 80, 97
Mirkin, 258, 316, 320
Mirman, 320
Mogilenski, 146, 149
Mogilensky, 186, 201
Mogilevsky, 212
Mogilinski, 320
Mogilnesky, 182
Mogilnesky-Magli, 182
Mohilever, 120, 121
Molchadsky, 318
Molchodsky, 320
Montefiore, 114
Morawicz, 11
Moritz, 320
Moshe The Schwartzer, 275
Moskovsky, 149
Moskowich, 289, 291, 320
Moskowitz, 259
Moskowski, 149
Movshowitz, 245
Mrochnik, 320
Mruchnik, 321
Muziricky, 323

## N

Naftalke Der Garber, 312
Napoleon, 88
Nasi, 44
Natan, 33, 40
Neter, 115
Nikolai I, 174
Nimele The Butcher, Xviii
Nir, 201, 320
Nishiozinski, 93
Nota, 93
Nowik, 205
Noyer, 202
Nuni, 319
Nybursky, 179, 180, 181, 182, 183, 184, 191, 195, 205
Nyomele The Butcher, 305
Nyumeches, 107

## O

Ogolnik, 245
Olshansky, 300
Oren, 316
Oren (Chwojnik), 257
Orkin, 121, 282, 283, 284, 285
Osipov, 133
Ozernicki, 202

## P

Papermaker, 306
Paras, 121
Pashnitzky, 320
Pekarsky, 321
Pepirmacher, 143, 151, 153, 157, 175
Peres, 317
Peretz, 135, 150, 152, 156, 161, 197, 300
Perlman, 321
Perlstein Levinson, Xii
Petia, 318
Pia, 275
Pilsudski, 186
Pinchas "The Yellow", 85
Pines, Xviii, Xix, 30, 32, 33, 34, 69, 71, 72, 73, 80, 81, 82, 83, 86, 95, 96, 97, 98, 99, 100, 103, 105, 111, 112, 113, 114, 115, 116, 117, 118, 121, 123, 127, 128, 137, 138, 152, 188, 194, 202, 208, 210, 212, 215, 265, 304, 305, 306, 316, 318, 319, 321, 322
Pinman, 317
Pinski, 173, 175
Pinsky, 179, 261
Pintlewich, 245
Pitkovsky, 153, 178, 180, 181, 184, 188, 194, 195, 198, 201, 202, 206, 226, 318, 319, 321
Pitkowski, 90, 158
Pitkowsky, Ii, Xiv

Pitkowsky Olshansky, Ii, Vi, Xiii
Podolsky, 280
Podrevsky, 184, 246
Polak, 92
Polik, 321
Pomerantz, 193, 194, 195, 198, 318, 323
Porat, 179
Posner, 318
Pripstein, 153, 181, 195
Privolsky, 321

# R

Rabbi Abba Swiaticki, 59
Rabbi Aharon, 42, 43
Rabbi Aryeh Leib Meyerson, 59
Rabbi Avigdor, 45
Rabbi Avigdor Charif, 45
Rabbi Avraham The Son Of Chaim Nasi, 44
Rabbi Avraham The Son Of Rabbi Chiya Hanasi, 66
Rabbi Avraham Yaakov, 58
Rabbi Avraham Yitzchak Hakohen Kook, 55
Rabbi Chaim Halevi Soloveitchik, 58
Rabbi Chaim Leib, 48
Rabbi David Oppenheim, 42
Rabbi Dov Ber, 48
Rabbi Efraim Zalman, 47, 48
Rabbi Elchanan, 41
Rabbi Elchanan Of Zelkow, 41
Rabbi Eliahu Hakohen Rappaport, 43
Rabbi Eliahu Of Lida, 77
Rabbi Eliahu Of Vilna, 46
Rabbi Eliahu Schik, 76
Rabbi Eliezer, 44, 45
Rabbi Eliezer Harkavi, 59
Rabbi Elinka Of Lida, 77
Rabbi Gershon, 14
Rabbi Heshel Of Krakow, 44
Rabbi Hirsch, 92
Rabbi Itzhak Isaac Chaver, 304
Rabbi Jonathan Bar Joseph, 304
Rabbi Lima Epstein, 46
Rabbi M. G. Yaffa, 50, 51
Rabbi Maimon, 67
Rabbi Manoach Hendel The Son Of Rabbi Shmaryahu, 44
Rabbi Matityahu Delacroti, 44
Rabbi Meir Gimpel, 56, 57
Rabbi Meir Idel, 92
Rabbi Meir Of Padua, 48
Rabbi Menachem Eliezer, 45
Rabbi Menachem Nachum Za'k, 22
Rabbi Mendel Of Shklov, 46
Rabbi Mordechai Epstein, 46
Rabbi Mordechai Gimpel, 48, 52, 54, 55
Rabbi Mordechai Gimpel Jaffee, 304
Rabbi Mordechai Gimpel Yaffa, 48, 49, 50, 52, 55, 56, 58
Rabbi Mordechai Wallach, 56
Rabbi Mordechai Ziskind, 41
Rabbi Moshe Almoshnino, 44
Rabbi Moshe Nathan Halevi, 52
Rabbi Moshe Rabinowicz, 47
Rabbi Moshe Tzvi Halpern, 46
Rabbi Moshe Zeev, 42, 43
Rabbi Nathan Hakohen, 42, 43
Rabbi Richtschreiber, 59
Rabbi Shabbtai Wallach, 304
Rabbi Shabtai, 58
Rabbi Shabtai Wallach, 46, 56, 57, 58, 59, 67, 80, 92
Rabbi Shalom, 23
Rabbi Shaul Wohl, 48
Rabbi Shimon, 22
Rabbi Shimon Bar Yochai, 47
Rabbi Shimon The Son Of The Holy Martyr Yisrael, 14
Rabbi Shlomo, 41
Rabbi Shlomo Charif, 41
Rabbi Shlomo Luria, 41
Rabbi Shlomo Mohilever, 52
Rabbi Shlomo Zalman, 41
Rabbi Shlomo Zalman Murkish, 45
Rabbi Shmaryahu, 44
Rabbi Shmuel Of Vilna, 45
Rabbi Tovia, 18, 23, 45
Rabbi Tzvi Hirsch, 41
Rabbi Tzvi Hirsch Kalisher, 50
Rabbi Yaakov Chaver, 46
Rabbi Yaakov Meir, 46
Rabbi Yaakov Meir Padua, 48
Rabbi Yaakov Moshe Of Slonim, 46
Rabbi Yechezkel, 41
Rabbi Yechezkel Katzenelboigen, 41, 42
Rabbi Yechezkel Landau, 45
Rabbi Yechiel Michel, 208
Rabbi Yehonatan, 44
Rabbi Yehonatan Eibeschutz, 42
Rabbi Yehonatan The Son Of Rabbi Yosef, 42, 43, 44
Rabbi Yehuda, 45
Rabbi Yehuda Eidel, 42, 43
Rabbi Yehuda Leib Hakohen Maimon, 55
Rabbi Yehuda Yudel Landau, 45
Rabbi Yerucham Fishel Pines, 48, 52
Rabbi Yisrael, 18, 22, 45, 46
Rabbi Yisrael Eisenstadt, 41
Rabbi Yisrael Halpern, 45, 46
Rabbi Yisrael The Son Of Rabbi Chaim, 45
Rabbi Yisrael The Son Of Rabbi Shalom, 11
Rabbi Yisrael Yaffa, 41

Rabbi Yitzchak Izak, 45, 46
Rabbi Yitzchak Izak Chaver, 46, 47
Rabbi Yitzchak Izak The Son Of Rabbi Yaakov Chaver, 46
Rabbi Yitzchak Yaakov (Samsonowich), 257
Rabbi Yochanan Sandlar, 213
Rabbi Yoel, 41
Rabbi Yomtov Lipmann, 45, 46, 58
Rabbi Yomtov Lipmann Epstein, 58
Rabbi Yomtov Lipmann Halpern, 46, 47
Rabbi Yomtov Lipmann Heller, 58
Rabbi Yosef, 43, 44
Rabbi Yosef Chaver, 47
Rabbi Yosef Jaski, 43
Rabbi Yosef Shlomo, 23
Rabbi Yosef The Son Of Yaakov, 41
Rabbi Zalman, 47
Rabbi Zalman Weiss, 58, 59
Rabbi Zeev Wolf, 257
Rabbi Zev Wolf, 41
Rabbi Ziskind, 48, 58, 59
Rabbi Ziskind Richtschreiber, 58
Rabbi Ziskind Shachor, 48
Rabinovich, 244, 321
Rabinovitch, 115, 307
Rabinowich, 175, 176, 178, 182, 183, 184, 187, 193, 194, 197, 198, 200, 201, 215, 216, 245
Radzominsky, 322
Rappaport, 11, 43, 316, 322
Reb Elinka, 78
Reb Elinka Of Lida, 78
Reb Shimon The Son Of The Martyr Reb Yisrael, 9
Reb Shlomo Charif, 41
Reb Tovia, 14, 15, 21, 25, 26
Reb Tovia The Son Of Yosef, 9
Reb Yisrael, 14, 15, 21, 22, 25, 26
Reb Yisrael The Son Of Shalom, 9
Rechtshendler, 322
Reiner, 322
Reizin, 134, 135
Reuven The Weaver, 71
Reznik, 251, 323
Rishon, 69, 83, 317
Rizkin, 149, 178, 184, 188, 199, 202, 206, 316
Rodcki, 175
Roditzki, 318, 322
Roditzky, 318
Rodler, 322
Rodtzky, 245
Rokach, 11
Roschowsky, 269
Rosenfeld, 266
Rothschild, 50, 120
Rothstyn, 149
Rotner, 139, 154, 245
Rotstein, 163, 206, 322, 323
Rozanitzky, 246
Rozen, 149
Rozenblit, 210
Rozenfeld, 253
Rozenschein, 175, 176, 211, 212
Rozenstyn, 149, 156
Rozin, 205
Rozman, 324
Roznik, 323
Roznitzky, 245, 322
Rubenstyn, 162
Rubinowich, 179, 180, 181, 183, 190, 195, 202, 271, 272, 286, 287, 288, 316
Rubinowich-Enis, 191
Rubinowich-Ines, 1, 267
Rubins, 202
Rubinstein, 121, 205, 322
Ruchmas, 316
Ruchmis, 30, 283
Rudabsky, 121
Rudetski, 177
Rudetsky, 176, 178, 194, 195, 281, 317
Ruhzansky, 283
Runik, 323
Rushkin, 1, 67, 90, 92, 179, 180, 181, 182, 184, 188, 202, 211, 262, 265, 267, 322
Ruszkin, 161
Rutman, 317
Ruzansky, 322

# S

Sacrobosco, 66
Salomon The Watchmaker, 232
Samsonowich, 257
Sapeiha, Vi
Sapieha, X, 6, 8, 24
Sapir, 181, 190, 198
SAVULSKI, 312
Schmidt, 153
Schwartz, 202
Segal, 90, 184, 202, 292
Seidel, Vii
Selec, 152
Sellers, Ii, Xiv
Selman, 149
Sender The Shoemaker, 150
Senderovich, 321
Shabtai, 93, 292
Shachor, Xviii, 119
Shadmi, 322
Shamir, 322
Shamit, 209

SHAMSHANOVITCH, 312
Shamshonowich, 319
Shapira, 154, 177, 178, 184, 189, 212, 318, 322
Shayka, 105
Shefem, Xviii, 86
Sheivitz, 153, 154
Shekel-Ravich, 202
Shemes, 181, 194, 195
Shemesh, 322
Shemshinowich, 105, 212
Shepes, 247, 312
Sher, Xix, 134
Sher (Szereszewski), 134
Shereshbasker, 209
Shereshevsky, 29, 30, 31, 305, 320, 321
Shereshevsky (Brott), 154
Shereshevsky (Sher), 305
Shereshrevski, 207
Sherman, 152, 156, 216, 274, 275
Sherobsky, 322
Shershever, 153, 154
Shifrin, 94
Shihen, 100
Shimon, 93
Shimon The Shochet, 90, 136, 209, 212
Shimshoni, 126, 127, 253, 265, 266
Shimshoni (Shemshinowich), 1
Shimshony, 322, 323
Shipiancky, 322
Shipiatzky, 211, 319
Shipitzki, 180
Shipitzski, 149, 153, 154
Shipitzsky, 188
Shiva, 322
Shkolnik, 292, 319
Shlomo The Shoemaker, 37
Shmerel The Baker, 292
Shmerkovitz, 201
Shmerkowich, 182
Shmerl The "Long, 63
Shmerl The Tailor, 60, 61
Shmuel Itche The Wagon Driver, 37
Shmuel Leib The Shoemaker, 212
Shpiler, 318
Shulamit, 317, 318, 319, 320
Siduransky, 320
Simchowicz, 47
Sirkis, 320
Skliravitz, 153, 184, 187, 192
Skloiravitz, 154, 205
Skolnik, 33, 121, 154, 181, 184, 188, 195, 201, 202
Slonimsky, 217
Slutitzky, 107, 183
Slutzky, 184, 188, 202

Smolniskin, 161
Snapir, 319
Snobski, 321
Sobolsky, 162, 251, 320
Sokolovski, 310
Sokolovsky, 7, 30, 35, 39, 102, 177, 178, 179, 180, 181, 182, 183, 184, 190, 192, 193, 194, 195, 198, 202, 205, 214, 217, 219, 220, 221, 222, 228, 229, 244, 254, 255, 265, 266, 267, 280, 292, 318, 320, 321
Sokolow, 46, 140
**Sokolowsky**, I, 52, 56, 69, 107, 116, 123, 134, 143, 147, 148, 151, 158, 166, 172, 173
Solitarnik, 320
Solnik, 320
Solominsky, 320
Solomon, Xiii
Soltz, 30
Soroka, 91
Soytitzky, 320
Spartanski, 197
Spicha, 83
Starewolski, 74, 99, 124
Starewolsky, 73
Stein, 153, 176, 192, 275, 322
Stier's, 217
Stopnicki, 205
Strikovsky, 320
Sydlenitsky, 181
Szapira, 149
Szeresewski, 146, 149
Szereszewski, 175
Szipiacki, 151
Szkliravitz, 107
Szklirowicz, 151
Szliowsky, 316
Szracyk, 158
Szybyc, 151

# T

Taylor, Ii
Tidhar, 119, 120, 136
Timinski, 319
Trabgoda, 319
Tsar Nicholas I, 303
Tserbiticki, 195
Tshernikovsky, 66
Tshernikovsy, 35, 40
Tuchman, 193, 194, 195, 224, 225, 226, 228, 229, 231
Tukachinsky, 120
Turn, 149, 202, 212, 215, 275, 319
Tzadik (Mrucnk), 167
Tzchovoy, 319
Tzemach, 316

Tzirka, 239
Tzolis The Tailor, 38

## U

Urn, 275

## V

Vego, Xii
Vegotsky, Viii, Xii, Xiii
*Vegotsky Taylor*, Viii, Xii, Xiv
Velvel, 152
Vishnitzer, 179
Vitzes, 312
Vygodesky, 184

## W

Wallach, 35, 101, 102, 208
Warsaw, 76
Wasz, 75, 76, 77, 81, 82, 103
Weinberg, 132
Weingarten, 318
Weinstein, 318, 319
Weiss, 321
Wilensky, 37, 149, 176, 192, 275
Winter, 11
Wishnivsky, 153, 154, 202
Wissotzky, 215, 216
Witkin, 318
Wolf, Xx, 11
Wolfowich, 323
Wolk, 318
Wolodinsky, 318
Wolpiansky, 100
Wynitsky, 184

## Y

Yaakov, 127
Yaakov Chaim The Shada'l, 39

Yaakovi, 319
Yaari, 66
Yaffa, 35, 52, 55, 56, 99, 113, 121
Yatom, 183, 186, 187, 201, 211, 212, 319
Yehonatan, 44
Yehuda The Printer, 177
Yellin, Xviii, 32, 97, 118, 119, 120
Yona The Shoemaker, Xviii, 213
Yona The Shoemaker, 83

## Z

Za'k, Xiii
Zabursky, 140
Zagagi, 316
Zakem, Ii, Vi, Xi, Xii, Xiii
Zakheim, 11, 22, 34, 102, 132, 181, 184, 202, 318
Zaklad, 318
Zaks, 191
Zaltzman, 38
Zambrowsky, 158
Zandman, 318
Zazhvir, 184, 220
Zeev, 43
Zeidel, 153
Zemach, 181, 195
Zilberberg, 318
Zilberberg (Pitkovsky), 198
Zinskind, 144
Ziskind, Xx, 152, 155, 177, 184, 190, 211, 259, 260, 318
Ziskindovich, 318, 319, 322
Zisking, 89
Zlotner, 193, 318
Zmochovsky, 318
Zohar, 191
Zoltkovsky, 318

# Appendix of Material Not included in Original Yizkor book

www.ingramcontent.com/pod-product-compliance
Lightning Source LLC
Chambersburg PA
CBHW082002150426
42814CB00005BA/193